Nathaniel Hawthorne

Nathaniel Hawthorne, 1860

NATHANIEL HAWTHORNE

The English Experience, 1853–1864

‡

Raymona E. Hull

University of Pittsburgh Press

Published by the University of Pittsburgh Press, Pittsburgh, Pa. 15260
Copyright © 1980, University of Pittsburgh
All rights reserved
Feffer and Simons, Inc., London
Manufactured in the United States of America

Library of Congress Cataloging in Publication Data

Hull, Raymona E
   Nathaniel Hawthorne, the English experience, 1853–
1864.

   Includes bibliographical references and index.
   1. Hawthorne, Nathaniel, 1804–1864 — Homes and
haunts — England. 2. Hawthorne, Nathaniel, 1804–1864.
— Biography — Last years and death. 3. England —
Description and travel — 1801–1900. 4. Novelists,
American — 19th century — Biography. 5. Consuls —
Biography. I. Title.
PS1884.H8   813'.3 [B]   79-26616
ISBN 0-8229-3418-3

Publication of this book was assisted by a grant from the National Endowment for the Humanities.

Acknowledgment is made as follows for permission to reprint material in this book:

All writings of Hawthorne family, Manning Hawthorne for the heirs of Nathaniel Hawthorne. Letters of Nathaniel and Sophia Hawthorne, by courtesy of the Trustees of the Boston Public Library. Letters of Hawthorne family and Hawthorne English Account Book, Essex Institute, Salem, Massachusetts. Letters of Hawthorne and H. A. Bright, by permission of the Houghton Library, Harvard University. Hawthorne letters and Vol. V of French and Italian Notebooks, by permission of The Huntington Library, San Marino, California. Letters, pocket diaries, and journals of Hawthorne family, Henry W. and Albert A. Berg Collection, the New York Public Library, Astor, Lenox and Tilden Foundations. Letters and manuscripts of Hawthorne family, The Pierpont Morgan Library. Letters in the Nathaniel Hawthorne Collection (#6249), Francis Bennoch Collection (#7120), and the Peabody Sisters Collection (#6952), Clifton Waller Barrett Library, University of Virginia Library. Letters of Nathaniel Hawthorne and Ada Shepard and other related material collected by Norman Holmes Pearson, Collection of American Literature, Beinecke Rare Book and Manuscript Library, Yale University.

Letters from *Shapes That Pass*, by Julian Hawthorne (1928), and *Hawthorne and His Publisher*, by Caroline Ticknor (1913), by permission of Houghton Mifflin Company. Passages from *The English Notebooks of Nathaniel Hawthorne*, edited by Randall Stewart, printed with the permission of The Modern Language Association of America, as agents for Cleone Odell Stewart. Copyright © 1941 by The Modern Language Association of America; copyright renewed 1969 by Cleone Odell Stewart. Numerous passages from The Centenary Edition of the Works of Nathaniel Hawthorne, by permission of the Ohio State University Press.

Diary of George Brown and other documents about William Brown, Liverpool City Libraries. Portion of letter from *The Letters of Mrs. Gaskell*, ed. Chapple and Pollard (1967), by permission of Manchester University Press and Harvard University Press. Material from Annie Fields's 1859–1860 diary, Massachusetts Historical Society. Letters of Robert Temple, The National Library of Wales, Aberystwyth. Material from Bright Collection, including letters and parts of his American Journal, the Master and Fellows of Trinity College, Cambridge, and Elizabeth Lloyd, Malvern, Worcestershire; for Anne Ehrenpreis's edition of Bright's American Journal, *Happy Country, This America: The Travel Diary of Henry Arthur Bright*, Irvin Ehrenpreis.

Contents

Illustrations

Preface

A fit false dreame . . .
A diverse dreame . . .

that ydle dreame was to him brought
Edmund Spenser

IN THE CONCLUSION to his biography of his parents, Julian Hawthorne wrote that although his father "easily" and "inevitably produced an impression upon the observer," he was a difficult man to know. As Julian saw it, "Men like Hawthorne can never be touched and dissected, because the essence of their character is never concretely manifested." The true revelation of such men, he said, "will be made only to those who have in themselves somewhat of the same mystery they seek to fathom."

If Julian was right, an adequate life of Nathaniel Hawthorne may never be written. The task is further complicated by the fact that Hawthorne's widow, responding to his desire for privacy, spent her energies protecting his memory by creating the image she thought should be presented to the public and refusing to allow the publication of any biography. The rest of the family followed her example, although biographical sketches did appear after 1864, the year of Hawthorne's death. Finally, twelve years after his mother's death, Julian published the two-volume life of his parents as his answer to accounts that were not authorized by the immediate family, such as those by James T. Fields, H. A. Page, G. P. Lathrop, and Henry James. But Julian's volumes, in spite of some good qualities, are as biased and inaccurate as any outsider's work.

One reason for this present undertaking of a book on a portion of the lives of the Hawthorne family is the availability of new materials. Descendants of both the Hawthornes and their friends have recently presented collections of letters to libraries. In 1976 Hawthorne's earliest American notebook was found in a chest of drawers. Unpublished pocket diaries, journals, letters, and notes, scattered in libraries from the east coast to the west and in the British Isles, have become available only in the twentieth century. Still, there are gaps in existing information.

Preface

It is the purpose of this account of a little known but important period in the lives of the Hawthornes to let the family members tell their own stories as far as possible. This approach results, of course, in a heavy proportion of quotation, some of it, as from the *English Notebooks*, already well known, other parts never before printed. If there are errors in the story, it is because there were numerous occasions when, because of their reserve, family members either failed to record or destroyed some items, and research into the matter has proved futile.

The English period is a challenging one to investigate simply because it has been neglected. Hawthorne's contemporaries, such as James T. Fields, either ignored or minimized the significance of those years. During his consulship Hawthorne did no writing of romance. A short excerpt from his notebooks about the town of Uttoxeter and the preface for Delia Bacon's book on Shakespeare are the only two literary products of the first four years in England that were published at that time. *The Marble Faun*, a romance begun in Italy, was rewritten in England during the Hawthornes' second stay there and published not long before they departed for America. Therefore, I have made no attempt at criticism of Hawthorne's writings, but have only summarized briefly some of the reactions to his work written either in or about England during the last years of his life.

In the conclusion of his biography, Julian wrote of his mother, "She lived for her husband; and when he died, her love of life died also; but her children remained, and she stayed in this world for their sake." When any family is as close as the Hawthornes were, it is impossible to speak of one without involving the rest, unless the biographer is attempting only the literary career of the artist. Even then he must consider the life of the man as well as that of the artist. Hawthorne went to England for the sake of his family, and his political appointment there permitted no time for a literary career. But the English experience had a lasting effect upon his subsequent years that must be examined and evaluated.

The years abroad not only interrupted Hawthorne's career as a writer of romance, but also caused physical and emotional changes in himself and the rest of his family. His dream of achieving at the same time security for them all, a broader education for his children, and the delights of foreign travel involved the sacrifice of his writing career in return for four years of drudgery worse than any he had known before. In spite of his satisfaction in having carried out his responsibilities in Liverpool conscientiously and in having learned much from travels on the Continent, Hawthorne maintained such an ambivalent

attitude toward England and toward Italy especially that the inevitable
question arises: Did the benefits of life abroad justify his sacrifice?

Any attempt to deal with the English period must go beyond the
return of the Hawthornes to the United States in 1860. Hawthorne
blamed the Civil War for his unsettled condition in the years after 1860
and for his inability to complete any romances, and almost to the end of
his life continued to hope that a voyage back to "Our Old Home" would
somehow solve his health problems. Sophia blamed Italy for her
husband's physical deterioration. The ultimate effects of seven years
abroad on her and all the children except Una did not become evident
until long afterward. For this accounting an epilogue is necessary.

It was not until after Hawthorne's death that the rest of the family
thought of going back to Europe. Even then they did not seem to
realize that they were pursuing the same kind of hope that Hawthorne
had pursued. For Sophia and Una, "Our Old Home" was still a
dreamland and remained so. Rose and Julian were the only ones who,
like the Red Cross Knight, awoke eventually to face a different world.

Acknowledgments

SPECIAL THANKS SHOULD GO to a number of individuals in Great Britain who have provided valuable assistance in research: the staff of the British Library, London; the editor and his assistant at the *Dumfries and Galloway Standard*, Dumfries, Scotland; the staff of Ewart Library, Dumfries; W. Forster, Deputy Director, Department of Adult Education, University of Leicester; the staff of Liverpool Record Office, Liverpool City Libraries, especially Janet Smith and Naomi Evetts; Elizabeth Lloyd, Barton Court, Colwall, Malvern, Worcester; H. Moore, formerly District Librarian, Redcar, Yorkshire (now at Middleborough Central Library); David Timms, Department of American Studies, University of Manchester; the staff of Trinity College Library, especially Patricia Bradford, former cataloguer, T. Kaye, sub-librarian, and Rosemary Graham; and A. G. Veysey, Archivist, County Record Office, Rhyl, Wales. An extra expression of appreciation goes to James O. Mays, of Burley, Hampshire, for help in research, for photographs, and for reading parts of the manuscript.

Those people in the United States to whom I am particularly indebted for help in research include Maurice Bassan, Department of English, San Francisco State University; Dorothy Potter and Barbara Adams Blundell, former members of the staff of Essex Institute, Salem, Massachusetts, and the present reference librarian, Irene Norton; the entire staff of Rhodes Stabley Library of Indiana University of Pennsylvania, especially Richard Chamberlin, reference librarian; Barbara Mouffe, of Boulder, Colorado; the staff of the Owen D. Young Library, St. Lawrence University, Canton, New York, including Andrew Peters, retired chief librarian, his successor, Mahlon Peterson, and Mary Lou Mallam, former reference librarian; Lola Szladits and her assistants at the Berg Collection in New York City; and Donald Gallup, Curator of American Literature at the Beinecke Library of Yale University, and his staff.

Acknowledgments

This book would not have been possible without the special help of several persons. The late Norman Holmes Pearson first started me on the project and encouraged me by a continuing correspondence and by permission to use his own copies of Hawthorne letters. Many of my quotations from Nathaniel Hawthorne's letters are taken from Mr. Pearson's transcripts made for an edition of the letters that he did not live to complete.

The late Claude Simpson, of Huntington Library, also provided valuable assistance from both his own knowledge and useful materials that he had contributed to the Center for Textual Studies at Ohio State University.

To the present associate editor at the Center for Textual Studies, Neal Smith, I am greatly indebted for help of all kinds, ranging from information in letters to the loan of films and mimeographed materials to corrections on my original manuscript. Like Mr. Pearson before him, Neal Smith has constantly encouraged me in my efforts.

To the late Arlin Turner, of Duke University, go my thanks for his hours spent carefully reading the revised manuscript, for his correction of details, and for his kindly advice on the work as a whole.

To Manning Hawthorne, grandson of Julian, I am greatly indebted for permission to make use of Hawthorne family writings, for his friendly advice, and for the gift of a family photograph.

I wish also to thank these friends in Indiana, Pennsylvania, for their help: Dorothy Lucker, former colleague in the Department of English, Indiana University of Pennsylvania, for many hours spent reading, suggesting revisions, and proofreading the entire manuscript; David L. Young, Department of English at Indiana University of Pennsylvania, for his expert work in photography; Elizabeth Wilhelm and Karol Hutton, my neighbors, for assistance in proofreading; Darla Sisko, my typist, for her patience with my own erratic typing; and Faith Ferguson, former colleague in the Department of English, for her careful work in proofreading and indexing.

Finally, I wish to thank the staff of the University of Pittsburgh Press for the helpful advice and editorial work so essential to the production of this book.

Nathaniel Hawthorne

‡ 1 ‡

Departure and Arrival

IN 1853 when Nathaniel Hawthorne, then at the height of his literary career, accepted the post of U.S. consul at Liverpool, it was with great expectations for the financial future of his family and himself. Hawthorne was approaching his forty-ninth birthday and had already published nearly all his best-known fiction—three romances, two collections of short stories, and several children's books. In addition to his early nonfiction, he had edited the *Journal of an African Cruiser* by Horatio Bridge, one of his college classmates, and had written the campaign biography of another college friend, Franklin Pierce. It was this biography, published in 1852, that led directly to the Liverpool appointment, a position thought to be the most lucrative of all such foreign posts.

The life of Pierce was not the kind of writing that Hawthorne was accustomed to doing. Years later, after Hawthorne's death, his son-in-law wrote that in spite of misgivings about his ability to do this task, Hawthorne had completed a conscientious piece of work.[1] In the short time allotted he had done his best to help the man whom he had known since college days at Bowdoin and who would continue to be his close friend to the end of his life. When the biography was published, Whig opponents criticized it for glossing over facts not favorable to Pierce; Democratic friends, however, rejoiced in the results that it brought. Soon after Pierce was inaugurated he submitted Hawthorne's name for the most suitable foreign post with the highest income. Hawthorne had expected some reward and was glad to accept the consulship in a country that he had always wanted to visit.

It seemed at the time that Hawthorne's reward was an appropriate one that would make him financially independent, perhaps for the rest of his life. He had never been one of the hugely popular writers who earned large sums of money; he was rather a respected literary man with an adequate income. His family had been able to manage on a thousand dollars or less per year, but circumstances were changing. Realizing that it would take more than royalties from his books to finance a good education for three children, he accepted the consulship as a way of accumulating enough savings to provide for future security. Added to this aim was the hope that the family could enjoy travel on the Continent after his four-year appointment came to an end.

When the Senate confirmed the appointment, the *Home Journal* commented on Hawthorne's good fortune in a way that reflected the opinion of his friends and most understanding readers:

> It seems to us, that in selecting this lucrative post for his friend, General Pierce has displayed excellent sense. Honour and glory Mr. Hawthorne has already, in abundance. No office whatever could increase his fame, or elevate his position. Money, on the contrary, is the precise commodity of which he stands in need, and money, therefore, has been placed within his reach. To a literary man, pecuniary independence is a blessing beyond estimate. It bestows upon him that leisure in which alone immortal books can be composed, and that freedom from care which he, beyond all other men, requires, for the cheerful elaboration of his works.[2]

Hawthorne himself probably had no premonition that while he was in Liverpool the consulship would keep him from all literary work except the manuscripts that much later became the *English Notebooks*.

Though a literary man by choice, Hawthorne was already accustomed to the political system. From 1839 to 1841 he had served as weigher and gauger in the Boston Custom House, and from 1846 to 1849 he had been surveyor in the customhouse at Salem. Dismissal from this second post, a result of the spoils system, led to the writing of *The Scarlet Letter*, with its controversial opening chapter, "The Custom-House." From these two experiences Hawthorne should have realized that during periods of government work he could accomplish almost no writing. However, he had looked upon the income from such appointments as a means of tiding him over until he could return to more creative work. In 1853 he had no way of foreseeing how far reaching and devastating the effects of appointment to the Liverpool post would be.

Four busy months would pass between the date of the confirmation and the Hawthornes' departure for Liverpool. The previous consul, Colonel Thomas Crittenden, wished to complete four full years of service by staying abroad until August 1. Hawthorne, for his part, had many preparations to make before leaving. First, he must go to Washington, D.C., in April. On that trip he was accompanied by the publisher William D. Ticknor, who was fast becoming Hawthorne's business manager as well as intimate friend and who was to sail to Liverpool with the family. In Washington, Hawthorne was entertained as well as briefed. During his stay he also secured the Manchester post, which, according to Ticknor, added $3,000 annually to his income. "This he would have lost, if he had not come on. I am very glad for his sake."[3]

Meanwhile Hawthorne had already begun to realize that his new position would entail a different and more expensive way of life. He must have clothes for formal occasions. At the end of March he wrote to Ticknor, "My best dress-coat is rather shabby (befitting an author much more than a man of consular rank); so, when you next smoke a cigar with our friend Driscoll, I wish you would tell him to put another suit on the stocks for me — a black dress-coat and pantaloons; and he may select the cloth. I shall want them before we go to Washington."[4]

Equally as important as personal preparations were the arrangements to be made concerning the Wayside, the house in Concord that Hawthorne had purchased only the year before from Bronson Alcott and to which the family would return after the consular years. Ephraim Bull, a neighboring farmer, agreed to look after the small acreage. The Peabodys, Sophia Hawthorne's family, would care for the house itself, and various relatives would stay there in the intervening years.

The Hawthornes had lived in the Wayside barely one year before they left the United States. But ten years earlier Sophia and Nathaniel had spent a glorious extended honeymoon at the Old Manse, which they rented for more than three years, and therefore knew Concord as well as they would ever know any of their places of residence except their native Salem. At first Nathaniel had been completely delighted with the Wayside. When George Curtis, who had known Hawthorne at Brook Farm, was planning to write a chapter on Hawthorne for *Homes of American Authors,* Nathaniel invited Curtis to come and see it for himself. Later Curtis described Concord as

> one of those quiet New England towns, whose few white houses, grouped upon the plain, make but a slight impression upon the mind of the busy traveller hurrying to or from the city. . . . Except in causing the erection of the railway building and several dwellings near it, steam has not much changed Concord. It is yet one of the quiet country towns whose charm is incredible to all but those who, by loving it, have found it worthy of love.[5]

‡ 5 ‡

When he came to details about Hawthorne's home, Curtis based his account on his own visit and on Hawthorne's description given in his invitation. Hawthorne wrote that Alcott, the previous owner, had made many changes in the house some time before he sold it: "He added a porch in front, and a central peak, and a piazza at each end, and painted it a rusty olive hue, and invested the whole with a modest picturesqueness; all which improvements, together with its situation at the foot of a wooded hill, make it a place that one notices and remembers for a few minutes after passing it."[6]

After describing the hillside and its thicket of trees, Hawthorne gave Curtis a picture of leisure in his favorite retreat: "I spend delectable hours there in the hottest part of the day, stretched out at my lazy length, with a book in my hand or an unwritten book in my thought. There is almost always a breeze stirring along the side or brow of the hill."[7] Had he not felt obliged to leave Concord for the sake of increased income, who knows what romances the "delectable hours" might have produced?

But the children were now old enough to cause their father to think about providing for their futures. Una, the first-born, was nine when they set out for Liverpool; Julian was seven; Rose, called "Rosebud," "Baby," or "Bab," was two. Their mother was forty-four, despite Nathaniel's later statement, and in better health than she had been at the time of their marriage.[8] At forty-nine, Hawthorne himself was a vigorous man.

Final preparations for the departure were well planned. In May or June Nathaniel sent Sophia to Boston to look over the various ships, and on her recommendation he booked passage for July 6 in the Cunarder *Niagara*. Two servants, Mary and Ellen Hearne, were to accompany the family. The heavy baggage was sent off on July 3. One of Nathaniel's last acts before leaving was to make provision for his only living sister, Elizabeth, to receive $200 per year during his absence.[9] When "Uncle Manning," from the Hawthorne side of the family, offered to come and help them pack, Nathaniel wrote that they had no spare bed, for they were sleeping "in borrowed sheets," but that he could oblige them by meeting them in Boston and bringing with him the bird that Dora Golden, Julian's former nurse, had given to them. Hawthorne added that Sophia's brother, Nathaniel C. Peabody, would also be in Boston to see off the family.[10]

Sophia's brother came with their father, Dr. Nathaniel Peabody. (Sophia's mother had died that spring, and neither of the sisters, Mary Mann or Elizabeth Peabody, could come.) The two Peabodys, father and son, went to the dock, together with James T. Fields, Ticknor's junior partner, to say good-by. Since Ticknor was sailing with the Hawthornes and would stay abroad long enough to see them settled and to attend to publishing matters in London, Fields performed the double duty of friendship and business. There was "a long gun salute" as the ship left the wharf and "sailed majestically" out of the harbor. When Julian saw the last point of land disappear, he said to his mother, "That, I suppose, is the end of America! I do not think America reaches very far."[11]

Julian, writing long afterward, recorded these impressions of the ship itself:

> Seventy-three years ago the *Niagara*, old Sam Cunard's prize ship, was a little paddle-wheeled thing, two hundred feet or more long and of corresponding tonnage. There was a brood of hens on board, and you could sit in the stern and hear them clucking in the bows. There was a cow, too, whose milk supplied the passengers during the voyage. The carpenter sawed and planed in an eight-by-five box forward of the main hatch; I spent many pleasant hours in his company. The saloon, twenty-feet long, was panelled with polished wood and upholstered in crimson plush; it was dining-room and sitting-room, with a library of twelve books, bound in red cloth, on a shelf at the end. There were, I believe, ten state-rooms, but I never saw but three, which the Hawthorne family of five persons slept in; they were the size of the cases in which upright pianos are packed; there was no running water, either hot or cold, and such a thing as a bath didn't exist in those times, either afloat or ashore. . . . There was no accommodation for second-cabin people, still less for steerage.[12]

Julian's remark about the number of staterooms shows a typical child's viewpoint: The boy was concerned only with his immediate family circle. Actually there were numerous rather distinguished persons aboard who must have had first-class cabins, and there were evidently some second-class accommodations. The total number of passengers indicates that the ship was well filled: 140 left Boston, including 16 scheduled to get off in Halifax, Nova Scotia, and 124 to go on to Liverpool. In addition, 17 more passengers embarked at Halifax.[13]

The captain of the *Niagara*, Captain Leitch, seemed to the Hawthornes a remarkable man. Afterward Julian remembered him as "a small, active man with bright eyes and very thick black whiskers; a genial, debonair, entertaining little gentleman." Sophia and Ticknor, who were among the group at the captain's table, commented on

Leitch's personality and skill. He was "a man of intelligence," wrote Ticknor, "and a gentleman, disposed to do all in his power to make the passage agreeable to his passengers." Sophia, who was timid about sailing, was more enthusiastic and naive in her praise:

> The minister [J. F. Crampton, British minister to Washington, en route to Halifax] told me that he sailed with him five years ago, when the captain was very young, and he was then astonished at his skill and power of command; . . . It was good to see his assured military air, as he walked back and forth while we moved out of the beautiful harbor. He made motions with such an air of majesty and conscious power. His smile is charming and his voice fine.[14]

Since the Hawthornes were his most distinguished American passengers, Captain Leitch naturally was as courteous as a British host at a social affair would have been. He was described by Julian as "very courtly to my mother, and pranksome with my two sisters and myself; with my father he had much grave talk. I suppose—since my father's dealings during the coming four years were to be with seamen chiefly—that their condition afloat and ashore was the main topic."[15]

What the two men did discuss we shall never know, for the only Hawthorne who kept a journal of the crossing was Sophia, and her interests were far from the troubles of seamen. She recorded some details of the first day out, but left her journal incomplete after the departure from Halifax. While the ship docked there one night to discharge and take on passengers, the two Hawthornes and Ticknor went ashore for a short time. But the darkness was relieved only by torchlight, and they could see no farther than the crowds standing on the pier and along the streets. The next day when Sophia tried to record her impressions of Halifax, she found them to be as indistinct as the light had been. Since the motion of the ship made writing almost impossible, she ended her journal abruptly.[16] The rest of the voyage she recorded later in letters sent home to her family.

After the *Niagara* left Halifax, Ticknor recorded those seated at the captain's table, in addition to the Hawthornes and himself, as "Mr. E. [Enoch] Train and wife and daughter, Mr. [Honorable J. S.] McDonald, speaker of Canadian Parliament, Mr. [W. G.] Hodgkinson and daughter, of England; all very intelligent and social people."[17] He acknowledged that he became friendly with only a few passengers: Train, the well-known shipowner, his wife, and son, Enoch, Jr.; W. J. Reynolds, Boston bookseller; and Arthur Gilman, architect. In view of Ticknor's naturally reserved manner, it is not surprising that he had comparatively little communication with passengers other than those whom he listed as enjoyable companions.

By contrast, Sophia apparently did a great deal of talking with various passengers. The two maids looked after the immediate needs of the children, who ate at a separate table in the women's cabin. Sophia therefore had freedom to enjoy the smooth passage of the vessel in beautiful weather; she read, wrote letters, observed the children playing, and chatted with passengers who were not at the captain's table. Evidently she too became acquainted with Ticknor's architect friend, for on an incomplete page of her shipboard journal is a sketch that she labeled "By Arthur Gilman."[18]

One British passenger whom Sophia singled out for comment was Field Talfourd, brother of the writer Thomas Talfourd, famous in his day for the tragedy *Ion*. "I had very charming conversations with him. He was a perfect gentleman, with an ease of manner so fascinating and rare, showing high breeding, and a voice rich and full." For at least a page she extolled his enunciation, evidences of his fine education, and his prowess "as a gymnast," ending with the remark that the sum of his qualities was not "very often met with in America. It seems to require more leisure and a deeper culture than we Americans have yet, to produce such a lovely flower."[19] Sophia did not refer to Talfourd again in her letters, but from her long description it is obvious that he summed up all the excellent qualities that she was expecting to find in English gentlemen.

One American whom Sophia conversed with frequently was a passenger from Salem, an ordained minister probably known to her at least slightly before the voyage. William Silsbee did not appear healthy, and Sophia was concerned about him. "Mr. Silsbee," she wrote, "looks so thin and pale that I fear for him; but I will take good care of him." Later she persuaded him to move to the "gentlemen's cabin where the air was better." It is possible that Silsbee was traveling for the sake of his health, for he stayed abroad more than a year. Late in August of 1854, when he was on his way back home, he visited the family in Rock Park, and Sophia commented on how much stronger he was then.[20]

When Sophia was not chatting with other passengers, she supervised the children's diet, even though they ate in a separate dining room. According to her notes, the children were not accustomed to eating meat, but "past rules have to be modified on the sea." "Julian eats nobly [including chicken broth and lobster meat] but Una is rather dainty." At first the milk from the cow on board was diluted before serving, but when Sophia complained on Rose's behalf, the steward said that Sophia was to have anything she wanted. Rose was immediately supplied with undiluted milk. Sophia's resulting comment reveals her recognition of their new status: "It is very convenient to have rank with these English people. It commands good service."[21] Between mealtimes Una read an advance copy of her father's new book for children, *Tanglewood Tales,* and occasionally walked or raced the upper deck with Julian. While these two children spent hours playing together, Ellen, one of the maids, looked after Rose. Sophia, when she had time to herself, sat on deck in the sun or in the shadow of the red and black funnel, and wrote letters and read.

Meanwhile Mr. Ticknor was fast becoming an indispensable friend to the Hawthorne family. Though this kind and thoughtful man deserves a description all to himself, he can hardly be thought of separately from Fields, his junior partner, who did not make this trip, but did sail with the Hawthornes when they returned to the States in 1860. Julian pictured Ticknor as "one of the most amiable of men, with thick whiskers round his face and spectacles shining over his kindly eyes; a sturdy, thick-set personage, active in movements and genial in conversation."[22] "Mr. Ticknor," wrote his son Howard, "was nervously quick in every action; his smile was brilliant, and his blue eyes, although kindly and humorous, were direct and piercing." Then the younger Ticknor proceeded to compare his father with Hawthorne: "Unlike as the two men were in physical and intellectual constitution, they yet coincided in so many spiritual correspondences, that no friendship could have been better for Hawthorne than this."[23]

Quiet and retiring—in that respect much like Hawthorne—Ticknor was practical and businesslike. He provided the conservative balance in the publishing firm. Though his chief concern seems to have been financial and technical matters, on this trip abroad he was apparently planning to negotiate with some British authors for publication of their books, a task more often assumed by his junior partner. Fields, the exuberant one, has been more widely discussed for a number of reasons: His outgoing personality brought him in contact with many famous writers, in the United States and abroad; his house on Charles Street was a social gathering place for many of these people (he and his wife delighted in their opportunity to entertain Dickens, for example); and he himself was a lecturer and writer, and later an editor of the *Atlantic Monthly.* Fields was undoubtedly better known than his retiring senior partner, but together these two men created the first American firm to become internationally famous as publishers of the best English and American writers of their day.[24]

In matters of friendship, however, it was to Ticknor that Hawthorne wrote the larger number of letters. And it was to Ticknor that Sophia turned for advice as long as he lived. Certainly she did not forget his kind attention on shipboard, for in 1854, a year after Ticknor had been the Hawthornes' houseguest in Rock Park, Sophia was still expressing her gratitude that he had made the voyage with them and been so kind to them.[25]

Sophia was the letter writer of the family. Her own Peabody relatives, especially her father, heard from her often. Nathaniel, on the other hand, seldom corresponded with his sister Elizabeth or with his Manning relatives. As a result there are no shipboard letters written by him that reveal his opinions about the voyage or his feelings about the future. He did not begin the notebooks until he took office in Liverpool on August 1, and there are almost no backward glances either in these notes or in the letters he wrote early in the Liverpool period.

As this peaceful voyage with pleasant company neared its end, the Hawthornes must have had mixed feelings about the experiences facing them, but we can only guess at their speculations on what lay ahead. What did they know about the country that was to be their residence for more than five years? Nathaniel especially knew the England of the past and loved it. But did he know the England of his own times? If his vision of the country led him to expect only picturesque villages, ancient churches, and neat gardens, he was ill-prepared for the poverty and grime of a city controlled by merchandising and shipping interests.

Because the Hawthornes were descendants of English-born Puritans, there was a strong British influence on their lives. Their anticipation of finding common ties in "Our Old Home" did not prepare them for a changing Britain. Like other Americans of the Victorian era, the Hawthornes probably thought of the "mother country" as a unified and growing power, with customs and ways of living resembling those in the United States. They could scarcely be expected to foresee England's complexities or conflicts. Though prosperity may have seemed general in England, there were still thousands of wretchedly poor people, some of whom Nathaniel was to see at close range in Liverpool. Universal suffrage was still far off. The working class had not yet shown its strength in unionism. It was a period of quick rise to wealth on the part of manufacturers and of accelerated growth of the great middle class in a society already divided into classes to a degree that the Hawthornes had never before known. The ambivalence toward these changes that Hawthorne later showed in his notebooks and sketches of English life arose inevitably from conflicts within both the country and himself.

In spite of periods spent in Boston, the Hawthornes were not accustomed to urban life, especially the conditions of a big industrial city. Liverpool to them was not merely the port by which they, like most Americans, entered England; it was to be the center for Hawthorne's work for four years. Their introduction to the city was a grim experience.

In contrast to the delightful weather of the voyage, the sky above Liverpool was gray. Their arrival was exciting, especially to Julian, but it must have been depressing to Sophia after the peaceful crossing. Long afterward Julian described the scene as they reached the harbor: "Heavy mists and clouds enveloped it as we drew near, and ushered us up the Mersey into a brown omnipresence of rain. The broad, clear sunshine of the Atlantic was left behind, and we stood on wet docks and were transported to sloppy wharfs by means of a rain-sodden and abominably smoking little tug-boat."[26]

Because of Sophia's delicate health, this must have seemed an inauspicious beginning to her life abroad. To Nathaniel it may have been a foretaste of what he described two years later, after the dreary work of the consulship had often made him wish to resign, as "this black and miserable hole."[27] This was certainly the wet city of the Liverpudlians!

‡ 2 ‡

Liverpool

1853

"ON SUNDAY MORNING, at an early hour, the British and North American Royal Mail Steamship *Niagara*, Leitch, arrived in the Mersey from Boston and Halifax with 147 passengers and a small quantity of specie on freight. . . . Amongst the passengers by the *Niagara* was Mr. N. Hawthorne, the new United States Consul for this port" (*Liverpool Chronicle*, July 23, 1853). The early hour was, according to Ticknor, 6 A.M.[1] Although the weather was miserable, the Hawthorne family's transition from ship to dock to hotel was so quick that none of them could have gotten very wet. Customs officials did not open the "little mountain" of their baggage, but passed it along with "polite smiles and gestures." Julian was impressed: "I knew my father was the greatest man in the world, but I didn't know that they knew it." A cab took them through the "grey drizzle" to "a massive grey stone structure—the Waterloo Hotel."[2]

The hotel, at Ranelagh and Bold streets, was in the heart of the city, near the railway station, in what was then an "open, airy part of the town."[3] Inside this typically English and Victorian building the Hawthornes found "a dingy, carpeted duskiness" and "courteous attentions from serviceable persons." They climbed narrow stairs to their apartment, which consisted of several bedrooms and a parlor that contained "tinkling glass candelabras with candles, and a small fireplace with a grate full of black coal-lumps, to which one of the attendants applied a sulphur match. 'Liverpool!' We congratulated one another, exchanging pregnant glances."[4]

In spite of the high cost of room and board, the Hawthornes' stay at the Waterloo extended to ten days because their accommodations at Mrs. Blodget's boardinghouse, where they had already arranged to stay, were not ready. The children were fascinated by the Waterloo, for it was their first experience in a hotel. They explored all its areas from bedrooms down to the kitchen, where the cook sometimes handed them "titbits on the tip of a long skewer." The beds were great canopied four-posters with "swelling feather mattresses," regarded by Americans as "unsanitary." Each room had its bedside stand with brown metal candlestick for use in the dark hours. An intriguing sight outside was two washtubs of salt water, each containing a large turtle destined to become soup. The animals' size was a total surprise to Julian, accustomed to little mud turtles in the brook at Concord.[5]

Sophia was more interested in the service, especially that provided by Mr. Lynn, the "head of Waterloo House":

> [He] is a venerable-looking person, resembling one's idea of an ancient duke—dressing with elaborate elegance, and with the finest ruffled bosoms. Out of peculiar respect to the Consul of the United States, he comes in at the serving of the soup, and holds each plate while I pour the soup, and then, with great state, presents it to the waiter to place before each person. After this ceremony he retires with a respectful obeisance. This homage diverts Mr. Hawthorne so much that I am afraid he will smile some day. The gravity of the servants is imperturbable. One, Mr. Hawthorne calls our Methodist preacher. The service is absolutely perfect.[6]

Away from the table, however, the servants were less grave and formal; in fact, it seems they petted and indulged the children. When a Punch and Judy show came down the street, the chambermaid held Julian in an upstairs window while she explained this strange form of entertainment. But in spite of the indulgence, the service, and the comfort, the hotel was too confining for children. "Julian, in this narrow, high room," wrote his mother, "is very much like an eagle crowded into a canary-bird's cage."[7] Outside was the great smoky city, no place for a woman and three children to go exploring. The whole family longed for the green countryside.

Hawthorne still had two weeks before beginning his work at the consulate and had intended to go to London with Ticknor. But since he did not wish to leave Sophia and the children alone in the hotel, he instead divided his time between his family and the consular office where he was soon to begin his new work.

During this period, the Hawthornes welcomed their first visitors. The day after their arrival, Colonel Crittenden, the outgoing consul, had called and offered to give Nathaniel the instructions he would need before assuming his duties. Two passengers from the *Niagara*, William Silsbee and Orlando Wight, also stopped in. Silsbee was starting his year's stay abroad by touring the city with his new acquaintance, another ordained minister. Then the first of the Liverpool merchant families called on Sophia: Mrs. William Rathbone, her daughter, and her sister-in-law, Mrs. Richard Rathbone, "author of The Diary of Lady Willoughby." Mrs. William Rathbone invited Sophia and the children to tea and to view the grounds of their estate, Green Bank, and on the afternoon of the day when the Hawthornes moved from the Waterloo, Mrs. Rathbone sent her carriage for Sophia, Una, and Julian. Sophia reacted enthusiastically to the hospitality of English people, who, "if they once open their doors and admit guests into their sacred homes, are delightful people." "There is such an ease, such cordiality."[8]

In the meantime Ticknor stayed on in Liverpool to help Nathaniel arrange his affairs until Wednesday morning, July 20, when he took the train to London. There was not much to be seen in Liverpool, he felt, "except the Docks and their Commercial buildings. I would not have remained twelve hours, but for Hawthorne. He wished me to stay by him as long as possible."[9]

The Liverpool of 1853 that seemed to Ticknor so uninteresting was a far different city from the modern one. Its most impressive nineteenth-century buildings were not yet in existence. St. George's Hall, designed as a concert hall, was just being completed; when it opened, it also became headquarters for the assize courts. The cornerstone of the William Brown Library was not laid until 1857, during a ceremony in which Hawthorne was the American representative. Walker Art Gallery was not opened until 1877. Liverpool Cathedral, Metropolitan Cathedral, and the Liver Building, with its twin liver birds on top, are twentieth-century constructions.[10] The great showplace of the early nineteenth century, the Town Hall, where the mayor's dinners were usually held, was considered the most elegant building in Liverpool.

The docks, of course, saw a great deal of visitor traffic, not only because of the many berths for passenger-carrying steamships, but also because of the hundreds of berths for merchant ships from all over the world. Even in those days the docks extended for miles along the right, or Lancashire, side of the River Mersey. It was port traffic that had created the wealth of Liverpool and made it the second largest city in England, with a population, according to the 1851 census, of about four hundred thousand.

Hawthorne was completely familiar with docks after his two previous work experiences in Boston and Salem, but the docks of those places had been smaller and somewhat cleaner. He was not interested enough in Liverpool docks to give them more than brief mention in his notebooks. Then he commented that the Mersey itself was not crowded, since only the small black ferry boats plying the river made up "the chief life of the scene. . . . The Mersey has the color of a mud-puddle; and no atmospheric effect, so far as I have seen, ever gives it a more agreeable tinge."[11]

The Hawthornes did not look at this sprawling city with the romantic view that Herman Melville had shown in *Redburn* only a few years before. Melville's depiction of the heart of Liverpool as a contrast between flourishing trade and horrifying poverty may have intrigued Nathaniel, but Sophia shrank from such scenes of misery. It is highly probable that she never read the novel, especially the descriptions of the dockwall beggars, the "Booble Alleys," and the starving mother and children in the cellar below Launcelott's Hey. One may argue that Melville's descriptions were fictitious, but the alley is still there (now spelled *Lancelot's Hey*), and other accounts of Liverpool suggest that Melville did not exaggerate the bad conditions.[12] Sophia was no social reformer; whenever possible, she ignored the unpleasant parts of the city and overlooked the fact that the fortunes of the millionaires in the suburbs whose social life she regarded with envy and delight had been made possible by the trade that also produced the beggars whom she avoided.

Liverpool was so different from Boston that neither Nathaniel nor Sophia ever adjusted to this great shipping center.[13] Boston was one of the oldest cities of the New World, the starting point of the Revolution and, to the Hawthornes, seemed full of antiquities. Liverpool appeared not to have any. It did not even have any evidence of Roman occupation; Hawthorne looked for that later in Chester, across the river. But the greatest contrast between Boston and Liverpool was the apparent absence of any cultural life in Liverpool. Bostonians might be laughed at for feeling that their city was the "Athens of America," but there is no denying that until the middle of the nineteenth century Boston was the center of the writing and publishing worlds. Both Nathaniel and Sophia had lived part of their early lives in Boston in the midst of such an atmosphere. They had been married in the back parlor of 13 West Street, where Sophia's sister Elizabeth had her bookshop and where Margaret Fuller held her "conversations." Nathaniel had felt most at home in the Old Corner Bookstore. It was some time before he found a real bookstore in Liverpool—Young's—and then it was far different from that familiar bookstore of Ticknor and Fields.[14]

The upper classes in Liverpool recognized Hawthorne as the author of *The Scarlet Letter*, but most of the wealthy merchants who invited Nathaniel and Sophia to dinner did not talk about literature. Their interests were commercial. Matthew Arnold was probably right when he said that Hawthorne was "perpetually in contact with the British Philistine; and the British Philistine is a trying personage."[15] The seeming absence of any concern with "culture" did not help to make Hawthorne feel at home in Liverpool, and he looked forward to London as the real center of English culture.

Sophia, the social one, was fascinated by the glitter and pomp of a life she had never experienced before. Still, she was lonely in Liverpool and soon came to dislike this unfamiliar city where the streets were narrow, crowded, and always muddy. In an early letter to her sister Mary she described the streets as "black" and declared that she did not like "a bit" to go to the city.[16] The central section, where she shopped, was a crowded area filled with gloomy brick or wooden buildings. The U.S. Consulate, which she seldom visited, was in the Washington Buildings, on Brunswick Street at the corner of Gorce Piazza, a small square near the docks.[17] From that square, Brunswick Street led directly to an open space, now called George's Pierhead. Here late in the day commuters lined up on the dock to board ferryboats that would carry them across the Mersey to Cheshire.

The Hundred of Wirral, that part of Cheshire across the river, was a popular suburb often referred to as the dormitory of Liverpool's middle class.[18] One serious disadvantage to living in Cheshire was the winter fog that often made crossings difficult or impossible. On the other hand, houses across the river were less expensive than those in the northern and eastern suburbs, and the Hawthornes therefore gave serious thought to living in the Wirral. But during the first weeks there was no time for house-hunting, and as a temporary arrangement, the Hawthornes left the Waterloo Hotel and began a nine-day stay, until early August, at Mrs. Blodget's, 153 Duke Street.[19]

The Hawthornes were happy to move out of the Waterloo, for the novelty of hotel living had worn off, and they were looking forward to the sociability of a boardinghouse. Mrs. Blodget's was described as "a brick building" on a "respectable street" within walking distance of the docks, with houses on only one side. The other side of the street had open spaces, warehouses, and yards. Upon entering the house, one faced a staircase leading to the first floor, where there was a large Victorian parlor. Julian immediately "didn't care for it"; he preferred his bedroom with a window on the street that made him "a citizen of the world."[20]

Mrs. Mary Blodget, wife of Samuel Chase Blodget and former resident of Gilbraltar, was the owner of this famous boardinghouse, a place frequented almost entirely by American sea captains and shipping men (and sometimes their wives). Her assistants were her niece, Miss Maria, "a little wisp of a woman" who may have been about thirty years old, and her younger sister, Miss Anne Williams. Mrs. Blodget was such an impressive figure to Julian that years later he recalled her vividly as a solid woman in her fifties, five feet four inches tall, and weighing about "twelve stone; into such limits were her virtues packed."

> Her dark hair was threaded with honorable gray. Her countenance was rotund and ruddy; it was the flower of kindness and hospitality in full bloom; but there was also power in the thick eyebrows and in the massy substance of the chin—of the chins, indeed, for here, as in other gifts, nature had been generous with her. There was shrewdness and discernment in the good-nature of her eyes; she knew human nature, although no one judged it with more charity than she. . . . She was clad always in black, with a white cap and ribbons, always spotless amid the grime of Liverpool; in her more active moments—though she was always active—she added a white apron to her attire.[21]

Other people writing about Mrs. Blodget's boardinghouse have agreed on her extraordinary qualities in making a temporary home for Yankees. Not only did she set an excellent table, she also turned what might have seemed a formal atmosphere into almost family living. In the evenings after dinner, the men gathered together to smoke and exchange stories; the ladies conversed in another room. The place was so popular that requests for reservations there had to be made far in advance.[22]

On August 1, while the Hawthornes were still at Mrs. Blodget's, Nathaniel began his official duties at the consulate. Although the Washington Buildings themselves have been demolished, Hawthorne left a graphic description of his gloomy quarters in the building on the corner of Brunswick Street:

> My apartment (about twelve feet by fifteen, and of a good height) is hung with a map of the United States, and another of Europe; there is a hideous colored lithograph of General Taylor, life-size, and one or two smaller engraved portraits; also three representations of American naval victories; a lithograph of the Tennessee Statehouse, and another of the

Washington Buildings, Goree Piazza, ca. 1928

Steamer Empire State. The mantel piece is adorned with the American Eagle, painted on the wood; and on shelves there are a number of volumes, bound in sheepskin, of the laws of the United States and the Statutes at Large. Thus the consular office is a little patch of America, with English life encompassing it on all sides. One truly English object, however, is the Barometer hanging on the wall, and which, to-day, for a wonder, points to Fair. (*EN*, 3)[23]

Of the work carried on by Hawthorne, his vice-consul and head clerk, James Pearce, and his junior clerk, Henry Wilding, Nathaniel himself has left a record in his notebooks. His notes, however, consist of anecdotes and informal jottings; they do not explain precisely what the consul's functions were. Only from government documents does the reader learn that the responsibilities of consuls had changed little from the time the regulations were first set down in 1792. Basically, all consuls had, since that year, assumed the same powers and duties: to receive protests and declarations from Americans, both crewmen and passengers; to care for stranded American vessels; to relieve distressed seamen; to require masters of ships sold abroad to pay the sailors' passage home; to authenticate copies of documents; and to take charge of and settle the estates of Americans who died abroad. "Such added powers as might be inherent in the office" were also referred to, but these were not clearly defined.[24]

In the first half of the nineteenth century only one major change was made in the work of U.S. consuls: A regulation passed in 1818 stated that consuls were required to certify invoices for goods that were to be imported into the United States so that the correct duties could be charged. The signing of such papers enabled consuls to collect fees, to pay a portion to the government, and to retain a portion for personal income in place of a salary. An early notation of Hawthorne's describes one good day's receipts as a total of nineteen sovereigns and thirteen shillings. Since a steamer was departing on that day, an unusual number of invoice certificates had to be signed, each of which brought him the sum of two dollars. "The autograph of a living author has seldom been so much in request at so respectable a price. Colonel Crittenden told me that he had received as much as £50 in a single day. Heaven prosper the trade between America and Liverpool!" (*EN*, 11).

Early in the summer before Hawthorne took office, a bulletin was issued by the Department of State requiring all American consuls, "whenever practicable," to employ no foreign clerks "to assist in the discharge of Consular duties."[25] Hawthorne disregarded this directive when he continued to employ the senior clerk, Mr. Pearce, and the junior clerk, Mr. Wilding, both Englishmen. Because of their knowledge and experience, these men were too valuable to be dismissed by their superior, who in spite of his years working in customhouses was new to consular duties.

Hawthorne found that though his assistants could handle financial matters, it was frequently his responsibility to attend to the affairs of American seamen and passengers. The notebooks describe some callers who were frauds, such as the young Englishwoman pretending to be an American who "fooled" him "out of half-a-crown." Others were unfortunate cases, such as the insane young man found wandering around in West Derby, the seaman of the *John and Albert* who was accused of assaulting the chief mate and remanded to America for trial, and Captain Auld, who died in a Liverpool boardinghouse. Hawthorne felt it his personal duty to attend the captain's funeral, to notify his widow in New Orleans, and to see to it that the dead man's belongings were shipped home.[26] At the end of only one year Hawthorne was already "sick and weary" of the office: "What with brutal ship masters, drunken sailors, vagrant Yankees, mad people, sick people, and dead people," he decided that the office was "full of damnable annoyances." Every day he felt "beset with complainants who I wish were all at the devil together. But I can get along well enough with men, if the women would only let me alone."[27]

Less irksome, though often dull, were the many formal calls paid by visitors: foreign diplomats, Americans entering the port or returning home, and Englishmen of all types and occupations. On one of his first days in office, Hawthorne received, among others, William Butler Ogden, a Chicago millionaire en route to London and the Continent; the captain of the Collins steamer *Pacific*; and an American shipmaster. The innumerable visitors that Hawthorne greeted during his years of service put a strain on this naturally unsociable man. Bored by the formalities of the consulate, Hawthorne was exasperated enough at the end of his four years to write to Ticknor, "I have received, and been civil to, at least 10,000 visitors since I came to England; and I never wish to be civil to anybody again."[28]

Even in the early days of his career, Hawthorne began to detest the monotony of his consular duties. If it had not been for the pile of sovereigns, he would have resigned long before his four-year assignment was over. But he had counted on saving enough money in four years for his family's future, and so he endured grimly, escaping from the burdensome job by walks in the city, by evenings and weekends with his family, and, after the end of the first arduous year, by frequent short vacations.

During his lunch hours, Nathaniel often walked the streets of Liverpool frequented by the poorer classes and so was able to record many long descriptions of ragged and diseased people: of unkempt women nursing their babies and of hopeless, careworn, but doggedly patient men. Sometimes he found women sewing or knitting at the entrances to their hovels or cellars. Other women, barefooted, went around the streets with baskets of cheap wares to sell. And always in the streets were dirty children playing, many of them unattractive and lackluster. But the little children took care of other little children in a way that made Nathaniel say, "I must study this street-life more, and think of it more deeply" (*EN*, 17).

On the ferry he encountered other unfortunate people moving among the commuters and begging. He watched one man try to sell a single dirty copy of the *Times*. After Hawthorne refused him and felt guilty for failing to give the man something, he reflected on the universality of beggars and then wrote a *P.S.*: "From subsequent observation, I think him a humbug" (*EN*, 49).

It seems strange that Hawthorne should have intentionally sought out the poorer sections of Liverpool. Perhaps it was a relief from the formalities of rich dinners with the mayor and other dignitaries. He may also, of course, have been gathering material for what he hoped to write some day—a romance with an English setting.

Nathaniel's guide during visits to the suburbs and the countryside was Henry Arthur Bright, the man who became his first close friend in England. According to Sophia, Henry Bright and Francis Bennoch were the only two Englishmen whom Nathaniel regretted leaving behind when he departed for the States in 1860.[29] In July of 1853 Nathaniel had not met Bennoch; the two did not come to know each other well until Hawthorne was in London during the spring of 1856. Bright and Hawthorne, however, had met in Concord in 1852 when Bright made a trip to the States with Thomas Henry Carr Burder, a friend from Trinity College, Cambridge, as his companion. The two young men were touring America in much the same way that many other young Englishmen traveled around the Continent in the year after graduating from Oxford or Cambridge. The difference was that Bright, whose family was Unitarian, could not receive a degree at that time because of the ruling on dissenters from the Church of England.

(Five years later he and his cousin, James Heywood, who was a prominent advocate of university reform, were the first two Noncon-formists to be granted degrees from Trinity.)[30]

In May of 1852, the screw steamship *Great Britain*, rebuilt after an accident five years earlier, made its first voyage to New York. This prize ship, then owned by the company of which Henry Bright's father was a partner, was hailed for its rapid passage of 13 days, 5½ hours.[31] Bright was aboard the vessel as a sort of unofficial representative of the owners, but his subsequent land tour was purely for his own pleasure. After a short stop in New York, he and Burder traveled through parts of the South, the East, the Midwest, and Canada. They enjoyed contacts with prominent literary people like Longfellow, Emerson, and C. E. Norton and with Unitarian ministers, such as Dr. William Furness of Philadelphia, and their friends. Bright's journal, which he evidently wrote for his family, recounts details of his travels.[32]

Bright's early impressions of Hawthorne and of New Englanders in general were not favorable. In a letter to Robert Temple, a college friend then living in Wales, Bright reported that although he had not yet been to Boston, he was told that "the conceit, the intellectual pride of the Bostonians is insufferable." He had heard such opinions from New Yorkers and from Southerners who hated Boston because it was the stronghold of Abolitionists. (Though Bright did not believe in slavery, he felt that the Abolitionists actually did "more harm than good.") He changed his opinion of Bostonians after visiting there and discovering how friendly some of the literary people he met could be. Then he regretted having to leave the city so soon.[33]

From Boston, Bright and Burder, accompanied by William Synge, a friend from the British Legation in Washington, took the train to Concord, where they stopped first to see Emerson. The village of Concord pleased Bright because it looked so much like an English village: "White cottages, covered with creepers, border the lanes which are shaded with huge drooping elms; from the branches of one of them, larger than the rest, swings jollily as Mrs. Lupin's Blue Dragon, the signboard of the little inn, and a short way on and you come to Emerson's house in the midst of a pine plantation."[34]

Emerson took the three Englishmen to call on Hawthorne in his "old queer house," where, Bright wrote to Temple, Hawthorne lived "the life of a recluse shrinking from all society and occasionally behaving with a strange rudeness originating from extreme shyness." The details of Bright's letter gave a frank picture of this first meeting:

Henry Arthur Bright

He received us with the most frigid manner, but asked us into his house, and that was nearly all he said, except in answer to a question, while we were there. Emerson was much amused, and made all the play in conversation, while Hawthorne listened. At last we rose to go, and had bidden the cynic good bye when he suddenly asked Synge and myself to come and look at an old arbour he had in his garden; Emerson and Burder had gone on, and Hawthorne then condescended to talk a little more, and he has, I feel very sure, great powers of conversation, as of everything, would he only give himself a fair chance; but Emerson tells us he hardly ever does unbend to any one. . . . He is an odd looking person with a fine massive head and the most wonderful black eyes I ever saw except Daniel Webster's.[35]

Bright's journal filled in a few details not contained in his letters to Temple. The conversation in the garden was at least partly about England. Hawthorne spoke of how he longed to see the country and "how deeply he and all New Englanders felt towards it." Bright's last comments about Hawthorne in the journal concerned the children and Hawthorne's political future; he mentioned "long-haired red-haired Una, and a beautiful glorious boy called Julian." Bright added, "Hawthorne is a democrat and will be promoted by his friend Pierce, perhaps (as T. Appleton says) 'as minister to some aesthetic court.' "[36]

Hawthorne seemed in good spirits when he joined the group later on the same day for four o'clock dinner at Emerson's house. But unfortunately, somebody made an embarrassing remark about the attitude of Fredericka Bremer, the visiting Swedish author, toward Hawthorne. Nathaniel replied stiffly that his interview with Miss Bremer had not been a successful one and vanished just as dinner was being announced. Emerson was amused; Bright was annoyed, for he wanted to see and hear more of this shy man.[37] They did not meet again until the following summer.

When Hawthorne reached Liverpool in July of 1853, Bright had just begun to work in his father's company and was starting to write articles for periodicals. In college he seems to have shown some talent in writing: One manuscript entitled "Characteristic Differences of Ancient and Modern Civilization" bears an undated note signed "HAB" to the effect that it won the English Essay Prize at Trinity.[38] Bright's earliest writings, such as the journal, were not published in his lifetime.

Bright's first significant publication was a pamphlet that resulted from observations he made during the 1852 tour. It was entitled "Free Blacks and Slaves. Would Immediate Abolition Be a Blessing. A Letter to the Editor of the Anti-slavery Advocate By a Cambridge Man."

Below the title a line from Milton, "They also serve who only stand and wait," implied Bright's general attitude toward slavery: that noninterference was the best policy for the time being. He was opposed to immediate abolition, not out of love for slavery, but because he felt that "external pressure" would only support the system that it was trying to overthrow. In other words, he advocated a wait-and-see attitude that was fairly typical of an upper-class Englishman.[39]

While there is no evidence that Hawthorne ever read the pamphlet, he might have agreed with Bright that the Abolitionist Movement was an unwise one. As the two men grew to be friends, they must have talked about slavery, for they had many lively discussions on the state of affairs of both America and England. Ten years later Nathaniel paid tribute to Bright as he had appeared at the consulate in those first days:

> He used to come and sit or stand by my fireside, talking vivaciously and eloquently with me about literature and life, his own national characteristics and mine, with such kindly endurance of the many rough republicanisms wherewith I assailed him, and such frank and amiable assertion of all sorts of English prejudices and mistakes, that I understood his countrymen infinitely the better for him, and was almost prepared to love the intensest Englishman of them all, for his sake. . . . Bright was the illumination of my dusky little apartment, as often as he made his appearance there.[40]

At that time Rose Hawthorne was too young to know anything of Bright's literary or political interests, but years later she recalled a vivid childhood impression of his frequent visits to their house: "He and my father would sit on opposite sides of the fire; Mr. Bright with a staring, frosty gaze directed unmeltingly at the sunny glow of the coals as he talked, his slender, long fingers propping up his charming head (over which his delicately brown hair fell in close-gliding waves) as he leaned on the arm of his easy-chair."[41] Sophia wrote more about his personality than about his appearance. She was especially charmed by his ability as a conversationalist and said that she wished Nathaniel could always have such agreeable visitors.[42]

Bright's first visits to Hawthorne and his family were rather formal, as was the tone of his letters. "My dear Sir," was the salutation of his letter of September 1, 1853, written from Coniston, in the Lake District, where Bright had gone on a vacation trip with his parents and younger sisters.[43] If Henry Bright had been aggressive in his attempt to become better acquainted with Hawthorne, Nathaniel might have withdrawn in shyness. However, Bright's approach was to try to be helpful on practical matters and to wait for Hawthorne to respond. A brief comment written in November of 1853 to C. E. Norton, in America, shows the slowly developing friendship: "I see a good deal of Hawthorne and like him better every time I see him, for every time he is less shy, and more pleasant. What a wonderful fellow he is!"[44]

Hawthorne's early reputation for shyness preceded him to England. Arthur Hugh Clough, for example, had met Hawthorne several times in Concord and was, as he said, beginning to "feel my way with him"; yet the English writer still pictured Hawthorne as too shy to be sociable at all. "Do you hear anything of Hawthorne?" Clough wrote to Longfellow. "I suppose he hides himself sedulously in a corner of the Consul's office at Liverpool, and will very likely return to America without coming up to London."[45]

At first Hawthorne must have felt socially ill at ease, especially among the wealthy class of Liverpool. In July of 1853, George A. Brown, a member of the American branch of the Brown family of bankers and a cousin of the famous William Brown, M.P., was invited to breakfast with Hawthorne, "our new consul, author of the Scarlet Letter and Seven Gables." Hawthorne appeared to him to be "a very unpretending simple-minded man." Two years later Brown made a similar comment: "He is a very retiring man at all events appears so — Every indication of Genius in his countenance — in a tete a tete I am sure Hawthorne would shine." A few days later he wrote, "Nathaniel Hawthorne dined with us yesterday alone — He is shy, can't decide: Have read his 'Scarlet Letter' am now reading 'House of the 7 Gables.' "[46] Brown was correct: In a group Hawthorne was usually silent; alone with one or two good friends, he could be drawn out. Frequently Sophia attempted, not always successfully, to get her husband to participate in conversations, but she was the sociable one. At the beginning of the Liverpool period the visitors, aside from the Liverpool merchants' wives, were mostly Americans whom the Hawthornes already knew, such as Mr. and Mrs. Sam Hooper and their children and the writers Grace Greenwood and Charlotte Lynch.[47]

The only consistent visitor to the Hawthorne residence was Henry Bright. On his first outing he took the Hawthornes to Norris Green, the home of his uncle, John Pemberton Heywood, and then to his own home, Sandheys, in West Derby. Sophia was ecstatic to see green lawns, flowers, fruit trees, and rich gardens: "After smoky, grimy Liverpool you may imagine our relief and refreshment."[48]

According to Julian, it was Henry Bright who suggested that the Hawthornes consider the suburb of Rock Ferry as a place to live when he discovered that Nathaniel preferred a rather inaccessible place, like the Wirral, where family life could be separated from consular business and there would be fewer social affairs to attend. Sophia, however, wrote that Mr. Bird of Dingle Priory had recommended Rock Ferry to them.[49] Whoever advised them, on August 6, the Hawthornes moved across the Mersey to the Royal Rock Hotel in Rock Ferry. There they stayed for nearly a month until they found the house that became their first English home.

‡ 3 ‡

Rock Ferry

1853–1855

ROCK FERRY, called a "watering place" in Victorian days, was and still is commuter country. Beginning early in the nineteenth century with the quick and safe crossing of small steamers, it and similar communities along the Cheshire side of the Mersey River grew rapidly. Liverpool merchants built houses and promoters established bathing resorts. In addition to its own ferry, the town of Rock Ferry had easy access by land to Birkenhead, a larger suburb downriver, from which more ferries operated to Liverpool.[1]

Royal Rock Hotel, a resort hotel near the waterfront and facing the pier, had "flowering gardens, lawns, and shrubberies round it, and an extensive pleasure garden close by, full of enchanting arbors, flowers, trees, and broad gravel walks."[2] There was an esplanade along the waterfront upstream. There was also a row of bathhouses, although the river would appear, from Hawthorne's numerous comments, to have been too muddy for pleasant bathing.

At the hotel, where they spent most of August, the Hawthornes occupied several bedrooms and a large parlor with a bay window that looked out over the river toward Liverpool and north to Birkenhead. From that window the family watched the traffic on the river: ferryboats chugging to the city; merchant ships laden with goods; a Cunard passenger steamer mooring once a week to a "large iron-buoy in the middle of the river"; frequent mail boats; an American steamer of the Collins Line saluting the Cunarder once a fortnight; and, most fascinating of all, a Chinese junk looking as if it were "copied from some picture on an old tea cup" (*EN*, 21–22).

From the window they also watched the Gibbs, Bright & Co. steamer *Great Britain* preparing to depart on a first voyage to Australia. One afternoon Henry Bright gave the Hawthornes a tour of this largest ship in the world. Nathaniel was struck by what he imagined as the "tedium and misery of the long voyage to Australia," for he noted especially the fifty pounds' worth of playing cards, at two shillings per pack, stowed away for the passengers' entertainment. There was also a "small, well-selected library" (*EN*, 10). Sophia reflected on the risks taken by 450 passengers on such a long voyage. She felt that Bright's father would find great pleasure in such a business venture, in spite of the fact that his company had already lost $200,000 on the vessel.[3]

Besides the novelty of watching the river traffic, there were many other pastimes for the family. The children played in the gardens of the hotel or went for walks with their nursemaid Ellen Hearne. Occasionally they took penny donkey rides in the park. The Hawthornes also had a number of visitors while they were house-hunting and making arrangements for the lease of a place to live. Mr. Barber, president of the Liverpool Chamber of Commerce, came in his carriage to take them to his residence, Poulton Hall, about three miles from Rock Ferry. Then the Hoopers and their children, whom the Hawthornes had seen the month before, arrived back in Liverpool. They had been on a visit to Wales before starting on a tour of England and the Continent. Nathaniel took Mr. Hooper and his son Sturgis to the city. Sophia, no doubt feeling that their American friends would be glad of an opportunity to see a typical British country home, took Mrs. Hooper and her daughter, along with Julian and Una, to see Poulton Hall.[4] Most of the house was closed for the winter, since Mr. Barber and his two sisters had gone to Scotland, but Sophia had permission to show friends around whenever she pleased. The mansion was not an impressive one, according to Nathaniel, but he wrote a long description of the very beautiful gardens and lawn (*EN*, 6–9).

After the Hoopers left, a neighbor family, the Squareys, took Sophia to the assizes in St. George's Hall. Ladies were not admitted to criminal trials, but they could visit the civil court. Describing the details in a letter to her father, Sophia said that this was only her second experience in a courtroom; once before, when Daniel Webster was counsel for the defense, she had attended court in Concord.[5] Her description implied much more elegant furnishings in the Liverpool building than in the Concord court, for this was a new showplace in the city.

By the end of the month the Hawthornes had already met and entertained several Americans who were waiting to return to the States on steamers from Liverpool and who preferred to stay overnight in the hotel at Rock Ferry instead of in the city: Dr. and Mrs. Gamaliel Bailey, for example, who were waiting for the *Atlantic* to sail. One wonders how much discussion of the antislavery movement took place while this famous editor of the *National Era* was at the hotel. Perhaps he was glad of a rest from politics, since he had reportedly been abroad for the sake of his health.

On a rainy Thursday, September 1, the Hawthorne family moved at last into what was to be their only real home in England, 26 Rock Park. Here they maintained for nearly two years a complete household in many ways typical of a middle-class suburb. We can only speculate on why they chose a house as large as 26 Rock Park. A great deal has been written about Hawthorne's concepts of house and home and about his own restlessness in moving from place to place. Circumstances had determined most of the changes in family residence in the United States; not only was it cheaper to rent than to buy, but also the climate was seldom satisfactory. The same factors seem to apply to the Hawthornes' experiences in England. The truth for Nathaniel lay in a comment that he wrote from England to his friend Pike in Salem: He was seldom homesick, for he carried his home with him wherever he went.[6] In choosing his first home in England he merely fitted family needs to what he thought were the demands of his position as a diplomat. He would be expected to entertain many more visitors than the family had ever entertained in the States.

Since the Hawthornes could not afford to live in a suburb made up of estates like those owned by the wealthy merchants of Liverpool (mostly on the other side of the river), they chose the next best locality, one consisting of comfortable houses built for rental purposes. Rock Park, a section of Rock Ferry close to the waterfront, consisted of one long winding drive forming an irregular loop, lined with semidetached houses and a few detached villas. The road was curved in such a way that the houses were built at slight angles to one another. They were also situated on several different levels. Those on the riverfront were lower, but still a little above the esplanade. Footpaths gave access to the esplanade.

Number 26 was a gray stucco house, "fashioned in a castellated style, with grounds in perfect order and surrounded by thick hedges." "Behind [it]," Sophia wrote, "is a lawn and garden with rare roses and fuschias, and carnations and many other flowers and a few fruit trees, and a strawberry bed." The semidetached house was about halfway between the lodge gates at the upper entrance of Rock Park and the lower end. According to Sophia, it was a four-minute walk from the house to the hotel and the pier.[7]

The house consisted of three stories with four good-sized rooms on each floor. Sophia described the large drawing room with "one end almost all a window opening upon the lawn and garden." The large

Hawthorne House, 26 Rock Park, Rock Ferry

dining room also had long windows opening upon a "nice piazza—into the garden again." The breakfast room looked out on the court in front, and on the other side were the kitchen and the butler's pantry. The second floor, besides having four chambers and a bath with hot and cold water (a rarity in those days), included a tiny room "with a fire place in it to run into from the bath to dress, in cold weather." The third floor had two large and two small rooms.[8]

A Miss Sheppard served as agent for her sister, the owner. At first, the rental price of the house, furnished, had been set at £200, but when the agent learned that it was the U.S. consul who wanted the house instead of "Mr. Nobody," she reduced the charge to £160. "So much influence has rank and title in dear old England," said Sophia. She added that Miss Sheppard did not know that Nathaniel was an author.[9]

Both the Hawthornes were well aware that Rock Park was likely to prove an expensive section of the suburb. Nathaniel emphasized that it was called "private property," an estate with residences for professional people and merchants, "the quietest place imaginable, there being a police station at the entrance; and the officer on duty admits no ragged or ill-looking person to pass." Payment at the lodge gates of a toll for carriages also kept out unnecessary traffic (*EN*, 22).

The choice of such a home raises a number of unanswered questions about the Hawthornes' ideas on their new status. Nathaniel's predecessor, Colonel Crittenden, had not maintained a house of his own, for he was a young man with no children. During their first years in England, he and his wife had lived at Mrs. Blodget's. But Hawthorne had three growing children to consider. In addition, he was a famous author as well as a diplomat and his situation was therefore different from Crittenden's. Later, when it began to look as if the consul's income would be limited, Nathaniel defended his position when he wrote to Ticknor, "No consul can live as a gentleman in English society, and carry on the official business on those terms."[10] The emphasis on "gentleman" and Sophia's frequent remarks about rank in England provide clues to the Hawthornes' concepts of their new status.

In setting up such a household, the Hawthornes found that a large initial expenditure for extra equipment was necessary, even though the house was, according to the lease, completely furnished. Kitchen utensils, crockery, blankets, quilts, and mattresses were supposed to be included in the furnishings. But the family account book reveals some costly expenditures: kitchen equipment, silver of all kinds, a complete tea and dinner service, glasses and tumblers, and many other housekeeping items. Sophia also bought materials for making table linen, sheets, pillowcases, slipcovers, "doylies," and antimacassars.[11] These expenditures suggest that the cost of setting up and maintaining a household for five family members and three servants was one of the reasons why Nathaniel decided ultimately in 1855 that they could all live more cheaply by renting rooms at a lodging house and providing their own meals.

The size of the house, the upkeep of the garden, and the care of three children demanded not only a regular staff of three women servants, but also the occasional help of a hired man and the weekly services of a laundrywoman. The wages for the servants were all fairly standard for those days. Emily, the cook, received eleven pounds annually for her work; Mary Hearne, the housemaid, was paid ten pounds; Ellen Hearne, nursery maid and general helper, received eight pounds. Ellen seems to have done most of the ironing. King, who had been butler for the former occupants of the house, helped out when the Hawthornes entertained at dinner; he also did some gardening, for which he once received six shillings for three days' work. The laundrywoman's payments ranged from three to five shillings per week. Nathaniel insisted on paying Mary two pounds more than housemaids usually received. Since there was no housekeeper, Mary probably had more responsibility than was usual for a housemaid. Her importance is indicated by her being summoned from Ireland, where she had gone in July to visit relatives, as soon as the Hawthornes decided upon the Rock Park house.

No doubt Sophia took upon herself many of the functions that a housekeeper might have performed. After one month's experience in managing a household of this size, she wrote, "It takes a great while every day to keep so large a house in proper order." But, she emphasized, "Oh no, dear father, we do not live in 'great style'—neither do we intend to have much company. We really could not afford it."[12]

In managing her household, Sophia seems to have supervised expenditures more carefully than did most Victorian women of her class, and therefore she must have been more active in planning and buying. The typical Victorian household in England patterned itself after that of the queen—close family ties, strong parental authority, and the function of the wife as a sort of general manager. It was her business to hire and dismiss servants, to supervise the education of the children (usually by means of hiring a governess), and to maintain social life by making "morning calls" as well as by giving occasional evening dinners. "The most successful mistresses," wrote Mrs. Beeton in her book on household management, "are those who, as in other walks of life, make themselves *felt* rather than seen or heard."[13] In her quiet way Sophia must have exercised firm control over the servants.

The Hawthornes had always been accustomed to one maid-of-all-work, from the earliest period at the Old Manse to the time of their departure from the States. But this maid had hardly been treated as formally as a British servant would have been. The recently discovered diary kept by Sophia for a month at the Old Manse shows that the family's relationship with Mary O'Brien was most informal, and the American notebooks also suggest that this "member-of-the-family" relationship was true with their other maids.[14] However, their first experience with three servants, each with different duties, in a much larger household, must have been somewhat different. In many households of the nineteenth century, the cook assumed control of the meals—with the approval of each day's menus by her mistress—and contracted for purchases of food from an egg woman, a vegetable woman, a butcher, and other persons who delivered their wares. At Rock Park, Sophia seems to have supervised the purchases herself, for she recorded in her account book every single expenditure, at first item by item in daily lists.

This unpublished account book represents the only financial record of the Hawthornes' way of life in England. Fragmentary and incomplete as it is, with only scattered entries in the latter half, it still makes significant contributions to the picture of life at Rock Park. If the reader succeeds in deciphering the hundreds of seemingly trivial items, he can make some general assumptions about food, clothing, education, recreation, travel, cost of services, and medical expenses. After making some attempts at totaling the expenditures, he may well conclude that the Hawthornes were living with too many household expenses to fulfill their expectations of saving money.

When he accepted the appointment, Hawthorne estimated that he could save at least $30,000 from his consular experience. He eventually realized that an annual expenditure of £700 ($3,500) for the household alone—the approximate total for 1854, minus part of the rent, which Sophia forgot to record—would not allow him to save as much money as he had counted on. In addition to paying his own clerks, Nathaniel also gave or loaned money to distressed people who came to the consulate, much of which was never returned to him.

After a year's experience he was still optimistic enough to think that he could comfortably save $20,000. He admitted, however, that he ought to accumulate more than that, for he saw that once the family returned to Concord, it would not be "quite so easy to live on a thousand dollars, or less, as it used to be. I am getting spoilt, you see."[15]

In the beginning the account book expenditures, though recorded almost daily, were not sorted in any way. The reader cannot reconstruct menus of any kind but can determine that the Hawthornes' diet was similar to that of the British except that the traditional beef and mutton were missing, probably because of their high cost. Instead, there were many purchases of local items such as chicken, fresh fish, pork, and occasionally rabbit. Foods listed most often were potatoes, milk, butter, eggs, as well as barm (yeast) and flour for making bread. The locally grown fruits and vegetables were only rarely supplemented by oranges or other imported fruit.[16] Since the account book records an astonishing number of jars of preserves, honey, jam, jelly, and marmalade (all purchased, not made at home), it is no surprise to find that Emily devoted much of her time to baking bread.

Tea, in spite of its high cost—one dollar per pound—was the usual family beverage.[17] There is no mention of coffee at this time. Though Sophia did not usually drink any alcoholic beverages, Nathaniel presumably had wine at dinner. Again the account book shows a moderate amount of money spent for wine and beer (and once for champagne), but no more than would be needed for the amount of entertaining that the Hawthornes did at Rock Park.

The planning of meals was a complicated task, since the children had their main meal at midday, when Nathaniel was away. (Sophia said she had only a "morsel of bread" at that time.) In the evening they ate supper before the adults' dinner. This meant setting and clearing the table four times a day.[18]

In the matter of household furnishings, the Hawthornes were, on the whole, well satisfied. The house was supplied with the elaborate and heavy furniture of the period. Sophia described for her father the damask curtains hanging from gilded cornices "with a valence of fringe," the flowered Brussels carpet, the ponderous mahogany chairs and tables, and the large portraits of John Campbell and other previous occupants.[19] One important difference between the Hawthornes' English house and their previous houses in America was the open fireplaces for burning coal, which was cheap in England, instead of the ugly airtight stoves that they had had in Concord.

Equally elaborate from the modern point of view were the clothes made by a dressmaker for the females in the household. It has been said that the parts of Sophia's letters in which she describes either the costumes of other ladies at the dinners she attended or her own specially made outfits might have served as pages for *Godey's Lady's*

Book.[20] Most of her dressmaking expenditures were for everyday clothes, which seem ornate if we consult the fashion magazines of those days. The account book shows large amounts spent for fabrics, buttons, and trimmings of all kinds. Many of the items had to be bought ready-made: shoes for fast-growing children, "India rubbers" for the wet climate, and a variety of accessories. For Nathaniel, and for Julian as he grew older, a tailor had to be engaged to produce "saques" and "pantaloons."

Like most women of her time Sophia was an experienced seamstress, but Mary and Ellen Hearne were not capable of doing more than very plain sewing. With her other household responsibilities, Sophia did not have time to do all the sewing herself. A professional dressmaker did the major portion of the work. Sophia took pride in clothes and was happy to have the children well dressed. Nor could she, as the consul's wife, afford to look shabby.

Because of the number of hours Sophia devoted to supervising the household, the education of the children in the Rock Park house was rather unsatisfactory. It was often interrupted by social life. The Hawthornes hired no governess until 1856. Sophia taught some lessons to Una and Julian daily at ten unless there were guests. Una was by nature a great reader, and Nathaniel also read aloud to the family in the evenings, but during the daylight hours Julian seems to have preferred physical activities. Sophia minimized her own efforts when she wrote that although the two children had some arithmetic and geographical science and Julian had had some Latin, she taught them "a little about shells and flowers, because at their age *objects* are particularly interesting." "When they look pale and heavy [because of the climate] I cannot urge study." In this letter Sophia's attitude was clearly expressed: Exercise and physical well-being were of utmost importance; when children drooped, "let learning go by the board."[21]

The most time-consuming and expensive lessons took place in Liverpool. Una went to the city for music lessons two days a week, and Sophia had to accompany her each time. Then Una began dancing lessons—one session at Birkenhead and one in the ballroom of the Royal Rock Hotel—but these did not last long. Julian was interested in drawing and wanted to learn music; Sophia proposed dancing lessons for him, too, but his father thought he should have fencing lessons instead. The problem was solved by the advice of Dr. Drysdale (whom Nathaniel always called *Dr. Dryasdust*). He said that Una was growing too fast; her brain needed rest in order to keep up with her body. Instead of dancing lessons, she should do calisthenic drills and get outdoors every day. The result was that both children took gymnastics with M. Huguenin two days a week in Liverpool, but this still required that Sophia make trips back and forth with them. It was a task she hated, for there was nothing for her to do during the lessons except hunt for sewing materials in the shops along the dreary city streets. "It is very depressing to go to Liverpool—to steam over the muddy water in a dirty boat and walk up into the city through the black streets, shopping wearily and dragging back all grimy and tired."[22]

Eventually in the fall of 1854, as fogs made crossing the river difficult, Una moved into Liverpool to board with Mr. and Mrs. Husson and to study French and music with them. She stayed in the city until Christmastime and then came home for the holidays. Presumably she did not go back to the Hussons' to board, but resumed the trips to Liverpool.[23]

If the cost of so many private lessons seems extravagant, we have only to recall that American children abroad in those days did not usually attend British schools; in fact, upper-class English girls were commonly educated in the home. A private school for Julian was considered, but the plan was abandoned as too costly. It was easier and less expensive for Sophia to supervise the children's reading of standard British schoolbooks such as Mrs. Markham's *History of England* or Milner's *Geography*. She did teach more than "shells and flowers," but her rather unsystematic way of educating her children was not calculated to prepare them adequately for the future.

At the same time, there was such close supervision of activities that the children were overprotected. They were never allowed to go anywhere alone, even to play or walk outside the grounds of their own house. Such treatment was characteristic of the age and circumstances, especially for girls. It was as much a part of a close-knit family life as the circle in the evenings when Nathaniel, like most fathers of his class, read aloud from books such as Scott's novels, *Don Quixote*, or *The Faerie Queen*. Though the Hawthornes spent very little money for recreational reading, they obtained books from several sources, such as friends, the nearby public library, or the Liverpool Book Society, to which Nathaniel had been elected.[24]

The evening hour for reading had always been an event eagerly anticipated by the children. They adored their father and looked forward to his return from Liverpool each day, even if the time that he could spend with them after his dinner was brief. Rose, who probably went to bed before the reading hour, enjoyed the earlier round of games, especially blindman's buff. Her later description of her father's hilarious laughter and agile movements in the game paints a very different picture from the usual one of him as a silent, shy person.[25]

This was a happy family, living rather simply and seldom entertaining upper-class Liverpool people. Social life was usually limited to friendly neighbors, Americans on tour, and the frequent visits of Henry Bright. Herein, of course, lies a contradiction that neither of the Hawthornes seemed to recognize. They understood that they were expected to entertain, but Liverpool people were not the ones who visited them at Rock Park. We can assume either that Nathaniel was bored by the city merchant class or that Sophia was overwhelmed by the Rathbones', the Hollands', and the Heywoods' style of living and felt unable to compete with them. Whatever the reason, none of these people, so far as we can tell, ever came to dinner at Rock Park.

Nathaniel said that one of his chief reasons for moving to Rock Ferry was to avoid social life in Liverpool as much as possible. He wanted and got relaxed suburban Sundays with the family as well as quiet evenings at home. Sometimes Sophia attended chapel service in Liverpool with either or both of the two older children. In fair weather on Sunday afternoons the two adults, with Julian and Una, took long walks to Bebington, Eastham, and other small Cheshire villages. Often Julian and his father went by themselves. It was then that Nathaniel related the fanciful tales of General Quattlebum that were never recorded. The mythical general vied with Hawthorne in performing magical deeds, but Hawthorne always won. Long afterwards Julian said that the telling of these stories extended over three or four years and that it was a pity that he was too young to write them down. He cited the tales to controvert the general impression that his father was "a sombre, unplayful person."[26]

Rose, who was too little to be taken on long walks, generally went out with Ellen Hearne while the other children were having their lessons. During the week, while their father was at the consulate, Una and Julian also painted and sketched, and Rose played with dolls and blocks. It was very much an at-home family, for the Hawthornes took no vacation trips until the second year. "We have lived very quietly here," Sophia wrote in her diary the first autumn and then mentioned only some calls from Liverpool women and Rock Ferry neighbors.[27]

It was not until 1854 that entertaining and being entertained became burdensome. At that time Hawthorne became more and more adept at refusing invitations, particularly to evening affairs in the city. Some years after this, a bookseller and publisher in Liverpool, who had come to know him as a customer rather than as a visitor, recorded his early impressions of the man who was generally regarded as somewhat "aloof from the residents of Rock Ferry":

> My first recollection of Mr. Hawthorne is of a dark-haired, retiring, and gentlemanly-looking man, who came to see me, and without a word to anybody or from any one to him, proceeded to investigate the books. In a little while he took from the shelf an uncut copy of "Don Quixote" in two volumes, illustrated by Johannot, asked me the price, paid me the money, and requested that the books be sent to 'Mr. Hawthorne at the American Consulate.'
>
> Then he began coming almost daily, after a long time growing somewhat familiar. He would inquire much about books, in which he took the keenest interest. . . .
>
> When the family finally left England, Mr. and Mrs. Hawthorne, and, I think Miss Una Hawthorne, called to shake hands and say good-bye. Hawthorne's personal appearance and demeanor very strongly reminded me of Dr. Martineau, and Mrs. Hawthorne's sprightliness was a delightful set-off to her husband's extreme diffidence and quietude.[28]

This description of both Nathaniel and Sophia seems to capture the impression that many people had of the Hawthornes, that of a couple reluctant to engage in much social life with the English. Americans, however, were occasionally welcomed as overnight guests. In the autumn Ticknor was the first to arrive, but because sociability and business had kept him in London longer than he had intended, his visit at Rock Park was too short for the Hawthornes. While he was in London, Ticknor decided to go to Paris for a few days and then make a quick trip to Edinburgh. Hawthorne had already made at least two different reservations for Ticknor on ships leaving for the United States in September. At last a stateroom was arranged for him on the *Canada* departing from Liverpool on October 1.[29]

Ticknor could spend only four days with the family. He arrived on Tuesday, September 27, bringing gifts for everyone: a book of engravings, *The Country Year Book*, for Julian; a leather portfolio and stationery for Una; a wax doll for Rose; a set of monogrammed razors for Nathaniel; and monogrammed scissors and a book of flowers for Sophia. The next evening there was a dinner party for him to which Henry Bright was invited. On Friday the entire family had planned a visit to Chester in order to show Ticknor the cathedral, but the weather that morning was too uncertain for Sophia to consider taking the children on such an outing. Instead, Nathaniel and Ticknor spent their last day together by themselves at Chester.[30] On Saturday morning,

October 1, to the great regret of all the Hawthornes, Ticknor sailed from Liverpool. Later in the day Nathaniel wrote in his notebook, "His departure seems to make me feel more abroad—more dissevered from my native country—than before" (*EN*, 31).

But there was not much time for regrets. That evening at six, Hawthorne joined ten or twelve other guests at a dinner party at the home of John Aiken, a wealthy Liverpool merchant, where he was introduced to Colonel and Major Burns, sons of the Scottish poet. After the ladies had left the dinner table, the sons of Burns entertained the men with some of their father's songs. According to Nathaniel's report to Ticknor, they liked him partly because of "the affection which I showed for the whisky-bottle." This remark is typical of Hawthorne's frequent comments implying an undue fondness for liquor. Such a reference appeared occasionally in his letters and may have been part of an attempt to cover up his shyness.[31] In his notebooks he merely stated that although the Burns men drank a good deal, "Neither of them (nor, in fact, anybody else) was at all the worse for liquor. I liked them both, and they liked me" (*EN*, 31).

The party lasted until midnight, and since it was a stormy night, Hawthorne stayed in Liverpool, returning to Rock Park for breakfast on Sunday morning. Sophia said in a letter to her father that since dinners lasted so late, Nathaniel had determined to refuse all invitations to evening affairs in Liverpool during the winter.[32]

However, the Hollands' dinner party later in October was in Liscard Vale, which was on the Cheshire side of the river and easily reached by cab. This was the first of the elegant dinners that so much impressed Sophia. She devoted numerous pages to descriptions of the headdress she wore, the drive to Liscard Vale, the servants, the twelve guests, the elaborate menu, including at least six different kinds of wine, and Mr. Harold Littledale, the "rich country gentleman" who escorted her in to dinner.[33] Nathaniel, by contrast, referred only to a remark of Littledale's about Dickens (*EN*, 36). Evidently the conversation was not of interest to him, and the dinner was too typical of the numerous affairs in Liverpool that as consul he could not avoid.

Dinners given by the mayor were the most notable occasions that Nathaniel was forced to attend. The first one, given in honor of the judges and grand jury during the assizes, was held on Friday, August 12, at the Town Hall. As "Mr. America," Hawthorne, of course, was toasted and expected to reply. His speech, he said, was not more than "2 or 3 inches long." He had previously considered speechmaking an almost impossible task to face, but he said that once started he was not embarrassed and went through it "as coolly as if I were going to be hanged" (*EN*, 12). This was the first of many such speeches, a duty that Hawthorne dreaded, but one that he performed adequately. It was a formality, the speeches were seldom reported, and presumably no one listened carefully or recalled, except vaguely, what had been said.

Hawthorne refused an invitation to another formal dinner party, to be given by Mr. and Mrs. William Rathbone, on the grounds of Sophia's poor health and the illness of Julian. Sophia's trouble was no doubt the cough that grew worse from that first autumn and that seems to have developed into chronic bronchitis. Julian had supposedly caught cold from sitting on wet grass. Nathaniel's letter is a good example of his ability to write a diplomatic refusal when necessary.[34]

Even Lord Dufferin of Ireland did not succeed in persuading Hawthorne to take time away from his work. Lord Dufferin wrote on two different occasions in November of 1853, inviting Hawthorne to his estate at Clandeboye, eight miles from Belfast. The first note said that his aunt, the Honorable Mrs. Norton, would also be delighted to receive Hawthorne at her house on Chesterfield Street. Hawthorne politely refused both invitations, for Clandeboye was four or five hours from Liverpool, and the visit would have involved not only several days away from the consulate, but also a journey by sea in foggy, disagreeable weather.[35]

There were no other English dinner parties that year, and only two overnight visits by Americans were recorded. In November came Mr. Ogden, "the large-hearted western gentleman," a friend of Elizabeth Peabody. Sophia said Mr. Ogden was "overflowing with life" and seemed "to have the broad prairies in him." He had called at the consulate and been invited to Rock Park. After dinner he entertained the family with accounts of the Lord Mayor's Dinner in London and of his own short excursion to Bacon's grave with Delia Bacon, whom Hawthorne would come to know three years later. In his notebooks Hawthorne did not mention Ogden's visit to Rock Park, but Sophia's descriptions suggest that the occasion was for her a bright spot in a month of increasingly dull, foggy weather.[36]

The other American visitor to spend the night was the famous actress Charlotte Cushman, who came at the end of December. A year before the Hawthornes left Concord, Nathaniel had been introduced to Miss Cushman and had liked her. When she came to call on him at the consulate while she was visiting her married sister and family at Rose Hill Hall in Woolton, south of Liverpool, Hawthorne asked Sophia to invite her to dinner and to spend the night. The next morning she sat down at Una's piano and sang a Spanish ballad among other songs. It was not an unusual performance for Miss Cushman, for she had begun her career years before as an opera singer in New Orleans.[37]

Long afterward Julian was indignant to read a description of her as a homely woman. He praised the beauty of her expression, her voice, her figure, and her stately carriage. "In our little drawing-room she was only simple, sincere, gentle, and winning. Born actress though she was, her horizon was by no means restricted to things histrionic; she talked well on many subjects, and was at no loss for means to entertain even so small and inexperienced a person as myself."[38]

Earlier in December the Hawthornes also had two English callers from London: William Jerdan, the journalist, and Francis Bennoch, merchant-poet, whom Hawthorne had invited to Rock Park since he himself could not go to London. Jerdan apparently dominated the scene as he told anecdotes of his meetings with famous people. Rose sat speechless upon his knee and stared gravely at him until he finally got her to smile. In a sketch of this scene written years later, Julian concentrated on a characterization of Jerdan and did not mention Bennoch at all. Sophia likewise wrote of Jerdan at some length but only remarked about Bennoch that he was "a patron of poets and artists, and as pleasant, merry, and genial as possible." In remembrance of this visit to Rock Park, Bennoch sent Sophia as a gift from both visitors a copy of *Letters of Laura D'Auverne* by Charles Swain. Jerdan's presence at Rock Park was only a single incident in the lives of the Hawthornes, whereas this initial contact with Bennoch, the unobtrusive guest, developed into an enduring friendship.[39]

In the following month the Hawthornes missed connections with an English writer whom they never did meet—Elizabeth Gaskell. James Martineau, Unitarian minister in Liverpool, and his wife called on Sophia to invite the Hawthornes to their silver wedding anniversary party at their home in Prince's Park. Another guest, they said, would be Mrs. Gaskell. But the night fogs were too heavy for Sophia to travel across the river; she wrote to her father that it would be "madness" to go. Two days before the party, Mr. Martineau and Mrs. Gaskell called at Rock Park. They brought a note from their friends, the Misses Yates, asking Sophia to dine and stay overnight with them in Prince's Park so that she could attend the Martineau party the following evening. Unfortunately, when the callers arrived at the house, Sophia was in Liverpool shopping for a Christmas present for her father, and though she regretted having to refuse the invitation a second time, she was more concerned that she had missed a meeting with Mrs. Gaskell.[40]

As the foggy weather grew worse, the Hawthornes stayed very much at home. Even Henry Bright, who was accustomed to the climate, stayed overnight with the family after he had dinner with them on Thanksgiving Day. When he promised to come to dinner, Bright did not know that it was "a festival day," but, Sophia wrote, "We are going to observe it in memory of the fatherland."[41] The account book records the purchase of a turkey, and we can assume the usual trimmings.

Christmas that year was rather uneventful. The Hawthornes observed the season by following as far as they could the British traditions of Christmas, New Year's Day, and Boxing Day. Even though Sophia did not mention this last holiday, the account book records the cost of a number of holiday boxes for servants and merchants. What Sophia described in most detail in her letters was the sound of bells in Liverpool on Christmas and New Year's Eve. There were also mummers who gathered at their gate on Christmas Day. Ticknor sent the family a barrel of apples to remind them of holiday times in New England.[42]

Hawthorne did not refer to Christmas in his notebooks that year. Aside from consular business, which he said had almost worn him out, his chief concern was the weather. Earlier in the fall Sophia had implied that he was not affected by English climate: "Mr. Hawthorne does not mind fog, chill or rain. He has no colds, feels perfectly well, and is the only Phoebus that shines in England."[43] The notebooks indicate, however, that he was depressed by the gloom, probably because foggy weather was responsible for keeping him indoors. There were no walks to Cheshire villages during the months of November, December, or January. Pages written during these months describe people whom he saw on the ferry and on the streets of Liverpool; other notations involve the consulate. An entry for November 14 sums up the typical weather for that time of year: "There is a heavy dun fog on the river, and over the city, today; the very gloomiest atmosphere that ever I was acquainted with"(*EN*, 38). To Ticknor he wrote, "You speak of the 'wretched climate' of New England. God forgive you! You ought to spend a November in England."

After the fogs of November and the chilly mists of December came a cold spell, with frost, and on January 1 there was a rare snowfall of several inches (*EN*, 43). A letter of Nathaniel's written early in January referred to the cold weather as about "the same temperature as our mild winter-weather; but the atmosphere is so moist that it penetrates to the bone."[44] He described the winter darkness in a way that must have represented Sophia's feelings as well:

> At this season, how long the nights are—from the first gathering gloom of twilight, when the grate in my office begins to glow ruddier, all through dinner-time, and the putting to bed of the children, and the lengthened evening, with its books or its drowsiness,—our own getting to bed, the brief awakenings through the many dark hours, and then the creeping onward of morning. It seems an age between light and light. (*EN*, 44)

In spite of his inability to take walks away from the city on weekends, Hawthorne had not forgotten two long-standing intentions: to see a great deal of the English countryside and in the process to attempt to find some trace of his ancestors. His reference to Hawthorne Hall in the nearby Hundred of Macclesfield occurs at the end of his notes for December 1, at a time when he could not yet have toured the countryside. Previous entries show that he had been reading Ormerod's *History of the County Palatine and the City of Chester* (London, 1819), but modern biographers have shown that he was mistaken in looking for ancestors in Cheshire. Had he read other books, he would have discovered records in Bray, Berkshire, an area he never visited.[45]

Hawthorne's search for his ancestors was part of the total interest in English antiquities that he revealed in many scattered references in the notebooks and in the descriptions of towns visited later during his stay in England. His interest in the past led him to visit churches, cathedrals, and castles; his love of English literature took him to places connected with such authors as Johnson, Scott, Burns, and Shakespeare; and his hope of someday writing an English romance caused him to record many detailed observations of people and places.[46]

Fortunately for Hawthorne's vacation plans, beginning in 1855, all his interests formed a happy combination, even though in pursuing them he never did find his ancestors. During this first year, however, he took no vacations, and the walks so necessary as relief from the drudgery of the consulate did not resume until February of 1854. With the warmer weather came the renewal of social life. There was, in fact, one pleasant day near the end of January when Sophia took Una with her to return four calls to people living in Liverpool suburbs, but it was not until late February and early March that the dinner parties resumed.

The first dinner party was at Sandheys, the Brights' home in West Derby, in the third week of February. Hawthorne did not mention the occasion, but this was Sophia's first overnight visit in an English home, and she made careful arrangements for it. Nathaniel, Sophia, and Una were to meet the Martineaus at Sandheys and spend two nights there. At the Rock Park house, Ellen would look after Rose and Mary after Julian, who had enough to keep him busy with maps to paint, a pile of books, and a popgun. As a safeguard the Hawthornes asked King, the ex-butler, to stay all night. "It was really safe enough," Sophia wrote, "only you know mothers have unfounded alarms."[47]

At the party on the first night, Sophia was escorted in to dinner by Samuel Bright and James Martineau. Henry Bright's father, Samuel, was described as "about fifty," "very handsome and gracious, his wavy hair beginning to be silvered, his eyes and complexion dark, his manners princely." "He looked more Oriental than English." The Heywoods were also present. Mrs. Heywood tried to get Nathaniel to agree to go to her costume ball, but he did not accept the invitation. (Sophia had refused immediately on grounds of family responsibility.) When dessert was served, the younger Bright children came in—the girls in their pretty muslin dresses with long sashes—and were admired by Sophia particularly. There were eight children in the family, seven younger than Henry Arthur, though not all were present on that occasion. Sophia could see no signs of "wearing care" in Mrs. Bright's face. For Sophia the cordiality and informality of her host and hostess made this a completely satisfying visit.[48]

Mrs. Heywood must have tried to change Hawthorne's mind about not attending her ball by following up her spoken invitation with a note, for his written response was a humorous one begging her not to be offended that he could not go. His description of himself, though somewhat exaggerated, contained a great deal of truth:

> He finds himself, indeed, in the position of an owl or a bat, when invited to take a pleasure trip in the sunshine; he cannot deny that it would be a most delightful affair, but still feels it fitter for himself to stay in his dusky hole than to go blinking about among other people's enjoyments. The truth is, Mr. Hawthorne has all his life been under a spell, from which it is now too late to free himself;—or rather, he was *born* a solitary brute; and he can not otherwise account for his now being able to resist Mrs. Heywood's invitation.[49]

The next day he wrote to Ticknor that he wished the tailor had made him a consular dress before he left the United States, for "it would have been first-rate to wear to a fancy-ball, to which I am invited to-night. Having nothing to wear, I shan't go."[50] The note to Mrs. Heywood seems closer to actual facts; a fancy-dress ball was not his style of entertainment.

Late in February the Sunday walks began again. On the nineteenth, Nathaniel, Sophia, Una, and Julian took a characteristic family outing by walking to Bebington Church. While Sophia and Una attended the service, Nathaniel and Julian roamed "past many old thatched cottages, built of stone," "an old stone farm house," and "a small Methodist chapel, making one of a row of low brick edifices; there was a sound of prayer within" (*EN*, 46). The two walked through a wood and observed that there were already a few daisies along the wayside before they rejoined Sophia and Una in the churchyard. On this occasion as on other Sunday outings Nathaniel did not attend the services, not because he was irreligious, but because he was far more interested in the architecture and in their surroundings than in listening to sermons.

In the new year the first of the literary people to visit the consulate was William Allingham, a young Irish poet and former customhouse worker, who stayed only briefly. He was on his way back to London, where he would try for a second time to earn a living by writing. Hawthorne was pleased by the gift of Allingham's book of poems, but sorry that the visit was so short. "When you next visit Liverpool, you will not escape us so easily."[51]

Allingham's description of Hawthorne, though slightly inaccurate as to his age, described the impression the consul usually made on the English:

> I called on him at his Consul's office, a dirty little busy place on the line of docks, and was very kindly received. . . He is about forty-six years old, middle sized, hair dark, forehead bald, features elegant though American, cheeks shaved, eyes dark. He is very bashful in manner, and speaks little and in a low tone. He has not yet had time to visit London, but intends to do so sometime in Spring, when I hope to see more of him. He looked oddly out of place in Liverpool.[52]

No friendship seems to have developed from this meeting, for there is no further correspondence from Hawthorne except a letter in 1855. Nathaniel sent copies of Allingham's poems to Ticknor and Fields with the request that they try to promote the little volume in America.[53]

Allingham's hope that he would see Hawthorne in London probably came from Nathaniel's comments that he planned to visit London in the future, but in the spring the Hawthornes did not accept two separate invitations from George Sanders, the London consul. Sophia regretted Nathaniel's inability to leave his work, for the Sanders family lived conveniently in Portman Square and could have gained admission tickets everywhere for the Hawthornes.

There was one person whose invitations Nathaniel was unable to refuse. John Bramley-Moore came to the consulate and insisted on Hawthorne's dining at his home that very evening. A short time later Bramley-Moore repeated his visit to the consulate; this time he took Nathaniel home to a dinner party to meet Samuel Warren, author of *Ten Thousand a Year* and *The Diary of a Physician*. This dinner prompted some very uncomplimentary remarks by Hawthorne about his hostess. The food and beverages, he wrote, were "very praiseworthy," but the hostess, "the only lady present," was a "stupid woman, of vulgar tone, and outrageously religious—even to the giving away of little tracts, and lending religious books." "Mrs. Bramley-Moore must be an underbred woman; it is indescribably evident in her whole tone and manner; and, I suspect, an Englishwoman does not so readily overcome such disadvantages as an American would" (*EN*, 55).

His host, Hawthorne said, was "not quite a gentleman." He seemed rich, had been mayor of Liverpool and an unsuccessful candidate for Parliament, but he talked too freely about the cost of the wines he served and of various other possessions, "a frailty which I have not observed in any other Englishman of good station." As for the guest of honor, Mr. Warren, Hawthorne forgave him for talking a good deal about himself and his writings. Warren said "nothing brilliant," but he possessed a "talent of mimicry" and enlivened the evening with his anecdotes (*EN*, 56).

The total effect of this party, however, was not an agreeable one. When the Brights again insisted on Nathaniel's going to West Derby for dinner and staying overnight, he departed with "a powerful anathema against all dinner-parties, declaring he did not believe anybody liked them, and therefore they were a malicious invention for destroying human comfort."[54]

Throughout the month of March numerous visitors stopped briefly at the consulate and the house at Rock Park, but there were no visits of long duration until April. At that time John O'Sullivan, who had been appointed U.S. minister to Portugal, together with his family, stopped on his way to Lisbon. The visit turned out to be a seven-week stay, because English ships were being commandeered to carry troops to the Crimean War.

While the O'Sullivans waited, various excursions and dinner parties were held. One dinner included James Buchanan, minister to England, who was staying in Liverpool while waiting for his niece to arrive from the States. The Hawthornes' three servants, occasionally King, and Madam O'Sullivan's maid all helped with the parties. With Ellen Hearne absorbed in household tasks, Sophia was left to take complete care of Rose, and she had no opportunity to give lessons to Una and Julian. The children did not seem to object to two months' vacation; in fact, Una, who had been very homesick, was much cheered, especially by "Uncle John," as she had always called John O'Sullivan, her god-father.[55]

Such a long visit caused a strain on everyone. Madam O'Sullivan, John's mother, was frequently ill. Sophia had a violent attack of what she called a twenty-four-hour "cholera," which she concluded later was caused not by diet but by fatigue.[56] The most evident result of the strain was that Ellen Hearne became "impossible" to live with. By the time the O'Sullivans departed, she was so "arrogant, hateful, and bitter" that finally in June Nathaniel dismissed her. This act upset Sophia, for she said she had always treated Ellen like a sister. Sophia would have tolerated the girl longer, but Nathaniel insisted on letting her go.[57]

In June, after the O'Sullivans' departure, the whole family came down with whooping cough. The children seemed to be affected the most and for the longest period of time. To make matters worse, the weather was damp, and fires were still necessary to relieve the chill. When the doctor decided that the Hawthornes would benefit by a change of air, Nathaniel took them to the Isle of Man in the latter part of July for a two-week vacation. Because of his work at the consulate he did not stay after the first Sunday, but left Sophia and the children at the Fort Anne Hotel in Mona and returned the following Sunday. Although he wrote to Ticknor that he found the Isle of Man "the most interesting place" he had seen yet, the only other place he had visited was North Wales, where he had spent a weekend with Henry Bright earlier in July.[58]

One day while the rest of the family were on the island, Henry Bright took Nathaniel to meet Harriet Martineau, who had come down from her home at Ambleside to visit her brother in Liverpool. As a result of this short meeting Hawthorne recorded in his notebooks a vivid portrait of Miss Martineau:

> She is a large, robust (one might almost say bouncing) elderly woman, very coarse of aspect, and plainly dressed; but withal, so kind, cheerful, and intelligent a face, that she is pleasanter to look at than most beauties. Her hair is of a decided gray; and she does not shrink from calling herself an old woman. She is the most continual talker I ever heard; it is really

like the babbling of a brook; and very lively and sensible, too; —and all
the while she talks, she moves the bowl of her ear-trumpet from one
auditor to another. . . . All her talk was about herself and her affairs; but
it did not seem like egotism, because it was so cheerful and free from
morbidness. And this woman is an Atheist, and thinks, I believe, that the
principle of life will become extinct, when her great, fat, well-to-do body
is laid in the grave. I will not think so, were it only for her sake; —only a
few weeds to spring out of her fat mortality, instead of her intellect and
sympathies flowering and fruiting forever! (*EN*, 77)

When Nathaniel told Sophia about the meeting, she was far more
critical of Miss Martineau: "She has become quite infidel in her
opinions, and I cannot think her quite sane. It must be either a fool or a
madman who says there is no GOD. Perhaps mesmerism has unsettled
her wits."[59] If she had met Harriet Martineau in person, Sophia might
have been more generous in her comments, for actually Sophia did not
limit her admiration to conventionally religious people; she was usually
pleased with anyone's cheerful conversation and was seldom so caustic
in her remarks as on this occasion.

During the month of August only a few Americans arrived at Rock
Park for short visits. First came George Bradford, an old acquaintance
of Hawthorne's from Brook Farm days. He was on his way to Switzerland and then to Italy for the winter. While he was at Rock Park, Sophia
took him and Una to Liverpool to call on Barbara Channing, a friend of
Sophia's who was on her way home to the States from Italy. She was not
at the Angel Hotel when they arrived, but they did find William Silsbee,
who was also en route home, and they invited him to Rock Park. Later
in the day, as the Hawthornes were having dessert, he and Barbara
Channing came for a short call. Sophia's final comment on Silsbee at
this time referred to the improvement in his health since she had seen
him on the *Niagara* the year before: "Mr. Silsbee seems to be a stronger
person in every way—or rather the strength of his mind is responded
to better by his personal power. I am sure his friends at home will be
rejoiced in his aspect and manner. He has the force added to his
sweetness and goodness which just make them richer. I think it a pity
he does not stay till October and see the rest of things—but he thinks he
must return today."[60]

Sophia was unable to persuade Silsbee to stay, but Bradford spent at
least a week with the Hawthornes. On September 2 the Hawthornes
left Bradford in Chester, where he planned to take the train north to
see York Cathedral before going down to London and thence to the

Continent. Nathaniel's parting gift was a letter of introduction to Francis Bennoch, who, he was sure, would help entertain Bradford while he was in London. Hawthorne described his visitor as "an excellent fellow" and said that he was bringing with him a silver "fruit-shovel" that James Fields had sent over for Mrs. Bennoch.[61]

Nathaniel's notebooks described St. John's Church in Chester at length and then gave a detailed picture of Bradford that revealed his own characteristic mixture of feelings. Bradford was conscientious, he was the "best little man in the world," but he lacked dignity and "strong will"; he became troublesome by his "anxiety not to give trouble." Hawthorne included such homely details as Bradford's passion for huckleberry pudding. Perhaps the most vivid sentence was the statement: "He wanders about the house like a cat, noiselessly, in slippers" (*EN*, 75–76). The portrait shows Hawthorne's habit of observing human behavior in minute detail and pointing out faults, but usually being kindly in his criticisms.

Shortly after Bradford departed, the Hawthornes took a second two-week vacation, this time to Rhyl, a resort on the north coast of Wales. Dr. Drysdale thought that they all needed another change of air, for the whooping cough still hung on. Again Nathaniel spent only weekends with his family. Sophia and the children took a parlor and two bedrooms in a rooming house at Mona Terrace, 18 West Parade, a long promenade close to the beach.[62]

In spite of inconveniences connected with cooking in their quarters, Sophia felt that the trip was more satisfactory than the previous one to the Isle of Man. The children were freer because there were no dangerous cliffs; they could dig in the sand and hunt for shells on the long, wide beach.[63] Nathaniel, on the other hand, called Rhyl a "most uninteresting place — a collection of new lodging-houses and hotels on a long sand-beach, which the tide leaves bare almost to the horizon" (*EN*, 77). He much preferred trips to nearby places in Wales, such as Rhuddlan Castle, Conway Castle, the hill of Great Orme's Head, and the state mines.

Nathaniel came to Rhyl for a second long weekend to do more sightseeing. It was pleasant to be a tourist for a change, although end-of-summer business was so slow that he scarcely made enough money to live on. On Monday, September 18, he returned by train to Chester and thence to Rock Park. The rest of the family came the next day. There were still traces of whooping cough, but Sophia wrote optimistically about herself that she hoped the coming year would find her "quite acclimated to the damp and fog of England."[64] Of course it did not, but at the moment the Indian-summer weather at the end of September made life unusually pleasant and relaxed.

Two days after the return from Wales, the Hawthornes attended a brilliant social event, the soirée of Mayor Lloyd at the Town Hall. They saw not only "the elite of Lancashire society, but a very magnificent display of pictures by Turner, Wilkie, Leslie, Paul de la Roche, and Collins, a rising artist." Sophia wrote to her father at great length about the mayor's hospitality and her introduction to Richard Monckton Milnes, whom Nathaniel had already met at the Heywoods'. Sophia did not meet Milnes's wife, since she was not at the soirée, but Nathaniel had previously made her acquaintance at the Heywoods' and had liked her "extremely well."[65]

If we judge by contemporaries' accounts, it would have been hard to resist the charms of either Milnes or his wife. In the 1850s, Milnes (who did not become Lord Houghton until after the Hawthornes left England) was combining a parliamentary career with writing and with entertaining literary people, especially at breakfasts in London. His wife, the daughter of Lord Crewe, was a charming hostess for Milnes's social affairs, whether at their London house on Upper Brook Street or at Fryston, their Yorkshire home. Julian wrote years after he had come to know Milnes: "A more urbane and attractive English gentleman did not exist. . . . His manners were quiet and cordial, with a touch of romance and poetry mingling with the man-of-the-world tone in his conversations."[66]

Apparently Milnes took an immediate liking to Hawthorne. He called at the consulate after the soirée and early in November invited the Hawthornes to spend at least a weekend at Crewe Hall. As usual Hawthorne sent a carefully composed refusal, giving the reason that shyness prevented him from going anywhere except to dinners that he could not avoid. The correspondence that followed was cordial on both sides. Hawthorne asked Ticknor and Fields to send some American books to Milnes. After they came, he answered Milnes's inquiries about the authors, particularly Thoreau and Sylvester Judd. In return for his gift of books, Milnes sent Hawthorne a copy of his edition of Keats's poems. The relationship between the two men remained friendly, although Hawthorne did not accept any invitations from Milnes until later when he went to London by himself.[67]

In early October a note came from William Henry Channing, a Unitarian minister from the United States. He was moving his family to

Liverpool and wanted rooms reserved at the Royal Rock Hotel until he could find lodgings in the city. Since the position Channing had accepted was that of pastor at the Renshaw Street Chapel, Sophia did not urge him to look for a house in Rock Ferry, because his parishioners and friends all would be on the other side of the river. Sophia was sure that the English would like Channing "in spite of their conservatism." After the Channings moved to Liverpool, she saw a good deal of them, though she was critical of Julia for spoiling her handsome children, Frank and Fanny.[68] Sophia attended the Renshaw Street Chapel whenever possible and praised Channing's sermons. In the beginning Nathaniel had not been certain of Channing's success, "fearing that he might not be beefy and ale-y enough for the English taste." However, after hearing about the first Sunday service, Hawthorne admitted that Channing seemed "to have excited universal admiration."[69]

Meanwhile, early in the summer, a change occurred in the Rock Park household that was to make matters easier for Sophia, who for some months had had entire care of Rose. Fanny Wrigley, daughter of a cotton manufacturer who had lost his fortune, was hired as a nursemaid for Rose. Since Fanny had had no training as a governess, she applied for a position as a nursemaid. She had never worked outside her own family, but she had some experience in caring for her invalid stepmother. Exactly when she moved to Rock Park is uncertain, but it would have been after Ellen Hearne was dismissed in June.[70]

On September 2, Sophia wrote to her father that the English nurse was "not quite suited to the place." She had never been in service before and was too frail, "too unaccustomed to be with servants to get along comfortably," though to Sophia she was "very convenient."[71] Nevertheless, Fanny Wrigley proved to be the one servant who stayed with the Hawthornes—except when they were in Italy—until they returned to the States.

Years later Julian paid tribute to Fanny in a long portrait:

> I think she was Lancashire-born; she typified a large part of the ancient population, rooted in the early times: people neither high nor low, whose deeds would never be recorded, but who were made of sterling stuff. . . . She took the world—the English world—for granted: things as they were—English things—were right, and all other things were probably wrong, but certainly unimportant. She had innumerable little special knowledges and aptitudes—plain sewing, making tea, child-care (indulgence, rather), dusting furniture, boiling eggs, making responses at

church of England services, household medicines, handling of invalids; she was the victim of endless timidities, mostly irrational; and was heroic before dangers faced on behalf of those she loved.[72]

The children soon came to love Fanny, whom they nicknamed "Fancie" or "Moony Fanny." As Julian described Fanny, she was not prepossessing in appearance. This new nurse was tall and thin with prominent nearsighted eyes and "a mass of brown hair, vaguely massed on top of her small head, hairpins insecure, and strands escaping." She also suffered "constantly from little physical ailments, headaches, toothaches, pains in the back, coughs: but she never complained; a mild sunshine always emanated from Fanny." Her concern for other people's troubles and her need to be useful turned this inexperienced girl into a reliable part of the Hawthorne household. One of Julian's last comments on Fanny indicates her relationship with the children: "She found us adorable, and I believe I can say we appreciated her."[73]

Rose became especially attached to Fanny because the girl was hired as her nurse, much as Dora Golden had been Julian's nurse in America. Since Rose was still too small to keep up with the others on their walks, on sunny days Fanny used to take the child on short strolls in the country. Years later Rose described to her aunt Elizabeth Peabody the delights of those rambles when Fanny helped her pick wildflowers along the ditches that bordered the lanes.[74]

Before the end of 1854, Fanny had already become an essential part of the household as the family settled down to face another foggy winter season. But this year fewer complaints about the weather appeared in anyone's letters. November was a busy month for Sophia. She went to the city twice a week to take her daughter to dancing school, and the two also went to chapel on Sundays. Julian was kept busy with his studies at home after Sophia decided against sending him to a dames' school in Rock Ferry. By December, a daily routine was established: lessons from ten to twelve; a walk before lunch at one-thirty; after lunch, study until four; exercise in the gym for half an hour; and then dressing "to receive papa." There was a brief social time with Nathaniel by the fire until the adults' dinner. Games afterward lasted until Rose went to bed; then Nathaniel or Sophia read aloud.[75]

Family preparations for the Christmas season were not elaborate. Each year it was the custom to place Christmas presents on a table in the parlor. "Sometimes they were on the large centre-table, sometimes on little separate tables, but invariably covered with draperies; so that we studied the structure of each mound in fascinated delay."[76] The presents were always inexpensive ones, sometimes gifts made by the children. The accounts for the year show that in addition to small sums allowed the children for their gifts, the adults spent moderate amounts on presents such as ninepins and a paintbox for Julian, a gold necklace for Una, and blocks for Rose. Sophia recorded buying an onyx signet ring "for Papa." Also listed in the account book were holiday boxes for such people as the muffin girl, the newsboy, and the butcher boy.

Christmas Day in 1854 was rather mild. The children went out to the garden and picked wallflowers, pansies, and pinks; they also got a beautiful rose from the garden of the hotel. Still, it was cool enough for fires in the fireplaces, and three days later, following a rain, it was cold enough to freeze the surface of the pools. During the evening chill, as he sat by the fireside, Nathaniel looked back over the year that was ending and wrote: "I think I have been happier, this Christmas, than ever before. . . . More content to enjoy what I had; less anxious for anything beyond it, in this life. My early life was perhaps a good preparation for the declining half of life, it having been such a blank that any possible thereafter would compare favorably with it" (*EN*, 98).

His satisfaction was marred, however, by a dream that had been recurring over a period of twenty or thirty years. In it he had failed to make progress in life as his contemporaries in school or college had; he had met some of them and felt ashamed and depressed. "How strange that it should come now when I may call myself famous, and prosperous!—when I am happy, too!—still that same dream of life hopelessly a failure!" (*EN*, 98).

The dream was symptomatic of Hawthorne's increasing worries over political difficulties. There is no one date when his concern began, but ever since he had heard rumors from Washington of a change in the financial setup of consulates, Hawthorne's aim of saving enough money from his consulship to live on for the rest of his life had begun to seem less attainable. Various proposals were discussed in Washington, and the rumblings were threatening, but no action came until a bill was presented for vote in Congress in the spring of 1855. The bill proposed to do away with the fee system and to substitute a flat salary—in Hawthorne's case, $7,500. Feeling that such a salary would never compensate for the drudgery of the consulate, for a time Hawthorne was determined to resign. The uncertainty of his situation is revealed in letters to Ticknor over a period of some months, but he made no decision until later in the year.[77]

Money was not his only concern; there was always Sophia's delicate health. Nathaniel would not agree to her enduring another English winter. Added to that worry was the shock of her father's death. All during the autumn of 1854, Dr. Nathaniel Peabody had been in failing health. Sophia sent him a New Year's present of ten pounds, to spend any way he wanted. There is no information as to whether it arrived before he died on January 1.[78] When the news of his death reached England several weeks later, Nathaniel told Sophia as gently as he could.

Because of the loss of Nathaniel Peabody as a correspondent, the picture of life in the Hawthorne household becomes less sharp after the end of 1854. Sophia's letters to her sisters, Elizabeth Peabody and Mary Mann, were never as long and detailed as the accounts she wrote to keep her father entertained. For two or three months in 1855, in fact, Sophia wrote very few letters to anyone. She went into a brief period of traditional mourning, and because Nathaniel's letters during this period are concerned chiefly with financial problems, there is almost no record of family activities except as one can guess at them from expenditures listed in their account book. There we find recorded the purchase of a mourning bonnet, black silk for dresses, and a "mourning band" for Julian's new hat. Sophia did not accept invitations even from the Brights. Nathaniel wrote refusals for her and the children.[79] His own notebook entries from January to April deal with affairs at the consulate and official dinners that he could not escape.

First, he was invited to a dinner at the home of William Brown, M.P., for James Buchanan, minister to England, who had come from London to Liverpool for a short visit. Buchanan had brought his niece, Harriet Lane, who was serving as his hostess in London and who was to be a bridesmaid at the wedding of one of the daughters of Washington Jackson, an Irish-American merchant. Brown was doing the entertaining because it was his grandson, a Mr. Hargreaves, who was being married to Jackson's daughter. The Hawthornes were invited to the wedding, but they could not attend since they had to go to the funeral of a young American woman who had died in childbirth. "We went to the house of mourning, rather than to the house of feasting" (*EN*, 101). If she had received the news of her father's death before this date, Sophia would not have attended the funeral; Nathaniel would have gone alone, as he did at other times during the year.

In February he again attended a mayor's dinner at the Town Hall.[80] By this time he had become somewhat used to speechmaking, and though critical of civic banquets in general ("What should we think of them in America!"), he evidently enjoyed the food—turtle soup, salmon, woodcock, and oyster patties, among other delicacies—and the elegant surroundings. When the mayor toasted him, he responded with adequate patriotic fervor. "After sitting down, as usual I felt that there might be great enjoyment in public speaking; but, while up, my great object is to get down again as soon as possible" (*EN*, 103).

Only one event in mid-spring was of significance to Nathaniel in later life. Both the Hawthornes had listened to the Hopwood trial at St. George's Hall,[81] and Nathaniel had also attended a luncheon on board the *Donald Mackay*, at which Austen Henry Layard, the famous archaeologist and author of *Nineveh*, was the chief speaker; but the major event to Hawthorne was a dinner at the Heywoods'. Here he met Mr. and Mrs. Peter Ainsworth of Smithill's Hall, Bolton le Moors, and heard for the first time the story of the Bloody Footstep. Mrs. Ainsworth invited him to come to see Smithill's Hall and the footmark, but he did not go until late in the summer. The dinner, the story, and the subsequent visit left such an unforgettable impression upon him that he made use of the footstep theme in the romances published posthumously. It was also at this dinner that he entertained the group with the story "The Ghost of Dr. Harris." His later dedication to Mrs. Heywood gives the place and date of completion of the manuscript as "Liverpool, Aug. 17, 1856." The story had evidently been in his mind for some time before he told it or wrote it down. It is the only tale that Hawthorne wrote while he was in England and was not meant for publication.[82]

Meanwhile, in March, Congress passed the Consular Bill, to become effective in January of 1856, and Hawthorne's letters were filled with speculations and possible plans. The injustice of the bill, according to him, was that incumbents were not allowed to complete their four years under the old system with the income they had anticipated when first appointed. Extending Hawthorne's original contract to August 1, 1857, would have been a contradiction to the terms of the bill. He also pointed out that the bill did not take into account consuls' extra expenditures, such as money given or loaned to stranded or needy persons. He added that his successor would have to forget the "beggars" and "tourists without funds" and find methods of cutting down on the clerical labor.[83]

Hawthorne analyzed his financial situation by saying that though he had already economized, he had spent thousands of dollars in addition to the initial expenditures of setting up a household. Later he wrote that he could not hope to live on less than $6,000 a year and that no salary of less than $10,000 would be an adequate return for the drudgery of the office.[84]

Nevertheless, by the end of March he had made up his mind not to resign immediately. Instead, he planned to collect as much as he could before the new bill became effective and practice strict economy in his household arrangements, so that he could still visit for a year or two in Italy before returning to the States. In order to save money he decided to give up the house in Rock Park as soon as possible and take lodgings. "This will abridge the number of servants, and make it impossible for me to entertain people—which is very expensive here." He would keep his two assistants, Pearce and Wilding, who would look after business matters when he was absent from the office, as he planned to be in the summer of that year.[85]

So far Hawthorne had taken no vacations from his labors, except a few long weekends, during a period of nearly two years. Now he planned for the family to leave Rock Ferry early in June and set out on short trips to areas close enough to Liverpool that a day's travel would bring him back to the consulate when necessary. "I rather think matters will go on about as well as if I were constantly on hand. At all events, I have a right to some recreation—for I have had very little hitherto."[86]

In deciding not to resign immediately and making plans for greater economy, Hawthorne was somewhat cheered by the thought that he could still save for the future, although not as much as he had expected. And after all, there was the additional possibility of going back to his writing once he was relieved of consular responsibilities. Late in the spring he wrote to his old friend, Horatio Bridge: "I shall have about as much money as will be good for me. Enough to educate Julian, and portion off the girls in a moderate way, that is, reckoning my pen as good for something. And, if I die, or am brain-stricken, my family will not be beggars, the dread of which has often troubled me in times past."[87] How fortunate that Hawthorne could not see the years ahead!

In May, while he was discussing the financial setup of the consulate in a letter to Pierce, Hawthorne summed up changes in his family since the president had seen them in Concord: "My family are well, although Mrs. Hawthorne suffers somewhat from the climate. Julian has grown amazingly, and is stronger than any English boy of his age, or two years above it. He is a sturdy little Yankee, and holds himself always ready to fight for his country's honour. Una is already taller than her mother, and little Rose is twice as big as when we left America—which she has quite forgotten."[88]

June of 1855, then, marked the beginning of what Hawthorne called their "ramblings." As yet they had no definite plans, though the suggestion of Sophia's spending the winter in Lisbon had been made by the O'Sullivans the previous year. Nathaniel did not decide on this, however, until sometime in late spring or early summer of 1855.

Since the lease on the Rock Park house did not expire until August, in May the Hawthornes advertised the place for rent for the summer.[89] It took them a month to pack and store most of their possessions. The account book shows that by June 15 the three servants were paid and the household bills settled. Hawthorne had arranged for Mary Hearne to exchange her services as a stewardess for her passage back to America.[90] There is no mention at this time of what happened to Emily, the cook. Fanny, the only servant they kept on, was to accompany the family from that time on.

If the new bill had not made strict economy so necessary and if Sophia's health could have withstood the winters in Rock Ferry, the Hawthornes might have remained there for the entire four years that Nathaniel was consul. Certainly they were happy in the house at Rock Park, in spite of the pressures of maintaining a large and expensive household. Describing this important chapter of their lives long afterwards, Julian wrote that life at Rock Park had more true English quality than they experienced in any other part of the country. He concluded his account of their years there with the nostalgia of a person looking back on a golden age:

> It was a good and happy life in Rock Park, and I think our father and mother enjoyed it almost as much as we children did. They were meeting people many of whom were delightful . . . and they were seeing towns and castles and places of historic and picturesque interest. . . , This was England; the Old Home, and the Old World, for the understanding of which they had prepared themselves all their lives previous. My father once said, "If England were all the world, it would still have been worth while for the Creator to have made it."[91]

‡ 4 ‡

Leamington, Lisbon, and London

1855–1856

AS THE TRAIN CARRYING the Hawthornes left Chester for central England, rain blurred the car windows so that they could not see the beautiful landscape. Sophia consoled herself by enjoying the luxury of a first-class carriage.[1] Any of the family thinking back over their experiences would have realized that several of their significant days in England had been gloomy: The Hawthornes had arrived in Liverpool in fog and drizzle, and when they moved into the Rock Park house, rain had made the transfer of their belongings a difficult process. Here they were again starting out in weather that was unkind to the health and spirits of all except Nathaniel.

By the time they reached Leamington, however, the sun had come out and the air seemed fresh and warm. With her usual optimism, Sophia described in her journal the "delightful weather" and the rich greenness of the countryside. She concluded that there was latent in Americans "an adaptation to the English climate which makes it like native soil and air to us."[2] In her enthusiasm over the ideal summer weather, she forgot the disagreeable winters they had lived through for two years.

With his customary disregard for weather, Nathaniel was occupied by the practical matter of finding a suitable place to live for several weeks. As soon as they agreed to rent a house at 13 Lansdowne Crescent, he wrote to Ticknor and invited him to visit them anytime during the month. Ticknor could not come; nor did the Hawthornes stay a full month, but they evidently felt at home in the town, for it was a place to which they were to return twice in the following years—in the fall of 1857 and for the fall and winter of 1859–1860.

Nathaniel wrote very little to Ticknor about the house that they rented for this short period. His remarks were limited to general comments on the cost of a lodging house in comparison with that of the house in Rock Park or of boarding at Mrs. Blodget's: "Our whole expenditure here, with these ample accommodations, will not exceed seven guineas a week. We are beginning to get an insight into English economical customs. They know how to be comfortable and make a good appearance on a great deal less than Americans spend for a poorer result."[3] He might have added that such lodging houses were found for the most part in resort towns, where living was cheaper than in large cities. Seven guineas a week was his preliminary estimate of their economic needs. The account book is too fragmentary to demonstrate the accuracy of his estimate, for it devotes only 6½ pages to the Leamington period and does not mention rent or give totals. The entries are chiefly expenditures for food and sightseeing in nearby towns. Sightseeing was obviously why Leamington was chosen as a starting point for summer travels.

Royal Leamington Spa, "garden town of Shakespeareland," was then, and still is, the most convenient center for tourists visiting such historic places in Warwickshire as Stratford, Warwick, Kenilworth, and Coventry.[4] Though the presence of "saline water" was first recorded in 1586, the town did not develop much until after the Royal Pump Rooms were opened in July of 1814. For the rest of the century Leamington was considered a fashionable resort town. Since the buildings were comparatively new, the town impressed Hawthorne as being very clean.

Visitors not interested in the baths could enjoy the wide, tree-lined streets, the half-mile of shops along the Parade, the classical terraces, and the colorful gardens. The largest and finest of these, Jephson's Gardens, was named for Dr. Jephson, the nineteenth-century physician who treated a number of well-known people, including John Ruskin and the famous Dr. Parr of Hatton.[5]

In 1852 Leamington had built a new railroad station to serve the increasing numbers of people coming up from London to frequent the baths at the Pump Rooms or to establish themselves in the town for the purpose of touring other parts of Warwickshire. Tourists could go by rail to Coventry, only nine miles to the north; or they could hire a cab to Stratford, Warwick, or Kenilworth. And if anyone wished more exercise than strolling up and down the Parade, there were plenty of country walks to nearby places like Whitnash, on the outskirts of Leamington. (Whitnash proved to be one of Nathaniel's favorite spots because of the architecture and setting of St. Margaret's Church.) The Hawthornes had the advantage of a convenient location in

Leamington; Lansdowne Crescent is in a quiet area east of the Parade near the corner of Warwick Street and Lillington Road, and yet close to the business district.

Sophia wrote no details about the house in Lansdowne Crescent. It was one in a row of attached "villas" similar in style to, but on a much smaller scale than, the Royal Crescent in Bath. Nathaniel's description in *Our Old Home* is actually of the house that was their second residence (in 1857), at 10 Lansdowne Circus, around the corner from the Crescent. The third house, on Bath Street, where they lived during the fall and winter of 1859–1860 (the longest amount of time they spent in any of the Leamington houses), has long since been demolished, and there is little written about it.

The night of their arrival was spent at the Clarendon Hotel, on the upper end of the Parade. By the next afternoon, June 19, they had moved into the lodging house in Lansdowne Crescent and begun to set up housekeeping by purchasing food.[6] Hawthorne pointed out that moving into lodgings presented one disadvantage: They could not get even a cup of tea until they had "made some arrangements with the grocer. Soon, however, there comes a sense of being at home, and by our exclusive selves, which never could be attained at hotels or boarding houses" (*EN*, 121).

With Fanny as their only servant and with Sophia to supervise their simple household, they were comparatively free to enjoy Warwickshire in the best of English weather. Julian and his father began at once by taking two exploratory walks during the forenoon and afternoon of the first day in their new home. On Wednesday, Nathaniel, Sophia, Una, and Julian left Rose with Fanny and began their real sightseeing with the aid of a *Guide to England*, which they had purchased in the spring to help them plan their excursions. From then on the English notebooks became a record of country walks and of rides to Warwick, Stratford, and Coventry.

Sophia's impressions of Leamington, aside from the accounts found in her *Notes in England,* which were probably based on later visits, are chiefly references to the climate and the appearance of the countryside in summer. Many of Nathaniel's impressions are also later ones, summed up in various parts of *Our Old Home* as a compilation of his experiences in Leamington during their three different times of residence. This 1855 visit, as revealed in the notebook entries, was only an introduction to the town and its environs.

At the end of the second week, Nathaniel left his family in Leamington and returned to the Liverpool consulate. On the way he made a side-trip of two days to Lichfield and Uttoxeter for a visit to Dr. Johnson's birthplace and the scene of his penance, an experience recorded at some length in both the notebooks and *Our Old Home*.[7] It was a visit Hawthorne had long wanted to make; the descriptions are, therefore, far more detailed than the actual length of the stay would warrant.

Only a few days at the consulate were necessary for him to dispose of essential business, and he was glad to escape at the end of the week. His attitude about Liverpool is reflected in the famous note to Bright in which he said that he had come back to "this black and miserable hole" for a few days. Then he added a postscript to his short letter: "I don't mean to apply the above two disparaging adjectives merely to my Consulate, but to all Liverpool and its environs—except Sandheys and Norris Green."[8]

On Saturday, July 7, Hawthorne returned to Leamington and spent Sunday with the family. Meanwhile Sophia had packed up once more, and on Monday at noon they departed by train for the Lake District. Nathaniel said that he should not have taken more time off, but that he had an "official engagement" to attend to and was able to combine it with a pleasure trip. What the official business was he never explained, nor did Sophia. After stopping for the night at the Albion Hotel in Chester, they took the train again as far as Milnthorpe and then rode by coach to Newby Bridge, a small settlement at the southern end of Lake Windermere. Here, from July 10 off and on for several weeks, the Swan Hotel (Thomas White, proprietor) became a convenient stopping place for the Hawthornes while they made various short tours around the Lake District.[9]

There was little to do at Newby Bridge except take walks and visit Furness Abbey at nearby Dalton, so after three days the family started off on a short excursion. First they went by steamboat north on Lake Windermere to Lowwood Hotel, where they spent three rainy days; then Sophia took Una, Rose, and Fanny back to Newby Bridge so that she, Nathaniel, and Julian could go farther north by themselves. Nathaniel did not like the Lowwood, finding it crowded, and with accommodations that did not provide the "home-feeling" at Newby Bridge (*EN*, 161).

He was glad to move from the Lowwood to Brown's Hotel in Grasmere, which he called "a very good house, on a retired and picturesque site, with fine mountain-views about it" (*EN*, 165). This hotel became headquarters while they drove to Rydal Mount and Rydal Water and walked around Grasmere. The notebooks mention the

Wordsworth graves in the churchyard of St. Oswald's but not Dove Cottage. After Grasmere they took a phaeton to Ambleside and drove over Kirkstone Pass to Ullswater, stopping to see Aira Force and spending the night at the King's Arms in Keswick. A walk from the hotel to Greta Hall enabled them to see the grounds of Southey's former home, but the gardener could not admit them to the house because the owner, "Mr. Radday," was away.[10] However, they did see Southey's monument and grave in the Crossthwaite churchyard.

On this trip they did not go farther than the Vale of St. John, perhaps because they did not wish to stay away too long from the three left behind at Newby Bridge. It is a pity that the Hawthornes never saw the most northern and western parts of the Lake District, for Nathaniel would have appreciated their rugged features. By Monday, July 23, he had completed his record of the trip with the observation, "I am pretty well convinced that all attempts at describing scenery—especially mountain-scenery—are sheer nonsense." For this reason his record was mainly one of where they had traveled. He had enjoyed the literary associations of the places they had visited, but soon grew "weary of fine scenery," for he had "eaten a score of mountains, and quaffed down as many lakes, all in the space of two or three days; and the natural consequence was a surfeit" (*EN*, 182–183).

The three days that followed at Newby Bridge were rainy. There was nothing to do but watch from their parlor window the stagecoach arriving four times a day or read books from the landlord's somewhat limited collection. Nathaniel was amused by a volume of Ben Jonson's plays. How the others entertained themselves he did not say. There was one pleasant day near the end of the week when Julian and Una went fishing, and Una caught "a good-sized perch—her first fish" (*EN*, 183).

On Saturday the entire family left Newby Bridge and rode back to Brown's Hotel in Grasmere. By this time the pleasures of sightseeing had definitely palled for Nathaniel. In addition to weariness at seeing the same places, he felt the burden of traveling with a family of children; they allowed him "no separate and selfish possibility of being happy. Sophia, however, suffers far less from this impediment than I do, though she has to bear a great deal more of it." If Sophia had read these remarks, she might have admitted that she, too, grew tired of the responsibility of three children. Part of Nathaniel's objection stemmed from his dislike of hotel life, which was both expensive and not very comfortable (*EN*, 185).

By this time he was perhaps relieved that he had to leave his family in Grasmere and return to business matters in Liverpool. He settled down at the Rock Ferry Hotel instead of in the city, because for at least two months the weather would permit easy access to Liverpool by ferry. His letter to Sophia reporting his arrival suggested that she might come to Rock Ferry for a day or two and then go to Matlock or Malvern or wherever she wished; or if she and the children were happy in Grasmere, he could come back north for a weekend at least. Sophia answered that she did not like the Grasmere accommodations and would return to Rock Ferry as soon as possible. She said she had a headache from all the excitement: Julian had frightened them all by his boldness in climbing and by falling into a ditch and getting wet.[11] It was certain now that she was wearied by the responsibility of traveling with children.

Henry Bright came for dinner at the hotel to welcome the family back to Rock Ferry. In succeeding days, Julian and Nathaniel took some walks to Birkenhead Park and to Tranmere Hall, but the only incident of importance was Hawthorne's overnight visit on August 23 to Smithill's Hall at Bolton le Moors, the place to which he had previously been invited by the Ainsworths. Although he devoted a number of pages in his notebooks to the scene of the Bloody Footstep, he did not enjoy his visit. He was bored with everything except the house itself. When he left, Mrs. Ainsworth asked him to "write a ghost-story for her house," but his literary use of the Bloody Footstep was postponed for several years. His final comment at this time was that "a week or two might pass very agreeably in an English country-house, provided the host and hostess and the guests were particularly pleasant people. Otherwise, I would rather possess myself in a hotel" (*EN*, 199).

In outlining his plans to Ticknor after Sophia's return to Rock Ferry, Hawthorne insisted that although her health was improved, he did not wish his wife to spend another winter in England. He had by then asked for a leave of absence in order to escort the family to Portugal, intending to accept the O'Sullivans' invitation to visit them in Lisbon. His intentions changed somewhat when he received no answer to his request. In the meantime he had refused an offer, relayed from Washington by Horatio Bridge, of a post in Portugal, because, he said, he did not understand diplomacy or "the lingo." Since he could not take a leave of absence, Nathaniel and Sophia reluctantly decided that she would take the girls and Fanny with her to Lisbon for the winter and leave Julian with his father at Mrs. Blodget's in Liverpool. The women and girls would not sail from Southampton until early fall, and before their departure Nathaniel and Julian would accompany them to London for their first visit to that city. In the month that they would be in

London, Nathaniel would return to Liverpool whenever it was necessary for him to be at the consulate.[12]

On September 4 the family set out for London, stopping en route for an overnight stay at the Lion Hotel in Shrewsbury. The next day they arrived for approximately a month's stay at Mrs. Raynolds's lodging house, at 24 George Street, Hanover Square, a convenient location for sightseeing. Hawthorne returned to Mrs. Blodget's for the week of September 15 to 22 so that he could attend to matters at the consulate. The rest of the month was one long stretch of daily sightseeing in which he allowed for little social life except the necessary calls on diplomats, including Buchanan and the American consul, General Robert Campbell.[13]

Since Nathaniel did not want anything to interrupt the pleasures of his last days with Sophia and the children, he looked up only two literary people. One was the poet and jeweler W. C. Bennett at his place of business, 65 Cheapside. Through correspondence, Hawthorne had bought two "excellent watches" from Bennett and had received some of his poems, but the two men had not met before. Bennett, who had long been an admirer of Hawthorne's writings, proved to be friendly and helpful, and Nathaniel said he liked the man because he did not appear to be typically British: "It seems strange to see an Englishman with so little physical ponderosity and obtuseness of nerve" (*EN*, 223).[14]

The other writer was Leigh Hunt, whom Hawthorne probably would not have sought out if Mrs. Russell Sturgis, wife of the banker who gave the Hawthornes financial advice, had not arranged for her carriage to take them to Hammersmith for an afternoon call on the author. Hawthorne wrote of Leigh Hunt: "He is a beautiful man. I never saw a finer face . . . [nor] an Englishman whose manners pleased me so well" (*EN*, 255). Rather characteristically, Hawthorne attributed Hunt's best qualities to his American blood—"his mother was a Pennsylvanian" (*EN*, 255). Although he appreciated meeting Hunt, Hawthorne felt that the writer was "better suited for women's companionship than for men's because they can better give him the tender appreciation he needs" (*EN*, 255–56). Hunt omitted all mention of the visit from his autobiography, but he expressed his great pleasure in a note to Hawthorne and also in one to Barry Cornwall, who had written the letter of introduction for Nathaniel.[15]

Near the end of September, Hawthorne summed up his social experiences in London to Ticknor by saying that he had not introduced himself to people except for a few with whom he had business: "I wish during this visit, to see all the sights with as little interruption as possible. . . . On some future occasion I will come to London for the express purpose of seeing people." Earlier he had written much the same to Fields, stressing more, perhaps, his delight in the city: "It enables me to enjoy it the better, that I do not come here a green Yankee, but well trained in English life and customs."[16]

The truth may have been that his intensity in sightseeing was an attempt to escape from his dread of the coming separation from Sophia. This visit was the last opportunity for the whole family to be together until the following summer. It was the first time since their marriage that Nathaniel and Sophia had been separated for more than a few weeks at a time. Why, then, did they volunteer now to part for almost nine months? Nathaniel's was the greater sacrifice, for he would have no family life to save him from the utter boredom of the consulate, whereas Sophia, much as she might miss him, would be living with friends as part of a lively society in a climate that she hoped would improve her health.

The Hawthornes' marriage, often referred to as the perfect love story, was based on what might seem to us to be old-fashioned attitudes. In her journals of the honeymoon period at the Old Manse, Sophia called her husband "My Lord" or "My dear lord." He in turn called her "the angel from Heaven" who rescued him from the dismal garret of the Herbert Street house in Salem. From the first, each one put the other on a pedestal. Sophia did not publish her generalizations on marriage, but we have two passages by Nathaniel that show his attitude toward the position of women: One, "A Prayer for Woman," extols their virtues; the other, a newspaper quotation, refers to woman independent of man as "a monster." Although later, in *The Marble Faun*, he pointed out the need for more liberal customs for women, he still thought of the ideal woman as distinctively the homemaker, as Sophia very much was.[17]

Wherever they lived, Sophia had primary responsibility for the children and the management of the household. Nathaniel was the breadwinner. If he was unable to support his family by his writing, some other means, such as government work, had to be found. If her health was in jeopardy to the extent that the children were likely to suffer from her disability, then he must somehow provide for the likelihood of a cure. It was the state of her health in England that forced a decision upon both of them.

How many of Sophia's ailments would be labeled psychosomatic today no one will ever know. The idea that marriage had rescued her from the life of an invalid beset by recurring headaches and turned her into a healthy wife who never had a day's illness is certainly a false one.[18] Anyone who reads her letters and journals from the years abroad will find constant references to her headaches, her cough, and the need to lie down or stay in bed for the day and refuse all social engagements. Later in Italy, Sophia had energy enough to take daily walks to see the marvels of Rome and to nurse Una through a long siege of Roman fever. But as soon as they returned to England—to Redcar, Leamington, and Bath, where there was little to occupy her mind—the signs of invalidism recurred. However, the worsening of her health in winter, when England was damp and cold, suggests that the climate did play an important part.

Still, one cannot help wondering how much this twentieth-century statement about Victorian women applied to Sophia:

> It was pretty generally established—as a literary convention, at any rate—that weak health and timidity were attractive to the Victorian male. These afflictions, however, probably grew up out of the emptiness of the lives of girls and women among the newly well-to-do classes. They had been deprived of most of their normal occupations by the conventions which delegated to servants the tasks about which they themselves and their mothers used to be busy, and they had become a prey to imaginary fears about their own health and the outerworld, concerning both of which they were extremely ignorant.[19]

The Hawthornes were not in the well-to-do class, but they had always had a servant, and when Sophia was a girl at home she had had nothing to do except exercise her artistic talents. In England, whenever she had little to do except look after Rose, she seems to have complained the most about her ailments, though privately in her diary, not to her husband. When emergencies occurred, she could rise to the occasion, as became evident in later years. Moreover, both Nathaniel and Sophia were ignorant about their bodies as most Victorians were.

However serious Sophia's condition was in 1855, both of them felt that some sacrifice was absolutely necessary, for it seemed possible that another winter in England might permanently damage Sophia's lungs. For financial reasons Nathaniel could not resign his post immediately in order for them to depart for Italy sooner than originally planned. The only solution seemed to be for Sophia to accept the invitation for a winter in Portugal, which both of them hoped would cure her cough. So, on October 7, the Hawthornes left behind the delights of sight-seeing in London and took the train to Southampton. They spent the night at Chapple's Castle Hotel, and the next day they walked around the town before the *Madrid* was scheduled to sail in the early afternoon. Nathaniel recommended his wife to the captain for special care, since she was "unattended by any gentleman"; and before the ship weighed anchor, he and Julian departed, leaving the other four on deck. "My wife behaved heroically, Una was cheerful; and Rosebud seemed only anxious to get off. Poor Fanny, our nurse, was altogether cast down, and shed tears, either from regret at leaving her native land, or dread of sickness, or general despondency, being a person of no hope, or spring of spirits" (*EN*, 258).

Nathaniel and Julian then took the train to Worcester, where they spent the night and did some sightseeing on the following day. It was a dark rainy night when they reached Mrs. Blodget's in time for a late supper. As he reflected upon his new situation with a young boy to look after, Nathaniel recorded his first reaction:

> Julian bore the separation from his mother well; but took occasion to remind me that he now had no one but myself to depend upon, and therefore suggested that I should be very kind to him. There is more tenderness in his own manner towards me than ordinary, since this great event; and ever and anon he favors me with a little hug, or pressure of the hand; which I take as hints that I must now be father and mother both to him. (*EN*, 258)

Nathaniel needed what comfort he could get from a child whose interests at the moment were in events going on around him. Julian was too active to sit around bemoaning the loss of his mother; he wanted to see and do everything. In the months that followed he took dancing lessons from M. Victor Regnier, instruction from an unnamed drawing master, and gymnastic training from M. Huguenin, a powerful "Swiss champion." In addition, Nathaniel attempted to teach him Latin, but Julian was no scholar. He much preferred going to the consulate or sliding down the banister at Mrs. Blodget's to a perch from which he could watch the American captains at dinner and snatch forbidden tidbits with a fork as the maid went past with her loaded tray.[20]

Hawthorne made sure that Julian's time was well spent, but he left it to the women—Mrs. Blodget, Miss Williams, and Miss Maria—to see that the boy was kept clean and well dressed. Another boarder, Mrs. Howes, wife of Captain Howes, also took upon herself the task of keeping Julian "within some bounds of decency." "Julian," she would say, "your hands and fingernails!" But, Julian concluded, "Dirt and disorder seemed to seek me as their home."[21]

If his academic education was somewhat neglected, this was nothing new. Actually the children had not had lessons since they left Rock Park. Sophia offered her sister Mary the explanation that she did not have Mary's ability to teach, but thought that even though the children could not study when they were moving around so much, they were getting "a general culture which is apparent at every turn." In the same letter she spoke of Julian's "intellect," his "power of observation," and his "profound insight."[22] Even if this was not a mother's prejudice, it is evident that Julian seldom applied whatever powers he had to formal study. He was more interested in shell-collecting, which he could scarcely do in Liverpool, and in people, whom he could observe in two busy places—the consulate and Mrs. Blodget's.

As an old man, Julian looked back upon this period with great fondness. At the consulate he sat in a corner watching his father interview the claimants who came for government funds. About noon-time Nathaniel would stop work and take Julian to a baker's shop half a block away. There on the scrubbed wooden counter were "a giant pyramid of fresh, sweet butter" and a heap of rolls hot from the oven. Each customer was given a knife and allowed to eat as many rolls with butter as he could for tuppence. Apparently Nathaniel himself seldom ate between breakfast and the six o'clock dinner, but after he had introduced Julian to the shop, he would often give the boy a tuppence and let him go there by himself.[23]

When Julian spent the hours at Mrs. Blodget's, he entertained himself, sometimes by reading Philip Gosse's new book, *The Aquarium*, which his father had given him, and sometimes by watching the world from the front window of his own little bedroom. Like most children he had an "unfailing appetite." Breakfast for him was "finnan haddy, muffins and crumpets, and [Dundee] marmalade; sometimes fresh-broiled mackerel." He had lunch—actually his dinner—by himself at one o'clock, and supper at five-thirty before the rest of the boarders had dinner. Sometimes he was allowed in the dining room when nuts and raisins signaled the end of the dinner, but meanwhile his favorite perch was on top of the post at the foot of the banisters. Once Mrs. Blodget surprised him there and admonished, "Never slide down the balusters, Julian; you might fall off and break your bones." Julian reflected, "I never broke any bones, but I broke the rule daily, and without remorse. What are balusters for?"[24]

In the evening after dinner the captains gathered in the smoking room for cigars and card games. Julian was allowed to take part, but promptly at eight o'clock Mrs. Blodget appeared in the doorway to summon him away, and the others went on with their "yarn spinning" and "jesting of a salt-sea savour," which he maintained any boy or woman might have listened to "comfortably."[25]

With intervals of visiting at the Brights' or the Channings' homes, daily life for Julian during the winter and spring continued to be full of interest. Usually he did not care much to visit the Channings. Though he admired Frank, who was two years older than he, neither Frank nor Fanny became his close friends. The Channing adults made Julian feel that his manners were clumsy, and therefore he was much subdued when he was in their home.[26]

By contrast, the Bright family and their home, Sandheys, in West Derby, had a great attraction for him. Years later he described the mansion with its "wide lawns, grouped trees, ordered flower beds and green houses, and the little white-washed stone huts of the tenants." When he was taken to the cottages to visit, he relished having a cup of tea with the tenants and sitting on a fireplace bench munching toast.[27] It is obvious that with so much to keep him busy in and around Liverpool, Julian was never particularly lonesome. There is no indication that he missed his mother or his sisters very much.

It was otherwise with Hawthorne. After a wearisome day at the consulate, he took part in the evening activities at Mrs. Blodget's, enjoying her "Gargantuan" dinners, the yarns of the captains, and an occasional cigar with them, but his heart was in Lisbon. To Ticknor he wrote that Sophia, a month after her arrival, reported being homesick, and he speculated on the effects of such a long absence from America on the whole family. He was also still concerned that Sophia's health might have been "radically impaired" by their residence in England. "These are gloomy thoughts, growing out of my solitary bachelor-state, I suppose."[28]

The letters to Sophia at first stressed Nathaniel's need for Julian; he could not bear the separation if it were not for his son's company. "He is really a great comfort and joy to me, and rather unexpectedly so; for I must confess I wished to keep him here on his own account and thine, much more than on my own. We live together in great love and harmony, the best friends in the world." Other letters refer to the fact that Julian was rapidly outgrowing all his clothes, that his haircut made him look like a real boy, and that his manners were improving. "I do not at all despair of seeing him grow up a gentleman."[29] But as winter came on, not even the Christmas festivities at Mrs. Blodget's helped to dispel Nathaniel's loneliness, and he made clear to Sophia his real feelings. Excerpts from *Love Letters* reveal the passion that still existed after thirteen years of married life:

February 7, 1856:
One thing, dearest, I have been most thoroughly taught by this separation—that is, the absolute necessity of expression. I must tell thee I love thee. I must be told that thou lovest me. It must be said in words and symbolized with caresses; or else, at last, imprisoned Love will go frantic, and tear all to pieces the heart that holds it. . . .

Oh, my love, it is a desperate thing that I cannot *embrace* thee [The word *embrace* has been crossed out and *see* substituted.] this very instant. Dost thou ever feel, at one and the same moment, the impossibility of doing without me, and also the impossibility of having me? I know not how it is that my strong wishes do not bring thee here bodily, while I am writing these words.[30]

From London, April 7, 1856, upon hearing of Sophia's illness in Madeira:

What a wretched world we live in! Not one little nook or corner where thou canst draw a wholesome breath! In all our separation, I have never once felt so utterly desperate as at this moment. I *cannot* bear it. . . .

Oh my wife, I do want thee so intolerably. Nothing else is real, except the bond between thee and me. The people around me are but shadows. I am myself but a shadow, till thou takest me in thy arms and convertest me into substance. Till thou comest back, I do but walk in a dream. . . .

Really, dearest wife, I have a heart, although, heretofore, thou hast had great reason to doubt it. But it yearns, and throbs, and burns with a hot fire, for thee, and for the children that have grown out of our loves. . . . But the first moment, when we meet again, will set everything right. Oh, blessed moment![31]

Only to Sophia did Hawthorne admit that this was the lowest point in his misery. To everyone else his letters were rather matter of fact. He did confess, but not to Sophia, that his health had not been good. When Mrs. Heywood invited him to dinner at Norris Green, he answered that he could accept only provisionally, for he found himself occasionally "ailing—in a sort of half-way condition between health and illness." He went to the dinner, probably in an attempt to revive his spirits.[32] Other guests were the James Martineaus and John Mansfield, a Liverpool magistrate. A week or so later Mansfield conducted Mrs. Heywood, "another lady," and Hawthorne on a visit to the West Derby Workhouse, which Hawthorne described in his notebooks and later in a chapter of *Our Old Home*. Details of the first account, written at the time, show that he was making an effort to distract himself from his own depression.[33]

The major portions of Nathaniel's letters to Sophia were concerned with newsworthy bits: Julian's activities, casual mention of meeting former neighbors on the ferry, a dinner at the Brights', talk of possible war between England and America, O'Sullivan's character, the arrival of Dallas, the new minister to England from the United States, and finally the opportunity of leaving the "mud and fog of Liverpool" for a trip to London. He never forgot to mention the girls: "Give my love to Una" or "Don't let little Rosebud forget me" were characteristic endings.[34]

In his letters to Ticknor and others, Nathaniel usually spoke of Mrs. Hawthorne and "the children." If it seems sometimes in the notebook entries that he paid more attention to Julian, it was because he wanted his son to be a real boy, not dominated by three females as he himself had been in his youth. From Nathaniel's letters to Una, from her replies, and from Rose's *Memories*, it is certain that he was idolized by his daughters as well as by his son. In keeping with Victorian traditions, however, the two girls came more directly under their mother's supervision.

At that particular time, Una and Rose, seven years apart in age, had relatively little in common. Though she was four years old, Rose was still called "Baby." She was a red-haired little beauty admired by visitors for her liveliness and grace, but she had a quick temper and a stubborn streak. Her father's letters to her in Lisbon contain humorous hints that she was not always "a good girl": "I am sure you never get into a passion, and never scream, and never scratch and strike your dear Nurse or your dear sister Una." He went on to say that if when she came back to England, Mamma reported that she had never done any such things, he would be "very glad," but if he were to hear that she had been naughty, he "would feel it his duty to eat little Rosebud up!"[35] In the years immediately after the return from Lisbon, she and Julian often had little quarrels, which their parents tried to let them settle by themselves.

Una, a quiet, withdrawn girl, was approaching the difficult period of adolescence. Apparently she had neither the beauty nor the charm that she had possessed in early childhood or that little Rose now had. In later years her mother admitted that when they were in Liverpool, Una found fault with everything and everybody.[36] Her prolonged homesickness suggests that she was not adjusting to life abroad. Her father's letters to Sophia in Lisbon reveal his concern that Una was growing up without his having the pleasure of seeing her mature, and that when she returned she might be a very different person. He also worried that she might be growing too attached to the "forms and ceremonials" of the Church of England. The letter in which Nathaniel expressed these concerns seems to be the only one written at this time revealing that there had been a close tie between father and daughter and that he was afraid it was being weakened by the separation.[37] Subsequent events were to demonstrate that the tie was not broken.

There is no doubt that Sophia's answers to Nathaniel's letters were more restrained than his. The letters themselves were probably destroyed, but there is evidence that her writings were never passionate. This tendency to restraint was in keeping with her conventional idea of what was proper. In later years she edited out those parts of her husband's writings she felt he would not have wanted made public. Her whole attitude toward personal feelings was decidedly Victorian, as we define the term today.

In her letters to Julian, Sophia always tried to be cheerful, chatty, and objective. She entertained him by lively descriptions of such social events in Lisbon as her presentation to the king and the opera she attended with the O'Sullivans. Any misery occasioned by the long separation is not evident in the letters. She must have found compensation in the hope that her health would be greatly improved by the climate in Portugal. Sophia was always optimistic about the future, and no doubt she rejoiced in the thought that Nathaniel would be cheered by the visit to London he was planning. That he was is due solely, as he himself confessed, to the efforts of Francis Bennoch.[38]

In planning his London trip, Hawthorne kept in mind the government ruling against absence from a consular post for more than ten days in any one quarter. He wrote to Ticknor, "About the twentieth of March, I mean to pay a visit to London, and shall probably remain there twenty days—ten in the first quarter of the year, and ten in the second; so that Uncle Sam will not be able to grab my salary on plea of over-absence. There is a pleasure in getting around such a mean old scoundrel as Uncle Sam."[39] He planned to leave Julian in Liverpool to visit the Brights and then the Channings. In explaining his arrangements to Sophia, Nathaniel wrote that Julian would be well taken care of: "I rather think he can do without me better than I can without him."[40]

On March 20 at 10 P.M. Nathaniel arrived at the London railroad station and took a cab to a lodging house at 32 St. James's Place, where his friend Mr. Bowman was expecting him (*EN*, 281). Nathaniel wrote little about Bowman except that he was "an agreeable companion," that he gave free use of his drawing room, and that he took time out from work at his counting house on Old Broad Street to tour the city with Hawthorne for a week. They arranged to meet early in May for a short trip to Scotland. The notebook entries for late March are concerned entirely with where the two went and what they did in London.

Hawthorne also hunted up Francis Bennoch, whom he had not seen since the brief meeting in Rock Park in 1853, at his company office on Wood Street. Bennoch invited Nathaniel to lunch at his company headquarters and then took him to see more sights. They were joined later in the day by Bowman, and the three made an expedition to Greenwich Fair. After this Bennoch took both men home to dinner at his house in Blackheath. The other dinner guests that night were the son of Benjamin Haydon, the painter; and Philip Bailey, the author of *Festus*; plus "one or two ladies." When Mrs. Bennoch came down to join them for dinner, Nathaniel described her as a "pleasant person, but in poor health, and looking older—at least more worn—than her husband." The dinner was good, but not elaborate, "befitting a prosperous tradesman of London; for I suppose that is Mr. Bennoch's rank, though he deals only by wholesale." The main course of roast lamb and jugged hare (with "no side dishes") was accompanied by port, sherry, and claret, and was served by one "female-servant." Nathaniel concluded that probably on formal occasions Bennoch put on "greater state" (*EN*, 287–91). After an evening of conversation with the Newton Croslands, who had dropped in, the group walked to Greenwich Station, where Hawthorne and Bowman got the train back to London.

Nathaniel was not so far particularly entertained by any of his London experiences. At the end of the week with Bowman, he was still somewhat depressed and, according to Bennoch, ready to go back to the consulate. Then Bennoch really took him in hand, determined to make life more pleasant by keeping him busy. The notebooks devote some thirty-five pages to details of their travels in and out of London. To Bennoch it meant taking a complete vacation from his responsibilities as senior partner in his wholesale silk and ribbon business. For ten days he generously gave all his time to Hawthorne, who was then almost a total stranger to him. By the end of this period the two had begun a friendship that was to last until death. This friendship reminds one at once of the relationship between Hawthorne and Henry Bright, his other close English friend.

As Julian said later, England would never have seemed "our old home" to his father without the companionship of these two men. "Both were genial, true, and faithful; but in other respects they were widely dissimilar." Certainly they differed greatly in appearance and age. Bright was then a very tall, thin young man in his early twenties, with brown hair, light blue or gray eyes, and a prominent nose. Bennoch was forty-four, only eight years younger than Hawthorne. Julian pictured him as "broad-shouldered, straight, and vigorous, massive but active, with a mellow, joyful voice, an inimitable brogue, sparkling black eyes, full of hearty sunshine and kindness, a broad and high forehead over bushy brows, and black wavy hair." Rose described Bennoch as "short and fat, witty and jovial." Just how tall or plump he was is hard to tell from portraits, but there is no doubt about the black hair, sparkling eyes, and facial features that made Julian call him "one of the handsomest men in England."[41] He was apparently a charmer, the complete antithesis in both appearance and manners to the American's stereotype of a Scot.

Julian went on to say that one naturally spoke of Bennoch in "superlatives; he was the kindest, jolliest, most hospitable, most generous and chivalrous of men, and his affection and admiration for my father were also of the superlative kind." It must have been his personality as well as his good looks that caused him to rise to a prominent place in London business and politics. Unlike Bright, who had money, education, and high social standing, Bennoch was a self-educated man from the farming class, who had started his career in London without any university degree. His financial success in life was due to a tremendous amount of energy and enthusiasm.

To date no biography of this remarkable individual has been written, probably because information about him is limited chiefly to records of his commercial and civic activities. The following thumbnail sketch explains partially how Bennoch came to be called a poet-business man:[42] For years his parents lived and worked on a tenant farm that was part of the Drumlanrig estate of the Duke of Buccleuch and Queensbury. The sixth in a family of nine children, Francis found little opportunity to do more than herd sheep. For this reason at the age of sixteen he departed for London, where he first served an apprenticeship as a clerk. Nine years later he had saved enough to establish his own business. He married Margaret Raine, a girl from the English-Scottish border country, and together they had a long, happy, but childless life. For the rest of his working career Bennoch was senior partner in Bennoch, Twentyman, and Rigg, wholesale dealers in silks and ribbons, at 77 Wood Street, City.

As an energetic young man with literary ambitions, Bennoch submitted his first poetry to John McDiarmid, editor of the local paper in the town of Dumfries, not far from Bennoch's birthplace. As long as he

Francis Bennoch

lived, McDiarmid, who was himself a poet, continued to publish Bennoch's work, but the first collected verses were privately printed in London. Wordsworth, to whom Bennoch sent a copy of the collection, advised the young man to stick to business and keep writing as an avocation. Bennoch accepted the advice. He made the wholesale silk business his livelihood, but kept on publishing poems written in his leisure hours. Partly through the Burns Society, he developed contacts with other literary people and gave some financial help to artists. Eventually he became known for entertaining large numbers of writers, including some Americans, in his home. On a journey to the States in 1848 he met numerous literary figures, among them Bryant, Longfellow, Bayard Taylor, and James T. Fields. He did not meet Hawthorne at this time, because the latter was then working at the Salem Custom House. In England, Bennoch also became acquainted with such authors as Southey, Landor, Kingsley, Dickens, Ruskin, and De Quincey, but it seems that those whom he entertained in his home and knew best were minor writers such as Charles Swain, the Howitts, the Croslands, and many others of the period. He might be called a lesser Richard Monckton Milnes or Samuel Rogers.

Bennoch's civic and political activities—writing pamphlets and articles on city affairs and serving as common councilman and as deputy of a ward—plus his success in the wholesale silk business led to his election in 1852 to membership in the Royal Society of Arts, a 100-year-old organization devoted to the promotion of arts and industry. In this group, too, he was an active worker; in fact, the week after Hawthorne's visit to London in the spring of 1856, Bennoch delivered his first paper to that Society's meeting. "On Thread or Fibre Gilding," a paper that led to much discussion among the members, reveals technical knowledge based on extensive experience and reading.

Such a busy life makes one wonder how Bennoch had time for all his social activities. However he managed his affairs, it is certain that when Hawthorne arrived at the Wood Street office, still depressed in spite of his sightseeing with Bowman, Bennoch decided to spend the rest of Hawthorne's vacation with him. When the two met, Bennoch commented, "I never saw a man more miserable. . . . London was detestable. It had only one merit; it was not so bad as Liverpool." For this reason, the effervescent Bennoch made every effort to entertain his guest, first by taking him out of the city on a trip. At the end of their experiences Bennoch wrote, "I found Hawthorne utterly prostrated by depression. I hoped to lift him out of himself, and I think I succeeded."[43]

This strangely matched pair set out from London by train for a series of short stops in the south of England. Years later in his description of the trip, Bennoch wrote that Hawthorne did not know where they were going and that he left all decisions to Bennoch, although the notebooks indicate that Hawthorne was perfectly well aware of where they were going.[44] How do we reconcile two versions so different in tone and point of view? The answer seems to be that Hawthorne recorded his impressions of events almost immediately after they happened and was interested chiefly in collecting notes for future descriptions of English people and the countryside. There are only a few mentions of his personal feelings. Bennoch wrote his description some thirty years after the events. The time lapse cast a glamorous light on the journey and made Bennoch remember how happy he had been to help his friend. It was a case of exaggeration rather than misrepresentation, for the outline of events is the same in both accounts.

The most significant incident occurred when the two friends went to visit Martin Tupper, the popular author of *Proverbial Philosophy*. At the station in Albury, Surrey, they were met, according to Hawthorne's account, by the twelve-year-old son of Tupper. They walked to Tupper's house and were greeted at the door by the author himself, who held out his arms to Bennoch and then embarrassed Hawthorne by his effusiveness. As they were introduced, Tupper exclaimed, "Oh, Great Scarlet Letter!" Hawthorne was too nonplussed to reply. The Tupper family had been waiting breakfast for them; so, though it was then ten o'clock and Bennoch and Hawthorne had already had two chops each earlier at Camp Aldershot, they all sat down at the table, "seven children inclusive." The rest of the day was devoted to sightseeing in the area (*EN*, 293–99).

Hawthorne's reaction to Martin Tupper grew less favorable as the day progressed: He was a fussy little man with "no dignity of character, no conception of what it is, nor perception of his deficiency." In spite of Nathaniel's recognition that Tupper was a kindly soul who meant well, the man bored him. "I liked him, and laughed in my sleeve at him, and was utterly weary of him, for certainly he is the ass of asses." By the end of the day Hawthorne was glad to depart. He left, feeling that the Tuppers were all very kind people: "I heartily wish them well" (*EN*, 300–06).

Either Tupper was a good actor or he did not realize how Hawthorne felt about him until long afterward. When years later he read Hawthorne's account, which Julian quoted in the biography of his father and mother, Tupper exploded that Julian had had bad taste to publish such disparaging remarks.[45] Worse yet, Hawthorne had actually been guilty of ingratitude. Tupper in a scathing denunciation claimed that on that occasion Hawthorne had shown envy of their old house for having more than seven gables, and of its owner for affluence as well as fame as an author. "That we did not take to each other is no wonder." Tupper concluded: "This, then is my answer to the unkindly remarks against me in print by one who has shown manifestly a flash of genius in 'The Scarlet Letter'; but, so far as I know, it was well nigh a solitary one."[46]

One incident in their short excursion shows considerable variation in the points of view of the three who described it. After the visit to the Tuppers, Hawthorne and Bennoch spent a quiet Sunday at Tunbridge Wells and devoted the next morning to touring Battle Abbey and Hastings. Bennoch wrote his version of what followed to Sir Theodore Martin, the central figure involved. Bennoch stated that on Monday before lunch he suggested to Hawthorne that they call upon some friends of his who were then staying in St. Leonard's, a section of the town of Hastings. At the same time, Bennoch wrote, he knew perfectly well that the Martins were expecting them for lunch. Sir Theodore greeted the two warmly and proved to be an ideal host. His wife proceeded to make Hawthorne feel so much at ease that he talked freely and evidently enjoyed himself immensely. Later, as they were on the train returning to London, Hawthorne told Bennoch that he did not catch the names of his host and hostess. Bennoch hesitated in revealing their identity because, he said, that very morning Hawthorne had vehemently condemned the *Bon Gaultier Ballads* without knowing that Martin was one of the authors. Hawthorne, much embarrassed by the discovery, reportedly said to Bennoch that it was an experience he would never forget: "From this time I shall never condemn any man before I know him, however much I may disagree with his opinions."[47]

Hawthorne's account in the notebooks tallied exactly on the cordiality of his host and hostess, but said nothing of the morning conversation about the *Ballads*. His notes, recorded the day after the return to London, constitute only one long paragraph. After identifying "Mr. Martin" as author and lawyer and calling his wife, who was an actress, by her professional name, Helen[a] Faucit, he described them both briefly. The passage ends with comments on what delightfully informal people they were: "In truth, we had grown to be almost friends in this very little while. And as we rattled away, I said to Bennoch earnestly—'What good people they are!'—and Bennoch smiled, as if he had known perfectly well that I should think and say so" (*EN*, 310).

When Martin came to write the biography of his wife, he included an account of the visit much like Hawthorne's, even quoting two paragraphs from Sophia's edition of *Passages from the English Note-Books*. He made one or two minor additions: Martin said that while they were spending Whitsun holidays at St. Leonard's, a letter came from Bennoch, an old friend, saying that he would call upon them the next day with Hawthorne. After the quotation from Hawthorne, Martin went on to explain that it was impossible not to talk with their guest freely: "We had heard of his reserved and distant manner to strangers, but found him all cordiality and frankness, and with a brightness and charm of thought and expression calculated to give warmth to the respect with which we had long regarded his genius."[48]

This incident, so different from the encounter with Tupper, raises unanswerable questions: Was Bennoch correct in saying that Hawthorne did not realize who his host was until afterwards? There is one possible assumption that might explain Hawthorne's unusual behavior: With people whom he knew to be famous he was inclined to be as reserved as Martin had expected. Did Hawthorne's cordiality, then, result from his *not* recognizing his host and hostess as well-known people, making him less shy than usual? Or was it simply a matter of his meeting two people, who, like Bennoch, did everything possible to put him at ease, especially by conversation that did not refer to the fame of *The Scarlet Letter?*

In themselves these incidents are, perhaps, trivial, but they are also indicative of the great disparity in personality between Bennoch and Hawthorne. In looking back upon the whole series of events described from several different points of view, we may have a better idea of what kind of man Bennoch was and of why Hawthorne admired him. For Bennoch was no less effusive than some of the Englishmen, such as Tupper, whom Hawthorne disliked. Somehow Hawthorne must have felt from the first that whereas the others merely flattered him, Bennoch was a sincere friend. Hawthorne's impressions of him from the night of the first dinner to which Bennoch invited him in April of 1856 remained unchanged for the rest of his life: "Bennoch is an admirable host, and warms his guests like a house-hold fire by the influence of his broad, ruddy, kindly face, and glowing eyes, and by such hospitable demeanor as best suits this aspect!" (*EN*, 291–92).

The week in London following the return from their trip was a whirlwind of social events such as Hawthorne had never experienced before. On Tuesday, April 1, Bennoch gave a dinner at the Milton Club for sixteen guests. Among these were Charles Mackay, editor of the *London Illustrated News;* S. C. Hall, editor of *Art Union Journal;* William

Howitt, editor of *Howitt's Journal;* Tom Taylor, newspaperman and playwright; Herbert Ingram, newly elected M.P. for Boston; and Lieutenant Shaw, whom Hawthorne had met on his recent trip to Camp Aldershot. Although the dinner party lasted until eleven o'clock, Hawthorne went on afterward to a supper party at the Park Lane home of Eneas Dallas, editorial writer for the *Times*. Dallas's wife, the actress Isabella Glyn, coming in from her work at the theater, joined them for a late supper. This day of introduction to the social whirl left Hawthorne more amused than bored, for he recorded the details, especially of conversation, more carefully than he did on some occasions later in the week (*EN*, 310–13).

Two days after this, Mackay invited Hawthorne to dinner at the Reform Club to meet Douglas Jerrold, well-known writer and contributor to *Punch*. This occasion was marked by an embarrassing situation. During the discussion of American authors, particularly Thoreau, Hawthorne applied the term *acrid* to Jerrold's criticism of books. He admitted his mistake and felt that he did all he could to soothe Jerrold's feelings, but Mackay, in his own account written years later, was extremely critical of Hawthorne for being clumsy in his efforts at conversation.[49] Matters must have been settled amicably, for they all went on to the Haymarket Theater to watch a ballet by Spanish dancers.

On Saturday, April 5, Hawthorne returned to the home of Eneas Dallas for another supper party, at which he met Charles Reade, the popular novelist. Although Hawthorne described Reade as "of agreeable talk and demeanor," he apparently enjoyed the novels more than he did their author. Hawthorne devoted most of his notations on this party to his hostess, Miss Glyn (*EN*, 316–17).

On Sunday, Hawthorne, Bennoch, and Mackay took the train to Woking, where they were met by S. C. Hall's carriage and driven to Addlestone for dinner at Firfield, the home of the Halls. Hawthorne did not have much opportunity for conversation with his hostess, a writer, although he liked her immediately, far better than he did her husband. In fact, most of what he recorded about that Sunday was in praise of Mrs. Hall, a rare tribute when one considers his general attitude toward women writers (*EN*, 317–19).

The climax of the social round was the Lord Mayor's Dinner on Monday night. Again it was Bennoch who was responsible for the invitation and who accompanied his friend to the Mansion House. This was, according to Bennoch, a dinner primarily for men "eminent in literature," especially periodical literature. Among the guests he listed were Thackeray, Dickens, Tom Taylor, S. C. Hall, Douglas Jerrold, and Albert Smith. Hawthorne's notebook account of the affair has been much quoted and discussed, largely because of the "miraculous Jewess," the mayor's sister-in-law, who sat across from Hawthorne and who presumably inspired his later description of Miriam in *The Marble Faun*. Bennoch wrote that Mrs. Salomons was considered to be one of the most beautiful women in England, that Hawthorne was so fascinated by her that "he could not keep his eyes off," and that he whispered to Bennoch, "How lovely!"[50]

This is another occasion for which there are varying accounts of the circumstances. In his notebooks and in a letter to Sophia, Hawthorne made it clear that he knew he would be called upon to make a speech. He reported borrowing some "flummery" from S. C. Hall, who sat next to him, and changing the ideas around to suit himself. When he sat down afterward, he was greatly relieved, but later he began to feel that he had "made a fool" of himself, especially when he discovered that the newspapers had omitted all his best points and exaggerated his statements on "international kindness" (*EN*, 323).[51]

In his version of the incident, S. C. Hall went into detail about how surprised Hawthorne was to be called upon to speak and about the coaching that he gave to Hawthorne on how to overcome stagefright. Basically, the account is not very different from that in the English notebooks, except that Hall emphasized Hawthorne's nervousness and his own part in the performance. He went so far as to claim that only because of his coaching did Hawthorne make an "excellent speech,—which certainly he would not have done had he not accepted and acted on my advice."[52]

Hawthorne's letter to Sophia that described his reaction to the entire social whirl showed him at low ebb, trying to forget his loneliness. On the day of the Lord Mayor's Dinner he wrote to her, "They have found me out, these London people, and I believe I should have engagements for every day, and two or three a day, if I staid. . . . In short, I have been lionized, and am still being lionized; and this one experience will be quite sufficient for me. I find it something between a botheration and a satisfaction."[53] However, at the end of his sojourn in London, he acknowledged a feeling of indebtedness to Bennoch and a realization that he had enjoyed himself "owing principally to Bennoch's kindness."[54]

Out of fairness to both Bowman and Bennoch, Hawthorne divided his time between them on the final two days of his vacation. Tuesday, April 8, was devoted to Bennoch. They lunched together and then went to the House of Commons, where they spent the afternoon in the speaker's gallery. Mr. Ingram had invited them to dinner at the refectory of the House. Most of the notebook entries are comments on Ingram, who in his vulgarity reminded Hawthorne of Bramley-Moore and some other Liverpool people. He admitted, "This was really snobbish in me." From the House they went to Albert Smith's lecture on the ascent of Mont Blanc. The evening was concluded by a visit to Evans's supper rooms, "where there was a crowded audience, drinking various liquors, smoking, eating Welsh rabbits, and listening to songs and other entertainments" (*EN*, 325–26).

Hawthorne's thank-you note written the next day to Bennoch confesses to a mild hangover and treats the previous night's affair with typical humor:

> Albert Smith is certainly a trump—the very ace of trumps—but he ought not to have come it quite so strong over my Yankee Simplicity as to make me drink four!!!!—and upon my honor, I believe it was five!!!!!—five "goes" (is that the phrase?) of whisky toddy! Having never heard of this drink before, I naturally supposed that it was some kind of teetotal beverage; for in America, a lecturer (like Mr. Albert Smith) is looked upon as own brother to a clergyman, and is invariably a temperance-man. Do you think the respectable Mr. Evans could have deceived him by putting spiritous liquor in my tumbler? At any rate, I have a suspicion that hot whisky-toddy, when taken in considerable quantities, has a slightly intoxicating quality. Please to tell Mr. Albert Smith so, and he will be on his guard how he gives it to his friends in future.
>
> Well, good bye. I shall return to Liverpool tomorrow, with such small remnants of a moral character as your evil guidance has left me.[55]

Hawthorne did not see Bennoch again that week, for on Wednesday he lunched with Bowman at Birch's and had dinner at Vermont House in Camden, the home of Henry Stevens, American book collector. Here he met Tom Taylor again, and after dinner a small reception followed for other guests. Some of those listed by Hawthorne included the Halls, the Howitts, and the Mackays; John Marston, the dramatist; Arthur Helps, writer; John E. Jones, sculptor; and George Godwin, architect. Howthorne had little to say about any of these persons; his last comment was, "Of all my London experiences, I think this evening was the most tiresome" (*EN*, 326–28).

Hawthorne lunched with Bowman on Thursday and traveled back to Liverpool, leaving himself the weekend to meditate on his twenty-day vacation, which seemed in retrospect to have given him greater satisfaction than he had acknowledged earlier. In his notebooks he concluded that it had been an experience "rich in incident and character, though my account of it be but meagre" (*EN*, 328).

Mention of the dull life of the consulate to which he returned is omitted from the notebooks. After a paragraph about Mrs. Blodget, he proceeded to describe his long account of a trip to Scotland with Bowman, which began on May 2. Apparently this was an exploratory excursion, for Nathaniel planned to take Sophia to Scotland sometime in the future. He and Bowman concentrated on Scott country: Glasgow, Loch Lomond, Inversnaid, Lake Vennachar, Stirling, Edinburgh, Melrose Abbey, Dryburgh Abbey, and Abbottsford. Then they went south to Newcastle, where Bowman stopped to attend to some business. They met again in York for a visit to the cathedral. At that point the week's vacation ended. Bowman went on to London; Hawthorne returned to Liverpool and began recording his impressions in the notebooks (*EN*, 329–49), but he found that "they lost immensely by not having been written day by day, as the scenes and occurrences were fresh."

From that time until June, when Sophia returned from Lisbon, only one incident was recorded in any detail in the notebooks. This was a dinner in Manchester on May 22 to which Bennoch invited him. When Hawthorne arrived at the Albion Hotel in the afternoon he found that Bennoch was attending to some business matters. While Hawthorne waited for him, he took a walk in the heart of the city and decided that it was no better than Liverpool: "It is a dingy and heavy town . . . being like the latter, built almost entirely within the present century" (*EN*, 350).

After Hawthorne returned to the hotel, Bennoch came in "with the same glow and friendly warmth in his face that I had left burning there, when we parted in London." The sentences that follow are one of the strongest tributes that Hawthorne wrote anywhere: "If this man has not a heart, then no man ever had. I like him inexpressibly, for his heart, and for his intellect, and for his flesh and blood; and if he has faults, I do not know them, nor care to know them, nor value him the less if I did know them" (*EN*, 350).

The other dinner guests that evening were three men who impressed Hawthorne by their knowledge and appreciation of Americans. Naturally, then, he felt more at home with this group than with the Liverpool merchants. First to arrive was Charles Swain, poet and engraver, whose works Hawthorne had read, but did not remember well. Swain was a quiet man who would, Nathaniel felt, have talked more had the two been alone or only with Bennoch. The second guest to appear was Alexander Ireland, editor of the *Manchester Examiner,* and, except for Bennoch, the greatest talker in the group. He had entertained Emerson and managed that writer's tour of England in 1847–1848. He talked about Thoreau, Margaret Fuller, and the *Dial* magazine, which he knew well. Hawthorne said little about the third guest, Charles Watson, except that he was a merchant, "a very intelligent man," and the only Englishman he had met who admitted that his countrymen cherished "doubt, jealousy, suspicion, in short, an unfriendly feeling, towards the Americans" (*EN*, 351).

The conversation was long and lively, and after the others had retired, Bennoch and Hawthorne sat talking at some length. It was then that Bennoch first proposed to Nathaniel that after Sophia returned, the Hawthorne family should occupy the Bennoch home in Blackheath for two months in the summer while he and his wife traveled in Germany. Nathaniel said he would leave the matter to the two wives for decision.

Before the men parted the following morning, Hawthorne invited Bennoch to come to Liverpool sometime in the future for a dinner at the Adelphi Hotel. Bennoch replied that although he could not spare the time that spring, he would accept at another date (*EN*, 352). The dinner did eventually take place, postponed until autumn of that year.

While Nathaniel was waiting for Sophia to return, Bennoch sent a letter from London asking him to write a sketch for the *Keepsake,* an annual to which he himself had already contributed a number of poems. The editor, Marguerite Power, was a friend of his who would appreciate such a favor from Hawthorne. In response Nathaniel sat down and, as he said, "dressed up" a little sketch of his pilgrimage to Uttoxeter, based on the notebook account of his side trip from Leamington in July of 1855. He sent it to Bennoch with the following comment:

> Though of little worth, the article is what money would not buy — so difficult is it for me to put myself in writing trim, after so long an interval. If it does not suit Miss Power's Annual, she will of course have no hesitation in rejecting it.
>
> If I had delayed writing it one day longer, I should have been in a state of too high ebullition to write anything; for I received a telegraphic message last night, announcing Mrs. Hawthorne's arrival at Southampton! Julian and I will set out thitherward to-day.[56]

The letter ended with a request that information be sent to him at the Castle Hotel about any place in a southern county where he might leave

Sophia and the rest of the family for as long as two weeks while he went back to Liverpool. Then on July 1 they could move to Bennoch's house in Blackheath.

On the day after the telegraphic message, Hawthorne made arrangements at the consulate for an absence of no more than ten days, after which he and Julian set out on an overnight trip to Southampton via Birmingham, Leamington, and Oxford. They arrived in Southampton the next night "between seven and eight o'clock." The last notebook entry for Wednesday, June 11, sums up Nathaniel's feelings upon the reunion: "I cannot write today" (*EN*, 355).

Upon meeting Sophia, Nathaniel handed her a copy of Coventry Patmore's *The Angel in the House*. The poem, describing the love, courtship, and marriage of Felix Vaughn and Honoria Churchill, daughter of the Dean of Sarum Cathedral, is a picture of idealized love based somewhat on Patmore's own life. One section in particular must have brought back powerful memories to Hawthorne: In "The Railway," Honoria and her father depart on a trip to London; her absence and its effects upon Felix suggest the reason for Nathaniel's gift of the book to Sophia. Actually, the whole situation in this typically Victorian poem illustrates Hawthorne's attitudes toward women, love, and marriage. It was a most appropriate gift to Sophia at a time when his own words were inadequate to express his feelings.

For two days after their reunion the whole family remained in the Castle Hotel, waiting for a wind and rain storm to subside. In the meantime, Bennoch had answered the request for information on a place to stay, and on the fourth day they called on Mrs. Hume, a friend of Bennoch's, who lived in Clifton Villa, Shirley, about two miles from Southampton. Here the Hawthornes planned to board for about two weeks. The next day, leaving Fanny and the children at the Castle Hotel, Sophia and Nathaniel, accompanied by Mrs. Hume, made a one-day excursion to Salisbury and Stonehenge. Upon their return on June 17, the Hawthornes moved from Southampton to Mrs. Hume's. There Nathaniel left his family while he went back to the consulate for a week.

At first Hawthorne was tolerant enough to say that his only criticism of Mrs. Hume, who was head of a "school for young ladies," was that she was not accustomed to feeding men with healthy appetites. Mrs. Blodget's meals had not prepared him for thin bread and butter, plus a "simple joint of mutton, at two-o'clock, which this good lady sets before us" (*EN*, 363). By the end of their stay he was exasperated to the point of recording a whole paragraph on the economies of mistresses of boardinghouses. It explains why, except for Mrs. Blodget's boarding-house, he preferred to live in lodging houses, where the Hawthornes could order their own meals:

> For Mrs. Hume's sake, I shall forever retain a detestation of thin slices of buttered bread. She is an awfully thrifty woman, and nobody can sit at her table without feeling that she both numbers and measures every mouthful that you eat; and the consequence is, that your appetite is discouraged and deadened, without ever being satisfied. She brews her own beer, and it is inexpressibly small, and is served out (only to the more favored guests) in one very little tumbler, with no offer or hint of a further supply. There is water in the milk, and she puts soda into the tea-pot, thereby to give the tea a color without adding to its strength. Human life gets cold and meagre, under such a system; and I must say that I cordially hate Mrs. Hume—a little, bright, shallow, sharp, capable, self-relying, good woman enough. (*EN*, 371–72)

There is no evidence that he passed on his opinions about her to Bennoch, but he was glad to leave Clifton Villa.

He had previously written to Bennoch that they would all depart from Southampton at 11:30 A.M. on July 1, arrive at Waterloo Station at 2:30 P.M., and wait for Bennoch to instruct them how to reach his house at Blackheath. "If it rains, we shall not come."[57] Either it rained or they were not packed and ready to leave, for it was Wednesday, July 2, before they departed. One of Bennoch's clerks met them at Waterloo and either conducted them or told them how to go by train to Blackheath and by cab to the house, where they arrived at 5 P.M.

Unfortunately, they found that Bennoch's house was not "so big as his heart," and Mrs. Bennoch was troubled over how to accommodate so many guests. The next day Nathaniel solved the problem by finding rooms for Fanny, Una, and Rose in a house nearby, where they could sleep and eat by themselves as "a separate family," "with only a daily visit or two to us old folks" (*EN*, 372).

It is no wonder that Hawthorne found the house too small for his family. Although the house at 4 Pond Road, Blackheath Park, has been remodeled since then, it still seems big enough to have accommodated only the Bennochs themselves and their two servants. We can, how-ever, with the use of imagination, picture the many social affairs enjoyed there, especially in the large garden. Today this small two-storied stucco house stands on a corner lot, almost hidden by lofty trees in front and closed in behind by a high brick wall on three sides of a long, rather narrow garden. Attached to the left side of the house at the front is a one-car garage, which looks as if it is a replacement for a carriagehouse of the nineteenth century. Though there is no mention that the Bennochs owned any kind of conveyance, their predecessors in the house may have.[58]

Identification of the house is unmistakable, marked as it is by a round blue-and-white plaque centered in the front wall above the second-floor windows. Official records show that it was placed there in 1933 by the London County Council. The notation reads simply:

L.C.C.
NATHANIEL HAWTHORNE
1804–1864
STAYED HERE IN 1856

The Bennochs, who had previously lived in Greenwich, rented the house at 4 Pond Road in 1850 and lived there for seven years until they moved to a house in another part of the same town.[59] Blackheath was then a growing community of commuters, far different from the place it had been in the earlier era of footpads and highwaymen. In the eighteenth century the inhabitants joined together to suppress the lawlessness for which the area was notorious, and thereafter, as the railroad system developed, the town became a desirable location for the residences of both business and professional people of London. It was quiet, open countryside, far from the smoke and dirt of the city, yet accessible by good train service.

The house, though small, was comfortable, and the garden a pleasant spot in which to relax, especially during the summer heat. Hawthorne wrote to Ticknor from Liverpool about three weeks after their arrival in Blackheath: "If I could only spend my whole time there, I should ask nothing better for the next two months. I got into a new vein of society, on this last visit to London, and have seen a good many interesting people. It is much pleasanter than stagnating in this wretched hole; but I must come back hither, now and then, for the sake of appearances."[60]

Such time as he could spare from work in Liverpool was divided between sightseeing in London and socializing both in the city and in Blackheath, for a number of the literary people, some of whom he had already met, were residents of this suburb. Before the Bennochs departed for Germany there was a round of social affairs. First there was a "conversazione" at the Newton Croslands', where the only interesting person, according to Hawthorne, was Philip Bailey, author of *Festus*, whom he had previously met at the first dinner at the Bennochs' home in April. On another occasion Nathaniel and Archibald Bennoch, his host's nephew, paid a visit to the vaults of a wine merchant at London Docks. Later the same day Hawthorne and Francis Bennoch made calls on various people in London. The next day Dr. Simpson, reputedly an expert on "diseases of the throat and lungs," came to Blackheath at Bennoch's invitation for a social visit, but he also delivered an optimistic opinion on the state of Sophia's health. During this week Bennoch and Hawthorne spent much of their time, presumably in the evenings, strolling around Greenwich Park (*EN*, 374–75).

On Tuesday, July 8, they were all invited to a soirée at the S. C. Halls' London house, at which Jenny Lind was the guest of honor. In spite of her pleasant conversation, Hawthorne was not particularly interested in her. He devoted more space in the notebooks to some of the other guests: Dr. Mackay; Catherine Sinclair, a "literary lady"; Mr. Stevens, the book collector; Joseph Durham, the sculptor; and Geraldine Jewsbury, another writer. The small supper room was so crowded that the Hawthornes, arriving late, could find nothing but sponge cake and champagne, neither of which Nathaniel liked. Of the evening's conversation he wrote, "I did not say—and I think that I did not hear said—one remarkable word" (*EN*, 377). The long, unexciting evening ended for the Hawthornes at midnight.

The next evening Hawthorne was invited to dinner at the home of Mrs. Heywood, Bright's aunt from Liverpool, who during the season maintained a London house at Connaught Place, overlooking Hyde Park. Most of the guests were relatives or friends of Mrs. Heywood and unknown to Hawthorne. The only three people whom he recognized from previous parties were Tom Taylor and Monckton Milnes and his wife. Hawthorne enjoyed hearing Mrs. Milnes talk about Tennyson, and he praised the lady as he had done before when he met her in Liverpool (*EN*, 377–79).

The result of his meeting with the Milneses was an invitation to one of Milnes's famous breakfasts two days later. On this occasion the list of guests was impressive: the Marquess of Lansdowne; George Ticknor, American historian of Spanish literature; Mrs. Nightingale, mother of Florence; John Gorham Palfrey, an American on a visit to England to do research in the State Papers Office; Joseph Hunter, a gentleman of "antiquarian pursuits"; and, most significant to Hawthorne, the Brownings. In addition, Hawthorne had a glimpse of Macaulay, who sat next to Milnes, but evidently there was no opportunity for conversation with him. Hawthorne had been assigned to conduct Mrs. Browning into the breakfast room, and he enjoyed their first conversation while he sat next to her. Browning came over and introduced himself to Hawthorne, and though there is no suggestion by any of those involved that they admired one another's writings, a friendship did develop when they met two years later in Florence (*EN*, 382).

Meanwhile, the Bennochs departed for the Continent, and Nathaniel, feeling the necessity of another trip to Liverpool, left his family in Blackheath from Monday, July 14, to Saturday, the twenty-sixth. Mrs. Blodget's was so crowded with guests that the lady had to put Hawthorne in a small back bedroom. She expressed the hope that he would not be disturbed by the ghost of a former occupant, and this remark led to Hawthorne's reference to a meeting with Henry Bright when the latter related a ghost story that had been told to him by Mrs. Gaskell (*EN*, 385).

In spite of his feelings about the "detestable Mersey" and "the black hole" of Liverpool, Hawthorne had not lost his sense of humor. In a letter to Julian he recounted with obvious exaggeration all the good food he had enjoyed at one of Mrs. Blodget's dinners: "chicken-pie, roast duck, fried tripe, boiled chicken, boiled salmon, fried soles. Also green peas, string beans. Puddings, tarts, custards, Banbury cakes, cheese-cakes, and green gages. . . . I did manage to eat some currant pudding, and a Banbury cake, and a Victoria cake, and a slice of a beautiful Spanish muskmelon, and some plums. If you had been there, I think you would have had a very good dinner, and there would not have been nearly so many nice things left on the table."[61] The emphasis on food is reminiscent of his previous scornful comparison between Mrs. Hume's thin bread and butter and Mrs. Blodget's sumptuous meals. Until late in his life Nathaniel had a healthy appetite and enjoyed good food, as the notebook comments make evident again and again.

Upon his return to London, Hawthorne made his first and only call on Delia Bacon at her boarding place at 12 Spring Street, off Sussex Gardens, between Bayswater and Paddington (*EN*, 386). This visit of July 26 came about as a result of correspondence begun in May, when Delia appealed to Hawthorne for aid, feeling that he as a literary man representing the U.S. government would listen to her theory on Shakespeare and sympathize with her efforts to prove it.

After a rather successful lecture career in America, Delia had gone to England in an effort to substantiate her gradually developing theory that the plays attributed to Shakespeare were written, not by that actor-writer, but by Francis Bacon or a group working under his direction. This theory, she claimed, could be proved by Bacon's letters and by papers buried in either Bacon's or Shakespeare's grave. At the time Delia met Hawthorne, the manuscript she was writing contained only analyses of Bacon's letters and some of Shakespeare's plays; she had not compiled any external evidence. Mr. Ogden revealed during his Rock Park visit that she had been prevented from opening Bacon's tomb. In August of 1856, she moved to Stratford with hopes of investigating Shakespeare's grave.

Although Hawthorne did not agree with Delia's theory, on finding her to be an intelligent woman and seeing her complete devotion to her cause, he promised to try to get her book published. Hawthorne's description of her in the English notebooks was retained as part of a chapter in *Our Old Home*:

> I expected to see a very homely, uncouth, elderly personage, and was rather pleasantly disappointed by her aspect. She is rather uncommonly tall, and has a striking and expressive face—dark hair, dark eyes, which shone as she spoke; and, by and by, a color came into her cheeks. She must be over forty years old—perhaps, towards fifty—[She was forty-four.] and, making allowance for years and ill health, she may be supposed to have been handsome once. (*EN*, 387)

The most effective point in Delia's appeal for help was the eliciting of Hawthorne's sense of duty toward stranded Americans. As with all the others he had assisted when he was in the consular office, the money for printing the book would have to come from his own pocket. Delia did not know this, and he never let her discover that he paid the entire printing bill. In fact, Francis Bennoch was the only one who realized what a costly enterprise this was to Hawthorne in both time and money.

When Delia asked Hawthorne to write a preface for her book, she had expected him to express support for her theory. In order to avoid doing this, he emphasized her right to be heard publicly and quoted her statement on the necessity of accepting internal evidence for her theory in the absence of external evidence. The resulting breach between them ended in Hawthorne's turning over to Bennoch the task of seeing the book through its publication and distribution. Delia had temporarily refused to have anything more to do with Hawthorne. Bennoch then became both literary agent and editor.

Delia had long since given up the idea of digging in Shakespeare's grave; she decided for some unexplained reason that the evidence would have to rest on Bacon's letters and the plays themselves. Readers did not accept this evidence. Hawthorne, Delia's brother, and many critics believed that the book would have been far more effective if she had contented herself with her analyses of the times and of the plays. The theory concerning Bacon alienated critics and other readers and made the book a financial failure, finally driving Delia to a state of insanity.[62]

Hawthorne could have been bitter about her condemnation of his preface, but he treated the matter with humor and tolerance. To Bennoch he wrote that he could think of one appropriate title for the book: "A Rasher of Bacon," for "it was a degree more than rash (in me) to get the book published at all. What a horrible pun!" A month later he said of himself, "A fool and his money are soon parted." "However, I do not repent what I have done." His final comment was somewhat stronger: "This shall be the last of my benevolent follies, and I never will be kind to anybody again as long as I live."[63]

In spite of their disagreements, Hawthorne retained in later years his admiration for Delia's intellect and perseverance; he felt that though she denied Shakespeare credit for writing the plays, she had "recognized a depth in the man whom she denied":

> And when, not many months after the outward failure of her life-long object, she passed into the better world, I know not why we should hesitate to believe that the immortal poet may have met her on the threshold and led her in, re-assuring her with friendly and comfortable words, and thanking her (yet with a smile of gentle humor in his eyes at the thought of certain mistaken speculations) for having interpreted him to mankind so well.[64]

When Delia left London for Stratford, Hawthorne was in Liverpool attending to consular business and making investigations about a seaside resort where his family might spend the next year. He made a trip to Southport, north of Liverpool, on Friday afternoon, August 22, and was satisfied by his brief visit that the place would do as a temporary residence. He returned to Blackheath on Tuesday, the twenty-sixth.

In his journal account of the rest of that week, Hawthorne noted one incident of importance to him. Bennoch, who had come back alone from the Continent, leaving his wife there to improve her health, spent an evening talking with Nathaniel: "He told me something about [Martin] Tupper that gives him an aspect of pathos and heroic endurance, very little in accordance with the ludicrous attitude in which I have sketched him. The thing is not [to] be recorded; but Tupper is a patient, tender, Christian man" (*EN*, 398).

Such a serious note is certainly in contrast to Nathaniel's earlier comments about Tupper, especially his humorous account of August 6, when both families, meeting by accident in London, ate "ice-creams" in a confectioner's shop. To Hawthorne's great amusement, Tupper and his wife ate from the same dish (*EN*, 393–94). The reader cannot help wondering about Tupper's problem and wishing that Tupper could have read Hawthorne's latest statement about him in addition to the previous ones that turned the little man against Nathaniel.

The final social event before the Hawthornes left Blackheath was a trip to Oxford, in the company of Bennoch, as guests of Richard Spiers, who had been mayor of Oxford in 1853. S. C. Hall's family and Joseph Durham, the sculptor, were also among the guests. Apparently Spiers' house was not large enough to accommodate so many people, for though the meals were at his house, the guests stayed across the street. The days that followed included tours of several colleges, an excursion to Blenheim, and one to Stanton-Harcourt. On Friday, September 5, Spiers gathered together in his garden those guests who had remained until the end of the week. There he arranged them in a group for a photograph made by Philip De La Motte, an artist-photographer.[65] After that, the party broke up. The Hawthornes and Bennoch returned to Blackheath, and Nathaniel recorded in his notebooks a twenty-six-page account of their activities that he had been prevented from completing while they were in Oxford (*EN*, 398–424).

That weekend Nathaniel and Sophia both wrote notes to Ticknor asking that a complete set of Hawthorne's works be bound and sent across the Atlantic as a gift to Spiers. When the eleven volumes arrived months later, Nathaniel found that they had been handsomely bound in green morocco with gilt edges. "To R. J. Spiers, Esq." was stamped on the cover of each. Someone, perhaps Sophia, later painted a water-color design of a coat of arms and pasted a copy in each volume. On December 26 Hawthorne was pleased to send them on to Spiers in return for his hospitality.[66]

The Hawthornes had been invited to Blackheath for the summer months only, and in September they had to depart. Nathaniel and Julian left for Liverpool ahead of the others; the rest of the family followed within a few days. They stayed at Mrs. Blodget's until they were ready to move to Southport: "And so finished our residence at Bennoch's house, where I, for my part, have spent some of the happiest

Ex-Mayor Spiers and His Guests, Oxford, 1856. From left to right: Sophia Hawthorne, Mrs. Spiers, R. Spiers, Jr., Fanny Hall, Mr. Addison, S. C. Hall, Mrs. Hall, R. Spiers, Sr. (behind her), and Nathaniel Hawthorne. (Sophia who disliked having her pictures taken, obliterated her face on this photograph.)

hours that I have known since we left our American home. It is a strange, vagabond, gypsy sort of life, this that we are leading; and I know not whether we shall finally be spoilt for any other, or shall enjoy our quiet Wayside as we never did before, when once we reach it again" (*EN*, 424).

A week later he added another ominous note: "I do not know what sort of character it will form in the children, this unsettled, shifting, vagrant life, with no central home to turn to, except what we carry in ourselves" (*EN*, 425). Undoubtedly this feeling of unsettled life was partly responsible for his appreciation of Bennoch; one wonders what else entered in. In an attempt to answer the question we are led to make further comparisons between Bennoch and Bright.

Age inevitably made some difference. Bright was about half Hawthorne's age; Bennoch was only eight years younger than Nathaniel. The social circles of the two men were also very diverse. In Liverpool, Bright's guests were more likely to be nonliterary people. Bennoch, though a business man, entertained almost exclusively literary and artistic guests, although for the most part they were minor figures of the time. One Englishman went so far as to say that Bennoch was a "*parvenu*," scorned by the best people because of his seeming attempts to buy his way into London literary society; he knew "a number of the wrong people."[67] Such a judgment depends upon how one defines "the wrong people." As for buying his way in, Bennoch did not put on lavish affairs, for he was not rich as some people supposed.

Perhaps Bennoch's worst fault was that he was overzealous in trying to please, to help others, and to manage their social lives. His comparison of himself with Hawthorne reveals his feeling of inferiority: "Throughout the whole of our intimacy there was, on his part, such a strange self-abnegation as to make me frequently very uncomfortable. The contrast between his enormous powers and lofty position in literature, and my own comparative insignificance, was so indubitable that in our familiar intercourse when I used to tease him, which was not infrequently, I wondered at my impudence."[68]

Bennoch was wise enough to know that Hawthorne felt at ease with him, and that he himself, as a patron of literary people, was in the best position to see that his friend met other Londoners. Monckton Milnes tried, but Hawthorne was unaccustomed to nobility and unwilling to change his ways for such a host, cordial though Milnes was; Milnes felt this and was somewhat hurt.[69] Bennoch, who did not expect his friend to be a lion at social affairs, compensated for Hawthorne's shyness by his own irresistible effervescence, and Nathaniel apparently accepted rather than resented Bennoch's oversolicitousness.

Hawthorne's comment written at the conclusion of his visit to London in the spring of 1856 still stands as his lasting judgment on Bennoch: "If he has faults, I do not know them, nor care to know them, nor value him the less if I did know them" (*EN*, 350). Nor did he value Bright the less after he had come to know Bennoch. The two remained different and separate friends in "Our Old Home." One dominated the Liverpool social life; the other, that of London—until the Hawthornes left England for the Wayside. Thereafter, Hawthorne's friendship with both men had to be maintained by correspondence.

‡ 5 ‡

Southport
1856–1857

HAWTHORNE'S RELUCTANCE to leave the Bennochs' home in September is understandable. At Blackheath his family had comfort, convenience, an interesting social life, and opportunities for sightseeing. Even though living there involved a long train ride back and forth to Liverpool, he was happy to escape the drudgery of the consulate whenever possible. Now the Hawthornes were planning to settle down for the autumn months in a town close enough to Liverpool that commuting to Nathaniel's office by train would take scarcely an hour. In the end, he was forced to acknowledge that living in Southport, like so many of his experiences abroad, was not what he had envisioned. It was fortunate that he could not foresee how barren would be the ten long months in this dull seaside resort. Without the stimulation of social life and of walks in a picturesque countryside, he had nothing to relieve the monotony of the consulate except the evening reunions with his family in a house too temporary to be a real home. The whole experience would prove to be the dreariest period of Nathaniel's life in England.

During the few days that he waited for Sophia and the girls to join him at Mrs. Blodget's, he was glad to be invited out to dinner twice. On Wednesday he dined with Henry Bright at the Monk's Ferry Hotel, where Bright was staying while his family vacationed in Scotland. For the most part, the conversation consisted of speculations based on gossip provided by another guest, a Mr. Crawley, about Mr. Spiers of Oxford.[1] The second invitation was to an informal dinner for Nathaniel and Julian at the home of Henry Wilding, chief clerk at the consulate. Hawthorne's journal account is the only glimpse we have of the personal life of the man upon whom he depended for accurate bookkeeping records. On a salary of "less than a thousand dollars" Wilding maintained a small house at New Brighton, a suburb across the Mersey at the tip of the Wirral. It was a "comfortable" place with a lawn and a kitchen garden. The only items inside the house that Hawthorne mentioned were a piano and a "fair collection of books." Wilding had a family—a wife and one child—but "he is temperate—abstemious, I should think," and managed his small salary carefully. It was dark and misty when Nathaniel and Julian took the 7:30 P.M. ferry back to Liverpool (*EN*, 424–25).

On Saturday, September 13, Sophia, Fanny, and the two girls arrived from Blackheath, and by Tuesday the family was ready to move: "Vagabonds as we are—we again struck our tent and set out for Southport" (*EN*, 425). They intended to stay only three months, but spent instead the entire winter and spring and almost half the following summer there.

The place they chose to rent was part of a semidetached house at 15 Brunswick Terrace, Promenade, where they obtained three bedrooms at ten and sixpence for each bed and a parlor for twelve and sixpence. The landlady, Miss Jane Bramwell, was pictured by Nathaniel as "a tall, thin, muscular, dark, shrewd, and shabby-looking mistress." The parlor, he said, was equally shabby, but "a fair specimen of what lodging-house parlors generally are in England." The floor of the fifteen-foot room was covered by an old carpet. The furniture consisted of a square table in the center of the room; half a dozen chairs, including two that were supposedly comfortable; a sofa that was not soft, but long and broad and "good to recline on"; a "beaufet, in which we keep some of our household affairs[;] and a little bit of a cupboard in which we put our bottle of wine, both under lock and key." The decorations included two glass vases on the mantel, a looking glass over it, a colored print of a lake or seashore, and two colored prints of Prince Albert and Queen Victoria (*EN*, 425–26).

Two days after they moved in, Hawthorne wrote that they had the option of a better parlor at the end of the week. They apparently did not move, but simply expanded to occupy more space in the same house, for their address remained unchanged, and payments for rent were slightly higher.[2] The arrival of their piano explained the need for a larger parlor, and an additional bedroom was required for the governess who came in October. In the months that followed, one more bedroom became necessary for servants. Later records reveal that the Hawthornes took over at least two floors of this three-story house.

Though the house was not very attractive, it was cheaper and more private than hotel rooms would have been. The English lodging house, Nathaniel wrote, is, "nevertheless, a contrivance for carrying the domestic cares of home about you . . . and immediately you have to set about providing your own bread and cheese and tea and coffee, and eggs and chops—and all such necessaries—even to the candles you burn, and the soap on your washstands" (*EN*, 425). At first, Fanny took the responsibility for much of the housekeeping, and the family settled down to a relaxed, but dull, life.

Nathaniel disliked Southport almost from the start, and after the initial novelty of seaside living wore off, Sophia too complained of the dullness. She wrote that her sister Elizabeth would "die of ennui in such an utterly stupid, uninteresting, lonely place, where there is no society, no life, no storied memories, and no scenery—except the horizon and the clouds."[3] Aside from housekeeping and sewing, there was nothing to do except take salt baths, ride in a donkey cart, or walk the sands when the weather permitted. Part of the time it rained; much of the time it was windy. Nathaniel found the high winds depressing in gloomy weather, but exhilarating on sunny days, especially after the summer visitors "began to depart to Liverpool, Manchester, and the neighboring country-towns." Even though he enjoyed walking on a sunny, windy day, he found the scenery uninteresting—"an interminable breadth of sands, stretching out to the horizon—brown or yellow sands, looking pooly or plashy in some places, and barred across with drier reaches of sand" (*EN*, 425–26).

It was not a "fashionable watering-place," Hawthorne said. "Only one nobleman's name, and those of two or three baronets" adorned the guest list in the weekly *Southport Visiter*. The few people they saw on the beach and the Promenade had "at best, a well-to-do tradesmanlike air." There were no public amusements, and "solitary visitors must needs find it a dreary place" (*EN*, 428). This was not Hawthorne's idea of pleasure.

So many changes have taken place in Southport that it is difficult to picture the beach and the Promenade as they were in 1856. Brunswick Terrace was the name applied to "a pair of semi-detached houses, three stories each, with a bay window to each floor." Number 15, occupied by the Hawthornes, was the first house from the south end of this wide street.[4] At that time the expanse of sands began at the edge of the Promenade. Since then a short, narrow street, Scarisbrick Avenue, has been cut through from the main street to the Promenade; the Marine Lake has replaced a large section of the sands; and there are now bridges from the Promenade across an expanse of gardens to the beach.[5] The "interminable breadth of sands" that Nathaniel found so monotonous is no longer even visible from that section of

Southport Promenade, 1856. The Hawthornes stayed in the house second from the right.

the Promenade, but nowadays in the autumn, after the tourists have departed, the beach in the distance is almost as deserted as it was in Hawthorne's day.

Nathaniel found the area between Southport and Liverpool, which he crossed daily on the train, to be equally dull—a flat expanse of land, as far as one could see. After a month of not socializing and of commuting to the city over this vast waste stretch, he wrote to Ticknor, "I must confess I sigh for London, and consider it time mis-spent to live anywhere else."[6]

If life in Southport was so dreary, we can scarcely help wondering why the Hawthornes had come in the first place and why, finding themselves disappointed, they stayed on for ten months. The primary reason was, of course, Sophia's health. Dr. Gibson, her physician in London, had recommended the town because of the mild sea air. Southport was miles from the foggy river climate of Rock Ferry, more accessible to Liverpool, and less expensive for the most part than Rock Park.[7]

At first Sophia reported that she was not sure what effects salt air and seashore would have on her lungs. At Blackheath she had not been well "at all during the whole two months, though it was inland and salubrious." She revived as soon as she reached Southport and was not so tired as she had been in the summer, but she could not walk long at a time. (The doctor had specified a limit of thirty minutes.) However, she and the children could ride in a donkey cart (at a cost of one shilling per hour), or take salt baths (at sixpence per person) in the bathhouse, "where there are nice accommodations, long deep baths of white china tiles, woolen carpets, and warm fires in true English comfort and nicety."[8]

During this early part of their stay, Sophia wrote to her sister Elizabeth that Dr. Gibson had said she should be "self-indulgent." Then she paid tribute to Fanny for being so helpful in taking care of their lodgings: "She is the most useful and convenient person in the world for me. . . . She is a famous nurse, too, having been well disciplined by an invalid stepmother."[9] These pleasant comments were evidently written during the first few weeks of the Southport stay, for gradually the absence of social life became tedious enough to cause a change of tone in Sophia's letters.

For Nathaniel life was only slightly different. Consular affairs were as dull as ever, and after the descriptions of Southport, the notebook entries for the autumn of 1856 concentrate on the only two social events that relieved the monotony. The first of these was the dinner that Nathaniel had promised to Bennoch in return for his hospitality. Bennoch came to Southport for the weekend of October 3 to 5, and on Saturday night Hawthorne entertained him at a big and expensive dinner party at the Adelphi Hotel, the largest in Liverpool.

The Hawthornes had never stayed at the Adelphi, for it was the most expensive hotel in the city. Earlier in the century, James Radley, the manager, had bought a block of terraced houses along Ranelagh Place at the foot of Mount Pleasant and gradually combined them into a single large hotel building. His personality is said to have been responsible for the enormous success of the Adelphi: "By his purported charm and polite, easy manner, coupled with the experience gained while he was operating in London as an Hotelier, and a rare talent for organization, he managed to make his hotel the most popular in Liverpool and it soon became famed throughout Britain and Europe."[10]

At Hawthorne's dinner party he was surprised to find that

> Radly [*sic*], our landlord, himself attended at table, and officiated as chief waiter. He has a fortune of £100,000 — half a million of dollars — and is an elderly gentleman of good address and appearance. In America . . . he would never conceive the possibility of changing a plate, or passing round the table with hock and champagne. Some of his hock, by the way, was a most rich and imperial wine, such as can hardly be had on the Rhine itself; — and of a most deceptive potency. (*EN*, 429)

When Charles Dickens, before departing for America on the *Britannia* in 1842, enjoyed his last meal at the Adelphi, he praised both the dinner and his host, Mr. Radley, "my faultless friend." The meal, he wrote, was "undeniably perfect"; it included "turtle, cold Punch, with Hock, Champagne, and Claret, and all the slight et cetera usually included in an unlimited order for a good dinner."[11]

The dinner for Bennoch sounds very similar. When Hawthorne referred to it in a letter to Ticknor, he enclosed a menu, on the back of which he listed the names of the guests. The dinner was his way of returning the hospitality not only of Bennoch, the guest of honor, but also of Henry Bright and Charles Swain, two of his literary friends. The other guests were mostly Liverpool merchants to whom Hawthorne had long been indebted. Their names were probably written in the order in which they sat:

Mr. Hawthorne

Mr. F. Bennoch	Mr. Joseph Pollock
Mr. C. Swain	Mr. Charles Holland
Mr. H. A. Bright	Mr. Albert Mott
Mr. Ely	Mr. Geo. Melly

Mr. Babcock

The menu, dated October 4, listed ten turtle dinners and included the following items:

> Haunch of venison &c.   Sherry & Biscuits   1 B Punch   2 Hock
> Sherry   Ale   4 Champagne   2 Moselle Cup   Dessert & Grapes
> Ice Creams & Cakes   Brandy   Liqueurs . . . 1 B Port   3 Claret
> Teas and Coffees   Cigars   Brandy   1 B Madeira.

To this was added a charge of 10s. 6d. for waiters. At the end were these entries:

> Brandy No 55   Rum   5 Bfts & Ham   Bedrooms   Servants Attendance
> Total £22-10-0   J. S. Kemp for J. Radley[12]

In other words, the evening's festivities cost Hawthorne over $100. It was the only occasion on which he entertained lavishly.

Bennoch, the guest of honor, spent part of Sunday with the family at Southport and then departed for London. Sophia had no responsibility for arranging the Saturday night dinner party; she merely recorded the total cost in the account book after Bennoch left.[13]

In the second important event, however, Sophia was involved as hostess. A month after the affair at the Adelphi, Herman Melville arrived in Liverpool en route to the Mediterranean and spent two days with the Hawthornes at Southport. Like Sophia, Melville was having problems with his health. In the five years since the Hawthornes had left the Red Cottage in Lenox, Massachusetts, where the two authors' friendship had begun, Melville had completed a tremendous amount of writing; in fact, he had worked so hard that a rest was absolutely necessary.[14] For this reason he had left his family with his father-in-law in Boston and sailed from New York to Glasgow. After traveling south by train, he arrived in Liverpool looking for a ship going to the Mediterranean that would take him as a passenger.

Hawthorne and Melville had apparently not seen each other since the latter visited at the Wayside in Concord in the fall of 1852.[15] Meanwhile, Hawthorne had tried to assist his friend twice, both times unsuccessfully, by recommending him for a position that might bring him a larger income than his writing did. Melville undoubtedly did not know that in 1855 Hawthorne had suggested him to Commodore Perry as a possible editor of his notes (*EN*, 98). How much Melville did know about Hawthorne's efforts in the spring of 1853 to persuade President Pierce to give him a consular appointment is uncertain. By the fall of 1856 Melville must have realized it was not Hawthorne's fault that the appointment did not go through, but Nathaniel still felt embarrassed by his failure to be of service.

Probably because of the weather, Melville waited a day in Liverpool before trying to locate the Hawthornes. He had arrived in the city early in the afternoon of Saturday, November 8, and had registered at a commercial hotel, the White Bear on Dale Street, not far from the Exchange and the docks. Since it was raining, he stayed inside the entire evening, and it was not until Sunday afternoon that he took a boat to Rock Ferry to locate the Hawthornes. There he learned that the family had long since moved from Rock Park, and he had to wait until Monday before finding Nathaniel at the consulate. Hawthorne invited him to stay at Southport for as long as it took him to find a suitable ship. The next afternoon, after exploring the docks and looking over the steamers that were in port, Melville rejoined Hawthorne at the consulate. Together they took the train to Southport.[16]

Melville's account of the two days that followed is a brief series of jottings:

> Wednesday Nov 12 At Southport. An agreeable day. Took a long walk by the sea. Sands & grass. Wild & desolate. A strong wind. Good talk. In the evening Stout & Fox & Geese. — Julian grown into a fine lad; Una taller than her mother. Mrs. Hawthorne not in good health. Mr. H. stayed home for me.

> Thursday Nov 13. At Southport till noon. Mr. H. and I took train then for Liverpool. Spent rest of day pressing inquiries among steamers, & writing letters, & addressing papers, &c.[17]

Hawthorne's account goes into much more detail about Melville and the "good talk." First of all, Nathaniel was impressed by his guest's ability to travel with only a small bundle, "which, he told me, contained a night-shirt and a tooth-brush. He is a person of very gentlemanly instincts in every respect, save that he is a little heterodox in the matter of clean linen." Melville had, of course, left his other belongings in Liverpool, but even later when he took ship he carried with him only a carpetbag. Hawthorne's marveling at such economy in baggage reflects his repeated annoyance at his own burdensome accumulation of luggage.

Hawthorne's reference to Wednesday's walk on the sands tells us far more than Melville's sentence or two. As they sat in a hollow of the sands, smoking cigars,

> Melville, as he always does, began to reason of Providence and futurity, and of everything that lies beyond human ken, and informed me that he had "pretty much made up his mind to be annihilated"; but still he does not seem to rest in that anticipation; and, I think, will never rest until he gets hold of a definite belief. It is strange how he persists—and has persisted ever since I knew him, and probably long before—in wandering to-and-fro over these deserts, as dismal and monotonous as the sand hills amid which we were sitting. He can neither believe, nor be comfortable in his unbelief; and he is too honest and courageous not to try to do one or the other. If he were a religious man, he would be one of the most truly religious and reverential; he has a very high and noble nature, and better worth immortality than most of us. (*EN*, 432–33)

With the exception of a sentence written when Melville departed from Liverpool, this is Hawthorne's last testimony to Melville's quality of character. It may serve as a partial rejoinder to those critics who have theorized that after the end of the Lenox period, the relationship between Melville and Hawthorne became decidedly cool. Circumstances had separated the two men, and in view of the relative failure of Melville's later writings to achieve popularity, it is not surprising that he may have been somewhat diffident about approaching Hawthorne.[18]

Melville's visit at Southport was a short one for two reasons: Hawthorne could not spare much time away from the consulate, and Melville had not yet located a ship. Evidently on Friday, November 14, he did find one that was to sail on the following Monday, for on that day he had his passport for Constantinople, via Malta and Gibraltar, and the Continent signed by Hawthorne at the consulate. He also obtained his Turkish visa at "Consulat Ottoman."[19] While he was at the U.S. Consulate, he was introduced to Henry Bright, who had stopped in to see Hawthorne. Bright invited Melville to his club for lunch and afterward took him to see the Unitarian Church, the Free Library, and the cemetery.[20]

On Saturday morning Hawthorne and Melville started out on an all-day trip to Chester. Melville's *Journal* refers briefly to an omnibus ride to Toxteth Park and to a visit to see the organ at St. George's Hall. This was a short expedition made alone either before or after the Saturday expedition with Hawthorne. Strangely, he did not even mention the trip to Chester. By contrast, Hawthorne, in his relief at escaping from the dullness of the consulate and Southport, devoted pages of his journal to an enthusiastic description of Chester—"the only place, within easy reach of Liverpool, which possesses any old English interest." It was a cloudy day with occasional rainy spells, but the two men managed to tour the walls and the Rows and, after lunch at a confectioner's shop, to visit the cathedral and enjoy cigars in the bar of the Yacht Inn, Watergate Street, which Jonathan Swift had made famous by his visits. At 4 P.M. they left Chester for Liverpool, where Hawthorne took the 6:30 train to Southport, leaving his friend to return to the White Bear Hotel (*EN*, 433).[21]

In anticipation of the ship's sailing on Monday, Melville spent Sunday packing his trunk for storage in Liverpool. However, Captain Tate delayed the departure of *The Egyptian* until Tuesday, to Melville's great disappointment. Hawthorne, who met him again on Monday, wrote somewhat optimistically about his friend: "He said that he already felt much better than in America; but observed that he did not anticipate much pleasure in his rambles, for that the spirit of adventure is gone out of him. He certainly is much overshadowed since I saw him last; [Hawthorne is obviously referring to the days in America, not to the visit of the previous week.] but I hope he will brighten as he goes onward" (*EN*, 437). Hawthorne concluded with a further comment on Melville's economy in taking only the carpetbag with him: "He learned his travelling habits by drifting about, all over the South Sea, with no other clothes or equipage than a red flannel shirt and a pair of duck trousers. Yet we seldom see men of less criticizable manners than he" (*EN*, 437).

When Melville sailed on Tuesday, he left his trunk at the consulate. It has been assumed by some that because Hawthorne wrote nothing more about Melville, the two friends never saw each other again. Melville's *Journal*, however, reveals that when he returned to Liverpool from his seven-month voyage on May 4, 1857, he met Hawthorne once more at the consulate. He also called on Henry Bright after he had secured passage home on the *City of Manchester*. Records of any meetings between Hawthorne and Melville that might have taken place later in America (and they would be unlikely because of later circumstances) apparently vanished long ago. Melville's letters do not include any such references, and Hawthorne's letters to him, according to Melville's own testimony, were destroyed.[22]

A few weeks before Melville's visit, the first governess the Hawthornes ever hired arrived from London. Miss Browne, who had been recommended by Mrs. S. C. Hall, was engaged for only three months because the Hawthornes were not then certain of staying in Southport beyond the end of 1856. But however unsatisfactory the lady proved to be, she was kept on until spring in order to relieve Sophia of some responsibilities.[23]

In some respects Miss Browne was not typical of English governesses, who were as a class generally not much above female servants. Sophia wrote that she was "a lady by *birth* and breeding and will teach Una French and Music. She has been three years in France, and can also teach drawing and dancing." Her use of the English language was said to be "irreproachable." A week after Miss Browne arrived, Sophia said of her, "She has authority with great sweetness, and they [the children] all are very happy and obedient. She has method and looks like order itself, without being prim."[24]

By the end of two months Sophia had become somewhat disillusioned: Their governess had been misrepresented; except for French and music she was a "nothing." Miss Browne was simply ignorant in many ways; she could not cope with Una, who had always been a great reader. Though she had lived in France, she did not have great command of the language. Una and Julian were being taught to "write, spell and cipher" and were also learning "geography, French, music"; "and they draw at stated times—though Miss Browne can give them no help." The children did not know facts, Sophia admitted, but they had read a great deal, and Miss Browne had not. "She has never heard of Spenser or other literary men."[25]

For the most part, Nathaniel agreed with Sophia on Miss Browne's qualities, but he looked at the matter from a broader point of view. Miss Browne was not "at all below the common level of governesses":

> It would be idle to expect her to teach music, drawing, and other accomplishments, so well as the scientific professors of those matters. The defect belongs to the system of instruction by governesses. . . . Miss Browne is a nice, humdrum little woman, with no talent whatever, and about as much education as gentlewomen usually get in England; for, except as regards the highest masculine education, the standard seems to be lower here than in America. She will serve very well, for the present, as

a finger-post to point the children on the way they should go. They like her, and so does my wife; and, for my part, as a member of my family, I like her ten times as much as if she could put me out [of] countenance with her wit and erudition. We have no idea of discarding her as long as we remain in England.[26]

Julian's picture of Miss Browne, written years later, was somewhat scornful of her limited knowledge, but his memory of her may have been refreshed by a rereading of family letters:

At Southport we had a queer little governess. . . . She was barely five feet in height, and as thin and dry as an insect; and although her personal character came up to any eulogium that could be pronounced upon it, her ignorance of the "branches" specified was, if possible, greater than our own . . . and although we liked little Miss Brown [sic] very much, she speedily lost all shadow of control over us; we treated her as a sort of inferior sister, and would never be serious. "English governess" became for us a synonym for an amiable little nonentity who knew nothing. . . . Miss Brown did not outlast our residence in Southport.[27]

To help Miss Browne in her teaching, Sophia invested in a few more school books: an atlas, Mrs. Markham's *History of France,* and various guides, plus copybooks, drawing paper, and pencils. Since there was no mention of the purchase of a geometry text, the book they used was apparently one sent over by Elizabeth Peabody. Julian was amused at Miss Browne's attempts to decipher the explanations in the text, but Sophia took the matter as one more indication that Miss Browne was not efficient enough for the Hawthornes to consider taking her to the Continent with them.[28]

Aside from lessons, life for the children continued as it had since they first arrived: salt baths, drives in donkey carts, and walks on the sands. Most of the time Sophia apparently took Dr. Gibson's advice about being "self-indulgent." Nathaniel did not mention increased expenses brought on by the addition of two servants, but not long after Miss Browne came it was evident that Sophia could not cope with all the housework without Fanny Wrigley's help. Much against her own wishes, Fanny had left the Hawthornes to live with her sister, who had asked her to come to York. Una was left to act as nursemaid to Rose. When more help was needed, Sophia somehow persuaded Emily, the cook at Rock Park, to return. She also hired an English housemaid, Mary [Sumner?], who was not only very pretty, but far superior to either Mary or Ellen Hearne.[29] Once again the English account book showed expenditures for servants' wages and allowances of tea, as well as for food. With Emily's return, breadmaking was resumed for the first time since Rock Park days.

Because there were almost no guests to entertain at Southport, it seems that the Hawthornes were able to be more economical than they had been at Rock Park. Less money was spent for rent and food. Possibly less was spent for clothing, in spite of the sewing materials that were bought and the seamstress who was occasionally hired. Omission of totals and some missing pages in the account book make the entire record of finances at Southport somewhat incomplete.

As the fall season advanced, Sophia continued to find Southport a dull town, but Una was pleased that they had settled down once more. She liked Miss Browne and she enjoyed the quiet life they led, which was only rarely varied by small incidents. One weekend Una went to visit the Brights, and a month later Henry Bright came to the Hawthornes' house for dinner. When the weather was bad, the children played battledore and shuttlecock indoors after lessons were over. Julian was not much interested in reading of any kind; Una was always happy to curl up with a book. She even liked Southport in the winter: It was odd, she said, that "a place so near Liverpool should be so entirely different."[30]

While the rest of the family lived rather uneventful lives, Nathaniel was too much occupied with business at the consulate and with Delia Bacon's book to be concerned with household matters. Once or twice he took walks in the countryside as far as Ormskirk, but he found little of historic interest there in comparison with Chester. In the late fall months his only social life consisted of a few dinners in Liverpool—one a banquet at the Town Hall given by the new mayor, Mr. Shand. Nathaniel noted that he had already described many similar banquets in the past. He appreciated the turtle, the American canvasback ducks, and the wines, and after dinner he was toasted as usual and made his customary response. In a letter to Ticknor, however, he said that he intended this to be his "last appearance on such an occasion." He was merely keeping a record of these events in order "to preserve all the characteristics of such banquets; because, being peculiar to England, these municipal feasts may do well to picture in a novel."[31]

The holiday season that year was ordinary. Neither Nathaniel nor Sophia referred to Christmas in letters sent to America, and Nathaniel's comments in the notebooks were brief. He wrote of the displays in the markets in preparation for the holidays and of the crowds who stood gazing at the hanging carcasses of animals they would buy for their Christmas dinners. "They [the English] are very earthy people. They love to eat, and to anticipate good fare, and even to hear the details of other people's good dinners" (*EN*, 441). He might have applied this description to himself!

The paragraph that followed referred to carolers, to Christmas boxes (in which one shilling was expected as a gift), and to the holly and mistletoe hung about the house. He concluded by contrasting the Christmases of 1856 and 1855: There were "no such kissing licenses as last Christmas at Mrs. Blodget's" (*EN*, 441). The account book records the one-shilling gifts to the postman and the lamplighter, but makes no specific reference to other recipients. However, when Una wrote to her "Aunt Lizzie," she included a list of all the family gifts. One of special importance to Julian was a microscope and a book on how to use it, given to him by his father. The microscope provided entertainment for him at least until the family left England a year later.[32]

The only midwinter event of significance was the arrival in early January of Dr. Channing, who came to baptize the children. Sophia's letter to her sister Mary was full of the details.[33] Characteristically, Nathaniel did not mention the event.

The next date in his notebooks is March 1, 1857. He had, therefore, failed to record one of the most important acts of his lifetime—his formal resignation in February from his position as consul. References to his resignation occurred in his letters again and again, however, especially those to Horatio Bridge. Hawthorne wanted to make it clear that Pierce's successor in office, James Buchanan, could feel free to let him go before the end of August 1857, if the president so desired; but he hoped that he could stay on to complete four full years. Since he knew Buchanan personally and was on friendly terms with him, he saw no reason why the president should insist that the resignation become effective on an earlier date.[34] Buchanan's refusal to accept his immediate resignation enabled the Hawthornes to go ahead with their plans to see more of England before leaving for Italy. Later circumstances, however, were to necessitate some modifications in their plans.

Hawthorne had written so often before about possible dates for his resignation that when the time came for the submission of a formal letter, he took the entire matter for granted. Of far more immediate interest to him was the burglary that took place at the house on Wednesday, February 18. It was described first by Nathaniel:

They entered by the back window of the school-room, breaking a pane of glass, so as to undo the wooden fastening. I have a dim idea of having heard a noise through my sleep, but, if so, it did not more than slightly disturb me. Una heard it, too, she being kept awake by Rosebud, who had burnt her leg; and Julian, being unwell with a cold, was also wakeful, and thought the noise was of the family moving about, below. Neither did the idea of robbers occur to Una; Julian, however, called to his mother, and the thieves probably thought we were bestirring ourselves, and so took flight. In the morning, the cook and housemaid found the hall-door and the school-room window open, some silver-cups, and some other trifles of plate, were gone, and there were tokens that the whole lower part of the house had been ransacked; but the thieves had evidently gone off in a hurry, leaving some articles which they would have taken, had they been more at leisure. (*EN*, 443)

Later Sophia explained why the robbers did not find as much as they might have expected: This was the second robbery; the first had happened at Mrs. Blodget's when one of her servants had opened two trunks and stolen "almost every piece of plate we possess—all the spoons, forks, indeed nearly every single bit!!!!!!!!" As a result, Sophia said, there was not much for the robbers to steal this second time.[35]

When a police inspector and a constable came to make out a list of the stolen articles, Hawthorne discovered that in addition to the cups, boxes, and trinkets, his boots and overcoat were missing. A few days later he and the servants were summoned to identify the stolen property, which the thieves had attempted to pawn. Since he wished to avoid publicity, he was unwilling to prefer any charges. However, James and John Macdonald, brothers, were arrested and tried. Sophia's letter to her sister reported that one of the thieves was sentenced to be "transported," and the other was "condemned to prison."[36] The newspaper's final report on the disposition of the case was printed on April 2.[37]

Because of the excitement generated by the robbery, several other incidents were unmentioned except by Una. On her thirteenth birthday, March 3, John O'Sullivan, who had been in London on business, came to Southport as a surprise for her. She said little about the celebration except that one of her presents was the three-volume *Life of Washington* by Washington Irving. Equally important to her and the rest of the family was the news that Fanny Wrigley did not like living with her sister, and would return to Southport.[38] Una was probably the one most relieved by the thought of having Fanny back again; playing nursemaid to Rose was not an especially pleasing occupation, as was shown by her impatience with the child.[39]

In spite of some lack of congeniality between the two sisters at that age, Una really preferred living in Southport to traveling around the country with her parents. However, her comments on travel are a bit inconsistent. When Nathaniel decided to take Sophia and Julian to York for Easter, Una wrote that she would like to go, but that her parents could not leave the house or Rose alone with nurse. Sophia's letters to Una, by contrast, are rather critical of her older daughter on the matter of travel, saying that although Sophia hesitated to go away without her, Una herself was responsible for being left at home: She got tired too easily with sightseeing, she apparently did not like to look out train windows, and she would rather read a book. Una's own letters to relatives in America expressed a wish to stay put in one place instead of leading the wandering life; in other words, though she did not admit it, she supported her mother's point of view.[40]

On April 10, then, the two adults and Julian, leaving the girls with Miss Browne, departed by themselves. They took the train to York by way of Skipton, Bolton Priory, and Leeds, reached the cathedral city on Saturday night, and established themselves for the weekend at the Black Swan. On Easter morning, Nathaniel deviated from his usual policy of not attending church by sitting through the long service, though he complained that he thought it would never end (*EN*, 451). Although it rained all day on Monday, the three Hawthornes went to see the cathedral again before they set off by train for Manchester at four in the afternoon. Besides his long description of York Cathedral, Nathaniel's other comment of particular interest concerned the Black Swan. It was, he said, a "good specimen of the old English inn, sombre, quiet, with dark staircases, dingy rooms, curtained beds, all the possibilities of a comfortable life, and good English fare, in a fashion which cannot have been much altered for half a century, past. It is very homelike, when one has one's family about him, but must be prodigiously stupid for a solitary man" (*EN*, 456).

On the way back to Southport the Hawthornes stopped in Manchester overnight and long enough the next day to visit the cathedral, where they observed the wedding of six poor couples. The group ceremony took place, Nathaniel said, during the Easter season because no marriage fees had to be paid then. Some months later Nathaniel reported that he saw a wealthy bridal couple coming out of the same cathedral. The second notebook passage refers only briefly to this wedding service, but when he was back in America, Hawthorne made the most of the contrast in a passage from *Our Old Home,* which was quoted years later at some length in the *Manchester Guardian.*[41]

On April 15, immediately after their return from York, Hawthorne became involved in an event of great importance to the city of Liverpool—the laying of the cornerstone of the Free Library, which was being built with funds donated by William Brown, M.P. The library, completed in 1860, was to become an outstanding addition to the city's buildings, and was significant because it represented an outgrowth of relationships between England and America. Brown, Shipley & Co., and W. and J. Brown & Co., importers in Liverpool, were branch houses of the American-based firm of W. and J. Brown of Baltimore. Alexander Brown, a Belfast linen merchant who had emigrated to America during the troubles in Ireland at the end of the eighteenth century, had built a fortune of $2 million before his death in 1834. Two of his sons opened branches in Philadelphia and New York, while a third son stayed in Baltimore. In 1810 William Brown, probably this third son, established the Liverpool headquarters, which became one of the leading importers of cotton in England. Brown added to the family fortune, built a home in Richmond Hill, served as M.P., and when the plan for a library was brought before the town council, volunteered to finance the venture if the city would provide the land. The first library, on Duke Street, had opened in 1852 and proved to be too small to house newly acquired collections. Land for a new building became available to the city corporation when the potteries on Shaw's Brow moved away, the houses were vacated, and the crest of the steep bank on Shaw's Brow, opposite St. George's Hall, was cut down. A new street was thereby created with open space beyond it that was suitable as a site for several buildings.[42]

The celebration on April 15 was such a historic occasion for the city that a booklet was published describing the ceremonies. From it we learn that after a series of addresses at the Town Hall at 11 A.M. there was a procession at noon along Castle Street, Lord Street, Church Street, and Lime Street to Shaw's Brow. The procession was not very "striking," Hawthorne wrote that night, for the only "characteristic or professional costumes" were the "flat cap and black silk gown" of the Bishop of Chester and the full uniform "with a star and half-a-dozen medals" of Sir Henry Smith, the general of the district. "Mr. Brown, himself, the hero of the day, was the plainest, and simplest man of all; an exceedingly unpretending old gentleman in black, small, withered, white haired, pale, quiet, and respectable. I rather wondered why he chose to be the centre of all this ceremony, for he did not seem either particularly to enjoy it, or to be at all incommoded by it, as a more nervous and susceptible man might" (*EN*, 458). Photographs of the scene verify Hawthorne's description, especially of Brown himself, who appears in the center of one picture.[43]

After this ceremony a banquet followed in St. George's Hall at 2 P.M. It was, as Hawthorne described it, a "cold collation," for it would have been impossible to provide a hot dinner for 900 people from the rather remote kitchen facilities (*EN*, 459). With the printed bill of fare given to each guest was a list of expected toasts, among which was Hawthorne's name, to be proposed by Monckton Milnes. The two had already met and renewed acquaintance earlier in the day at the Town Hall, but in St. George's Hall, Hawthorne was seated so far from Milnes that he could not hear what was said about himself—whether he was toasted on his "own basis or as representing American literature, or as Consul of the United States" (*EN*, 460). The published booklet, however, gave not only Milnes's introduction, but also Hawthorne's reply, which proved to be an appropriate one.[44]

Milne's toast included all the references that Hawthorne had guessed at, stressing the friendly relations between America and England. It was a speech most optimistic about the future, ending with this prophecy: "Thank God, these two great nations, speaking the same great speech, carrying out in the main the same great institutions, are the hope and the blessing of mankind—the hope of the future world, and, under Providence, a blessing to the nations. I give you 'Nathaniel Hawthorne and the United States of America.' "[45]

Hawthorne's reply emphasized that he appeared at the ceremony, not on the strength of his own merits, but as a representative of his country, especially of its literature, and that he was, therefore, speaking in behalf of all American literature. Circumstances, he said, had directed Americans' abilities to more active pursuits than writing, but Americans had at least shown that they came "from the same stock as the great writers of the past."[46] This was Hawthorne's favorite theme, the English inheritance of his countrymen. In the last part of his speech he paid tribute to William Brown's connection with America by blood, friendships, and interests. Brown was, therefore, Hawthorne said, an excellent example of the cordial relationships between England and America. Hawthorne's conclusion, like Milnes's, looked to the future: "In considering the means by which he [Brown] should best promote human happiness, he found no means so powerful as by diffusing knowledge among men. It is good for us to praise him now as we have done, while his living ears may hear us. Coming centuries—the future, the far future—will praise him much better than we can do."[47]

Hawthorne's speech was followed by brief remarks by Brown and Alderman S. Holme, representing the mayor. After the toasts, "the organ struck up the national anthem, and the company dispersed shortly before six o'clock."[48]

The Liverpool ceremonies took place on a pleasant, dry day, when the city streets were free of their usual mud, but the early part of the month that followed brought only raw east winds. Nathaniel saw little difference in Southport as spring approached, since there was still nothing but the vast stretch of sand, now beginning to be dotted with people. It was at this point, after nearly nine months there, that he spoke of Southport as the most "stupid" place he had lived in: "I cannot but bewail an ill fortune, to have been compelled to spend these many months on these barren sands, when almost every other square yard of England contains something that would have been historically or poetically interesting. Our life here has been a blank" (*EN*, 461).[49]

"Spring fever," he wrote to Ticknor, had been making him restless for some time, and the York trip, though "pleasant," did not satisfy him. He was now planning a trip to Lincolnshire and a later one to Scotland.[50] Bad weather caused the Lincolnshire trip to be postponed until Friday, May 22. As before, the girls were left in Southport, this time with both Miss Browne and Fanny Wrigley to care for them. After traveling by train through "dreary" country via Manchester and Shef-field, the three arrived in Lincoln that evening and registered at the Saracen's Head. They spent most of Saturday touring the cathedral, and after the rain stopped on Sunday afternoon, they took a carriage drive to see the rest of Lincoln. On Monday a steamer took them down the river to old Boston, once the home of the Reverend John Cotton, in whose honor a side chapel of the local church was to be restored by means of American contributions. The Peacock, where the Hawthornes stayed in Boston, was, though reportedly the best hotel in town, a "poor one enough," according to Nathaniel (*EN*, 474). He wrote nothing further about it, and not a great deal about Boston itself.

Peterborough was another cathedral town where the Hawthornes stopped overnight. The Railway Hotel was a "wretched and uncom-fortable place," which Nathaniel was glad to leave, and perhaps for that reason he devoted small space in his notebooks to Peterborough. Nottingham seemed far more comfortable and interesting, for within ten miles of the George the Fourth, "an excellent house," was the entrance gate to Newstead Abbey. Nathaniel wrote a long description of Byron's former home, then owned by Colonel Wildman, sheriff of Nottingham (*EN*, 486–91). Again Nathaniel's interests were in the romantic past. Sophia also recorded a detailed description of Byron's home, and included an interview with their landlady, who came to their hotel parlor and talked about Byron's daughter.[51]

In a letter to Ticknor summing up their trip, Nathaniel wrote that he was recording in his journal for future use what he saw of interest on his travels: "I have now hundreds of pages, which I would publish if the least of them were not too spicy. But Mrs. Hawthorne altogether excels me as a writer of travels. Her descriptions are the most perfect pictures that ever were put on paper; it is a pity they cannot be published; but neither she nor I would like to see her name on your list of female authors."[52]

Sophia did, of course, publish her account years later, when, after her husband's death, she was hard-pressed financially. A comparison between her journal written in 1857 and the later version published in *Notes in England and Italy* shows that she always edited out most personal elements, even calling the children *J--, R--,* and *U--* when it was necessary to refer to them at all. Her description of the visit to Newstead Abbey shows how omission of the informal parts resulted in an account that differed little from those in traditional guidebooks. A long passage from her original manuscript, omitted from the published *Notes,* describes Julian's being stung by nettles and afterward compensating for his short-lived terror by devouring a large chunk of bread that he bought at the "Hut," the entrance-gate building at Newstead Abbey. Although none of the three Hawthornes had eaten since breakfast and it was then six o'clock, Sophia wrote, "Papa and I sublimely awaited our dinner at the George the Fourth."[53]

Nathaniel no doubt chuckled over her humorous description of Julian's escapades, for it is the informal kind of writing that he included in his own journal, but like Sophia he did not intend his for publication either.

On the way back to Manchester from Nottingham, they stopped off at the Bath Hotel in Matlock, Derbyshire, in order to see the Derwent Valley and the "Grand Cavern." Nathaniel appreciated the beauty of the Derwent Valley, saying, "I have never seen anywhere such exquisite scenery as that which surrounds the village." But he was not much pleased with the "dreary" cavern and was somewhat bored by their subsequent shopping expedition for souvenirs (*EN*, 491–94).[54]

The next day while Sophia visited the Great Exhibition in Manchester, Nathaniel took Julian with him to Liverpool, where he had an

appointment at the consulate. His record ends with critical comments
of the kind that later offended his British readers:

> Thus ended our tour; in which we had seen but a little bit of little
> England, yet rich with variety and interest. What a wonderful land! It is
> our forefathers' land; our land; for I will not give up such a precious
> inheritance. We are now back again, in flat and sandy Southport, which,
> during the past week, has been thronged with Whitsuntide people, who
> crowd the streets, and pass to-and-fro along the promenade, with a
> universal and monotonous air of nothing-to-do and very little enjoy-
> ment. It is a pity these poor folks cannot employ their little hour of leisure
> to better advantage, in a country where the soil is so veined with gold.
> (*EN*, 494–95)

The only incident recorded in the notebooks during the two weeks
that followed their return was the arrival of the American "war-
steamer" *Niagara*. (This was apparently the same ship in which the
Hawthornes had sailed to England; it had been converted and was later
used in early unsuccessful attempts to lay the Atlantic cable.) Hawthorne took Captain Hudson and the purser, Mr. Eldredge, to the
mayor's office. Then because the captain was an old friend of Mrs.
Blodget's, Hawthorne showed the two "naval gentlemen" the way to
her house. Mrs. Blodget and her sister, Miss Williams, were delighted
to see the captain, for it gave them all a chance to talk over old
acquaintances and life at Gibraltar in the days when Mrs. Blodget was
said to have been "a rich lady" there with "a whole navy-list at her
table." On the following day when Hawthorne made his official visit to
the ship moored on the Mersey River, Mrs. Blodget, Miss Williams, and
several American captains' wives went along. Hawthorne was impressed by the pleasant manners of the ship's officers and pleased to
find Americans with no concern for growing rich. However, he concluded with a note of disapproval: They did not seem to profit from the
advantages of travel, for their experience was "world-wide, though not
world-deep. . . . They get to be very clannish, too" (*EN*, 496–97).

Meanwhile, in two separate letters Nathaniel had begged Francis
Bennoch to accompany him, Sophia, and Julian to Scotland, but
evidently London business matters would not permit Bennoch a vacation at this time.[55] The Hawthornes were forced to depart without him.
As before, the two girls stayed at home, with Fanny and Miss Browne to
look after them.

This time Nathaniel extended his travel plans to include far more of
Burns and Scott country in the southern part of Scotland. The three

Hawthornes spent their first weekend at Mauchline. From there they went on to Ayr, to Glasgow, "a noble city," to Dumbarton, and then by steamer to the head of Loch Lomond (*EN*, 517). By the end of the first week they had seen Inversnaid, Rob Roy's cave, the Trossachs, and Loch Katrine. Wherever they stopped off, Nathaniel did a good deal of walking, Julian fished without much success, and Sophia sketched or took notes for her journal.

By the following Tuesday they had arrived in Linlithgow after visiting Stirling Castle. It was during Wednesday's walk around the Linlithgow palace that Hawthorne reviewed in his mind the story of one of Bennoch's ancestors, who had led a group of Scots in seizing the castle from the English. The legend, which he did not relate in the notebooks, is that William Bunnoch [*sic*] hid eight men in his wagon under a load of hay and stopped the wagon halfway through the castle gate, so that the portcullis could not be closed. Other Scots who were in hiding nearby responded to the signal. Together they killed the porter, overpowered the English garrison, and handed the castle over to Robert Bruce. It was one of the last two English strongholds to be taken over by the Scots in 1313.[56]

On Wednesday the Hawthornes reached Edinburgh and settled down for three days at Addison's Alma Hotel on Prince's Street, where they rented a parlor and adjoining bedrooms with a beautiful view of the street, the Old Town, and the Castle on the hill. It was, Nathaniel said, the most comfortable hotel in Great Britain. The Hawthornes spent the entire three days sightseeing by cab and on foot. They had intended to visit Dryburgh Abbey but gave up that idea when rain threatened. Instead, they took the train to Durham in order to spend their last free Sunday at the cathedral. Since it was the only way he could see the inside of the cathedral, Nathaniel attended a service as he had done at York, but this time he did not sit through to the end. During the sermon he walked around in the churchyard until Sophia came out (*EN*, 533–43).

The Hawthornes stayed only one day in Durham and then returned to York, where they spent Monday morning revisiting the cathedral. That night they were back in Southport, finding the place just as it was when they left. Neither sands nor sea had changed. It all was as monotonous as ever.

Shortly after their return, Nathaniel pointed out that July 16 was the fourth anniversary of his arrival in Liverpool. As he looked back over the four-year period, he wrote that the time had passed neither "unprofitably, nor unpleasantly," but he was not sorry that it was over.

"An official life is a hard one, though some people seem to think differently."[57] He reported to Ticknor that he had enjoyed his second trip to Scotland, that Sophia "received great vigor" from the excursion, and that he had "no further fears of her health." His only disappointment now was that neither Ticknor nor Fields nor any one of his American friends had come over to visit. He had dreamed one night of seeing Fields, but they had both grown so old that neither one recognized the other. His recollection of the dream led him to say,

> In good earnest, the cares and toils of office have given me a long shove onwards towards old age during these past four years. Italy may perhaps revive me a little. I never felt better in my life, however, than during my late tour to Scotland. It suits my constitution, to be idle and enjoy myself. I wish I were a little richer; and I doubt whether you would ever advertise another book by the "author of the Scarlet Letter." Still, I thank God for bringing me through this consular business so well.[58]

In writing this paragraph, Nathaniel had perhaps not accurately evaluated his own proclivities: He *had* enjoyed the climate in Scotland, he *was* weary of consular duties, but unlike the Southport people he had described walking on the sands, he would have been bored by complete idleness. So many years away from literary production had made him reluctant to think of returning to the writing of fiction. Instead, he was putting his energy into filling his notebooks so rapidly that, as he said, "I shall have it in my power to come down upon John Bull with a folio volume; but I have no such intention. My journal is too full and free ever to be published."[59] Actually, the only parts of the notebooks that would not bear printing at that time were those in which he expressed his personal opinions of British people as frankly as he had done after the visit to Martin Tupper. Often he only implied his personal feelings, as he did at the end of July in 1857 when he summed up the dullness of seaside living. He concluded simply and cheerfully, "But we shall soon say 'Good bye' to Southport" (*EN*, 545).

‡ 6 ‡

Manchester, Leamington, and London
1857–1858

THE HAWTHORNES moved to Manchester from Southport on July 21 with one purpose in mind: to prepare themselves for a residence of one or two years in Italy by making a thorough study of the art treasures in the Great Exhibition of 1857. Sophia's previous stopover on their return from the Lincolnshire trip had enabled her to obtain a preliminary view of how much was to be seen. Manchester was close enough to Liverpool that Nathaniel could commute when necessary. The plan was for the family to spend approximately a month near the Exhibition, on the outskirts of the city, then move to London for a short stay, and finally proceed to Paris in September. However, the delay in the appointment of Hawthorne's successor, as well as the illness of Wilding, the chief clerk, made it necessary for Nathaniel to be in the Liverpool office periodically long after his term as consul expired at the end of August. As a result the Hawthornes stayed for seven weeks in Manchester before moving to Leamington and thence to London.

As they were preparing to leave Southport, Charles Swain, the engraver-poet who lived in Prestwich, near Manchester, arranged for them to rent part of a house on Stretford Road in the suburb of Old Trafford, not far from the site of the Exhibition. In his first notations written after moving, Hawthorne showed satisfaction with his surroundings:

> We are here, about three miles from the Victoria Railway Station, in Manchester, on one side, and perhaps nearly a mile from the Exhibition on the other. This is a suburb of Manchester, and consists of a long street, called the Stratford [*sic*] road, bordered with brick-houses, two stories high, such as are usually the dwellings of tradesmen or respectable mechanics, but which are now in demand for lodgings, at high prices, on account of the Exhibition. It seems to be rather a new precinct of the city; and the houses, though ranged along a continuous street, are but a brick border along the green fields in the rear. (*EN*, 545)[1]

The house in which Mr. Swain obtained rooms for the family was occupied by the Richmonds, who had never had lodgers before, although Hawthorne described the furnishings as typical of lodging houses.[2] The rent was six pounds, ten shillings per week, a higher rate than it would have been by the year. The location was fairly convenient, and the Hawthornes wasted little time in getting settled. They attended the Exhibition for the first time on Friday, July 24, though Julian and Nathaniel had taken a walk around the grounds on Thursday. As usual the Hawthornes provided their own meals, except that whenever they spent entire days at the Exhibition, as on that first Friday, they ate lunch or dinner there in the middle of the day. The recording of expenditures for groceries in Manchester began on July 21 and continued until September 7.[3]

Because the Richmonds' house did not prove satisfactory, the Hawthornes stayed there barely two weeks. Nathaniel wrote that the lodgings were "dear and inconvenient, and the woman of the house a sharp, peremptory housewife, better fitted to deal with her own family than to be complaisant to guests" (*EN*, 555). He did not explain how they found the second lodging house, but on August 3 they moved to a new place at 35 Boston Terrace, Chorlton Road, Old Trafford. The house was run by "a civil, pleasant sort of a woman, auspiciously named Mrs. Honey." She must have lived up to her name, for they stayed there until early September, and though the house was far from ideal, Hawthorne made frequent comments on the "kind disposition" of their landlady. He described the house as typical of poorer middle-class dwellings, with thin walls and wide cracks between the floorboards and over the doors, so that the place was full of drafts. The outer walls were so thin that sometimes the voices of people in the next house were audible. For such quarters they were obliged to pay five pounds per week (*EN*, 555–56).

Even so, this rent was a pound less than the Stretford Road house had cost; however, travel and other expenses mounted rapidly after they moved. Nathaniel made frequent trips by train to Liverpool and most of the family rode the omnibus to the Exhibition at a cost of one shilling per person round trip. Then Exhibition tickets were one shilling each, except on half-crown days. Fanny's wages were three pounds for two months. There were also such extras as programs for the Exhibition, fencing lessons for Julian, a few items of clothing, and meals eaten at the Exhibition Hall. Nathaniel was not concerned about the total as long as he was employed, but after August 31, the effective date of his resignation, he still had to travel back and forth to the consulate occasionally, without any pay, until late in the fall. He sometimes begrudged the money spent in these months, for if it had not been for consular affairs, they could have been enjoying Italy.[4]

Meanwhile, Nathaniel was making a strong effort to gain an appreciation of painting through visits to the Exhibition, sometimes with Sophia, at other times with Sophia and one or more of the children. On their first Thursday morning walk, Nathaniel and Julian merely surveyed the exterior of the building, a huge structure somewhat resembling London's Crystal Palace. Then they took a long walk past the Botanic Gardens and out through other suburban villages, all rather more picturesque than the Southport area. But it was a sultry day and Nathaniel did not really enjoy either the air or the exercise (*EN*, 546).

His lassitude in the "heavy air," even in this rural section, is typical of the reaction of the British themselves to the atmosphere of large industrial cities. A contemporary writer considering the suitability of Manchester as a place for an art exhibition wrote, "The atmosphere of Manchester is thick with coal dust; its factory chimneys overtop and outnumber the belfries of a medieval city." The city, he said, was the epitome of industrialism, in short, "the last place in the world in which we should have expected to see a glimmer of aesthetic taste." Yet, he admitted, Manchester people had already shown interest in good music, and some modern painters had secured "patronage."[5]

If the Exhibition was slow at first in attracting visitors, he wrote, it was because of the high cost of admission. As soon as the admission price was lowered, "crowds of the working population began to pour in; and now we have twenty thousand of a day spending their half-holiday in a scene where there is nothing to degrade or corrupt, or even passingly gratify the lower passions of humanity."[6]

By the time the Hawthornes had settled down in their second lodging house, the general admission fee had been reduced, and the entire family could afford to attend. Often, however, Rose stayed at home with Fanny; on some days Una and Julian accompanied their parents; and sometimes Nathaniel went alone. In order to study the artworks carefully, the Hawthornes bought several catalogues and programs. The children had no governess now and apparently no lessons from Sophia; the Exhibition was their education.

Hawthorne's first reaction to the Exhibition was much like that of a person visiting a large museum for the first time: "Nothing is more depressing than the sight of a great many pictures together. . . . There never should be more than one picture in a room, nor more than one picture to be studied in one day; galleries of pictures are surely the greatest absurdities that were contrived; there being no excuse for them, except that it is the only way in which pictures can be made generally available and accessible" (*EN*, 547). Thereafter, realizing that he was surfeited by too many paintings at once, he visited one gallery at a time over and over again. Nathaniel soon discovered that even when he attended the Exhibition with Sophia, who had studied painting and was herself an amateur artist, or with others in the family, he enjoyed the experience more if he went into a gallery all by himself and studied only what he wished to.

In so huge a structure there were plenty of opportunities to leave the others behind. The architectural plan of the building resembled that of a cathedral. There was a grand nave, called the Great Hall, with a transept, two large galleries parallel to the nave, three galleries beyond the transept, and an open court on the north leading to the entrance to the Botanic Gardens. The nave contained a display of ornamental art, the British Portrait Gallery, and the greater part of the sculpture exhibit. The transept held engravings, photographs, miniatures, and original drawings and sketches by the Old Masters. In the salons beyond the transept were the Hertford Gallery, the Oriental Salon, and a special watercolor gallery. Salons labeled A, B, and C, in the long gallery south of the nave, contained paintings of the Italian, Spanish, German, Flemish, and Dutch schools; salons D, E, and F, in the north gallery, held the collection of British painting from earliest days to the contemporary Pre-Raphaelites.[7] With such a variety to choose from, a student could easily spend weeks at the Exhibition.

The Hawthornes had missed (probably intentionally because of their dislike of crowds) two important events: the grand opening on Tuesday, May 5, and the queen's visit on June 30. The prince consort officially opened the Exhibition in a ceremony lasting half a day. Why the queen did not go to Manchester until the end of June is unclear, but when she did visit, the occasion was marked by a local holiday and much celebration. The ceremony on that day was similar to the one on the opening day, with addresses and a program of Handel's music.[8]

Although attendance fluctuated from the beginning, the Exhibition was regarded as highly successful. Experience with an earlier London attraction, the Crystal Palace, had taught the planners something about providing for the comforts of visitors. They worked hard in every way to make Manchester an example of the sophistication that could be achieved even in the provinces. Before the Hawthornes arrived, changes had been made to improve facilities. A hall at the side of the main building was converted into a coffee salon 430 feet long, extending from the "second-class refreshment room and the railroad corridor parallel with the south side" of the Palace. The western end of the salon had been fitted up with stalls as a "first-class confectionery room."[9]

Such class distinctions were ordinarily accepted by the Hawthornes without comment, but just before they left Manchester, Nathaniel made note of the separate refreshment rooms for first and second classes: "I have looked most at the latter, because there John Bull and his female may be seen in full gulp and guzzle, swallowing vast quantities of cold boiled beef, thoroughly moistened with porter or bitter ale; and very good meat and drink it is" (*EN*, 563). His remark may sound like a sneer at second-class citizens; though he always enjoyed good food and drink, he did not "live to eat," nor did he like to watch people stuff themselves. Sophia made no comment on signs of gluttony; instead she observed that in general the second-class people conducted themselves well with "no confusion, no noise, no rudeness of any kind."[10]

On a day devoted to the Old Masters, Nathaniel was studying his favorite Dutch painters when he met Alexander Ireland, a newsman reporting for the local paper, whom he had met at Bennoch's Manchester dinner in the spring of 1856. Ireland reported having seen Tennyson, accompanied by Woolner, the sculptor, in a nearby gallery. According to Nathaniel's record, Ireland did not know the poet laureate and therefore could not introduce Hawthorne, but Nathaniel was content to look at him. He studied Tennyson so thoroughly that the next day he was able to describe the poet's appearance in detail: his rather untidy black suit and white shirt; black "wide-awake hat"; long, black hair, "looking terribly tangled"; long, pointed beard a little browner than his hair; dark face, smooth, "but worn, and expressing great sensitiveness"; black eyes and a pair of spectacles (carried in his hand) through which he looked at the pictures (*EN*, 553).

Knowing how much Sophia would enjoy seeing the poet laureate, Nathaniel hunted until he found his family "under the music-gallery" and led them all, including Rose and Fanny, back to the picture gallery where they watched Tennyson for a short time. Later Hawthorne wrote that he would have been glad to see more of the poet, but could not bring himself to follow Tennyson, "for I must own that it seemed mean to be dogging him through the saloons, or even to have looked at him, since it was to be done stealthily, if at all" (*EN*, 554).

Sophia, by contrast, was not entirely satisfied with merely looking at Tennyson. She watched the whole family and studied the face of Mrs.

Tennyson. After the Tennyson adults had gone on downstairs, Sophia observed the maid and the two little boys stopping to buy a catalogue. "So then I seized the youngest darling with gold hair, and kissed him to my heart's content. And I was well pleased to have had in my arms Tennyson's child."[11]

Alexander Ireland's two versions of the incident reveal some variations. In his first account, sent to Fields twenty years after that day, Ireland said that he happened to meet Hawthorne in a gallery and had pointed out to him Tennyson and Woolner as they walked around the Exhibition Hall. Ireland had urged Hawthorne "to go forward and make himself known to Tennyson—a suggestion from which he shrank; and so the opportunity passed away of these two men of genius coming into personal contact."[12]

After another twenty years had elapsed, Ireland enlarged upon his account to Moncure Conway, who was gathering material for his projected biography of Hawthorne. Unfortunately, Ireland's recollection of the occasion must have become badly confused by this time, for he wrote that in an after-dinner conversation at Bennoch's Manchester party (which was in 1856, not 1857 as Ireland implied), he had offered to be Hawthorne's cicerone through the Exhibition because he had acquired "a pretty good knowledge of its contents" while writing his weekly analysis of the art treasures. Ireland said that when he and Hawthorne met by appointment the next day, he offered to introduce Hawthorne to Tennyson. To Ireland's surprise, Hawthorne flatly refused, in spite of Ireland's long argument (which constituted two pages of his letter to Conway). Ireland was greatly disappointed, but noted that all the time the two were discussing the matter Hawthorne was observing Tennyson's appearance so carefully that he could later devote several pages of his notebooks to a description of the poet.[13]

Whoever was right about the details of this incident, it shows how Hawthorne's habitual shyness resulted in his failing to meet most of the famous literary figures of England in his day.

In spite of many visits to the Palace of Art Treasures, Hawthorne realized that the development of art appreciation could not be crammed into a few weeks. Furthermore, his art study was interrupted by business in Liverpool and by a few social events. One afternoon he left the Exhibition at three o'clock in order to visit the engraver's office of Charles Swain, the poet, at 58 Cannon Street in the heart of Manchester. After a short stay there, the two men took the omnibus to Swain's house in Prestwich, four miles north of the city. Sophia and Julian had left home in the forenoon and spent the day with Mrs. Swain and the couple's four daughters. It was teatime before Hawthorne and Swain joined the group at the Prestwich home. As Nathaniel surveyed Swain's house he was glad to find that his host led a comfortable life in a well-furnished home. Hawthorne, who had tried to discover something good in the poet's work to account for his success ("because the man himself is so very good and loveable" [*sic*]), made to Swain the only diplomatic comment he could think of: He said that the poet had had favorable notices in American newspapers. This seemed to please Swain, and he asked for copies of American reviews (*EN*, 559–60).

Late in August, Nathaniel went by himself to a dinner at the home of Francis Haywood, a cotton broker and a "man of literature," who seemed to have some wealth but no great reputation in Liverpool. The country house of the Haywoods, Edge-lane Hall, in a suburb south of the city, was the scene of a pleasant, but to Hawthorne not very interesting, dinner party in honor of John Adolphus, barrister and author of a critical work on Scott, who was in the city to attend the assizes. Other guests included Emilia Gayangos, a "Spanish lady" who was said to have assisted both Prescott and George Ticknor on matters of Spanish literature, and two other "gentlemen of learning and culture, which did not particularly appear in anything that was said." Hawthorne was disappointed in both his host and the guest of honor. Haywood did not seem to have any conversational ability: "I never heard anybody say fewer rememberable things than he." The whole affair was dull and endless. Nathaniel spent a restless night at Edge-lane Hall and was doubtless glad to go back to the consulate the next morning (*EN*, 560–61).

Another dinner party, at an artist's home in Manchester, proved to be a very different kind of affair. One day on a visit to the Exhibition, Hawthorne happened to meet Judge Pollock of Liverpool, who introduced him to Charles Duval, a Manchester painter looking over the works at the exhibit, including two of his own. During the conversation Duval invited Hawthorne to dinner at his house, Carlton Grove, in a suburb of the city. There at 6 P.M. he found Judge and Mrs. Pollock, another lady whose name was not given, and two grown daughters and two sons of the Duvals. Although Hawthorne did not particularly like Duval's two pictures—satirical sketches called *Forgotten Vows* and *Recalled to Memory*—he enjoyed the man, the family, and the dinner. It was, he wrote, "the most sensible dinner I ever assisted at in England, because it was so comfortable, unpretending, and satisfactory for all the purposes of a friendly dinner." His hosts and guests were all "very sensible and natural people, truly refined and devoid of airs." This he attributed somewhat to their being mostly Irish, for a typical English party would have emphasized the meal itself rather than the conversation that accompanied and followed it. After the ladies had withdrawn, there was more good talk at the table, and then all adjourned to the drawing room for music by the daughters and the sons. At ten-thirty Hawthorne departed from the home of these kind people whom he said he should like better the more he came to know them. As in the case of Swain, however, he was surprised to find that an artist of no greater reputation than Duval could provide so comfortably for a large family (*EN*, 563–64).[14]

In the meantime, instead of going to dinner parties, Sophia was keeping herself completely occupied by visiting the Palace of Art Treasures and caring for the children. As she wrote to her sister Mary near the end of their stay in Manchester, she was "too stupidly weary to write" after a day at the Exhibition. Sophia was seeing to it that Una and Julian were exposed to art very gradually, for her principle was "not to wear out young twigs with hanging millstones on them. I want to be sure they grow upwards so as to come close against the sky—and to keep fresh and vigorous all the way. The tender brains—I fear to crowd them."[15]

Una seems to have accepted whatever plans were made for her, but Julian often showed signs of restlessness. He missed the beach at Southport, where he had especially enjoyed sketching shells found in the sand. Now he had to satisfy his scientific inclinations by visits to the Botanic Gardens and by playing with his microscope slides. He examined such items as a piece of tapioca supplied by his mother and some moldy cheese provided by the landlady, Mrs. Honey. He also took fencing lessons from a drillmaster, Sergeant Blair, who came to the house one afternoon a week. These activities he recorded in long letters to Una, who was spending a week, together with Rose and Fanny, in York.[16] The length, the tone, and the amount of detail in Julian's letters suggest that in the heat of late August days he was definitely bored.

Nathaniel, too, was becoming bored by the Exhibition, but the chief reason why the Hawthornes decided early in September to leave Manchester for Leamington was Sophia's health. Sophia reported to her sister Elizabeth that "the foul air of the manufactories" made her cough more, and "the moment Mr. Hawthorne perceived it, he decided to come away." Nothing but the Palace of Art Treasures would ever have kept them in "such a nasty old ugly place." "We thought we had pretty well studied the pictures and could afford to leave them now."[17]

On Tuesday, September 8, they were all glad to leave their "small, mean, uncomfortable, and unbeautiful lodgings at Chorlton Road, with poor and scanty furniture within doors, and no better prospect from the parlor-window than a mud-puddle, larger than most English lakes, on a vacant building lot opposite our house" (*EN*, 564–65). The rain poured down as they piled their baggage into two cabs and drove to the railroad station. Fanny had left a day ahead of them in order to secure lodgings that would be ready for the Hawthornes when they arrived.

The choice of Leamington was determined by substantially the same factors as in 1855. It was a center for travel in Warwickshire; it was a clean place in contrast to Liverpool and Manchester; and it was fairly close to Liverpool. The one great difference between their earlier stay in Leamington and this one would be that now Nathaniel was no longer subject to any ruling about absence, although he still went to Liverpool when necessary and could not leave the country until all consular affairs were settled.

In describing Leamington during his later visit, Hawthorne used the word *genteel:* It was a place where people with only "moderate incomes" could live. His description characterized the town during the entire century: "The tasteful shop-fronts on the principal streets; the Bath-chairs; the public gardens; the servants whom one meets, and doubts whether they are groom, footman, or butler, or a mixture of the three; the ladies sweeping through the avenues; the nursery maids and children; all make up a picture of somewhat unreal finery" (*EN*, 565).

Their rented house at 10 Lansdowne Circus was located almost in the center of a circle of small two-story houses most of which were of white stucco. In the middle of the Circus, surrounded by a driveway in front of the houses, was a circular lawn edged with shrubs. In front of each house was a tiny plot of grass and flowers, likewise enclosed by a low hedge of shrubs.[18]

Sophia wrote little to her sister Elizabeth about the house they had rented; instead, she described the town; the garden; the River Leam, with "trees bending over it"; broad walks; rich shrubbery; lawns; and the Jephson Gardens, with the lake full of white and gray swans, the temple with a marble statue of Dr. Jephson, seats of all kinds, and bowers for shelter, all "perfectly elegant and beautiful." What she did say about the location of the house revealed her usual enthusiasm: "We

Section of Lansdowne Circus, Leamington Spa, 1972. Number 10, Hawthorne's Old Home, is the left-hand house of the pair on the extreme right.

are in a charming little paradise of gardens, with a Park at the centre, towards which all these gardens converge. It is such a Paradise as the English only know how to make out of any given flat bit of land."[19]

Nathaniel, however, reviewing the charms of Leamington in a letter to Fields, was reminded of his own sense of homelessness: "My wife and children and myself are familiar with all kinds of lodgment and modes of living; but we have forgotten what home is—at least, the children have, poor things; and I doubt whether they will ever feel inclined to live long in one place."[20]

For the time being Nathaniel satisfied himself with recording the many details of their experiences in Leamington—the walks in Jephson Gardens and to villages near Leamington, and the excursions to Kenilworth, Warwick, Coventry, or Stratford. His accounts of life in Leamington were so much more pleasant than his descriptions of Southport that later historians were quick to note the difference. They observed that Hawthorne was a satisfied visitor and an enthusiastic walker, and they included his name among the prominent men who had lived in the town. In fact, several accounts represented him as living in Leamington for two or three years.[21] In this respect they were probably following Hawthorne's combining of accounts of three different visits to the town into one chapter, "Leamington Spa" (in *Our Old Home*), with emphasis on the house at 10 Lansdowne Circus.

Life in Leamington was not all pleasure, however. At the end of the first week Nathaniel was called back to Liverpool by the serious illness of Henry Wilding. Matters were further complicated by the delay in the appointment of a consul to succeed Hawthorne. The new man, Beverly Tucker, finally left New York for Liverpool on September 27, but it would still be some time before he could assume his duties. Hawthorne was forced to continue his travels back and forth to Liverpool at least until mid-October.

Back in July, in planning for a year or two on the Continent, the Hawthornes had hired by correspondence Ada Shepard as governess upon the recommendation of Horace Mann, who was then president of Antioch College. Ada, a recent graduate, had sailed to Paris in September in order to join the Hawthornes before they left for Italy.[22] Although she was to receive no salary, the position seemed ideal to her, for she had been offered a position teaching modern languages at Antioch, with the understanding that she was to perfect her knowledge of French, Italian, and German. This interim position would afford her that opportunity. She and her fiancé, Henry Clay Badger, who had graduated with Ada, would have to postpone their marriage for at least a year until they both returned to Antioch to teach.

When the Hawthornes found themselves forced to stay in England longer than expected, Sophia decided that the children needed more preparation in languages than Miss Browne had been able to supply and began arrangements with the U.S. consul in London for their new governess to leave her study of French in Paris and come to live with them in Leamington. Ada, however, was an independent young lady and too impatient to wait for the details to be worked out. "I'm going to England alone: are you astonished?" she wrote to Clay Badger. Unfortunately, Ada had not investigated any train schedules; when she reached London she found that there was no train to Leamington until the following day. Undaunted, she proceeded to Rugby, where she spent a rainy Saturday night at George's Inn. The Hawthornes must indeed have been surprised when Ada arrived in Leamington without warning on Sunday, October 4.[23]

Neither Nathaniel nor Sophia recorded any early impressions of their new governess. The only description of her appearance in 1857 was written years later by Julian: "She was a little over the medium height, with a blue-eyed face, not beautiful, but gentle and expressive, and wearing her flaxen hair in long curls on each side of her pale cheeks." He also remarked that at Antioch she had "imbibed" "all the women's rights fads and other advanced opinions of the day," but that by nature she was "a simple, affectionate, straight-forward American maiden, with the little weaknesses and foibles appertaining to that estate."[24]

Ada's first reaction to Sophia and the children was most enthusiastic:

> They seem to me thoroughly charming in every way. Mrs. Hawthorne has all the good qualities of Mrs. Mann without those which we do not so much admire, and with a thousand additional graces . . . . Una is the most remarkably developed child, to all appearances, that I ever saw, remarkably developed physically, mentally, and morally. Julian is a very Hercules in miniature. I believe I *never* saw so fine a physique in a boy as he has. And he has splendid great eyes, and beautiful chestnut locks; though his features are not handsome. Little Rose is a sweet creature, but less remarkable, evidently, than the other two. Ah! how I shall love these beautiful children![25]

Ada did not describe her first meeting with Hawthorne until the night of October 14, when he returned from Liverpool to the family circle:

Mr. Hawthorne came this evening, and I was quite surprised to see so *handsome* a man as he is. He has the most beautiful brow and eyes, and his voice is extremely musical. I do not wonder that Mrs. Hawthorne loved him any more than that her angelic loveliness attracted his poet-heart. Ah! what rare delight it is to see two rightly married![26]

A few days later Ada pictured for Clay an evening scene in the Hawthorne household in a way that revealed her initial enthusiasm for Nathaniel, Sophia, and the children:

It seemed very strange to look up occasionally from my book [*House of the Seven Gables*] and meet his eye as he sat ensconced in an easy chair in a meditating mood apparently, his eyes resting occasionally upon his lovely children as they pursued each some favorite pastime—Julian drawing shells for which he has the greatest passion, Una reading Scott's poems, and little Rose flitting about among her toys, while Mrs. Hawthorne, the beautiful mother of the interesting group, reclined on the sofa with the London papers in her hand. It was an almost perfect picture of domestic bliss. Not that any individual of this family circle is absolutely perfect, of course (although I hardly see how any one could approach perfection more nearly than Mrs. Hawthorne), but their relations to each other are so delightful that it does my very heart good to be among them.[27]

Such was her first impression. A year with the Hawthornes was to change her mind somewhat, though she never tempered her admiration for Nathaniel, and she remained fond of the children. For the time being she concentrated on trying to develop the abilities of the children in the areas that she was expected to teach. Their daily schedule of lessons sounds fairly rigorous: "Chronology" before breakfast at eight-thirty; arithmetic and French after breakfast until the one o'clock dinner; geography and Italian from two to four; tea at six; then anything they pleased in the evening, such as reading or being read to by Hawthorne.[28] After the children went to bed, Ada wrote her long letters to Clay, usually in front of the fire in the drawing room, where the Hawthornes sat reading. It was midautumn and a coal fire, Nathaniel's great delight while he was in England, was necessary, especially in the evenings.

In one of her many letters to Clay, Ada wrote that she had never before seen children who seemed to have led such a "natural" life. Mrs. Hawthorne had told her that until they came to England, she and her husband had never left the children in the care of other persons, "even long enough to go out to tea"; that their friends had opposed this practice; but that Mrs. Hawthorne was convinced it was the right way. Sophia said that it was "a mother's duty to devote herself to her children first of all" and that she lived up to this ideal completely. Her husband's position in England, she said, had robbed his family of the close association they had had before.[29] She did not comment on what was obvious: He was now able to devote all his time to the family except when he was required to make occasional trips to the consulate.

When, on a trip back to Liverpool, Hawthorne finally met his successor, Beverly Tucker, he prophesied to Ticknor that the new consul would be "very popular with the shipmasters and American residents; a bluff, jolly, good natured gentleman, fond of society, and an excellent companion—wholly unlike me in every respect. (He is not really so bad as you think him, but there is a likeness in the picture you draw, and if I were to lend him even a ten-pound note, I should be very doubtful of ever seeing it again.)"[30]

Since Tucker was not a successful business manager, he was lucky when he decided to retain Henry Wilding and to make him vice-consul in place of Pearce, who was leaving when Hawthorne did. Wilding had assumed entire responsibility for the bookkeeping; perhaps it was the heavy load that had caused his complete breakdown in health. But he was now on the way to recovery, and Hawthorne could breathe more freely, though he could not leave the country until the accounts were settled.

At the end of October, while the Hawthornes were doing their last sightseeing in Warwickshire, Nathaniel was corresponding with Bennoch about a lodging house in London. Bennoch, busier than ever at the moment, still took time to make arrangements for a place on Great Russell Street in Bloomsbury, a short walk from the British Museum.[31] By the time the family moved from Leamington, the beautiful October days had ended, and the usual dismal English November had begun.

Moving day, November 10, was another gloomy, rainy day. The Hawthornes departed on the 10 A.M. train, leaving most of the baggage behind in a van that broke down on the way to the railroad station. They carried enough hand luggage to tide them over until the next day, when the rest of their belongings would reach London. When their train arrived in Euston Station, Sophia and Rose took a cab to Bloomsbury. The others decided to walk to their lodgings at 24 Great Russell Street. The only recorded comment made about Mrs. Siever's house was written that night by Ada to Clay; she said that the accommodations were "rather less comfortable than ours in Leamington, and less so than the Hawthornes had expected from the account of the friend [Bennoch] who engaged them for them."[32]

Immediately after their arrival, Nathaniel, "restless and uncomfortable" after his train ride, set out for a walk, "without any definite object." In his wanderings around St. Paul's he happened to meet an old friend, Mr. Parker, formerly of Boston, who told him sad news of Bennoch, "the friend whom I love as much as if I had known him for a life time, though indeed he is but of two or three years standing" (*EN*, 590). Bennoch's bankruptcy was reported in the *Gazette* and in the *Times* on that very day, November 10. When he was corresponding with Hawthorne on the subject of a lodging house, Bennoch certainly must have known of his impending misfortune, but concealed the distressing news. W. C. Bennett, the poet-jeweler friend whom Hawthorne called on at his shop in Cheapside, confirmed the news of the bankruptcy, but denied the truth of a rumor that Mrs. Bennoch had died in childbirth the previous week. Hawthorne, who could scarcely believe this second rumor, since the Bennochs had never had any children, was relieved to learn that the news was quite false but distressed that the failure of Bennoch's firm was a certainty (*EN*, 590–91). The details were not fully published, however, until November 28, when the case went into bankruptcy court.

Hawthorne, hesitant about approaching his friend in person, sent a note and in the answer was requested to call upon Bennoch. It was an awkward task for Nathaniel; he walked down to the City and, after retracing his steps several times, reluctantly turned in at 77 Wood Street. Rigg, the junior partner, greeted him, asked him to wait a short time in the "confused and dismal" warehouse, and finally came back with an invitation to stay to lunch with them. Rigg conducted Hawthorne upstairs, leading him through winding passageways and around packing cases and boxes of silks, until they came to the dining room. Here Hawthorne recalled previous scenes when he had enjoyed the hospitality of the firm at the luncheon table (*EN*, 604–05).

At last Bennoch came in, "not with that broad, warm, lustrous presence that used to gladden me in our past encounters . . . though still he was not less than a very genial man, partially bedimmed. He looked paler—it seemd to me, thinner and rather smaller—but nevertheless smiled at greeting me, more brightly, I suspect, than I smiled back at him; for, in truth, I was very sorry" (*EN*, 605). Twentyman, the middle partner, then entered, looking as depressed as the others, and all four sat down to a good dinner, "such as ruined men need not be ashamed to eat," of roast beef and boiled apple pudding, with one decanter of sherry and another of port.

After the partners left, Bennoch sat by the fire with Hawthorne and explained that he blamed himself, as the founder and leader of the company, for not controlling his partners' speculations. He had not realized the extent of the company liabilities, for evidently he had been too much occupied during the past year to supervise carefully. While Bennoch talked, Hawthorne envisioned a dreary future for his friend: He would have to start all over again, "as he had begun twenty-five years before," and would not be able to achieve his political and civic ambitions. The only suggestion Hawthorne could make to Bennoch was that he go to America, but his friend did not seem to favor the idea, and Hawthorne concluded that he would regret seeing Bennoch "transplanted thither," "away from this warm, cheerful, juicy English life into our drier and less genial sphere; he is a good guest amongst us, but might not do well to live with us" (*EN*, 606).

Hawthorne underestimated his friend, for Bennoch was not so easily defeated; eventually he made a remarkable comeback and once more headed his company until he retired some twenty years later. Matters were settled when the partners decided "to leave themselves entirely in the hands of their creditors." The report of the creditors' meeting revealed that the private property of the partners, except that of Mr. Rigg, showed a small surplus. Mrs. Bennoch offered to help with her husband's debts by handing over to the creditors her sixty shares in the Gas Consumers' Company. The case ended with the solicitor, Mr. Reed, suggesting that a committee of four creditors be appointed to work out solutions, and this they apparently did.[33]

Although while in London he did keep in touch with Bennoch, Hawthorne was not one to inflict himself upon a friend who was preoccupied with recovering from financial disaster. As a result, the Hawthornes did not enjoy the same social life with the Bennochs they had before. Instead, they did what they expected would be their last sightseeing in England. Many of the days were spent at the British Museum, which was only a few steps from their lodging. Nathaniel's reaction to the museum was the same as to the Exhibition in Manchester: There was so much to see all at once that it was overwhelming.

They did not neglect other parts of London: The notebooks record visits to such places as the Tower, Westminster Abbey, the National Gallery, the Middle Temple, St. Paul's, and the Crystal Palace, which they toured under the guidance of Mr. Silsbee. He had apparently returned to London from a trip to the Continent and was happy to serve as a guide, but in spite of his enthusiasm about art, he bored Nathaniel by his constant talk. Sophia was a more interested listener when Silsbee brought with him to their lodgings a number of his letters to American friends which he delighted in reading aloud to the whole family.

Hawthorne preferred walking the streets of the city by himself, for he took pleasure in being lost among the crowds. The description in the notebooks is reminiscent of his earlier story "Wakefield":

> There is a dull and sombre enjoyment always to be had in Holborn, Fleet-street, Cheapside, and the other thronged parts of London. It is human life; it is this material world; it is a grim and heavy reality. . . . [There is] in short, a general impression of grime and sordidness, and, at this season, always a fog scattered along the vista of streets, sometimes so densely as almost to spiritualize the materialism and make the scene resemble the other world of worldly people, gross even in ghostliness. (*EN*, 607)

The foggy weather was not beneficial to the health of the household, for most of the Hawthornes and Fanny had the "flu" in November. Early in December, Nathaniel caught a cold, and Sophia had a "season of indisposition" for several weeks, presumably her old bronchial trouble, which fog and dampness always revived. To make matters worse, all the children came down with the measles. This was the final cause of delay in the Hawthornes' departure for Paris. Dr. Wilkinson came to the house frequently to attend to the women and children.

As a friendly gesture the doctor invited the Hawthornes to a party at his house, where much of the conversation was about spiritualism (*EN*, 616–17). Dr. Wilkinson also gave Hawthorne a letter of introduction to Coventry Patmore, who was then assistant in the Department of Printed Books at the British Museum, and Patmore called on the Hawthornes. Since Nathaniel and Sophia had both enjoyed *The Angel in the House*, they were glad to meet and talk with the author. Mrs. Patmore could not accompany her husband because of the "naughty behavior of their little boy," and the Hawthornes were disappointed in not seeing the lady generally regarded as the original of Honoria, though she herself denied any connection with the heroine. Ada's appraisal of Patmore was a very favorable one: "He is a young man; he is thirty-four only, he said. He is very plain-looking, with a long, forcible nose, a thin face, and rather slight figure, dark blue eyes and dark brown hair. His manners are delightfully simple and affable."[34]

Hawthorne had not sought sociability in these few weeks because the family had not expected to be delayed so long in London. "Had I thought of it sooner," he said, "I might have found interesting people enough to know, even when all London is said to be out of town; but meditating a stay of only a week or two, it did not seem worth while to seek acquaintances" (*EN*, 616). And so their last few weeks were rather lonely ones, since few people knew that they were still in the city.

On January 3 Hawthorne wrote that they were readying themselves for departure. Actually he had begun preparations some months before, first by applying for passports. He had sent a letter of application from Leamington in September, at a time when he expected to take his family to Paris, where they would remain until he was free to rejoin them. The application presumably was still good on Saturday, January 2, when Hawthorne went in person to Dallas's office to collect the passports.

Although written four months before their departure, the letter of application gives us an outline of the family members as they were when they left London. Hawthorne described himself as "age (I am sorry to say) fifty-one [if born in 1804, he was actually 53]; height five feet, ten and a half inches;—hair dark, and somewhat bald;—face, oval;—nose straight;—chin round. As regards any other particulars, I can put them in myself." Then he went on to describe Sophia: "Mrs. Hawthorne is forty-two years of age [she was probably forty-eight], five feet high, an oval face, light hair, ordinary nose, &c, &c, &c—her name is Sophia Amelia Hawthorne." He gave the children's ages as thirteen, eleven, and six. There would be no separate passports for them. He added that a governess would accompany them.[35]

Fanny had originally planned to stay with the Hawthornes until they reached Paris, but it turned out that she did not leave London with them. Two days before Christmas she received word from her own family that her father had drowned. She left immediately for York, to the great distress of the Hawthornes. Ada was the only one who said that the family had intended to take Fanny to Italy. The extra expense that would be involved in keeping on a nurse in addition to a governess suggests that Ada may have been mistaken in her assumption that Fanny would proceed from Paris to Italy with the Hawthornes. Nevertheless, it was a sad and unexpected farewell to make to a faithful servant, especially at the holiday season.[36]

One important preparation on Hawthorne's part was the packing up of all his English notebooks, which consisted of six manuscript volumes. At the end of volume six, he wrote on September 17 from Liverpool that he took pleasure in putting Mrs. Blodget's name "last in this last volume of my English journal" (*EN*, 573). It was not the very last volume, of course, for he apparently carried with him to Paris the one begun in Leamington.[37] The six notebooks were left with Henry Bright with the following letter:

Dear Mr. Bright,
Here are these Journals. If unreclaimed by myself, or by my heirs or assigns, I consent to your breaking the seals in the year 1900 — not a day sooner. By that time, probably, England will be a minor Republic, under the protection of the United States. If my countrymen of that day partake in the least of my feelings, they will treat you generously.

Your friend
Nath Hawthorne[38]

At that time the Hawthornes had no thoughts of returning to England and had made preparations to ship home whatever they would not need on the Continent. As early as July, when they were still in Manchester, Nathaniel had mailed to Ticknor several packages that were to be sent on to the house in Concord. Nathaniel wrote to Ticknor that it gave him "a slight sensation of home-sickness to be sending these things home, but I am pretty well contented to remain behind."[39]

Now at the beginning of the new year, the family were all eagerly waiting to leave the dreary English winter behind for sunny Italy. Hawthorne should have felt tremendously relieved after four years of toil. The reward that was so long in coming was finally within reach: a year or two in which he had no obligations except for the comforts of his wife and children while they were absorbing the culture of Italy. There is no indication that he asked himself at this time whether the four years' labor had been a worthy sacrifice for either the family or himself. At the moment he was experiencing a kind of numbness instead of the joys of anticipation; family illnesses, coupled with depressing weather, had completely dampened his spirits. After he collected their passports at the American legation and thought about the people working there, he discovered that he was happy at least in one respect: He was "a sovereign again, and no longer a servant; and really it is very queer, how I look down upon our Ambassadors and dignitaries of all sorts, not excepting the President himself" (*EN*, 620–21).[40]

Nathaniel's final act before departing was to say good-by to his two close English friends. On January 4 he wrote a short note to Henry Bright, asking him to help Wilding, who was in danger of being dismissed from his Liverpool post. At the end of his letter Hawthorne said, "I have hardly left myself room for a few parting words; and, to be sure, there need [be] none, for I hate leave-taking, in proportion as I value the friend from whom I part."[41]

On the last Monday evening Bennoch came to tea—his first and only visit to the Hawthornes since they had been at Mrs. Siever's lodging house. The two men spent the evening talking together at some length, but what they said to each other we shall never know. Hawthorne's impression was that whatever Bennoch's future might be, he would "never get all the sunshine back again." Bennoch would continue to endure, but he could scarcely enjoy life as he had in the past. As Nathaniel thought back on the scene several days later in Paris, he wrote, "But it seems most unnatural that so buoyant and expansive a character should have fallen into the helplessness of commercial misfortune; it is most grievous to hear his manly and cheerful allusions to it, and even his jokes upon it." In describing their meeting to Ticknor, Hawthorne relayed a message from Bennoch: "He bade me tell Fields and yourself that he is not dead yet, though beaten down."[42]

At 7 A.M. the next day, Tuesday, January 5, the Hawthornes took the train to Folkestone, setting out once again on a cold and miserable day.[43] They had had a wet introduction to the country in the summer of 1853, and now it was a wet and colder farewell. They had expectations of a warm, dry climate in Italy, but Hawthorne's last recorded thought in London expressed his real feelings as they were about to leave: "I have now been so long in England that it seems a cold and shivery thing, to go anywhere else" (*EN*, 621).

‡ 7 ‡

Italian Interlude
1858–1859

EARLY IN LIFE Hawthorne had acknowledged that all too often expecta-
tion and realization are completely different kinds of experience;[1] he
had also learned to accept both fortune and misfortune with equanim-
ity. But Sophia's customary optimism in facing problems underwent
severe strain before the end of the year and a half that the family spent
on the Continent. Limited funds, the climate, illnesses, and Nathaniel's
inability to complete any writing except the notebooks all made this a
difficult period. Much of this personal material Sophia later changed
in her edition of her husband's notebooks for 1858 and 1859 or
omitted altogether. The result was a volume of rather depersonalized
travel notes, similar in tone to her own publication, *Notes in England and
Italy*. The complete manuscript of Hawthorne's French and Italian
notebooks, not available until this century, now gives us a fuller story.[2]

When the Hawthornes reached Paris on January 6, Nathaniel began
his record of Continental travels by describing their departure from
London. If they had hoped for better weather as they left cold, wet
England, they were much disappointed. There was a footwarmer in
the carriage of the train from London Bridge Station to Folkestone,
but instead of warming the interior it provided only enough heat to
steam up the windows and shut out their last view of green fields. Then
it began to snow. "It seemed as if we had staid our English welcome out,
and were to find nothing genial and hospitable there, any more."[3]

Hawthorne's last glimpse of England was the white cliffs, which on
that dreary day did not seem at a distance either very white or very
imposing. Most of the family huddled on deck in spite of the cold. Rose
was afraid of seasickness and Sophia stayed with her, while Julian
pretended not to be affected, and Ada Shepard looked "quite desolate
and patiently miserable." Nathaniel found that the two-hour passage to
Boulogne was made bearable for him only by drinking brandy and hot
water with sugar in it (I, 117, MA587).[4]

As the train from Boulogne proceeded toward Amiens, the weather turned colder. Dusk came early on the short winter day, and frost covered the train windows. When Nathaniel could scratch a peephole on the glass, he saw that the fields of northern France with their patches of snow and ice more nearly resembled New England's brown fields than those green ones of England to which he had become accustomed during nearly five years. This was the first of the many comparisons of the Continent with England or with the United States that he was to make during the year and a half that followed.

In three or four hours they reached Amiens, where Hawthorne experienced his first troubles with customs officials who talked too fast in a language that he could understand only by reading. Ada Shepard came to his rescue, and they finally were able to proceed by omnibus to the Hotel du Rhin, where they shivered again for the rest of the day.[5] Hawthorne concluded his daily notebook entry by writing, "Really I do not know when I have been so utterly miserable as on this journey; and sooty, misty England seemed a kind and genial region in comparison" (I, 120, MA587).

The following day was not much better. If the cold had not dulled Hawthorne's senses, he might have enjoyed his rambles around the town. Even so, he devoted several pages of his notebooks to a description of the cathedral and recorded his first brief impression of Catholic worship: Even the holy water at the entrance was full of ice!

When they reached Paris at 5 P.M. after another ride behind frost-covered windows, they were still suffering from the unexpected cold. They took a suite of rooms on the third floor of Hotel du Louvre, Rue St. Honoré, for which, Hawthorne said, they paid twenty-five francs per day, plus four francs for a candle in each room. Ada was a bit more specific in describing their accommodations. Though she admitted the discomforts of travel, she was glad to "get away from that horrible lodging house in Great Russell Street, and to be ensconced in these nice French chambers with their neat and tasteful appointments." She made note of the green velvet carpets, the mahogany furniture, the red velvet coverings and cushions, and the bronze ornaments on the mantels. It was the only hotel she had seen so far that could compete with those of New York.[6]

In this hotel directly across the street from the Louvre the Hawthornes spent about a week, during which Nathaniel began to realize that touring the Continent with a family of young people was going to be more costly than he had counted on. He found that in addition to the price of rooms (between seven and eight dollars a day), meals were also expensive. "It is a terrible business, feeding so many mouths, and especially children, and most especially a boy, at a French table." Later he commented on Julian's complaint that the mutton chops were not enough: "I really think he would eat a whole sheep" (I, 126, MA587).

On the first afternoon, instead of dining at the table d'hôte they went into the restaurant of the hotel, where they could choose from the menu. This meal, ending with ice cream ("which I little thought to have eaten in this Arctic weather"), led him to compare the French and the English in the preparation of food, a topic he had always been interested in and which he continued to comment on during the rest of their stay in France:

> All the dishes were very delicate, and a vast change from the simple English system, with its joints, shoulders, beef-steaks and chops; but I doubt whether English cookery, for the very reason that it is so gross, is not better for man's moral and spiritual nature, than French. In the former case, you know that you are gratifying your coarsest animal needs and propensities, and are duly ashamed of it; but, in dealing with these French delicacies, you delude yourself into the idea that you are cultivating your taste while filling your belly. (I, 126–27, MA587)

Fortunately Hawthorne's sense of humor had not deserted him in spite of the weather and his own physical condition.

At sometime during those first days of 1858 he caught a cold; it was to recur in Rome and stay with him off and on for most of the spring months. This was probably why he felt his senses dulled and his desire for sightseeing diminished; ill health was a new experience for him. In contrast to the vigorous life he had led in England, he spent his first morning in Paris sitting at the hotel window because of persistent nosebleeds. Meanwhile, Ada and Sophia went to see about the luggage; Nathaniel did not go out at all until dinnertime. They decided to hunt for a restaurant that might be less expensive than the hotel, and on a walk through the neighborhood they found the Restaurant des Echelles, which thereafter became their regular dining place.

In spite of another nosebleed at dinner, Nathaniel recovered enough to walk around the streets and form some general impressions of Paris. Thus far, he said, it was "wholly unexpected," more like his image of St. Petersburg. The buildings were more impressive than those of London. He admitted that he had no sympathy with the French people, but that they did "grand and beautiful things, in the architectural way" (I, 131–32, MA587). In the days that followed he filled his notebook with comparisons between France and England—

the food, the buildings, the art galleries, the liveliness of people in the streets. He did not have time to become acquainted with any French people; hence he never developed any real understanding of their country.

The few persons who called on the family at the hotel were mostly Americans who were also visiting in Paris.[7] The most famous of these was Maria Mitchell, "the celebrated astronomical lady of Nantucket." Although she was not mentioned in the English notebooks, Miss Mitchell had brought a letter of introduction to Hawthorne in Liverpool while he was still consul. Now she asked the Hawthornes to let her accompany them to Rome. Sophia hesitated at first, because the group of travelers was already large and she was reluctant to assume any more responsibility, but she finally agreed with Nathaniel that Miss Mitchell seemed to be an independent woman who would not be an extra burden.

There is only occasional mention of Miss Mitchell in the French and Italian notebooks, but one of Ada Shepard's letters conveys an early impression of the astronomer: "Although reared on the hardy soil of Nantucket, she is very polished and delicate, has a nice sense of propriety and even a poetic taste. Her personal appearance is not very prepossessing to those who look on the outside only; but I liked her at once, and like her more and more the longer I see her."[8]

Unfortunately, in the published portions of her diary Miss Mitchell left no entries of her experiences in Paris. It is only later in her Roman notes that we have glimpses of the Hawthornes as she saw them.

The family devoted the remainder of that week in Paris chiefly to sightseeing. Nathaniel, however, had some business matters to attend to: a visit to the bank for French money; a courtesy call on the American minister, Judge Mason; and a call at the office of the American consul, Henry Spencer, to obtain a visa. Spencer advised the Hawthornes to go by steamer all the way to Civitavecchia, the port nearest Rome, rather than landing at Leghorn and traveling thence to Rome. Hawthorne accepted his advice and paid a fee of five francs and some sous for his visa. Later he wrote in his notebook that he supposed Spencer deserved the money, "but really, it is not half so pleasant to pay a consular fee as it used to be to receive it" (I, 161, MA587).

Meanwhile, he recorded more comparisons between Paris and England. The Champs Elysées might be pretty in summer, but now there was not a single blade of grass—nothing but hard clay covered with dust. The next day, however, the ground had softened as rain alternated with snow. Unable to find a cab, the Hawthornes were forced to walk back to the hotel through mud. The clouds and rain that continued for several days led Nathaniel to say, "England has nothing to be compared with it . . . no walks were possible" (I, 144, MA587). Had he forgotten the winters in Liverpool when walking was impossible?

Hawthorne had to admit that the Paris galleries were admirable not only for their fine architecture but for their collections. He had little to say about any of the paintings he observed, for Sophia seems to have taken him around the galleries until he became "wearied to death" and "began to have that dreary and desperate feeling which has often come upon me when the sights last longer than my capacity for receiving them." He was trying to make the most of their few days in Paris galleries, but he gave the impression of being merely dutiful. It was far more interesting to watch the crowds in the streets. "The city was livelier, on this sombre and misty day, than ever London was, in its gayest sunshine" (I, 155, MA587).

Their intensive sightseeing made the children tired, especially little Rose, whose short legs did not carry her along the streets as fast as her father walked. Julian was often bored. Una, too tired to go out, spent one whole day in the hotel room. Sophia caught a cold from walking in rain, snow, and mud, and Nathaniel's cold was not improved. Paris in January did not prove to be a very charming place.

By the end of a week the family seemed relieved to be starting out by train for Marseilles. Nathaniel's last walk was through the gardens of the Tuilleries, which were disappointing to him because the ground was bare, the branches of the trees were "naked," and everything was such a contrast to the greenness of England. He concluded about Paris that "nothing really thrives here; man and vegetables have but an artificial life, like flowers stuck in a little mould, but never taking root. I am quite tired of Paris, and never longed for a home so much" (I, 163, MA587).

On the way from Paris to Marseilles the train traveled through flat, uninteresting countryside as bleak as New England in late autumn. The family stopped overnight in Lyons and again in Marseilles, where Julian and his father took a walk around the city. Nathaniel recorded in his journal an explicit passage about the dirt in the city, including a reference to the "water closets" at the hotel and in the streets. Sophia, of course, later modified the passage in her edition of the notebooks so that it read, "The nastiness which I saw in Marseilles exceeds my heretofore experience. There is dirt in the hotel and everywhere else, and it evidently troubles nobody,—no more than if all the people were pigs in a pigsty."[9]

By contrast, the steamer *Calabrese*, which they boarded for the voyage to Italy, was "very clean and comfortable." The cool air and the voyage itself would have been very pleasant, but Nathaniel enjoyed nothing, "having a cold upon me, or a low fever, or something else that took the light and warmth out of everything." Since the ship pitched a good deal, he spent the first part of the voyage stretched out on the bed to give himself the "best chance of keeping my stomach in an equable state." He tried to record more of his impressions of Marseilles, but found little to say. It was the same problem he had encountered in writing his English notebooks: "After the first novelty is over, new things seem equally common place with the old. There is but one little interval when the mind is in such a state that you can catch the fleeting aroma of a new scene" (I, 177–80, MA587).

Whenever the ship put into port for a day, as at Genoa or Leghorn, Hawthorne joined his family in going ashore, although his physical condition was still not good. He quickly grew tired of sightseeing and found that his "receptive faculty" was very limited. Being forced to see so many things, he wrote, was like "having dainties forced down the throat long after the appetite was satisfied" (I, 185, MA587).

When the Hawthornes finally reached Civitavecchia, they had to spend half the day with customs officers, inspectors of passports, and *vetturini*, or coachmen. At last they arranged for a *vetturino* to take them to Rome in eight hours by means of a carriage with four horses at a cost of three napoleons (sixty francs, or probably about fifteen dollars). Since there were said to be robbers along the route, they were glad to have an armed government mail coach traveling ahead of them. In his account written years later Julian told how his father hid a good many gold coins in an umbrella, which was then fastened to the roof of the vehicle, while Miss Mitchell put hers into her stocking.[10]

At the gates of Rome, Hawthorne did what he had quickly learned was customary with travelers on the Continent: He gave the customs officers a tip sufficient to enable the party to pass through the gates without baggage inspection. They went to Spillman's, on Via della Croce, the only hotel that could accommodate them at midnight. Nathaniel's last comment in his first Italian notebook was that the family had arrived "half-frozen" and had been so ever since that date. "And this is sunny Italy and genial Rome!" (I, 189, MA587).

It was two weeks before he had energy enough to begin the second manuscript volume of his notebooks, written at Palazzo Laranzani, 37 Via Porta Pinciana. The apartment they found after several days of hunting was a suite of ten rooms occupying the second *piano* and reached by a flight of seventy stone steps. As in all such houses, the floors were uncarpeted and their suite had fireplaces in only one or two rooms. The yearly rental was about twelve hundred dollars. They had a servant named Lalla, who apparently prepared only breakfasts and teas; the dinners were brought in from a nearby restaurant in a stack of covered tin trays, kept hot by a charcoal brazier underneath.[11]

Hawthorne spent most of the first few weeks sitting in a corner by a fire, wearing his overcoat. He went out occasionally, he said, for an hour or so in the middle of the day when it was likely to be less chilly. Usually he sat and read, for his fingers were too cold for writing and his energy was at a low ebb. When, two weeks after their arrival, he began the second manuscript volume of his notebooks, he confessed, "I have seldom or never spent so wretched a time anywhere" (II, 1, MA588).

Gradually he became somewhat acclimated and began to feel that warmer weather might eventually reconcile him to Rome against his will. His first impressions, however, constituted a list of unpleasant items which he would have expanded had he been in the mood to write:

> Cold, mistiness, evil smells, narrow lanes between tall, ugly, mean-looking whitewashed houses, sour bread, pavements most uncomfortable to the feet, enormous prices for poor living, beggars, pickpockets, ancient temples and broken monuments with filth at the base, and clothes hanging to dry about them, French soldiers, monks, and priests of every degree, a shabby population smoking bad cigars—these would have been some of the points of my description. (II, 2–3, MA588)[12]

Maria Mitchell, who had taken a room at some distance from them in an old house in the Via Bocca di Leone, saw the Hawthornes nearly every day and joined them in their sightseeing. In addition, Ada often visited Miss Mitchell's apartment in the evenings after lessons and sightseeing had ended. A letter of Maria Mitchell's written home in February stated, "Mrs. Hawthorne walks with us, Mr. H. never."[13] About the same time she wrote in her diary that she thought Hawthorne could not have been very well, because he was so inactive. Then she recorded a short description of him as she saw him in the Palazzo Laranzani: "Generally he sat by an open fire, with his feet thrust into the coals, and an open volume of Thackeray upon his knees. He said that Thackeray was the greatest living novelist. I sometimes suspected that the volume of Thackeray was kept as a foil, that he might not be talked to. He shrank from society, but rode and walked."[14]

Miss Mitchell did not know Hawthorne well enough to understand his nature and to realize that though he gave her the impression of being "taciturn," he was not always so. It was weeks before he desired any sociability.[15] But the rest of the family made up for his inactivity. Even Sophia, who complained that her soul, as well as the fountains, had been "iced over," developed an early enthusiasm for the city:

> But I am in Rome, Rome, *Rome*! I have stood in the Forum, and beneath the Arch of Titus, at the end of the Sacra Via. I have wandered about the Coliseum, the stupendous grandeur of which equals my dream and hope. . . . I have climbed the Capitoline and stood before the Capitol, by the side of the equestrian statue of Marcus Aurelius. . . . I have been into the Pantheon, whose sublime portico quietly rises out of the region of criticism into its own sphere. . . . And I have been to St. Peter's! There alone in Rome is perpetual summer![16]

Nathaniel's first reaction to St. Peter's was less enthusiastic than Sophia's. He wrote that it was useless to attempt a description of such places: The building was so different from his expectations, based on his familiarity with the dim interiors of English cathedrals. And so he began his comparisons of England and Italy by expressing an attitude that did not change much during the year that followed: "I am glad I saw the castles and Gothic churches and cathedrals of England before visiting Rome, or I never could have felt that delightful reverence for their gray and ivy-hung antiquity, after seeing these so much older remains. But indeed, old things are not so beautiful in this dry climate and clear atmosphere as in moist England" (II, 7, MA588). (He had not yet experienced the humidity of summer in Rome!) There was no greenness here, he wrote; hence, the English ruins would always be more beautiful. Then he added a note that he emphasized later in *The Marble Faun*: After a thousand years there will be ruins in the United States, but "we can never have a Furness Abbey or a Kenilworth" (II, 8, MA588).

Another passage written after his first visit to St. Peter's appears later in *The Marble Faun*: a description of the confessionals with their signs designating the languages spoken by the different priests. "If I had a murder on my conscience or any other great sin, I think I should have been inclined to kneel down there, and pour it into the safe secrecy of the confessional" (II, 10, MA588). He then devoted considerable space to comments on the seeming need for confession and the value Roman Catholics place on their religion.[17]

The Hawthorne family's first experience with the Roman Carnival was a delight to the children and a bore to Nathaniel. He described the crowds of participants in the Corso, the spectators in the balconies, the "miserable bouquets fished up from muddy pavements," and the "sugar plums" filled with lime or "bad flour" (which he did not appreciate, particularly since one hit him in the eye). However, in comparing notes with Julian, Rose, and Una, he found that they all had enjoyed the experience. He concluded that "only the young ought to write descriptions of such scenes. My cold criticism chills the life out of it" (II, 26, MA588).

One sunny day when the Hawthornes had been in Rome for three weeks, they went to call on the Storys at their home in the Palazzo Barberini. The renewal of acquaintance with William Wetmore Story, American artist-writer whom Nathaniel had known some years before in New England, was the Hawthornes' introduction to the world of American artists in Rome. Until the middle of March, however, Story; C. G. Thompson, the painter who had painted Hawthorne's portrait in Boston; and Maria Louisa Lander, the sculptor who was to make a bust of Hawthorne, were the only three artists mentioned in Nathaniel's notebooks. (The Hawthornes might have met more artists sooner had they accepted Mrs. Story's invitation to her fancy ball.) On their first visit they stayed only long enough to admire the Storys' apartment — more for its views and the sunlight coming in the windows than for its size and furnishings.[18]

William Story had his studio in another building, situated in the "Via San Nicolo di Tolentino, which opened from the Piazza Barberini through the new quarter of Rome."[19] Hawthorne later spent many hours in Story's studio, for he liked this versatile poet, prose writer, lawyer, painter, musician, and sculptor, finding him "sensible of something deeper in his art than merely to make beautiful nudities and baptize them by classic names" (II, 28–29, MA588). The unfinished *Cleopatra* in Story's workshop became Kenyon's work in *The Marble Faun*, and in his preface to the romance Hawthorne freely acknowledged this fact in order to help promote his friend's interests.

At that time, however, Hawthorne had no definite plan for an Italian romance; he was only recording what he saw that might be of use later on in his writings. The first incident of significance to his future romance happened even before he had seen the statue of the faun. It was his and Sophia's visit of February 16 to the Church of the Capuchins, around the corner from Piazza Barberini, where they saw not only the skeletons and graves of monks long dead, but the body of one who had died very recently. Nathaniel's description of the bare feet and the brown robe ended with mention of "some blood oozing from his nostrils! Perhaps his murderer — or his doctor — had just then come into the church and drawn nigh the bier; at all events, it was about as queer a thing as ever I witnessed. We soon came away and left him lying there; a sight which I shall never forget" (II, 40–41, MA588).

A few days later they visited the picture gallery of the Palazzo Barberini, where Guido's portrait of Beatrice Cenci was located. Hawthorne found it impossible to describe, for its spell was "indefinable." There was such "unfathomable depth and sorrow" in her eyes; she was like a "fallen angel, fallen without sin." He wished that he could have seen the painting without a knowledge of the Cenci tragedy, but the portrait led him to supply his own interpretation later in his romance (II, 56–57, MA588).

There were other impressions of works of art and scenes that Hawthorne dutifully recorded in his notebook, but they were, for the most part, of less importance to his romance. The Pincian Hill, Miss Lander's studio, Guido's painting of Michael overcoming Lucifer, the Dying Gladiator, the calf in the field outside the gates of Rome—these were only a few of the items briefly noted. The last notation in this second volume deals with the celebration of Una's fourteenth birthday, when they hired a barouche and drove out the Appian Way to the tomb of Cecilia Metella. On their return they stopped at the tomb of the Scipios and the nearby Columbarium of Pomponius Hylas, where they descended into chambers so dark that a guide and tapers were necessary. This expedition and their subsequent visits to catacombs provided the background for the scene in the romance involving Miriam's model.

Una's birthday marked the first warm day they had experienced in Italy, and Nathaniel commented that it produced languor; Roman climate did not seem to be "healthy in any of its moods" (II, 90, MA588). Nevertheless, by the middle of March he felt that spring was actually beginning. In spite of his lingering cold he began to enjoy a little social life, such as the dinner given by Thomas B. Read.

Like Story, Read was both author and artist; he was also an admirer of Hawthorne's writings and paid tribute to his skill several years later in the introduction to his long poem "The Wagoner of the Alleghanies." All the guests at his dinner, besides Hawthorne and James Hooker, a banker,[20] were painters or sculptors. Next to Hawthorne sat John Gibson, the English sculptor who had been in Italy for about forty years and whose use of color on sculpture had created a great deal of controversy. The dinner party and Gibson's conversation stimulated Hawthorne to write in his notebook five pages concerning their discussion of art.

Shortly afterward Hawthorne was again expressing regret that he did not feel "inclined for walking, having been sick and feverish, for two or three days past, with a cold, which keeps renewing itself faster than I can get rid of it" (III, 9–10, Berg). But on a bright, mild day, he and Sophia went for a noontime walk to the Forum, across the Tiber, and to St. Peter's again. From then on for the next two months the pace of sightseeing and socializing increased. One day Sophia and Nathaniel called on two American ladies, the Misses Weston, at Palazzo Galitzin, and took a carriage ride after lunch to the Castle of St. Angelo. Another day they visited the studio of Joseph Mozier, an American sculptor. When the artist returned the call at their apartment, he launched into a condemnation of Margaret Fuller's Italian husband, Count Ossoli, to whom he had tried to teach sculpture. As a result of Mozier's conversation, Hawthorne included in his notebook an extensive passage about Margaret Fuller and her seemingly inappropriate husband.[21] At the end of the month they went to Gibson's studio to see his work and to meet a young American woman whom he had accepted as a student: Harriet Hosmer, or "Hatty," as her friends called her.

Hawthorne described Hatty as a "small, brisk, wide-awake figure, of queer and funny aspect, yet not ungraceful, nor to be rejected from one's good graces without further trial." She was dressed in a purple or plum-colored broadcloth man's sack (he was not sure whether she wore a skirt or "pantaloons"), a man's shirt and collar, and a cravat, fastened with a brooch of Etruscan gold. On her curls was a jaunty black velvet cap. Nathaniel was amused by her appearance, but kindly in his attitude; he felt that she seemed to be "frank, simple, straight-forward, and downright" (III, 52, Berg). However, it is unlikely that the Hawthornes were ever close to Hatty, for Sophia was not generally pleased by emancipated females. Nathaniel was more interested in the work of Story and Powers, and Ada, who was close to the sculptor in age, was not favorably impressed by her.[22]

When Easter came, the adults went to St. Peter's and in the evening were led to a spot on Monte Cavallo by another American sculptor, Paul Akers, for a view of the illumination of St. Peter's. Although Hawthorne enjoyed Akers's company, he was able to stay only a few minutes, for he was still feverish with the cold that he could not seem to get rid of. The cold kept him indoors all the next day, and at the end of the week on a visit to the Coliseum he was still complaining of the "malevolent, or at least not friendly" air of Rome (III, 77, Berg).

In the days that followed, the Hawthornes visited two more studios: that of George Loring Brown, an American landscape painter, a "plain, homely, Yankee sort of man," and that of Edward Bartholomew, an American sculptor. Then Frederika Bremer, the Swedish writer, called on them. Nathaniel wrote that she had changed little since her visit to their house in Lenox, when she went away "so dissatisfied with my conversational performances and so laudatory of my brow and eyes, while so severely criticizing my poor mouth and chin" (III, 86, Berg).[23] The real trouble at Lenox, he wrote, had been that he could not understand her Swedish accent. He then recorded one of his most revealing statements about himself: There had to be "close and unembarrassed contiguity" between his companion and himself, or he could not carry on a conversation with any meaning. "I doubt whether I have ever really talked with half a dozen persons in my life, either men or women" (III, 86, Berg). If Hawthorne talked to his close friends as he wrote to them, we can assume from his many informal letters to William Ticknor, Henry Bright, and Francis Bennoch that these men who played an important part in his life abroad were numbered in that group.

The third manuscript volume of the Italian notebooks, completed near the end of April 1858, concludes with Hawthorne's conception of the germ of an idea for a story. In the Capitoline Museum he studied the statue of the faun attributed to Praxiteles and wrote, "It seems to me that a story, with all sorts of fun and pathos in it, might be contrived on the idea of their species having become intermingled with the human race; a family, with the faun-blood in them, having prolonged itself from the classic era till our own days" (III, 88, Berg). Three days later he had resolved to describe the statue at some length in his fourth notebook because he would need the details for the "little Romance" he was beginning to think about. After a page of description he hit upon an important idea: The faun might be "refined through his feelings, so that the coarser, animal part of his nature could be thrown into the background, though liable to assert itself at any time" (IV, 14, MA589).

In the meantime, through the sociable Storys, the Hawthornes were introduced to several more visitors to Rome: Mr. and Mrs. Robert Apthorp, whose little son was studying music in Rome; Mrs. Apthorp's sister, Miss Sarah Hunt; and Mrs. Anna Jameson, the English art critic, whom Hawthorne was surprised to find so very cordial. One afternoon Mrs. Jameson took him for a drive to visit several churches and the tomb of Cecilia Metella. Their discussion en route centered on nudity in sculpture. When Hawthorne discovered that his hostess, like Gibson, objected to modern clothes on statues, he responded that rather than relying upon nudity, which he found unnatural, the art of sculpture should "perish" (IV, 32, MA589). Realism, not prudery, was his justification.

Had Hawthorne forgotten his earlier friends during these busy days in Rome? On March 16 his first letter to Bennoch explained that he had not written to anyone except his bankers since his arrival in Rome. He had nothing to report except news about his cold and the unfavorable impressions of Rome he had recorded earlier in the notebooks. Already the family was planning to move to Florence for the summer, but so far, Hawthorne said, he had made no definite arrangements.[24]

In April he wrote practically the same news to Ticknor, expanding a bit on their plans: They would summer in Florence and spend the winter of 1858–1859 in Rome, and then he supposed he would have to return to the United States. His reason was that the climate and the constant moving around prevented him from settling down to any "serious literary labor," though he admitted that he could have done so in England if he had had any leisure time. He did not then admit to Ticknor that he felt impelled to produce a substantial piece of fiction in order to supplement the insufficient savings from his consular years. Thus he was unconsciously justifying a future event that he did not yet count on: returning to England to write.[25]

In the last part of his letter he compared life in Rome with that in England, just as he had done in his letter to Bennoch:

> Rent is a good deal dearer [in Rome than in England]; and nothing is cheaper except maccaroni [sic], figs, bad cigars, and sour wine. Rome struck me very disagreeably at first, but rather improves upon acquaintance, and has a sort of fascination which will make me reluctant to take a final leave of it. I wish I were a little more patriotic; but to confess the truth, I had rather be a sojourner in any other country than return to my own. The United States are fit for many excellent purposes, but they certainly are not fit to live in.[26]

For the present, he put aside all thoughts of his own country and began, with C. G. Thompson's aid, to negotiate with various *vetturini* to move the family to Florence. Thompson, who was far more accustomed to dealing with Italians, went with Hawthorne several times. The prices were always too high. When they finally found a *vetturino* whom Thompson knew and recommended, Hawthorne signed a contract in which everything was written down, "even to milk, butter, bread, eggs, and coffee, which we are to have for breakfast; the vetturino being to pay every expense for himself, his horses, and his passengers, and include it within ninety-five scudi, and five crowns additional for buonomano" (IV, 43, MA589).

It would seem from his notebook entries that Hawthorne had forgotten his children as well as his friends, for he seldom mentioned any of them except when he noted that one or more had accompanied him to a gallery or a church. As a matter of fact, they were being kept busy with lessons for hours at a time—too many hours, according to Ada. Evidently she was confined to her teaching and the apartment more than she wished, for passages in her letters depict a rather restricted family life. On May 16 she wrote, "I am sorry that I cannot walk often in the evening here; but Mr. Hawthorne never goes out."[27] The evenings were spent chiefly at home, either reading or writing. After tea Sophia would read a chapter in the Bible to the children. When Rose had gone to bed, Sophia and Nathaniel, and sometimes Una, wrote in their journals. Ada was busy turning out page after page of letters, usually to Clay, not so often to her family. Frequently it was late before she finished, and she admitted that Sophia had to send her to bed at 11 P.M.[28]

Although she had only three pupils during these spring months, Ada found it necessary to give very different kinds of instruction because of their varied ages and attitudes. Una, an ardent reader, seemed very mature for her age. Julian, on the other hand, seemed to be no student at all (as he himself admitted many times). But Ada decided that he was like most boys of his age, to whom study "is a painful instead of a pleasant duty."[29] In Rome, Julian was busy hunting lizards and other interesting creatures or enjoying the companionship of Eddy Thompson, who was about his age. As for Rose, even at seven she was still called "Baby," and her formal education was apparently somewhat neglected. Though the child was affectionate with Ada, she did not seem to relish any kind of school work, nor did Ada make much effort to help her. Ada wrote that she called Rose her "pupil," but that her studies were not burdensome to either of them. "She only reads and spells a little and writes on her slate. She prints very nicely indeed, and lately she is learning to write."[30]

In spite of some dissatisfactions with Ada's teaching and with her spending so much time in interminable letter-writing, the Hawthornes were pleased enough with their governess to ask her to stay on for a second year. Though she missed Clay, it was too good an opportunity for her to refuse.[31] Nathaniel was also glad to have someone near to help him in the numerous situations that involved dealing with people who spoke a foreign language. Most of the time the parents left Ada and the children free to do as they pleased. Often the four walked around Rome and sketched; everybody in the family except Nathaniel carried a pad and pencil and frequently sat down to draw. It is doubtful that any of the children had much guidance or training in art. Sketching was simply the thing to do in those days, just as keeping a diary or journal was customary. The children's real education, as Sophia said in England, was in being exposed to the total culture of other nations.

Ada's report that Hawthorne never walked in the evenings was not quite accurate, for late in the spring the dinner hour was moved to 2 P.M. so that the family could have the cooler hours of late afternoon and early evening for walks. At the end of one busy day the three adults were invited to tea at Miss Bremer's apartment. Afterward they walked to the upper edge of the Tarpeian Rock. Hawthorne was sufficiently impressed by its height to record his thoughts about the old Romans "flinging political criminals" down over the edge to certain death, another image that was to be used later in his romance (IV, 51, MA589).

Sunday, May 23, was the Hawthornes' last full day in Rome until the following October. They had breakfast at the Storys', where the guests included Hatty Hosmer and William Cullen Bryant, who had called on the Hawthornes at dinnertime on Saturday. The Bryants were starting home from a European trip, and since they also stopped later in Florence, Nathaniel had more to say about the poet in a later notebook. The rest of the day was devoted to packing and to verifying the inventory of furniture in their apartment.

In the evening Una and her father took a farewell walk in the Pincian Gardens. After their conversation he expressed some dismay on hearing with what "alarming fervor" Una had spoken of her love for Rome and her yearning to come back. "On the other hand," he reflected, "nothing elevating and refining can be really injurious; and so I hope she will always be the better for Rome, even if her life should be spent where there are no pictures, no statues, nothing but the dryness and meagerness of a New England village" (IV, 55, MA589).

Early on Monday morning the troubles of departure began. A dispute arose with Lalla, the maid, and her mother over wages, and there was also an argument over money with the men who carried down the luggage and put it in the *vettura*. Lastly, Hawthorne wrote, they were "infested with beggars" hanging around the carriage and crying for money as the Hawthornes drove away in the middle of what he was sure was a "shower of anathemas." Finally, at 8 A.M., they passed through the Porta del Popolo, leaving Rome with somewhat mixed feelings. Hawthorne said he had less regret than the others, "yet we [all] felt the city pulling at our heart strings far more than London did, where we shall probably never spend much time again." Thus he admitted to a certain attachment to the city in spite of "disgust" at its bad features (IV, 57, MA589).

So began what Hawthorne described as the most carefree period, brief as it was, that he had ever experienced. Someone else was in charge of overnight accommodations, meals, luggage, and all the other disagreeable travel responsibilities he had always hated.

The route the Hawthornes took to Florence under the supervision and care of Gaetano, their *vetturino*, was the same as that commonly taken by English and American tourists: Terni (where they missed seeing the falls because of rain), Foligno, Spoleto, Perugia, Assisi, Lake Thrasymene (which Hawthorne said did not compare with either Windermere or Loch Lomond), Arrezzo, and Incisa. Almost every night Nathaniel wrote a brief description of the inn where they stopped, the historic spots they visited, and now and then the food they ate at dinnertime—a subject he had not discussed since the day they had arrived in Rome. Occasionally he also referred to the activities of the children.

When the Hawthornes reached the gates of Florence on Sunday, May 30, Nathaniel tipped the customs officers and the family passed through with no examination of the baggage. They drove at once to the Casa del Bello, where Hiram Powers, the American sculptor, had supposedly made arrangements for them.[32] But when Nathaniel found that the bargain for rental had not been completed, they spent the first night at Albergo della Fontana, a comfortable, moderately priced hotel. That evening Powers called on them, and though Nathaniel liked him immediately, he was too weary to be sociable.

The next day they set out to inspect the Casa del Bello, which was across the street from Powers's house.[33] They learned that they had a choice of apartments: the second *piano* at forty dollars a month or the first at fifty dollars. In spite of the higher rent, they chose the first floor because of its access to a terrace and a garden. Sophia wrote a detailed description of the apartment, an account that shows her interest in furnishings and housekeeping:

> It is a delightful residence. We have the first piano, which opens at the back upon a broad terrace, leading down into a garden full of roses, jessamine, orange and lemon trees, and a large willow tree, drooping over a fountain in the midst. We have thirteen rooms on the first piano,

besides four kitchen rooms beneath. . . . It is the very luxury of comfort. I have selected the best of the three parlors for the study. It is hung with crimson velvety hangings, and the doors are draped in that graceful way they have in Europe. . . . It has an ormolu table, two couches, four stuffed easy-chairs, candelabras, chandelier, and a Turkey carpet (an unusual grace). It gives upon the garden, and there is no sound but 'bird voices' that can reach it;—the very ideal of a study, such as the 'Artist of the Beautiful' ought to have, but which till now he has not found.[34]

At the moment they seemed to have the ideal location, and the weather, Hawthorne said, was "delightful": "too warm to walk, but perfectly fit to do nothing in, in the coolest of these great rooms. Every day I shall write a little, perhaps—and probably take a brief nap, somewhere between breakfast and tea—but go to see pictures and statues occasionally, and so assuage and mollify myself a little after that uncongenial life of the consulate, and before going back to my own hard and dusty New England" (V, 30, HM302).

At the end of the first week he still felt pleasantly relaxed: "Warm as the weather is getting to be, I never feel that inclination to sink down in a heap and never stir again, which was my dull torment and misery as long as I staid in Rome. I hardly think there can be a place in the world where life is more delicious for its own simple sake than here" (V, 32, HM302).

Near the end of the second week he was beginning to think that life might be more pleasant if the weather were not quite so warm. For the time being, however, the heat did not prevent the family from sightseeing, from becoming better acquainted with the Powers family, and from meeting the Brownings and a few visitors to Florence. It was a call from Robert Browning that really started the Hawthornes on a round of socializing. Browning came one afternoon to invite the adults to Casa Guidi for the evening to meet several other guests. Later Hawthorne wrote that Browning seemed "younger and handsomer" than he had in London two years before (V, 53, HM302).

That evening, Mrs. Browning seemed to Nathaniel to be different than she had been at Milnes's breakfast in London, probably because, as he said, "morning light is more prosaic than the illumination of their great, tapestried drawing room." Here she seemed to him "a pale little woman, scarcely embodied at all; at any rate, only substantial enough to put forth her slender fingers to be grasped, and to speak with a shrill, yet sweet, tenuity of voice" (V, 56, HM302).

This was the Hawthornes' introduction to Pen, the delicate little son of nine years, who sat quietly when he was not busy helping to pass strawberries and cake to the guests. Ada remarked that Pen had "long, fair hair, parted on his forehead, like a girl's, and hanging in waves around his head." His eyes, she said, were even more beautiful than his father's or his mother's.[35]

Among the other guests were Mr. and Mrs. David Eckley, wealthy Americans who had been traveling in the Near East; Fanny Haworth, the "English literary lady" whom Nathaniel had met in Liverpool; and Bryant and his daughter. Hawthorne described Bryant as "homely and plain of manner, with an old-fashioned dignity, nevertheless, and a remarkable deference and gentleness of tone, in addressing Mrs. Browning" (V, 57, HM302). (Because of her illness Bryant's wife was unable to be present.) Although the Hawthornes enjoyed their evening at the Brownings', conversation became dull before the end. There was nothing "startling" except that "disagreeable and now wearisome" topic of spiritualism.[36]

Hawthorne's boredom was only one sign that the heat was beginning to drain his energy. Before the end of one month he already had misgivings about his ability to do much work. He seemed to have "an affluence of ideas, such as they are," and an "impulse to be at work," but at the same time he felt a "sense of being unsettled." He wished that he could lock himself in a quiet room. "I need monotony, too—an eventless exterior life—before I can live in the world within" (V, 78, HM302). It took him two weeks to complete even the outline of the Italian romance he had in mind. One reason was that near the end of June he lost a week of activity because of a cold and fever. Though he said little about this, Ada thought that the situation was beginning to worry Sophia.

By this time Ada was so much a member of the family that Sophia called her "her eldest daughter." But Ada stood in awe of Hawthorne. He was so "over-critical," she wrote, "so extremely difficult to please, that a word [of praise] from him is worth a great deal."[37] After an entire page on the relationship between husband and wife, Ada summed up her attitude that Hawthorne was only slightly short of ideal: "He is a man after your own heart, perfectly true, rigidly upright, a perfect master of his passions and inclinations, delicate, tender and gentle in bearing, most regardful of the feelings of others—almost the best man I know, yet not a giant like Mr. Mann and Mr. Parker, my two idols."[38]

From her months of living so closely with the family, Ada had come to view Sophia more critically. In appearance she was not beautiful at all; "most people would call her particularly plain." What concerned

Ada most, though she afterward confessed that she should not even have mentioned it to Clay, was Sophia's "uncharitable" judgment of tradespeople with whom she dealt. She did not trust them because she was afraid of being cheated. Ada's last statement was the strongest: "Mrs. H. is just and upright to the fullest possible extent, but *she is not generous*."[39] In spite of her realization that all was not perfect in this family circle, when Ada decided to stay on with the Hawthornes, she recognized the advisability of adjusting to situations so as to avoid unpleasantness. Hawthorne himself showed no knowledge of any disagreements between the two women; wisely they kept such matters to themselves.

Near the end of June, the Hawthornes visited the mysterious woman who was to suggest their second place of residence and to become a friendly neighbor. Jane Isabella (or Isa) Blagden, "our lady of Bellosguardo," who rented the Villa Bricchieri on a hill outside Florence, was a hostess admired by many literary people. Her contemporaries, who knew little of her past life, were apparently charmed by her personality, for she had "no great assets in beauty, fortune, or literary ability."[40]

Other guests at Miss Blagden's who were mentioned in Hawthorne's notebook were Thomas Augustus Trollope, brother of the novelist Anthony, and Mr. Boott, an American musician, and his artist daughter. Hawthorne made few comments on the guests at this time, but after the Hawthornes moved, Miss Blagden and her friends reappeared in both the notebooks and Ada's letters.

The Hawthornes had been in Florence only a month when the heat impelled them to begin looking for another house somewhere outside the city. Miss Blagden suggested Villa Montauto, on the hill of Bellosguardo, and Ada supplied the means of communication, first by writing a letter in Italian to the owner, "Signore Conte Cavaliere Guilio Bambaloni da Montauto." Throughout the negotiations for a contract, Ada served as interpreter until at last the family moved into the villa on August 1.[41]

The move to Villa Montauto was an important event in the Hawthornes' lives, for the building and its setting contributed a major portion to the story of Monte Beni. Hawthorne recorded such a detailed description of their new home in *The Marble Faun* that all its readers are familiar with the general appearance of Villa Montauto.

Its eighty-five-foot tower was the dominant feature not only of the villa and its environs but also of the life experienced there by the family. It was the first place the Hawthornes explored and is the only part of the villa that Nathaniel described in much detail in his notebooks. The top portion was most important of all, for it provided a view of the entire countryside: the city of Florence, the valley of the Arno, scattered villas and villages, and "great tracts of cultivation, rich with the fig, the vine, the olive, besides Indian corn and other grains." The landscape lacked only streams and lakes. Nathaniel missed the "gleam of water" that makes a scene come to life. It gave him "a sense of oppressive sunshine and scanty shade" (VI, 50–52, MA590). Still, the tower became a favorite place for the family to watch the sunset behind the imperfect landscape.

The villa itself, though impressive for the vast number of rooms, could not compare to Casa del Bello in comfort and luxury. But there was space enough for every member of the family to have an entire suite of rooms if desired. On the ground floor Nathaniel had a dressing room, a large bedroom, and a "writing-closet," with elaborately frescoed ceilings throughout. In addition to his own quarters, he mentioned specifically only the kitchen, a chapel, an oratory adjoining Una's room, and the servants' room. As he looked around, he noted such religious objects as sacred prints, crucifixes, holy-water "pots" (a term changed to "vases" by Sophia in her edition), and a "naked" ("undraped," according to Sophia) little wax figure holding up a tiny heart. One object that appeared later in the Italian romance was a skull carved out of gray alabaster and placed upon a "sculptured cushion of white marble" (VI, 62, MA590). The rest of the Villa Montauto came alive in the romance later, for Hawthorne's memories of this place were as vivid as those of Rome, though more briefly recorded.

The grounds around the villa seem to have been more suitable than the bleak interior for entertaining guests. There were extensive lawns (not very green at this season), gravel walks, shrubbery, cypress trees, and a terrace on one side of the house. One "luxury" in particular pleased Nathaniel: He could for the first time since leaving the Wayside stretch out upon the ground without fear of catching cold. "Moist England would punish a man soundly for taking such liberties with her bosom" ("greensward" in Sophia's edition) (VI, 56, MA590).

Once the novelty of exploration wore off, there were few outstanding events for the next two months. William Story came over from Siena, where he and his family were spending the summer, and Isa Blagden brought over her companion, Annette Bracken. A friendship immediately developed between Ada and Miss Bracken, and these two, together with Miss Blagden, spent the long summer evenings reading and reciting Greek, Latin, and German.

Isa Blagden also took Sophia and Nathaniel to call on Seymour

Kirkup, an antiquarian interested in "spirit rappings." Kirkup ushered them into the library of his old house by the Arno and showed them a section of books on magic and the occult, a manuscript volume of Dante, and a plaster cast of Dante's face, which Kirkup believed to be a death mask. Hawthorne was particularly interested in a four-year-old girl named Imogen, a "pale, large-eyed" child, who "frisked through those shadowy old chambers, among the dead people's trumpery, as gaily as a butterfly flits among flowers and sunshine" (VI, 70, MA590). The entire incident was so intriguing to Hawthorne that later in his unfinished romances he developed fictional characters suggested by Kirkup and Imogen.

In his notations for September 1, Hawthorne wrote down an important item: He had finished "sketching out a Romance," a task that had taken him two months, and was putting it aside to be developed during the following winter (VI, 76, MA590). Meanwhile, he intended to revisit galleries and see whatever remained to be seen of Florence. From then until the family left Florence for Siena, the notebook contains mostly a record of visits to galleries. There were two exceptions: a long section on spiritualism and a description of wine-pressing. The section on spiritualism includes stories told by Powers; a ghost story told by Mrs. Baker, daughter of Major Gregorie, who had rented the nearby Villa Columbaria; and an account of the séances during which Ada served as a medium for writing messages.

The pressing of the grapes was a far more significant event to Hawthorne. However, he compared it unfavorably with cider-making in New England, which he thought much more picturesque. Although he took pleasure in the sight of huge bunches of grapes, a sample of the sour and bitter juice, "still lukewarm with fermentation," was, he said, "a wail of woe, squeezed out of the wine press of tribulation; and the more a man drinks of such, the sorrier he will be" (VI, 140, MA590). How different was the delicate, golden "sunshine wine" of Monte Beni!

After the last visits to the galleries of Florence, Nathaniel retired to the top of the tower to smoke a cigar and relax. It was a delightful evening, yet he did not regret having to leave Villa Montauto. Instead he was "impatient" to go, for "taking no root, I soon weary of any soil that I may be temporarily deposited in. The same impatience I sometimes feel, or conceive of, as regards this earthly life; since it is to come to an end, I do not try to be contented, but weary of it while it lasts" (VI, 158–59, MA 590).

When the Hawthornes said good-by to the Powers family in Florence, Nathaniel wrote that it was unlikely he would see them in the

United States, and he questioned whether they were wise in spending so many years abroad "in exile":

> In such a case, we are always deferring the reality of life till a future moment, and, by and by, we have deferred it till there are no future moments, or, if we do go back, we find that life has shifted whatever of reality it had to the country where we deemed ourselves only living temporarily; and so, between two stools, we come to the ground, and make ourselves a part of one or the other country only by laying our bones in its soil. (VI, 160, MA590)

So, although he had been away from America only five years, Hawthorne had already recognized what was likely to be his own fate.

On the way from Florence to Siena on October 1, the Hawthornes had to change trains at Empoli, and in the process Hawthorne's leather bag was mislaid. The next day he was delighted to retrieve the important possession, for it contained his journal and the manuscript book in which he had outlined his romance. As he thought about the annoyances and responsibilities of baggage, he jotted down a most characteristic remark: There was one comfort in knowing that "in the last, long journey we shall ever take; — we can carry no luggage along with us. There will be no luggage car, nor carpet-bags under the seats" (VI, 163, MA590).[42]

Aside from this near disaster, the visit to Siena was uneventful. The family saw all the noteworthy sights, but the town was so small that a tourist could soon exhaust its possibilities. They also spent whole days at Villa Belvedere, the house outside town rented by the Storys for the summer. Had the villa been located in England, Hawthorne might have been tempted to buy the place and stay there for the rest of his life, but Siena did not have enough to offer, especially to a family with children; "it would be terrible without an independent life in one's own mind" (VI, 170, MA590).

Before the end of two weeks, the family set out again, this time with Rome as their destination and with a very good *vetturino* to look after them. Their route south was different from that of the earlier journey north and was rather uninteresting to Hawthorne. Only one incident played an important part in his later writing: At Viterbo he ordered some wine of Montefiascone, "the genuine Est wine," which he described as "of golden colour, and very delicate, somewhat resembling still champagne, but finer, and requiring a calmer pause to appreciate its subtle delight. Its good qualities, however, are so evanescent that . . . the finer flavor became almost imperceptible before we finished it"

(VI, 247, MA590). Here, then, was the "sunshine wine" of Monte Beni!

The Hawthornes' arrival in Rome was far different from their first one, "when we crept towards Rome through the wintry midnight, benumbed with cold, sick, weary, and not knowing whither to betake ourselves. Ah, that was a dismal time!" (VI, 254, MA590). This time they approached the city on a pleasant autumn day with a comfortable feeling generated by thoughts of the house ready to receive them for a stay of six months. The Thompsons had made arrangements for the rental of seven rooms at 68 Piazza Poli, a quiet little square around the corner from the Trevi fountain.[43] In comparison with the vast spaces of Villa Montauto, this house was very small, with almost tiny rooms and a steep staircase, but Hawthorne felt that it was good for them to be prepared for their return to the crowded quarters of the Wayside.

As they settled down for what was to be six months of getting to know Rome thoroughly, Hawthorne resolved not to record their daily walks in detail, for since he had already described most of the places, there was no need to repeat and risk not doing it so well as the first time. Nor did he say anything about the resumption of his children's lessons. Ada explained about the new group of pupils who joined the Hawthorne children: Cora Thompson, a girl of Una's age, "very bright"; Eddy Thompson, Julian's age and "his bosom friend"; Herbert Thompson, barely ten, also "bright"; Lily Motley, oldest daughter of John Lothrop Motley, the historian; and Edith Story, who was given a special lesson at the Storys' apartment after the regular school hours of ten to three.[44]

For a very short time all went well, but soon the unfavorable effects of the Roman climate became apparent. First, Nathaniel caught a cold. In spite of his lack of energy he went for a walk, and as he sat down to rest, he meditated on the "Roman atmosphere": "All my pleasure at getting back—all my home-feeling—has already evaporated, and what now impresses me, as before, is the languor of Rome—its nastiness—its weary pavements—its little life pressed down by a weight of death" (VI, 264, MA590).

One Sunday a short time later, Una and Ada spent all day sketching at the Palace of the Caesars. Dismal, rainy weather followed, and Una seemed to have caught a cold. After a week, during which she was delirious part of the time, the doctor diagnosed her illness as Roman fever, or malaria. From November 2, when her father said she had her first attack, until the following spring, life was dreary for the whole family. The weather, Nathaniel wrote, was like an English November, except that there were no fogs, only "ugly, hopeless clouds, chill, shivery winds, drizzle, and now and then pouring rain." He would have welcomed an English coal fire to compensate for the "miserableness of the outside atmosphere," but that was impossible (VI, 266, MA590). Even his walks in the beautiful Borghese gardens did not save him from the miseries of the weather and from worry over Una's recurring attacks of fever. The notebooks stop suddenly in November and resume briefly at the end of February, then stop again when the real crisis for Una came early in April.

During this period Ada's letters provide what little information we have, for Nathaniel and Sophia wrote neither letters nor journals during the time of greatest stress. Ada's letters, as might be expected, talk about little except the family illnesses. Roman fever is a recurring disease, and Una's attacks returned for a week at a time about the middle of each month. She was seldom able to do any studying, but Ada continued class work with the rest of the children, except when she herself was ill with gastric fever. Ada worried about Una, especially because she probably felt some responsibility for having taken the girl on the sketching expedition that brought on the fever.

There was very little social life for the family in the winter months, for Sophia was too busy caring for Una, while Ada divided her time between teaching during the days and taking German lessons in the evenings, and Nathaniel read, wrote on his romance, and, when possible, took his daily walks. The Italian notebooks give no details about the book that Hawthorne was working on during this winter. However, his pocket diary for 1859 reveals that in spite of concern about the family, he had been writing steadily until almost the end of January. There was one day when he seemed unable to continue his "scribbling," as he called it, but at last on January 30 he finished the rough draft and put it aside, intending to rewrite it when he reached the Wayside.[45]

The work he had completed must have demanded a tremendous amount of self-discipline, but it had its advantages: Shutting himself up to write every morning was one escape from worry about Una. It was also a way to avoid the almost daily callers. They included friends who had moved to Rome for the winter, such as Charlotte Cushman, Annette Bracken, Robert Browning, and the Motleys, and two temporary visitors, Elizabeth Hoar from Concord, and the artist Christopher Cranch.[46]

By early spring almost everyone in the family except Una had been ill and recovered. First, Sophia and Rose had gastric fever. Then Ada spent more than two weeks in bed, probably with the same illness. Sophia not only tended her the whole time, but also wrote to her family to reassure them when Ada ceased to write her usual long letters. Dr. Franco, their English-speaking physician, made almost daily calls. Finally, early in February, Nathaniel suffered from gastric fever and for the first time since childhood had to lie in bed when the doctor came (P.D. [N.H.], Feb. 10, 1859). He stayed in bed for several days, and it was a week before he began to feel like himself again. No wonder Ada concluded later in the month that Rome was an unfavorable place to live as far as health was concerned. But she added a cheerful note: They had only about eight weeks left there. This was true according to their original plan, which was to leave the city in mid-April and travel for a number of weeks before returning to Paris. Then Ada would depart from Le Havre in June,[47] and the Hawthornes would stop off in England before leaving for home from Liverpool. But matters did not work out that way.

When Carnival time came again, Hawthorne's old friend ex-President Pierce and his wife arrived in Rome for an extended visit. The only aspect of the Carnival that made Nathaniel feel more enthusiastic than last year was that Una had recovered sufficiently to watch from the Motleys' balcony and to greet Pierce at the apartment when he first arrived to call on the Hawthornes. But the recovery was, as before, only temporary. It was fortunate that Pierce was in Rome to be of support to Hawthorne when they were all in the period of greatest despair over Una.

Pierce seems to have visited the family almost daily until he and his wife left Rome on April 19. Hawthorne was saddened to observe how much his friend had aged. There was rumor, Pierce said, of his being brought up again in 1860 as a presidential candidate, but he was not interested, and Hawthorne felt that such a nomination was unlikely. However, in spite of all the criticisms that Hawthorne had heard of the previous administration, he had not lost his faith in Pierce's ability and would "be glad to have it fully recognized" (VI, 289, MA590).

There were no journal entries during the darkest days of late March and April, but the pocket diary records how often Pierce called at the house. Sophia kept no journal either, only her pocket diary, and the pages were left blank between April 11 and 30. Later she wrote to her sister Elizabeth that Pierce had called three times a day and that she really owed to him her husband's life.[48] When the crisis came for Una, Dr. Franco told the Hawthornes that she had "quick consumption" and that she might not live beyond the first week in April. Nathaniel's and Sophia's reactions to Dr. Franco's diagnosis were almost identical. On April 5 Sophia wrote, "He has stopped my heart from beating by his revelations. He says she has florid phthisis—which is a rapid consumption, sometimes lasting only twenty-four hours—and all is over! GOD help us now!" Three days later Nathaniel wrote that the doctor seemed "to have very little hope. God help us!"[49] At that time none of the Hawthornes expected to take Una with them when they left Rome, but on the morning of April 9 the crisis had passed. It was to be a long, slow process of recuperation, a period when the family wearied of Rome, but were unable to leave.

The Hawthornes had hoped to accompany Pierce and his wife to Venice and then Trieste, but as soon as Una seemed likely to recover, they regretfully saw the Pierces depart. Nathaniel was especially grateful for what his friend had done:

> Never having had any trouble, before, that pierced into my very vitals, I did not know what comfort there might be in the nearby sympathy of a friend; but Pierce has undergone so great a sorrow of his own, and has so large and kindly a heart, and is so tender and strong, that he really did me good, and I shall always love him the better for the recollection of these dark days. Thank God, the thing we dreaded did not come to pass. (VI, 308, MA590)[50]

After Pierce left, Hawthorne wrote that he had found his old friend "inwardly unchanged." Then once more he prophesied the future in a way that proved later to be absolutely correct: "We have passed all the turning-off places, and may hope to go on together, still the same dear friends, as long as we live" (VI, 310, MA590).

Though Pierce had been the most faithful friend during the worst period of Una's illness, he was not the only caller to show concern. In fact, so many people came that Ada spent much of her time welcoming them and accepting the delicacies or the flowers that they brought; for Sophia, who watched over Una at night, had to snatch a few hours of rest during the day. Even Mrs. Browning came, though she very seldom went out and could scarcely descend the stairs safely.[51] Mrs. Thompson arrived one evening and stayed so that Sophia could have her first night's sleep in five or six weeks.

Once Una showed signs of improvement, the Hawthornes regained to some extent an interest in both sightseeing and socializing, but their experience of recent months had spoiled Rome for them.[52] When, in late May, Nathaniel took his last walk to the Pincian hill, he looked at everything "as if for the last time." Later he wrote that though he had been miserable in the Eternal City, he did not hate it; he might even have some love for it. "But (life being too short for such questionable and troublesome enjoyments) I desire never to set eyes on it again" (VII, 6, MA591). Ada likewise was glad to escape from Rome, "where it seemed as if some wicked spell were working, from which we could never set ourselves free. We all feel a wonderful exhilaration—all but Mrs. Hawthorne, who loves Rome better than the rest of us."[53]

From May 25, the day of their departure, to the last scattered items written in England, the final notebook shows Nathaniel's increasing reluctance to "journalize." He gave the briefest accounts of their travels north to Marseilles, Avignon, Geneva, Villeneuve, Lausanne, and Paris, stopping to write details chiefly when they visited the Castle of Chillon. At Geneva he attempted to analyze why his journal suffered: He had no energy, no curiosity, no "heart to enjoy" nor "intellect to profit" by all the things that had originally tempted him to travel abroad. "It may be disease; it may be age; it may be the effect of the lassitudinous Roman atmosphere; but such is the fact" (VII, 38, MA591).

Since Hawthorne himself never knew when, how, or why his gradual decline began, we cannot expect to answer the question either. But it is obvious that in Italy (aside from feeling the effects of Una's illness) he began to age, undoubtedly as a result of all his illnesses. In his notebooks and pocket diaries he seemed reluctant to acknowledge occasions when he had a cold or was generally unwell. Ada Shepard's letters reveal much more. As early as April, 1858 (when Hawthorne seemed to have recovered somewhat from his persistent cold), Ada wrote, "Mr. Hawthorne has been quite ill lately. Rome does not seem to agree with the family generally. I hope the air of Florence will prove more congenial." But Hawthorne was no better in Florence. Ada's letters record days when his illness was serious enough to alarm Sophia. Ada was genuinely puzzled by the state of Hawthorne's health: "It seems strange that, when he never was ill before in his life, he should suffer so much from colds, etc. in Italy."[54]

When the Hawthornes reached Paris on their way north from Italy, Nathaniel reflected on how much his appearance must have changed during the eighteen-month absence from England. However, in a letter to Bennoch summing up his dreary state he omitted mention of illness and wrote of other causes: "You will find me travel-worn, shabby . . . gray, wrinkled with time and trouble, and nowise improved except by a moustache, which has been the natural growth of Italy. Mrs. Hawthorne says it makes me look like a bandit."[55] Actually, it made him look older, as the photographs taken in London in 1860 indicate.

The letter to Bennoch was written to ask him to recommend a

different lodging house from the one on Great Russell Street where they had been in the fall of 1857.[56] It seemed possible that the Hawthornes' stay in London might be protracted, for though Nathaniel had sent a note from Switzerland to Henry Wilding in Liverpool asking for passage to Boston in mid-July or August 1, no reply reached the family until after they had arrived in London.[57]

They left Switzerland on Thursday, June 16, spent the long weekend in Paris, and departed on Tuesday for Le Havre, where Ada was to meet the Thompsons, who were also going home to the United States. After she boarded the *Vanderbilt* that night, the Hawthornes stayed at Wheeler's Hotel near the Quay Notre Dame, for the next day they expected to take a steamer to Southampton. The only person to give an account of Ada's parting from the family seems to have been Julian, as he recorded it years later:

> We were sorry to say good-bye to her; she had been a faithful and valuable element in our household, and she had become a dear friend and comrade. . . . She, too, was sorry for the parting. She once had said to me: "I think your father is the wisest man I ever knew; he does not seem ever to say much, but what he does say is always the truest and best thing that could be said."[58]

Since the *Alliance* did not sail for England until Wednesday midnight, the Hawthornes spent the day exploring Le Havre and at dusk went on board. They planned, upon reaching England, to stay for a week or two in London and then sail from Liverpool in July. Their return would be, Nathaniel estimated, six years from the date when they had first landed in England. His last journal entry from the Continent forecast a dubious future: They would go immediately from Boston to Concord, "there to enjoy (if enjoyment it prove) a little rest, and sense that we are at home" (VII, 62, MA591). This time none of his prophecy came true.

‡ 8 ‡

England Again:
Yorkshire, Leamington, and Bath
1859–1860

WHEN HAWTHORNE WROTE his expression of uncertainty about the return to Concord, he completed what he regarded as his record of travel on the Continent.[1] He still kept his pocket diary, in some ways equally revealing of himself and the family, in which he continued the story of the year 1859, but he ceased what he called "journalizing." After December of 1859 there is not even a diary to tell us what happened. These facts may help to explain why so little biographical material has been written about his experiences during this period. Only the letters complete the English experience, for Hawthorne's major efforts had gone to the writing of *The Marble Faun,* and by the end of that work he was tired out.

On Thursday, June 23, when the Hawthornes arrived in Southampton from Le Havre, they left their baggage at Goodridge's Hotel and spent the day sightseeing. Early Friday morning they took the train to London, where Nathaniel and Julian went first to Wood Street in order to get Francis Bennoch's recommendation on a lodging house. Nathaniel had had so few letters from him that he was still concerned that Bennoch would never recover from the effects of the bankruptcy. But he was pleased to find his old friend "well and cheerful." Bennoch directed the family to a very convenient boardinghouse, Mrs. Coxon's, at 6 Golden Square, off Regent and Warwick Streets near Piccadilly, a location that would put them within walking distance of many of the places in London that they wanted to revisit.[2] So began three weeks of relaxation and attempts to recover from the strain of Una's illness.

When Henry Wilding wrote from Liverpool that no staterooms were available for a July crossing, Nathaniel requested reservations to Boston for August 13 (P.D. [N.H.], June 30). What he planned to do in the interval he did not say, but for the time being he was making the most of what he thought would be his last visit to England. He had not, however, counted on an event that was to change his plans entirely:

James T. Fields and his second wife, Annie, arrived in England to begin a long European tour. Fields was too ambitious a man to pass up business opportunities even on a pleasure trip, and he immediately set to work arranging a contract for Hawthorne with a British publisher. By July 5 he had persuaded Smith and Elder to pay £600 "for the new Romance." It did not require much effort to persuade Hawthorne to stay in England long enough to rewrite the book and obtain a British copyright.[3]

At first Nathaniel thought that he could do the necessary revision by the autumn of the year, so that they could sail to the United States before winter set in. However, he must have realized from previous experience that writing and sightseeing did not mix, and that he, therefore, could not do any real work in London. Neither could he revise as rapidly as he had hoped. It turned out that they would have to spend the winter in England.

Before he could settle down to work, Hawthorne evidently was determined to enjoy himself, free from the pressures of a publication deadline. The pocket diary for the first week in London recorded days full of activities: visits to Westminster Abbey, the National Gallery, the Thames Tunnel, the British Museum, the Vernon Gallery, and St. Paul's; numerous strolls in St. James's Park; and a visit to the Bennochs at their home in Blackheath.[4]

On Friday, July 1, leaving his family at Mrs. Coxon's, Hawthorne set off on a weekend excursion with Bennoch and Fields. The itinerary included sightseeing at the castle and priory of Lewes; a dinner in Brighton with Sir Francis Moon, London's famous printmaker, at which Nathaniel made a speech; visits to Arundel Castle, the town and cathedral of Chichester, Portsmouth harbor and docks; then a trip to Farnborough, where Captain Shaw took them to Aldershot Camp for a visit from Saturday night until Monday. Before leaving in the early afternoon they watched an inspection of the troops by the Duke of Cambridge. As soon as Bennoch and Hawthorne arrived back in London (Fields seems to have left the group at Brighton), Nathaniel and Sophia went off to dinner at the home of the *Athenaeum* critic, Henry Chorley, at 13 Eaton-place West.[5]

During Nathaniel's absence Sophia had complained in her pocket diary of a "new kind of headache." After the dinner at Chorley's she went to bed for a day. Nathaniel wrote in his diary on July 6 that she "had had an influenza, but is better." Accumulated weariness plus the heat may have been responsible for her illness. Whereas Nathaniel noted each day that it was "warm," Sophia commented on the weather of July 10: "Red hot and brassy. I was too tired." As a result, pages of her diary for the next three days are blank.

In spite of the heat, Nathaniel was very busy. Henry Bright had arrived in London; so had Franklin Pierce. Between these two men and Bennoch, Hawthorne had all the activities he could keep up with: lunch with William Jerdan and others at Bennoch's company; visits to Westminster Abbey and Hall, Old Bailey, and the House of Commons; dinner at the Wellington and a play at the New Adelphi Theater; a trip to Richmond with Bright for dinner at the Star and Garter (Sophia and the girls went along, while Julian visited the Bennochs in Blackheath); dinner at the Oxford and Cambridge Club with Bright; a call on Mrs. Heywood at her home on Connaught Place; a day of sightseeing with Pierce; and a number of luncheons with Bennoch. One day while the rest of the family went to the Crystal Palace with the Pierces, Hawthorne and Bright had the day to themselves before dining with Barry Cornwall. There they met Leigh Hunt, A. W. Kinglake, Charles Sumner, Fields, and others, but unfortunately Hawthorne left no comments (P.D. [N.H.], July 12).

July 13, an "awfully hot" Wednesday was the Hawthornes' last full day in London. Nathaniel spent the morning at the British Museum, the afternoon walking with Julian and calling on Chorley (who was not in) and the evening with Henry Bright at the Workingman's College, where they met Tom Hughes, author of *Tom Brown's School Days*. On Thursday, Pierce called to say good-by before the Hawthornes took the train to Yorkshire to hunt for a place to spend the rest of the summer.

In their diaries neither Nathaniel nor Sophia gave any reason for the move, but Sophia's letter to Elizabeth Peabody from the Talbot Hotel in Malton, Yorkshire, explained why they had left London: Nathaniel had decided to finish his book in England because of the copyright, and they hoped the work could be done by October, because, if not, they could not start for the United States in the November fogs. Then she went on to say that "Una was fading in London, and so we have brought her here on our way to *Whitby,* a seashore old town, hard by the Holy Isle—Here Mr. Hawthorne will bring himself to finish his book—away from the world." In Malton they were to be joined by Fanny Wrigley, who had been living there with her family since her father's death in December of 1857. Sophia was relieved by thoughts of Fanny's help: "She will again become general of my army and aide de camp extraordinary, and I am going to sit down and rest. This I can do with her in the house."[6]

Whether or not Fanny had recommended Whitby as a result of her familiarity with towns in Yorkshire, the Hawthornes found it an impossible place; it was a fashionable resort and therefore too crowded and expensive. Sophia, Fanny, and Julian spent the afternoon of July 15 hunting for a lodging house. When after no success they returned to the railroad station at sundown, the family went to the Angel Hotel "a comfortable house of the commercial class" (P.D. [N.H.], July 15).[7]

Thereafter for a week while they stayed at the Angel, some of the group (usually the women) searched daily in or around Whitby for a place to live. Most of the time Nathaniel and Julian walked on the cliffs and the sands or visited the ruins of the abbey. Here it was that Hawthorne obtained the name for one of the four main characters of his Italian romance: Hilda, from St. Hilda, the seventh-century abbess. Hawthorne borrowed more than the name, for he spent some time investigating the history of the place and in the process acquired knowledge of the legendary material.[8]

He seems to have made use of some elements of St. Hilda's reportedly gentle personality in his portrait of Hilda in *The Marble Faun,* and he must also have heard or read the local tradition that at a certain time of the year, when the sun shone through the abbey ruins, it revealed the figure of a woman dressed in a shroud standing at one of the high windows. This was said to be St. Hilda in her "glorified state." A further popular belief was that as the sea birds flew over the ruins, they "dropped their wings" as a sign of respect for the abbess.[9] At the abbey ruins there was no tower; the ruins on the cliff above the harbor are actually much more impressive than Hilda's tower in the narrow, crowded Via dei Portoghese, and sea gulls are less romantic than Roman doves. Nevertheless, Hawthorne absorbed some of the traditions associated with the abbess's dim legendary past and transformed them to fit his Italian romance.

Apparently he was not interested in either the history or the atmosphere of this fishing town itself, and Whitby weather did not prove congenial to any member of the family. Nathaniel's diary entries for the week note "a rainy morning," "sunshine and mist," "dull weather," and a most descriptive phrase for July 20: "a misty moisty morning." He had nothing to say about the activities going on in Whitby, but he could scarcely fail to observe the fishing boats in the harbor and the tourists walking on the sands or parading along the cliff on what has since become West Cliff Drive. The only rambling he did around the streets of the town was in search of Simpson and Chapman, bankers of Grape Lane. Finally he located what was then known as Whitby Old

Bank in a very narrow little street near the bottom of the "church stairs," 199 steps leading up to the ruins of the abbey.[10]

Meanwhile, unknown to Hawthorne until later, Mrs. Gaskell was beginning work on a novel with Whitby as the setting (*Sylvia's Lovers*) and was planning to visit the town in order to obtain accurate information on life there in the eighteenth century. Henry Bright was eager to bring about a meeting between the two novelists, but his plan never worked out, for Mrs. Gaskell postponed her visit until fall and the Hawthornes departed from Whitby after one week. Once again, though she did not mention the fact, Sophia must have been disappointed in her failure to meet Mrs. Gaskell.[11]

In her diary entry for July 21, Sophia wrote, "We suddenly decided tonight to go to Redcar tomorrow—a watering place with a fine beach, old fashioned and quiet, thirty miles more north—at the mouth of the Tees."[12] The next morning was foggy and misty when they set off by omnibus to Guisborough and thence by train to Redcar. Sophia and Fanny went out to find lodgings, this time with greater success. On that Friday a tenant was moving out of Mrs. King's at 120 High Street, and the Hawthornes could move into the house on Saturday. They spent the interval at the Clarendon Hotel in the center of town, near the railroad station.

The next day at two o'clock, according to Nathaniel, they took possession of their lodgings, which seemed "comfortable" (P.D. [N.H.], July 23). Sophia was more specific in her letter to Elizabeth Peabody:

We live in a nutshell, divided into six apartments. The drawing room has a bow window and commands the sea. Mr. Hawthorne has a study commanding the High Street. Una has a nest, and Julian another,—I have a chamber of rather larger dimensions, and Fanny and Rose one not quite so large as mine. The landlady lends us her parlor to dine, sup, and breakfast in. It was the only house with six rooms to be had in Redcar on the day of our arrival; so we had no choice. All the watering places in England overflow at the season. We thought this would be out of the way and solitary, but we were much mistaken. It is, however, not quite so expensive as Whitby, which is more reasonable than Scarborough.[13]

If the Hawthornes had not reached the Yorkshire coast during the tourist season, they might have found living places easier to obtain and less expensive. They learned within two months that as soon as autumn set in, the sands became as deserted as they had been at Southport. The "gray German Ocean," Hawthorne wrote, tumbled within twenty yards of their house, their "resting place" for the time being. It was, he said,

Hawthorne House at 120 High Street, Redcar, Yorkshire

as bleak and dreary a strip of sand as we could have stumbled upon, had we sought the world over. . . . But the children like it, and the roses already blow in all their cheeks. It suits my purposes likewise; and I mean to write all the mornings, and moisten myself with the sea-spray (not to mention other liquids) in the afternoons and evenings. I have bought half a ream of letter-paper, and shall begin business in earnest tomorrow.[14]

Actually it took him two days—Sunday and Monday—to finish looking over the rough draft and meditate on the changes he needed to make. On Tuesday, July 26, he "began the Romance in good earnest," and thereafter as long as they were in Redcar he wrote steadily every day, including Sundays, for about six hours. The one exception he noted was a day when he and Julian made a trip to the bank in Middlesborough. The family had no visitors and no social life. They received numerous letters, and Sophia wrote some replies, but Nathaniel almost none. This was the kind of monotonous "exterior" life that Nathaniel had said was necessary to him if he was to lead an imaginative "inner" life.[15]

It was also the kind of outdoor life that delighted Julian especially. Here he could spend hours hunting shells on the wide beach and bathing in that gray ocean. Nathaniel's pocket diary recorded almost daily walks on the sands with Julian after the writing stint was finished for the day. Julian's memories of those hours remained vivid over the years:

He walked far along the sands, with his boy dogging his steps and stopping for shells and crabs; and at a certain point of the beach, where the waves ran over a bar and formed a lake a few feet in depth, he would set himself on a tussock of sand-grass, and I would undress and run into the cold water and continue my swimming lessons. . . . Both my feet were finally off the bottom, and I felt the wonderful sensation of the first cousin to flying. While I floundered there my father looked off towards the gray horizon, and saw the visions of Hilda, Miriam, Kenyon, and Donatello which the world of readers was presently to behold through his eyes.[16]

As a boy Julian could not have realized what these long walks meant to his father. Away from the disagreeable aspects of the Eternal City and the family's unfortunate experiences there, Nathaniel recaptured the atmosphere of Roman scenes with such vividness that readers would be able to follow precisely in his footsteps around the city.

Redcar was the perfect colorless place in which Hawthorne's romantic imagination could function best, both during and after his actual writing hours.

In the earlier part of each day, while his father was absorbed in writing, Julian continued the diary begun at Southport, which included drawings of the shells that he had collected. With childish aplomb he included in the first part of the Redcar section a statement that would have amused or perhaps irritated his father because of its failure even to mention his mother's or his sister's health: "We came here principally for my father to finish a book which he had been composing in Italy. I believe he came in one measure on account of myself, as I am, or will hereafter be seen a great lover of the sea and the objects therein."[17]

Rose also enjoyed the outdoor life, but she preferred playing in the sand. When weather permitted, she and a little girl named Hannah "pounded brick, secured sugary-looking sands of different tints, and heaped up minute pebbles" as products for sale in their imaginary grocery shop. If her father happened to encounter them as he was taking one of his solitary walks, he would "look askance" at Rose's "utterly useless, time-frittering amusement" as if "Baby" was a bit too old to be building castles in the sand. It was at times like this that her father seemed a distant idol, an adult merely tolerant of child's play, not the companion of Rock Park days.[18]

Una was not so easy to please as her sister. In spite of some walks, a number of days of horseback riding, and enough outdoor life to help restore her health, she found little to do except read books from a circulating library. There were no amusements beyond a visiting circus and one or two expeditions to nearby places such as Wilton Castle. The quiet life might have appealed to her if she had not been disappointed by her father's postponement of their return to the United States: "I begin to think we shall never go now. I do long to be settled once more, for I am heartily tired of tossing about hither and thither for so long."[19] But with characteristic obedience and good grace, she said nothing to her family and accepted the need for her father's work to be completed and her mother to have a year's rest.

Sophia's pocket diary for 1859 recorded in detail the weariness that resulted from months of caring for Una in Rome. The entries at Redcar ranged from "I lay down" or "too tired" (July 27), to "very ill" (September 2), "unable to go out" (September 7 and 8), and "not very well" (September 30). When Fanny was ill in bed for two days on August 12 and 13, Sophia must have recovered enough to look after the family's needs. Most of the time she rested, read, and occasionally composed letters. In a long letter to Henry Bright she wrote that fatigue accumulated from the anxiety of the last months in Rome prevented her from "showing any signs of life beyond breathing." Her complete lassitude was given as the explanation for her failure to answer his letter of July 29 until September.[20]

It was impossible, she went on to say, for her husband to do more than write the one letter that Bright had asked him to send to Milnes as an aid to him in giving a speech in Parliament on the mistreatment of sailors. This Nathaniel had done immediately, but social letters were out of the question since he was spending "six hours a day" on his romance:

> When he leaves his study after such a session, the thought of a pen or a sheet of paper makes him desperate, he is so very tired. This imaginative composition, going as he does beyond the lowest deep, wearies and also completely absorbs him. He walks on the sands and leans against the everlasting sea for rest all the afternoon and in the short intervals of the day and evening, he reads the stupidest book he can find upon which he may intellectually slumber and yawn. . . . Were it not for this complete occupation and abstraction of Mr. Hawthorne and my own inability for social intercourse, we should have most joyfully responded to your half thought of coming to Yorkshire.[21]

This letter tells us more than any other piece of writing from the Redcar period about Nathaniel's work habits and Sophia's sympathies. She did not forget that Henry Bright would also be interested in the children's activities, but mention of them was postponed until almost the conclusion of her twelve-page letter. At the end she thanked him for sending the newspaper with the account of her brother-in-law's death, which the family had already heard about from Russell Sturgis in London and from both Elizabeth Peabody and Mary Mann.

The distressing news of Horace Mann's death came at the end of the first month of rest for Sophia, days of doing nothing but reading and occasionally strolling on the long, broad sands. There are almost no comments in her pocket diary on the type or quality of the books she read during their two and one-half months in Redcar. There are only brief jottings of such titles as *Oliver Twist, All the Year Round, Life of Philip II, History of the Queens of England, Romany Rye,* Sir Thomas More's *Household,* and Disraeli's *Sybil* and *Venetia*. Then suddenly on Friday, September 9, she wrote, "My husband gave me his manuscript to read." For four days the only notation is, "Reading ms." The chapters represented, according to Nathaniel, more than half the book (P.D. [N.H.], Sept. 10). Sophia made no mention of the contents or of her reaction to it until much later, after the romance had been completed.

For Hawthorne the writing process, though inexorably scheduled for a large part of each day, was slow in the beginning and uneven in its movement. On July 28 he recorded "slow and poor progress"; the next day it was "scribbled fitfully till 2, with many idle pauses, and no good result"; July 30, "tolerably well"; August 1, "with middling success"; August 4, "a little more satisfactorily than heretofore"; then on August 6, "no great progress, but more interested as I get on." Thereafter the usual daily statement was, "Wrote till 3," and on some days he returned to the study after dinner. The work went on, occasionally with times of discouragement, but without interruption until October 5, when the family left Redcar for Leamington.

While they were making preparations to move, a letter from America brought news that was no surprise to them: Ada Shepard was now Mrs. Clay Badger. She had joined her husband on the staff at Antioch College as a teacher of modern foreign languages. Elizabeth Peabody, who had gone to see her sister Mary at the time of Horace Mann's death in Yellow Springs, Ohio, either gave Ada the Hawthornes' address or possibly enclosed Ada's letter with her own. In their diaries both Sophia and Nathaniel made mention of reception of the two letters, but it was Una who answered Ada's letter (P.D. [S.H.], Oct. 2).

The reason for the Hawthornes' decision to move away from Redcar was not explained in either pocket diary, but later in the fall various letters indicated one important reason: The coastal storms would be harmful to Sophia's health. Furthermore, Nathaniel had written enough of his romance to feel that he could finish it in a few weeks, and Leamington seemed an appropriate place in which to work. It was less secluded than Redcar, closer to London so that he could go back and forth if necessary, and lively enough to please the rest of the family. They had already spent one late autumn season in Warwickshire and knew what to expect of the climate. Julian and Rose, of course, were disappointed; they preferred the seaside. Una's feelings were mixed, as her note of October 4 to "Aunt Lizzie" revealed: "Our last day in Redcar . . . and a most lovely one it is. The sea seems to reproach us for leaving it. But I am glad we are going, for I feel so homesick that I want constant change to divert my thoughts. How troublesome feelings and affections are! When one ought to forget, they are strongest."[22]

Apparently the Hawthornes had made previous arrangements for a lodging house, since they were met at the station by Mrs. Maloney, their landlady in 1857, who took them to "21 Bath Street, Mrs. Mountford" (P.D. [S.H.], Oct. 5). The house was "in an unfashionable part of town," Sophia said, but the rooms were comfortable, except that they were so close to the railroad that there was "constant thunder." This section of the town must have been less expensive also, for Sophia's letters stressed their need for economizing. They had spent more money in Rome than they had anticipated, and they could not expect income from the book until it was published. They would have to "count the sixpences." Sophia wrote that they would "never be able not to do this . . . it is so expensive to live in England, and everywhere else except alone in Florence."[23]

In addition to the cost of living, Sophia was concerned about their need to save for the eventual enlarging of the Wayside and for sending Julian to college. For the last part of their stay in England, study at home under parental supervision was the least expensive kind of education for the children. Julian was studying Latin under his father and Greek with his mother. "He seems to have learned nothing of Miss S.," Sophia wrote to her sister Elizabeth, "but now he understands what he is about." Rose was learning to read, write, draw, and cipher as she had not done before. "She hated to read with Miss S." Una was studying Latin, French, Italian, and history.[24]

To Mary Mann, who was still interested in the staff members at Antioch, Sophia wrote the same criticisms of Ada Shepard's work that she had to her sister Elizabeth. Though this letter was not written until the next spring, it is evident that Sophia had not forgiven Ada for her failures. Ada was "no more qualified to be professor of French than Rosebud." Mary could have no idea of the limitations of Ada's intellect, but the Hawthornes knew from their two years of experience. She had taught the Hawthorne children really very little and even less in the second year when she took on the Thompson children. In her letter to Mary, Sophia was quite severe in all her criticisms, especially about the effects of Ada's teaching on the three children individually. True, Ada had shown her devotion in times of illness, but she had spent too much time writing letters to Clay, even during school hours. Ada had begun "well but ended ill."[25]

If Julian was studying Latin with his father, it must have been in the afternoon or the evening after the daily period of writing, for Nathaniel had not yet completed his work. He wrote the preface to his book on October 14 and sent the first part of his manuscript to Smith and Elder on October 17, but there were interruptions in his schedule before he finished the last eighty pages. On one day Hawthorne did not write at all because their Boston friend, George Hillard, stopped off for an hour's visit between trains (P.D. [N.H.], Oct. 20). Nathaniel met him at the station and took him to the house during that interval. The next afternoon Henry Bright came and stayed for the evening. Once again, on Saturday, October 22, Nathaniel "did not write"; he and Henry Bright took the train to Rugby, visited the school, saw Bilton Hall (the residence of Addison), watched a football game, and dined at the Royal George Hotel with Henry's cousin, Charley Bright, a student in his last year at Rugby. The two friends returned to Leamington for the night, and Bright evidently spent Sunday with the family, for it was Monday before Nathaniel went back to his writing and his afternoon walks with Julian. A few days before Hillard's visit, Bennoch had spent an evening with the Hawthornes, but he came after the daily writing period.

At last on Tuesday, November 8, Hawthorne recorded the event of most importance to him: "Wrote till 5 minutes of 12, and finished the last page of my Romance. 508 manuscript pages." The following day he sent off a letter and the second package of manuscript to Smith and Elder. The work had taken longer than he had anticipated, for, as he wrote to Fields, there was much more to do on the book than he had realized. He admitted also that the writing had worn him down a little, but the "bracing air of the German Ocean" had helped counteract any bad effects.[26]

Now that the gloomy days of November had begun, the climate of Leamington was not so pleasant as that of Redcar; but then winter in England was, as the Hawthornes well knew, not an agreeable time. The hardest work for Nathaniel had ended. He had only the matter of a title and the proofreading to attend to, and he had no need to travel out of town in bad weather. "We find nothing to complain of in the climate of Leamington. To be sure, we cannot always see our hands before us for fog; — but I like fog, and do not care about seeing my hand before me." It was always summer, he wrote, "by a bright coal fire," something he had greatly missed in Italy. The charm of Leamington, however, consisted in the walks and drives to interesting places in Warwickshire. He decided that if they later found such excursions to be impossible, they might consider moving to Bath or Devonshire after Christmas. For the time being he did not need to huddle in front of the fireplace as he had done in Rome.[27]

Una reassured the relatives at home about her father's health when she wrote that though he had been "unwell a great deal of the time" in Rome, as soon as they came to England he began to "regain his usual health and strength, and now he is perfectly well." She added that she liked Leamington, though she did not explain why.[28] It was not because of the climate, but because there was more to do here than on the bleak sands of Yorkshire. There were lectures to attend and programs of all sorts for tourists and residents alike. And Julian was happy to be taking weekly lessons from Major Johnstone in the use of the broadsword.

At this time Sophia said little about her own health. Between tutoring the children and reading her husband's manuscript (which she did before he sent it off to the publishers), she was well occupied. To Elizabeth she expressed no opinion of the book, for, she wrote, "You will soon see it now," and her sister could judge for herself. She continued that as usual her husband thought the book "good for nothing, and based upon a very foolish idea which nobody will like or accept. . . . I am used to such opinions. He has regularly despised each one of his books immediately upon finishing it."[29]

A major problem to Hawthorne was finding an appropriate title. He sent a number of suggestions to Smith and Elder. When they rejected all of them and chose *Transformation* (which he himself had once suggested and forgotten about), he responded by asking for a different title for the American edition. The proofreading was monotonous, but an easy task compared with the rigors of composition, which Hawthorne had always found an exhausting process. At first the proofs came through rather quickly, and he returned them at once. Then, as the mailing slowed, he concluded that since it was too late for the work to be finished in time for holiday sales, Smith and Elder was postponing publication until after the first of the year.[30] He did not object, but he wished that he had at least part of the money that would be due him. As he often did, he was forced to write to Ticknor for money to be deposited with Barings, his London bankers.[31]

Hawthorne would gladly have discussed some of his problems, such as titling his book, with Fields; but James and Annie, after a short stay in England and a tour of Germany and Switzerland, had gone to Paris until the end of the Christmas season. They would then proceed to Italy. Nathaniel's pocket diary for November 28 recorded an unusual entry, a letter from Fields in Paris to "my wife," and then: "My wife and I answered Fields' note."

The Hawthornes' responses contained a definite negative reaction to a suggestion by Fields that Sophia become a contributor to the *Atlantic Monthly,* recently purchased by Ticknor and Fields. Sophia's letter was the most positive statement she could have written: "I assure you most earnestly that nothing less urgent and terrible than the immediate danger of starvation for my husband and children would induce me to put myself into a magazine or a pair of book covers. You forget that Mr. Hawthorne is the Bellelettre portion of my being, and besides that I have a repugnance to female authoresses in general. I have far more distaste to myself as a female authoress in particular."[32] Then she showed her knowledge of Fields's persuasive ways by saying that though he was "eloquent, fascinating and of infinite good humor," she would oppose him with "as steady and immovable pertinacity as the biggest created rock would resist the raging sea or the sweet lapsing tides. You have no idea how inexorable I am. Neither the honied words of Nestor, nor the artful insinuations of Ulysses, in short no one and nothing would prevail, except the one prospective horror afore-mentioned. But I wish all prosperity to the Atlantic Monthly, and I hope Mr. Hawthorne will help you."[33]

Evidently Nathaniel read his wife's note before he commented in a similar, milder tone, adding praise for her ability to write travel sketches: "Perhaps I may yet starve her into compliance. I have never read anything so good as some of her narrative and descriptive epistles to her friends; but I doubt whether she would find sufficient inspiration in writing directly for the public."[34]

His letter to Bennoch, written on the following day with humorous intent, came closer to the truth of Hawthorne's attitude toward female writers in general and his wife in particular: "I don't know whether I can tolerate a literary rival at bed and board; there would probably be a new chapter in the 'Quarrels of Authors.' However, I make myself at ease on that score, as she positively refuses to be famous, and contents herself with being the best wife and mother in the world."[35] From such excerpts the reader may judge for himself which one of the partners in this Victorian marriage was more responsible for the refusal. Fields did not repeat his request; thus the matter ended until years later.

At the end of this letter to Bennoch, Hawthorne wrote that they expected him for a visit within ten days. But apparently Bennoch could not leave his work. Hawthorne wrote again on December 22 to say how much they were disappointed that his visit "did not come off' and to send Christmas wishes to both Bennoch and his wife.[36] Two days later Bennoch sent a barrel of oysters, which the family thoroughly enjoyed on Christmas Eve, though they would rather have seen the giver in person. That same evening, a very mild one for December, they had a "symposium of Christmas boxes" (P.D. [S.H.], Dec. 24).

Sunday, Christmas Day, was "rainy, dark, chilly." Fanny was ill in bed with influenza and did not come downstairs until the twenty-seventh. The ladies in the family dressed up for the holiday dinner at four o'clock: Rose in white muslin, Una in blue challis, Sophia in "starred brocade" (P.D. [S.H.], Dec. 25). After dinner and Nathaniel's usual walk with Julian, they all listened to a story by Julian based on the theme of "Sing a Song of Sixpence" (P.D. [N.H.], Dec. 25).

The week that followed was a succession of wet days, with few diary entries. In spite of the frequent rains, Nathaniel and Julian took their daily walks. Sophia's diary had blank pages for three days. Then came the night of December 31. Nathaniel's last diary entry was: "I went to bed at 11, partly on account of a cold. The rest of the family sat up till midnight to welcome in the New Year." Sophia's final notation was: "12 o'clock at midnight. The bells are ringing the NEW YEAR. We sat up and opened the door to the New Year." Thus ended all daily records of family life in England. From then on, infrequently written letters sum up the first months of 1860, which led to their departure for home.

Hawthorne wrote to Ticknor late in January that they were passing a dull winter because the weather was unsuitable for excursions; in addition, Sophia's health was not so good in the damp climate as it had been in Rome. He was certainly not exaggerating the state of Sophia's health; she had been ill since the beginning of the year. On February 27 she explained to her sister Elizabeth the reason for the lapse of almost two months between letters: She had been in bed for over six weeks and did not even dress and "creep into the drawing room" until the previous week. It was an attack of acute bronchitis, the longest illness she had experienced since her marriage. For all of those weeks she had had to be "head" of the household management because Fanny had "none at all." In addition, Fanny and all the children had been sick with a short-lived fever, probably from a "dirty and diseased house-maid [not her own servant] who went off to the hospital from here."[37]

Because Sophia was ill at the time, Nathaniel took Una with him in mid-February when he went to Coventry to dine at the house of John Bill, a ribbon manufacturer. The visit marked one of the few occasions when Hawthorne added a passage at the end of his French and Italian notebooks (VII, 65–71, MA591). Since it was not the first time he had been in Coventry, he thought there was little point in recording anything more about the town. Instead, he merely summed up a few highlights: a tour of the ribbon factory, including a climb to the roof for a view of the town; the visit to Mr. Bill's house—"unpretentious though he has an income of £3,000 plus interest in a former business"; and the dinner itself, at which there were several other guests.

The guests of most interest to Hawthorne were the Brays. Charles Bray was a philosopher and editor of the *Coventry Herald,* at whose home Emerson had once stayed while on a lecture tour of England. Charles's wife, Caroline, talked chiefly about George Eliot, "whom she had known intimately all her life," Hawthorne wrote. He was not quite accurate on this point, since Mary Ann Evans was twenty-two years old when she and her father moved into a house next door to Mr. Bray's sister, Mrs. Pears. Hawthorne was pleased to hear about the author of *Adam Bede,* a novel he greatly admired, but he made an erroneous assumption: He inferred that though she had been mistress of Mr. Lewes, they were "now married." In spite of comments suggesting that Hawthorne refused ever to meet George Eliot because of her daring action in going to live with Lewes, Hawthorne himself is said to have once remarked humorously that he would like to have met her, but that none of his lady friends were on an intimate enough basis with her to arrange a meeting. Regardless of what he had heard about her social position, he approved of her writing and was glad to hear about her from close friends of hers.

After that short excursion of only one day, he found himself once more settled at home, somewhat depressed by the weather and his inactivity. Heretofore, he said, he had had to go out daily: "Now this winter, I have chiefly moped by the fireside, and at most have ventured out for an hour or so in the day. It has been inconceivably depressing; such fog, such damp and rain, such sullen and penetrating clouds, such mud and mire; surely the bright severity of a New England winter can never be so bad as this. I have not really emerged into life through the whole season" (VII, 71, MA591).

Because of the damp climate, the Hawthornes were already planning to change to what they hoped might be a better location, that is, as soon as Sophia was able to travel. Both the Hawthornes thought the place should be somewhere closer to London. Sophia stressed that as soon as the book was published, Nathaniel should go to London by himself and enjoy the city as much as he could before they left England. The doctor had said that she herself could not risk crossing the Atlantic until June because fogs were bad at sea in the spring. But she confessed to a longing for home, "where there is no rent to pay and the garden will produce food."[38]

Two days later she sent almost the same information to Mary Mann, adding that the children, especially Julian, were also impatient to get home. Una had "variations of desire." (Sophia did not know how much Una had previously written to relatives in America about her homesickness.) Although Rose had forgotten Concord, she was looking forward to having "room to run on the lawns and in the woods, to feed chickens, and bring up a Newfoundland dog and a cat—and above all to have a garden of her own and cultivate flowers and beans."[39]

On the day that Sophia wrote to Elizabeth Peabody, Nathaniel had gone to London to sign papers for the British copyright. He stayed only one night and refused all social engagements there until later in the spring. At the moment he, too, was beginning to wish to get home, although he was sure that he would want to return to England: "I fear I have lost the capacity of living contentedly in any one place." As for living in England, he felt that all the pleasures were concentrated in London. He did not say so at the time, but it was obvious that this city was an impossible place for Sophia to stay in permanently. If he could have the same freedom in America, he told Ticknor, he would more readily live there. But the advantages of life abroad were that "You have no rights and no duties, and can live your own life without interference of any kind. I shall never again be so free as I have been in England and Italy."[40] Even though burdened with an ailing wife and three children in England, he was correct in his prophecy of having less freedom in America. Only time would tell how right he was.

On February 28, the day Hawthorne returned from London, Smith and Elder published the first edition of *Transformation* in three volumes, but since they did not send proofsheets to Ticknor and Fields until late January, the American edition of *The Marble Faun* in two volumes did not appear until March 7. However, the U.S. copyright was protected because no British copies of the book could be imported before Ticknor and Fields brought out their edition.[41]

While Hawthorne was waiting to see what kind of reception his book would meet with in England, the family celebrated Una's sixteenth birthday. It was a significant event to them all, for the previous birthday had been passed in Rome just before the crisis in her illness, and it seemed for a while that there might never be another celebration. Before he made his quick trip to London, Hawthorne had written to Bennoch reminding him of his promise to compose an ode for the occasion of the birthday. They would not insist upon an ode, but they must have some kind of verse. Bennoch complied with a six-stanza tribute "To Nathaniel Hawthorne on the Anniversary of His Daughter Una's Birthday," in which the theme was a contrast between winter and springtime, the season when the "miracle" of flowers repeats itself in new blossoms. Una was not named within the poem, but was referred to in the last two lines: "Thy Hawthorne into blossom broke, / Anticipating May." Later when the poem was included in Bennoch's published *Poems,* he inserted a paragraph footnote describing the circumstances of his friendship with Nathaniel Hawthorne.[42]

There seems to be no mention of presents, but Julian, not to be outdone by Bennoch, also gave his sister a verse, called "A Lay," in which he addressed Una as "beauteous and gay."[43]

When Hawthorne sent a thank-you note to Bennoch, he wrote that the poem had had a great success in Leamington, "and, unlike my Romance, it goes on growing better and better to the very end."[44] The remark is the first evidence that he had already recognized a source of criticism from his readers. Within a week of publication he had discovered from the reviews that some of his British readers were dissatisfied by his failure to explain events in the final chapter. After reading further criticisms, he finally agreed to write an explanatory chapter that would be inserted at the end of the third volume.[45] The Postscript, dated from Leamington, March 14, proofread on March 16, was inserted in the second British printing and thereafter also in American editions.

Still, even after the Postscript was printed, reviewers expressed an uneasy feeling that the last part of the romance was hazy. Even Hawthorne's good friend, Henry Bright, had some criticism of the plot of the romance. (His *Examiner* article was published before the Postscript was printed.) But apart from the plot, Bright wrote that the book had great power. He praised Hawthorne's style, saying that "few novelists in England, and none in America," could write as "clearly and purely." Bright added another note revealing his understanding of Hawthorne: The novelist was neither an antiquarian nor a historian; he wrote no photographic descriptions, but his own impressions. "He takes things as he finds them," Bright said, and the result was, here and there, pure poetry similar to the "outpourings of De Quincey."[46]

Previously, Bright, who was an ardent collector of autographs, had asked for some of the original manuscript, and Hawthorne had sent parts of it to him in Liverpool when the printing was finished. It was nearly the end of April before he mailed the last of the pages with the comment, "Here is the preface, which I somehow neglected to send with the former package of rubbish." Bright responded to the gift by having the manuscript pages collected into two leather-bound volumes; he then commissioned an artist to paint a title page in watercolors with hand lettering and design.[47]

The British reviews, in spite of some adverse criticisms, must have satisfied Hawthorne; in fact, he wrote to Ticknor that as far as he could tell the success of the book had been "good."[48] One of his most enthusiastic readers was John L. Motley, the historian, who, according to Hawthorne, had taken the romance exactly as its author meant it. If Motley's letter had come a few days sooner, the author would have been tempted to include it in the postscript, because Motley had expressed what Hawthorne himself "could only hint at." But Motley was another American living abroad, and to him Hawthorne could make a remark that would have made English people furious if they had read it: "These beer-sodden English beefeaters do not know how to read a Romance; neither can they praise it rightly, if ever so well disposed."[49]

While he was reading British reviews and waiting for Ticknor and Fields to send over some reviews from America, Hawthorne finally decided where his family should move from Leamington. Sophia had recovered sufficiently so that they could pack up for the last time before their sailing date. They chose Bath because it had a better climate and was still on a direct rail line to London, even though it was farther away than Leamington.

When the Hawthornes arrived at the station in Bath on March 22, the porter recommended they stay at York House. At the hotel they learned that this was not only the finest hotel in Bath, but one of the most famous in England. Sophia began to worry that it would take a year's income to pay their expenses for one day and night, but as it turned out, their bill was "more moderate than those of many inferior hotels all about England." After all her travel experiences, Sophia was still naive about luxury hotels, especially this one, in which the furnishings were rich and the servants impeccable. The family were given a sitting room "hung with crimson"; in the dining room they had the "finest cut crystal, and knives and forks with solid silver handles, and spoons too heavy to lift easily, delicate rose and gold china, and an entire service of silver dishes"; in addition, the food was simply "Apician." The Hawthornes invented a fine fiction to match their surroundings: Nathaniel and Sophia were the Duke and Duchess of Maine; Julian was Lord Waldo; Una was Lady Raymond; and Rose was Lady Rose. The attendants at meals were called "Sublime" and "Pensive"; the boy who tended to the coal fires "Soft," because he was a "noiseless apparition," always appearing at the right moment to revive a fading glow. After dinner Sophia relaxed in front of the fire in her large chamber, which was "draped with white muslin over rose color and drab damask."[50]

The next day she and Fanny, with Rose to help look for "to let" signs, toured the city in a bath chair in search of lodgings. At last they found a "modest house" at 13 Charles Street. Sophia admitted that though she was "very fond of splendor," she was much more comfortable and at home here than at the York House, "with its shaded grandeur."[51]

Nathaniel had very little to say about Bath. In a brief passage added to the French and Italian notebooks dated April 23, he explained why: "We have been here several weeks; but I have no longer any impulse to describe what I see, and cannot overcome my heavy reluctance to take up the pen. Had I seen Bath earlier in my English life, I might have spent many pages on it, for it is really a picturesque, and to people who are not weary, an interesting city" (VII, 75, MA591). He did make mention of the lack of antiquities, except for the abbey; referred briefly to Beau Nash; and said that he might describe the Pump Room at some other time, but it would be no matter if he did not. He never did, for he kept the journal primarily for his own use and any future English romance would apparently not include Bath.

Strangely enough, Sophia had little to say about the city, perhaps because it was similar to Leamington, though on a much grander scale and better known to readers of English literature. She remained concerned chiefly with her children and the family plans for the future. Since Mary Mann was now occupying the Wayside, it was to Mary that Sophia wrote what the family needs would be when they returned. Earlier in the spring she had explained that although they were bringing Fanny Wrigley with them, they would want a cook and a maid, for Fanny had too "feeble a constitution" to do that kind of work. She was accustomed to sewing, nursing, and taking care of the "business end of housekeeping." They were planning a simple way of life, and Sophia was looking forward to enjoying her "snuggery, for it is not comfortable to live in palaces except in hot weather. One can never be cosy in a palace."[52]

As soon as their passage was engaged for June 16, Sophia wrote further directions so that Mary Mann would know when to expect them and what arrangements to make. Nathaniel did not want the expense of a caretaker or any farm animals on the property. They did want a kitchen garden to supply their own table, but Mary should use her judgment on having a garden started before they arrived. Sophia summed up their needs by suggesting that the Hawthorne family had no intention of living "in style, but only with comfort and as much elegance as we have income for." This would not entail more than one or two servants.[53]

Evidently Mary Mann either recommended or hired a cook for them, for "Mrs. Kimball" was referred to in a later letter. They had no plans to hire more than the one servant until they saw how well Fanny worked out. She would not stay in America with them unless she became "strong and efficient." Then Sophia revealed her usual concern for economy: At present Fanny was not to be paid except for her passage, which would be deducted from the salary she would receive as soon as she proved herself able to work. The family relationship to Fanny became evident in a further statement of Sophia's: Fanny would not like to tend table "now that she has sat at it with us." In other words, Fanny was not really of the servant class, as Sophia brought out in her emphasis that the woman had an independent income.[54]

While Sophia was busily working out plans for the Wayside, Nathaniel was eager to make another trip to London. However, his wife again became ill and he could not leave the family until mid-May. He had agreed to go to Cambridge where Bright was to be awarded the M.A. degree on May 24. He would have gone to London early in May and perhaps stayed longer had it not been for Sophia's troubles, which began in April with a cold that sent her to bed for several weeks. In addition, Fanny was suddenly taken ill. Nathaniel wrote to Fields that Sophia was "in the hospital." Fields was back in England after months on the Continent, but he was not invited to Bath since the Hawthornes were in "no condition to make guests comfortable." Nathaniel promised to travel to London as soon as he could safely leave.[55]

During these spring weeks Sophia was somewhat defensive when she wrote about her health to Mary Mann. She explained carefully that her bronchial condition had not been caused by the whooping cough in Rock Ferry days, but by the damp climate, which had affected her from the first and was continuing to do so. She hoped the dry heat and clear cold of her native land would restore her. There were, she said, "no reserves between my husband and me about my health or upon any other subject and I would on no account conceal from him any truth." She knew his qualities from twenty years together and was certain that he understood her condition. Showing her impatience to leave, she concluded that they had only "twelve weeks more in England!"[56] Perhaps Sophia took too much for granted. Nathaniel understood her health problems, but his letters to others hint that beneath his recognition of the need for help and understanding there was a certain amount of restiveness.

After the years of dull work at the consulate and the months of exhausting writing on *The Marble Faun,* Hawthorne could at last think of England as a place where he was comparatively free of responsibility, and he looked forward to a London visit even though it was being cut short by family circumstances. His emotions had become a mixture of temporary homesickness and regret at having to leave England. The regret was a feeling that was to prove far from temporary. If he had not been forced to consider the welfare of Sophia and the children, he might have stayed in England indefinitely. But Hawthorne was a man ill-accustomed either to shirking responsibilities or to doing nothing. Wherever he traveled he had recorded what he saw as notes for future writing. Now the journalizing had ceased, and work on the English romance had been postponed until he reached Concord. For the present, the only consolation during the waiting period was to allay his fears about the future of his writing career by reading the American reviews of his romance that were sent over by Ticknor.

His thank-you note to Ticknor for these notices gave no clues as to what articles he had received in the mail. In general he was pleased by both American and English reviews:

> After so long absence and silence, I like to be praised too much. It sounds like a welcome back among my friends. But, in fact, if I have written anything well, it should be this Romance; for I have never thought or felt more deeply, or taken more pains. . . . I daily receive notes of congratulation and requests for autographs—which latter annoyance seems to be the great and ultimate result of literary reputation. I scarcely thought that these fat-brained Englishmen would have taken so wild a fiction in such good part. To say the truth, some of them do grumble awfully; for it is not every man that knows how to read a Romance, and if I were not myself the author, I doubt whether I should like this one.[57]

Aside from Motley's letter and the published reviews, Hawthorne probably never heard the comments made by some of his friends and admirers. Maria Mitchell, at home in Nantucket, asked of a correspondent, "Did you feast on 'The Marble Faun'? I have a charming letter from Una Hawthorne, herself a poet by nature, all about 'papa's book.' Ought not Mr. Hawthorne to be the happiest man alive? He isn't, though!"[58]

Longfellow, also at home in the United States, wrote to Emmeline Wadsworth that Italy was just the right country for Hawthorne to write about, "for he always sees everything in that magical twilight atmosphere, where fact merges into fable, which the prosiest person must find in Italy. His story has the same painful tone, deeper even than a minor key, which all his books have, as if written by a fallen angel, but which gives great power and true human pathos, if sometimes morbid, to his creations."[59] Longfellow's journal recorded a briefer, but similar, comment. He had read the romance all evening and all the next day. When he finished it, he wrote, "A wonderful book; but with the old, dull pain in it that runs through all Hawthorne's writings."[60]

From Rome in May, Harriet Hosmer wrote a paragraph full of praise in a letter to Wayman Crow, her patron and "second father" in St. Louis:

> I suppose you have read Hawthorne's new book. What a delicious one, as a picture of Italy and Italian life! It is only taking the words out of another's mouth, for me to say that Donatello's creation is one of the most exquisite poems penned. I don't know anything half so ideal and artistic as it is. Of course the plot is nothing, nor did he care that it should be, I fancy, but for perfection of writing, beauty of thought, and for the perfect combination of nature, art, and poetry, I never saw its equal.[61]

From Chester, Robert Temple, who had been reading some of Hawthorne's works since he had received the description of Bright's 1852 visit to Concord, sent a most enthusiastic comment to his old friend, Bright: "How grand a book is Hawthorne's Transformation. I never had the least wish to go to Italy before. Now I long for those Tuscan lawns [?]."[62]

Mrs. Gaskell's scattered comments on the romance were especially interesting because she had not read the book. She sketched the subject as she had heard it talked about and then stated that somehow after the murder one liked "Donatello the better!" Late in 1859 she wrote to George Smith, the publisher, "Do *you* know what Hawthorne's tale is about? I do; and I think it will perplex the English public pretty considerably." There is no doubt now that it did, but the interesting point is that Mrs. Gaskell at this time had only heard about the book, probably from Henry Bright, who had tried unsuccessfully to arrange a meeting between the two novelists.[63]

By mid-April, Hawthorne had decided that sales on both sides of the Atlantic must be going well. At the moment he was concerned about not hearing from Fields, for whom he had reserved a stateroom on June 16, and he was longing for the sailing date to arrive. "All my homesickness has fallen on me at once, and even Julian is scarcely more impatient than myself." Then in explaining that he anticipated their return to New England, which had a more healthful climate than England, he wrote to Ticknor that he looked upon the place now "as a Paradise," but he was afraid that he might change his mind after a few months. Nevertheless, he would do his best "to live contentedly at home."[64]

Unknown to the Hawthornes, Fields and his wife had arrived in London on April 23 for a short stay before starting north on the last portion of their vacation abroad. Hawthorne's letter to him reached their lodgings at 41 Jermyn Street, as shown by Fields's response of May 2. He regretted that he had not been able to go with Bennoch to visit the Hawthornes in Bath. He had business with the publisher John Murray that he could not leave. His reaction to Hawthorne's romance was one of flattering enthusiasm that must have pleased the author even though he understood the reason for Fields's exuberance:

> I am delighted with the Marble Faun as I knew I should be. . . . On all hands among the best people I hear golden opinions, and your Publishers here are very proud to have sent out your book. Your Boston publishers hold up their heads higher than ever now. You can't imagine what lots of attention I get in London from the fact that I am one of the boys who publish for you in America. I am sure that I have eaten the last week two dinners on the strength of my title page notoriety.[65]

Then Fields urged Hawthorne to come to London and meet more people, especially Anthony Trollope, who was glad to hear that Hawthorne enjoyed his books. Nathaniel finally did go ahead with plans for his trip, but his arrangements were made with Bright, Bennoch, and Motley. To Bright he wrote that he would go first to London, where he would stay with the Motleys for a few days before moving to Cambridge for commencement ceremonies.[66] The Motley family had rented for the season a small house at 31 Hertford Street, which Lady Byron had furnished for her granddaughter, Lady Annabella King. Hawthorne confessed to Bennoch that though he liked both the Motleys, he would feel freer staying alone in a lodging house. He hoped that Bennoch could help him get away for a few days to Blackheath.[67]

Before Nathaniel left Bath for London, the family celebrated Rose's birthday a number of days early, because her father would not be there on that special day, May 20. Rose received her birthday presents and was privileged to order what she wished to have for meals and to tell them all what to wear. Sophia wrote the details to Mary Mann, including the dinner menu of Rose's favorite foods—"turkey, cauliflowers, rice and potatoes, rhubarb, oranges, and biscuits for dessert." There was "no fowl at this time of year," her mother wrote, "so she settled for boiled beef."[68]

Since he kept no diary, details of Nathaniel's departure to London and his visit there must be pieced together from various letters. He arrived at the Motleys' on the afternoon of May 16 and went to dinner at Lord Dufferin's that evening. There at last he met Mrs. Caroline Norton, whom he had missed seeing in Rock Ferry days. The next day he breakfasted with Fields, met Field Talfourd, strolled in the park with Henry Bright, and dined at the home of Robert MacIntosh (former governor of St. Kitt's and related to Longfellow by marriage), where he met "Uncle John" O'Sullivan again. Nathaniel's letters to his wife suggest that he was really enjoying himself: "Thou wouldst be stricken dumb to see how quietly I accept a whole string of invitations, and, what is more, perform my engagements without a murmur." Then he added, "The stir of this London life, somehow or other, has done me a wonderful deal of good, and I feel better than for months past. This is queer, for, if I had my choice, I should leave undone almost all the things I do."[69]

His social life was interrupted by a day at the photographer's on May 19. Henry Bright made the arrangements, and John Mayall took three different photographs, an action that for some years confused people and resulted in conflicting accounts by those who did not realize that Bright, Motley, and Bennoch each obtained a print with a different pose.[70] These photographs were the first ones that show the moustache that Hawthorne had allowed to grow in Italy during the previous year.

Apparently the round of social affairs also included a breakfast at the Milneses', an evening at the Cosmopolitan Club, and dinner at the Oxford and Cambridge Club. Smith and Elder invited him to a dinner to meet the contributors to *Cornhill Magazine*, but Hawthorne declined, "being tired to death of dinners."[71]

While he was still at the Motleys', he added one more revealing entry at the end of his French and Italian notebooks: "I would gladly journalize some of my proceedings, and describe things and people; but I find the same coldness and stiffness in my pen as always since our return to England." He mentioned here only the dinner at Lord Dufferin's and his meeting with Mrs. Norton, but concluded that he could get "no color," "so I shall leave it here" (VII, 78–79, MA591).

As a result, we are left without Hawthorne's impressions of the people he met in London, and information on his few days in Cambridge must be reconstructed from letters and contemporary accounts. He had planned to go to Cambridge on Thursday, May 24, but his letters suggest that he did not "settle in" until Friday. At Trinity College he stayed in "an ancient set of college-rooms," which were "temporarily vacated by the rightful possessor." The rooms had been obtained for him by Lemprière Hammond, at that time a fellow and assistant tutor at Trinity. By correspondence with Bright, Hammond had also arranged for both Bright and Hawthorne to dine with him on Friday night to meet some friends. He hoped they would stay over Whitsunday, a "high feast day."[72]

In April, Hammond had written to Bright that if Hawthorne came in May he would see Cambridge at its best. "By that time the 'backs' ought to be looking their loveliest; and though I fear he may be too late to see a boatrace, yet there will be some amount of stir and life at the period of the May term."[73] Hammond was right: It was a busy weekend for Trinity. On Thursday there was a University congregation at which names of degree candidates were offered to the Senate after being confirmed by the University Council. The M.A. candidates included both Bright and his cousin, James Heywood, who together with him had been the first Nonconformists to be granted the B.A. degree in 1857. The university calendar showed that Thursday was the queen's birthday, an occasion for which there was a "Grand Tulip Show" of the Cambridge Horticultural Society on the grounds of Trinity College. Whitsunday, the twenty-seventh, was celebrated as "Scarlet Day," probably from the color worn by the Masters. Though Hawthorne left no record of his visit to the University, years later Bright recalled to Julian how delighted his father had been with Cambridge.[74]

From Cambridge, Nathaniel returned to London on Monday morning in order to meet Bennoch and make an overnight trip to Canterbury. Then he stayed at Blackheath with the Bennochs until Thursday, the thirty-first. Because Mrs. S. C. Hall had so urgently pressed him to accept a dinner invitation for Wednesday night, he did not go back to Bath as early in the week as he had originally intended. From their first meeting Nathaniel had admired Mrs. Hall and would have regretted leaving England without seeing her.[75]

Hawthorne left no account of the dinner at the Halls' or of his farewell to Bennoch, but it must have been a sad one, for Nathaniel felt the same about Bennoch as he did about Bright. In March, before he was invited to the Cambridge commencement, he had expected to say good-by to Bright in Liverpool, an action which, he wrote, would cause "a sharp pain. The sooner it is all over, the better."[76] Surely he would have said the same about his good-by to Bennoch.

As soon as Hawthorne reached Bath, he notified Smith and Elder that letters addressed to him should be forwarded to Mrs. Blodget's until June 16, the date on which he was to sail to America. In the next few days there was nothing else to do but pack and move to Liverpool.

There he wrote the last letters mailed from England. These were a note to Russell Sturgis in London, asking for his funds from Barings to be sent on to Ticknor; a thank-you note to Dr. John Brown congratulating him and thanking him for a copy of his story of *Rab and His Friends;* and one last note to his poet-jeweler friend in London, W. C. Bennett, who had written a series of three sonnets on *The Marble Faun:* "The very last act that I make of my pen in England is to thank you."[77]

After her packing, Sophia did little except rest and wait for Annie and James T. Fields to join them at Mrs. Blodget's. She had already written a last letter to Ticknor, expressing her regret that he had not come to England and would not be returning on the *Europa* with them: "I shall miss you on shipboard immensely, for you were always so kind and helpful and full of pleasant talk for us, and so unweariable in walking us up and down the deck." Fields, of course, would be with them, but he would be of little help, for he was always seasick. The letter concluded with her thanks to Ticknor for being such "a faithful caretaker" of their affairs.[78]

Obviously Sophia had not seen enough of Annie Fields to realize that she would provide excellent company on shipboard. Annie's diary of the year abroad is the best source for information about this last part of the Hawthornes' and the Fieldses' experiences in England. It shows that from London on June 4 the Fields couple had gone on a quick eight-day tour to the Edinburgh area, the Trossacks, Glasgow, Carlyle, and the Lake District. When they realized that the train from Windermere to Liverpool would not arrive until very late, they telegraphed Mrs. Blodget. At 1 A.M. they found both Mrs. Blodget and her sister, Miss Williams, waiting up for them. "What excellent ladies these two are," Annie wrote, "and how homelike and comfortable everything looked as we arrived. I know no other house in the world so nice."[79]

In her diary during the Liverpool stay, Annie made only two comments on the Hawthorne family. After dinner on June 14, she and her husband took a long walk with Julian and Una. The next day she stated that the Hawthornes were busy preparing for departure, which would be exactly one year from the day that she and James had arrived in Liverpool. She could scarcely believe they were going home. "Hawthorne is here," she wrote, "looking a melancholy, silent, grand genius—as he is." No doubt Hawthorne *was* melancholy, for much as he disliked Liverpool, it was hard to say good-by to England and his friends there. We can only assume that Henry Bright returned from London in time to say good-by to the Hawthornes before they sailed.

Early in the morning of that momentous day, Saturday, June 16, at

seven-thirty, according to Annie Fields, they all left Mrs. Blodget's for
the Cunard steamer *Europa*, where they were happy to meet Captain
Leitch once more. Annie was also glad to meet Harriet Beecher
Stowe and her two older daughters, who were bound for Boston on
the same ship.

On Sunday, June 17, the ship reached the last part of Great Britain
that Hawthorne was ever to see. They landed at Queenstown (now
named Cobh), and since the weather was pleasant and the ship would
remain in harbor for six hours, the Hawthornes and the Fieldses went
ashore together. The two families hired two "jaunting cars" and took a
"delicious drive round the island gathering flowers" on their way.

From that day on, the voyage was pleasant and uneventful to most
members of the two parties. The women read during the day, but in the
twilight hours Sophia and Annie had "delicious long talks cheating the
hours of their fancied power." Mrs. Stowe often joined the group, and
the women, at least, were thoroughly entertained. James Fields as usual
suffered "abominably," his wife said, "from dyspepsia."[80] Nathaniel
jokingly suggested all manner of fantastic edibles to quiet his friend's
stomach, but even Fields at his best could not have saved Nathaniel
from the melancholy slowly settling upon him.

According to Fields, Hawthorne kept repeating, "I should like to sail
on and on forever, and never touch the shore again." He spent much of
his time walking on deck, standing to watch the sunset, or pacing the
deck late at night. During the day he would often sit down beside Fields
as his friend lay in a deck chair and "commiserate" on the latter's
"unquiet condition." He himself was never seasick; he loved sailing,
and this time especially he could have stayed on deck "forever."[81]

To Annie Fields the return was a comfortable voyage with pleasant
companions and beautiful weather. Though Sophia did not write
about her own feelings, her actions as described by Annie imply that
she was delighted to be on the way home. She probably would not have
phrased her attitude as strongly as Nathaniel did when he wrote to
Fields earlier that England had been "disastrous" to his wife "from first
to last."[82] But she must have been glad to leave, if only for reasons of
health. In addition, there were ties to her sisters, her brother, and their
families, whom she had not seen for seven long years.

As for Hawthorne's feelings, we can guess at what he thought from
his constant talk of his desire to return to England, perhaps after he
had written another book.[83] Recollection of those last days in England
was still too pleasant for him to face the prospect of going back to

Concord. Dreamy days on the Atlantic merely postponed the inevitable reality. Years later, Julian, romanticizing as usual, wrote that from the moment of departure from Liverpool his father had leaned upon the ship's rail, looking "backwards towards the old home that he loved and would never see again."[84]

Concord Once More:
Memories of "Our Old Home"
1860–1864

TWO DAYS AFTER THE HAWTHORNES reached Concord following the docking of the *Europa* in Boston, Nathaniel was back in the city with Fields at the Old Corner Bookstore. Longfellow, who saw them there together, remarked that Hawthorne was tanned from his voyage and that Fields was still pale. Both looked "bewildered and sad," for they were "going through a schoolboy's Blue Monday."[1] Fields, recovering from his seasickness, was no doubt regretting the end of the glorious holiday he and his wife had spent on the Continent and in Great Britain. His companion, the good sailor, was never to recover from the effects of his seven years abroad, which in spite of the difficulties he had encountered still retained for him a pleasant dreamlike aura.

Hawthorne was escaping to Boston for a day rather than facing some unavoidable realities in Concord. He was already being confronted at home with a variety of problems, arising one by one at a time when he no longer had the vigor of his earlier days. As he wrote to Horatio Bridge, "My friends tell me that I am very little changed, but, of course, seven years have done their work."[2] There was more to the statement than he realized.

Long before, in letters from England, he had anticipated the task of remodeling the Wayside to accommodate the changed needs of his family. Now the problem had to be faced at once. His children were old enough to need separate bedrooms. He wanted a guest room, maids' rooms, and a more adequate place to work than the old first-floor study, which, according to new plans, was to become a library. A tower study where he could write without being disturbed was undoubtedly suggested by the tower at Villa Montauto. On June 28 he called in his next-door neighbor, Bronson Alcott, whose family had previously owned the Wayside. Plans were quickly developed; Wetherbee, the carpenter, arrived on July 7; and the remodeling work began early in August.[3]

But the outcome was far different from the original conception. Construction took all winter, and the interior was not completed until the end of May 1861. The cost, first quoted at $500, Hawthorne later estimated at more than $2,000 for construction and finishing work. To this amount would have to be added the expense of furnishings and carpets.[4] Such expenditures made it imperative that Hawthorne produce a substantial piece of writing, the income from which would augment his dwindling savings.

The noise and confusion of construction kept Hawthorne from settling down to work on the English romance. There was no quiet place to which he could retire for the concentration he always needed when writing seriously. To escape from the constant hammering and sawing, he retreated to the hillside behind the house, where he soon wore a path by treading back and forth as he meditated. It was December before he and Alcott could sit down together in the tower study for the first time.[5] During the summer months Hawthorne had done no writing except a sketch for the *Atlantic Monthly* on Robert Burns, based on notations from his English journals.

Other problems besides the remodeling prevented him from beginning his romance. Late in the summer Una experienced an illness that was either a recurrence of the old Roman fever or a result of accidental overdoses of quinine given to her by Dr. Franco. Details were not discussed in family correspondence. She herself admitted in letters merely that she had been ill. Her father was more explicit in writing to Ticknor: Una had recovered by means of "medical electricity," administered by Mrs. Rollins of Cambridge, the "Doctress." Without such help, Mrs. Rollins told the family, Una would have been "subject to life-long disease." As it was, she would eventually recover completely. During the illness Una herself despaired of her future. Concord, she wrote, was "a killing place. . . . Shall I ever, ever be well!" Her doubt was a better prediction than Mrs. Rollins's statement.[6] Una did recover for the time being, but she continued to have relapses, and her father continued to worry about her.

Because of her delicate health, Una was not expected to attend school, but by September the education of the two younger children became an important issue. For Julian, who had to be prepared for college, the matter was solved by the selection of Frank Sanborn's coeducational preparatory school. Although Sophia did not approve of coeducation, she talked the matter over with her husband and finally agreed to let Julian enroll in the school in September. This was Julian's first experience with formal schooling, and apparently he had to work hard to keep up with his classmates. But in later years all that he recalled about his preparatory schooling was the fun the pupils had. It is no wonder that his mother later objected to Sanborn's failure to stress academic work and to his overemphasis on social life. In a letter to the schoolmaster she protested that when she brought Julian home from England he had been "a sacredly folded bud . . . with a genuine reverence for woman," but that his experience at Sanborn's school had turned him into a "man of the world" who flirted and coquetted.[7]

In spite of her comments about "dissipation" at Sanborn's and her decision to send Rose to a girls' school, Sophia did not seem to object to her children's involvement in the social life of the town that included both boys and girls. When Una was physically able, they all took part in picnics, bathing parties, and boating on hot summer days, and in dancing and ice skating during the winter. They were friends with the Emerson children (especially with Edith and Edward, who were about the same ages as Una and Julian), with the three sons of Mary Mann, and with the Alcotts and other Concord young people. The children had much more freedom in social relationships in Concord than they had during their restricted lives abroad. Sophia's diary for 1861 suggests that none of the family except Nathaniel stayed at home very much.[8] She herself visited Mary Mann almost every day. At first, perhaps, escape from the confusion of the remodeling was necessary for the whole family. Still, Sophia and the children adjusted to a different kind of life more easily than Nathaniel did.

After his return Hawthorne impressed some people in the town as being more relaxed and genial than he had been previously, a change they attributed to his consular experiences. Others, such as Sanborn, who met Hawthorne for the first time in 1860, continued to refer to his shyness and preference for solitary walks on the ridge behind the Wayside.[9] The two impressions were not contradictory. Certainly Hawthorne met people more easily than he had before his years abroad, but gradually as he became more and more frustrated because of his inability to cope with financial difficulties by producing a satisfactory piece of writing, he withdrew from most social life except for an occasional meeting of the Saturday Club in Boston.

Before leaving England, Hawthorne had implied that his friend Motley would find himself virtually an exile if he stayed away from the United States too long. Adjustment to life in America would be almost impossible. "It is dreary to stay away, though not very delightful to go back."[10] Hawthorne was partly correct in his own case. Neither his relationships with friends nor his literary reputation had suffered because of his absence, but he was distressed over the changing conditions in his own country. As the nation drew nearer to division by war, he became more and more upset and found himself unable to carry through with the great writing project he had planned while he was abroad. He had been convinced that at a distance from the English scene he could complete a work that would involve American and English characters in interrelationships. Now the task seemed impossible. Readers, he said, were no longer in the mood for a romance, even if he could write one.[11]

While he was working in the Liverpool consulate, he had set down in his journal the "germ of a new Romance." It was suggested by his experiences with a number of American visitors who were attempting to trace their English ancestors, some in hopes of perhaps eventually laying claim to an estate in England. On April 12, 1855, he wrote:

> In my Romance, the original emigrant to America may have carried away with him a family secret, whereby it was in his power (had he so chosen) to have brought about the ruin of the family. This secret he transmits to his American progeny, by whom it is inherited throughout all the intervening generations. At last, the hero of the Romance comes to England, and finds that, by means of this secret, he still has it in his power to procure the downfal[l] of the family. It would be similar to the story of Meleager, whose fate depended on the firebrand that his mother had snatched out of the flames. (*EN*, 107)[12]

Three years later in Rome, Hawthorne had sketched out in a notebook further plans for the English romance, but left them unfinished when the family moved to Florence for the summer. As he jotted down his ideas, he noted that he had not yet "struck the true key-note" and that until he found it, he would write "nothing but tediousness and nonsense" (*The Ancestral Footstep*, CE 12, p.58). Back in Concord he struggled to develop those plans and in the process wrote two incomplete drafts (published later under the titles *Etherege* and *Grimshawe*). Within both manuscripts appeared many isolated comments giving directions to himself about plot, characters, and symbols, as well as some pages of summary. All of these indicate his uncertainty and dissatisfaction. In places where he reached an impasse, he queried "Who? why? how?" In one long passage interrupting his narrative he made numerous suggestions, each followed by "T'won't do." That section ends with the comment, "Nothing seems to do" (*Etherege*, CE 12, pp. 197–203). At one point, after completing a passage of dialogue, he broke off with, "Here I come to a stand still!" and a page later exclaimed, "Oh, Heavens! I have not the least notion how to get on. I never was in such a sad predicament before" (*Etherege,* CE 12, pp. 285–86). When nothing seemed to work right in the first version of his story, he threw it aside and started a second one (later to be entitled *Grimshawe*). That likewise was left incomplete. Twenty years later Julian pieced together the major portions of the two versions to form *Dr. Grimshawe's Secret.* It was a remodeling job as extensive as the Wayside had been, but the characteristic Hawthorne style remained.

It is as impossible to explain exactly why Hawthorne's writing failed him as it is to determine why his health and spirits failed, but a sentence from the second manuscript may give a partial clue. Within parentheses in the narrative he inserted this comment: "When the machinery of human life has once been stopped, by sickness or other impediment, it often needs an impulse to set it going again, even after it is newly wound up" (*Grimshawe*, CE 12, p.459). The sickness was Una's (his was not yet serious enough). Experiences in England had prepared him for the task and the need to write was urgent, but a sense of direction was lacking. All the details of plot and character that he had accumulated were merely trappings for a standard Gothic romance. There was no central theme, no meaning or moral, such as had unified his earlier works. His own comments, whether meant to mock himself or to be taken seriously, show that he did not know where he was going.

Was the war to blame? Was it his slowly deteriorating health? Or was his trouble a combination of factors? Whatever the cause, he himself was certain that he had not found the right way to work out his ideas. Frustration and dissatisfaction made him withdraw more often to his hillside during the years that followed. In the first six months after the return, he did not write a single letter to his two best friends in England, perhaps partly because he knew they were both concerned about the possibility of war, a subject he preferred to avoid. Finally each man wrote to him. In a sentimental vein in September, Henry Bright reminded Hawthorne of all the pleasures they had known together:

> Do you remember all our talks in that odious office of yours; my visits to Rockferry; my one visit, all in the snow, to Southport; our excursions into Wales, and through the London streets, and to Rugby and Cambridge, and how you plucked the laurel at Addison's Bilton, and found the skeleton in Dr. Williams's library; and lost your umbrella in those dark rooms in Trinity; and dined at Richmond and saw the old lady looking like a maid of honor of Queen Charlotte's time; and chatted at the

Cosmopolitan; and heard Tom Hughes sing the "Tight Little Island;" and—But really I must stop, and can only trust that now at last you will be convinced of my existence, and remember your promise and write me a good long letter about everything and everybody.[13]

The whole letter was teasing, characteristic of Bright, and meant to get a response from the recipient.

Francis Bennoch, distressed by Hawthorne's months of silence, waited until December before sending a letter addressed in care of Fields, who *had* written to him (including the news of Una's illness) and who, he was sure, would forward his note. Bennoch's letter consisted of a holiday greeting and a question: How should he answer all his English friends who were asking what he had heard from Hawthorne? The note crossed the Atlantic at the same time as Hawthorne's first letter to him. Hawthorne's letter, written on December 17, summed up recent happenings and also announced that he had designated the new guest room as "Bennoch's Room." Bennoch's immediate response contained a New Year's greeting and a discussion of the signs of approaching war in the United States, a subject that he was certain was making his friend unhappy.[14] How much so Bennoch could scarcely have realized, for he did not know how increasingly disturbed Hawthorne was to become, especially after the war began in April.

How much the rest of the family were disturbed by conditions in the nation is not clear from Sophia's diary for 1861, since it consists chiefly of brief impersonal jottings of all the Hawthornes' activities. On April 13 she recorded, "News of WAR!" A few days later: "Today we bade farewell to our band of heroes at the station." On April 21: "I can only think of the war." As time went on, aside from notes about her reading of war news in the papers and the indications that she and Una sewed for the soldiers, the daily entries were concerned mostly with the arrival of workmen at the house and the various social activities of the family. She herself, in spite of occasional bad days, seems to have been full of energy. She walked to the village, sewed, weeded in spring and summer months, supervised finishing work inside the house, entertained callers, and made a few trips to Boston to shop for furnishings for the new rooms; and still she had time to read a variety of nonfictional books. During the winter months, Scott's *Waverley* novels, sent to Concord from Ticknor and Fields, had provided pleasure for the family circle around the stove. When warmer weather returned, the reading aloud of Scott seems to have ended. The children were absorbed in social life, and Sophia was glad they were so busy. She said nothing about her husband's struggles to write in his tower study. Until summer only five notations referred to him specifically: January 26: "My husband went to Boston to dine [at the Saturday Club]." March 7: "General Pierce and Mr. Ticknor called to see us and took my husband to the Hotel to dine." March 14: "My husband sent a paper to the *Atlantic* [probably the second in the series of English sketches based on his journal]." April 17: "My husband is better. The good aconite benefitted [*sic*] him." June 1: "My husband went to Boston."

The April 17 entry marks Sophia's first indication that her husband had not been well. However, it has generally been assumed by biographers that his health began to decline soon after his return in 1860. Late in the spring of 1861, Nathaniel himself wrote to Ticknor that his health was better than it had been, thus implying that it had not been good in recent months; but he doubted that he would "ever again be so well" as he had been in England. He began to wonder whether he should have settled by the seashore instead of returning to an inland town, but it was too late to think of that: "I have fastened myself down by taking a house upon my back. It is folly for mortal man to do anything more than pitch a tent."[15]

When summer came Nathaniel must have been ill again, but it was Julian's sickness that Sophia recorded in her diary on July 11. When Julian appeared at noon, sick and dizzy, she wrote, "I am quite anxious about him. It seems almost a sunstroke." She must have used this incident to urge that both husband and son should take a vacation trip together, for near the end of the month the two started out for Pride's Crossing, on the coast of Massachusetts, not far from the farmhouse where Nathaniel's sister Elizabeth was boarding. In the correspondence between husband and wife from July 29 to August 8 only the last of his letters, announcing their return in two days, seems to have survived. However, two of her letters remain. The first, written at night on the day of Nathaniel and Julian's departure, shocks the reader by her frankness about the state of her husband's health. It proves that Nathaniel was worse off in 1861 than anyone had so far admitted: "Of all the trials, this is the heaviest to me,—to see you so apathetic, so indifferent, so hopeless, so unstrung. Rome has no sin to answer for so unpardonable as this of wrenching off your wings and hanging lead upon your arrowy feet. Rome—and all Rome caused to you. What a mixed cup is this to drink!"[16] She went on to beg him for everyone's sake to stay away as long as possible and not to worry about the money; it was better to spend money on a restful vacation than to pay it to doctors.

Nathaniel and Julian did stay a second week, but in his letter Nathaniel made no reference to his wife's worry about his health or to the amount of money the vacation was costing them. He wrote of Julian's activities and of the place itself: "The vicinity is very beautiful—insomuch that if I had seen it sooner, I doubt whether I should have built my tower in Concord—but somewhere among these noble woods of white pine and near these rocks and beaches. . . . We have nothing to complain of—except the heat, which would have pervaded any abode, unless it were an Italian palace."[17] Finally, on Saturday, August 10, Sophia recorded in her diary the simple statement: "My husband and Julian returned this afternoon."

For the next three weeks there were few entries in the diary. Then on September 3 Elizabeth Hawthorne arrived for a visit of almost two months, and this gave Sophia an opportunity to travel. Leaving Una and Nathaniel to look after his sister, Sophia and Rose departed for Brattleboro (Vermont), Salem, and Boston. It was late October before they settled down again in Concord, and then on the thirty-first Elizabeth Hawthorne went back to her boardinghouse near Beverly.

Somehow during the year, in spite of work on the house, which seemed unending, and in spite of all the other interruptions and his own poor health, Hawthorne managed to do a good deal of writing, very little of it, however, to his satisfaction. Having thrown aside the drafts of his English romance, probably by midsummer, he turned to plans for a story supposed to have taken place in Concord at the beginning of the Revolutionary War. Sometime early in 1861 he had outlined those plans to Fields, but they seem to have remained chiefly in his head until later in the year. That the story was at least planned early in 1861 may be assumed from two factors: his absorption in both the pleasures and the financial burden imposed by the Wayside; and in the beginnings of the Civil War as reflected in his hero's attitude—first, disapproval of fighting, then some involvement in spite of himself. The writing of a number of studies, a scenario, and two different drafts (at present published as *Septimius Felton* and *Septimius Norton*) occupied Hawthorne for about two years.[18]

Evidently he spent a longer period of time on this second romance than on the English one, and in spite of changes in names and identifications of characters he seemed to be more sure of his plot structure, at least in the first draft. In both versions there are fewer parenthetical directions to himself and no long pages of summary, probably because of the separate studies and the scenario. The first draft has a conclusion comparable to the ending of the scenario; the second one ends abruptly about two-thirds of the way through his plot. Obviously the author was dissatisfied with what he had produced.

The idea for the story had come from a remark once made to Hawthorne by Henry Thoreau that a former occupant of the Wayside had determined "never to die." This was all Thoreau knew of the man (Study 1, p. 499, CE 13). Hawthorne developed the ideas inspired by the remark into the story of the efforts of a young man, named Septimius in most of the manuscripts, to achieve immortality by experimenting with an ancient recipe for an elixir that would prolong human life. It was an old theme that Hawthorne had long ago made some references to or use of in short stories.[19] In the stories he had concluded that any attempt to achieve immortality would be unwise and would end in failure. That he had not changed his mind causes the reader to wonder why he pursued the theme once again. In a short passage at the end of his scenario, he speculated on the outcome of his romance: "Perhaps the moral will turn out to be, the folly of man in thinking that he can ever be of any importance to the welfare of the world; or that any settled plan of his, to be carried on through a length of time, could be successful. God wants short lives, because such carry on his purpose inevitably and involuntarily; while longer ones would thwart and interfere with his purpose, by carrying on their own" (CE 13, pp. 529–30). The reader must also wonder whether Hawthorne was convinced of his last point: Did God want shorter lives? Was he already thinking of his own fate?

Apparently not content with his elixir theme alone, Hawthorne added other Gothic devices, such as the bloody footstep and the return of the hero to England, which he had tried in the Grimshawe story. Once again they did not work. Perhaps Julian came close to the truth when he wrote years later that his father could not sympathize with "Septimius's infatuation." It was all too improbable. "The young man must be à fool; and Hawthorne finally decides that he is a fool, and makes him appear so."[20] Whether Julian was right or not, Hawthorne lost interest in his hero and abandoned the manuscripts, but not the idea of the elixir, for it was to become the theme of his last unfinished romance.

The initial scenes in the story of Septimius had been suggested not only by the Wayside itself, but by events at the beginning of the Civil War that brought to mind the importance of Concord in the Revolutionary War. The hero shows some of the same shifting attitudes about fighting that were concerning Hawthorne himself. It is difficult to trace Hawthorne's attitude toward the situation in the nation before and at the start of the Civil War, because he himself did not know where he stood. While he was in England it had been easy enough to look at the troubles of his country and be glad that he was not involved. As early as 1856 he had written to Ticknor, "I sympathize with no party, but hate them all—free soilers, pro-slavery men, and whatever else—all alike. In fact, I have no country, or only just enough of one to be ashamed of; and I can tell you, an American finds it difficult to hold up his head, on this side of the water in these days." Less than a year later he confessed that if it were not for the children, he would consider himself "a citizen of the world, and perhaps never come home."[21] In Italy his own troubles became such a heavy burden that he had little time to think of affairs at home, and during the following year in England he was totally occupied with the writing of his Italian romance. When he arrived in Concord, however, he could not overlook the signs of approaching war.

Like his own country, Hawthorne was torn by conflicting emotions. He did not approve of slavery—though he knew little about the slaves—but neither did he approve of war. After the actual conflict began, he confessed that no one seemed to be sure of what the fighting was really for. Though he felt that war was always a mistake, the spirit and enthusiasm of people around him was infectious. He wished that he were younger and could make himself useful. As it was, he would keep quiet until the enemy was within a mile of the Wayside.[22]

Once the war made some headway, he expressed disagreement with the early attitude of his friend Henry Bright that the Union must be preserved at any cost. The country would be better off if the South were allowed to go free. In fact, he must have said enough in agreement with the idea of secession that Horatio Bridge later felt called upon to protest Hawthorne's loyalty to the North. What distressed Hawthorne most in the letters he received from English friends such as Bennoch, Bright, and Henry Wilding was that though the English people as a whole were divided in their feelings about the war and did not approve of slavery, it was obvious that the commercial and manufacturing classes in that country favored the South. Whatever the outcome should be, he himself seemed to rejoice that the old Union was gone. "We never were one people, and never really had a country since the Constitution was formed." Even if the North were to win, the South should be cut adrift. This was written to Horatio Bridge, but he had expressed some of the same ideas to his English friends. Finally he included in the letter to Bridge a warning that none of his English correspondents except Bright (much earlier in his 1853 pamphlet on slavery) had mentioned: If the war continued, it would be necessary to prepare the Negroes for future citizenship by allowing them to fight and by educating them.[23] As we look back on the period now, it is not surprising that Hawthorne, distraught by conflicting emotions about the war, was equally distraught about his writing.

In spite of his wish to avoid the subject of the war in correspondence with his English friends, he longed for an opportunity to see and talk with both Bennoch and Bright. He tried to persuade each of them to visit America again. But Henry Bright was involved in family responsibilities. In June of 1861, Bright at the age of thirty-one finally decided to marry. Eleven months later the first of his children was born. A transatlantic trip was impossible.[24] Hawthorne turned, therefore, to Francis Bennoch, urging him, now that the guest room bearing his name was ready, to come over and "see America in time of war":

> Come and let us talk over the many pleasant evenings we spent together in dear old England. Come, and I promise that all distracting thoughts and disturbing circumstances shall be banished from us: and although our children are no longer children, I am sure they would unite with the elder folk, and enjoy the opportunity of showing that Yankee hearts never forget kindnesses, and long for the chance to repay them; — not as a cancelling of debt, but to prove how deeply kindly deeds are appreciated by them.[25]

Unfortunately, Bennoch could not comply with Hawthorne's urging. As a result, the "distracting thoughts and disturbing circumstances" occasioned by the war continued to plague Hawthorne all that winter. At last, early in the spring of 1862, he decided to learn something of the war firsthand by taking a trip to Washington at the invitation of his friend Horatio Bridge.[26] Accompanied by Ticknor, he stopped briefly in New York and Philadelphia and spent several weeks in Washington and Virginia. Hawthorne joined a group of men who were introduced to Lincoln; he toured army camps, including Manassas, the site of the Union defeat in the first battle of Bull Run; and he traveled as far west as Harper's Ferry. There he visited, among other places, John Brown's former blockhouse, used to house Confederate prisoners. Late in the month Ticknor went off on some travels of his own. Meanwhile, in letters to various members of his family Hawthorne wrote that he was well and having a good time.

He did not plan to stay in Washington so long, but the painter Emanuel Leutze took time from his mural at the Capitol to work on a portrait of Hawthorne.[27] The trip was evidently having a beneficial effect upon Hawthorne's health, for he wrote to Fields that he was enjoying the cigars and champagne that Leutze provided whenever he saw that the sittings were making Hawthorne tired.[28]

Not long afterward, when Hawthorne was at home working on an article about his Washington experiences, Concord people were saddened by news of the death of Henry Thoreau. It was scarcely a year since Sophia's nephew, young Horace Mann, Jr., had started off to Minnesota with Thoreau on a journey that would, it was hoped, benefit the latter's health. Since their return the previous July, however, Thoreau had steadily weakened until he became bedridden. When his death was announced, all Concord prepared to attend the funeral. Sophia and Nathaniel were among the crowd that filled the church, for though neither of them had enjoyed Thoreau socially, both had admired his writings and felt that he was worthy of more praise than he had received in his lifetime. A few days after the funeral, in a letter to Annie Fields, Sophia summed up her feelings by saying that Thoreau was "Concord itself in one man."[29]

At the same time Nathaniel wrote to James Fields that he was sending in an article for the *Atlantic Monthly* about his Washington trip. As usual, Fields was delighted to receive any contribution from Hawthorne. This time, however, he objected to one passage, a frank description of President Lincoln that Fields thought his readers might find offensive. Reluctantly Hawthorne agreed to have the passage deleted, though he thought it might have some historical value. He promised to insert his own footnotes, supposedly written by the editor, poking fun at the author for some of his statements.[30]

"Chiefly About War Matters by a Peaceable Man" hardly improved Hawthorne's literary reputation, but its details did reveal how much his life abroad and his trip to Washington had broadened his point of view. The tone was that of a humorous, sometimes satirical, yet serious-minded bystander. The article was an objective report of what he had seen, with comments interspersed that certainly could not have pleased his readers no matter what their sympathies were. Actually, the article was a protest against the war, as indicated by its title. In describing the devastation of the countryside by army encampments, Hawthorne compared the sites to "barren esplanades," like those of the squares in French cities, without a blade of grass.[31] The town of Harper's Ferry, with its "dismal ruin[s]," resembled an Etruscan city he had seen among the Apennines, "rushing, as it were, down an apparently breakneck height" (*CW*, 11:326).

When the article was published in July of 1862, Hawthorne carried out his promise to insert editorial footnotes criticizing some of his own comments. Speaking of John Brown in the text, for example, he concluded that any sensible man must have felt "a certain intellectual satisfaction in seeing him hanged, if it were only in requital of his preposterous miscalculation of possibilities." To this remark he appended the note: "Can it be a son of old Massachusetts who utters this abominable sentiment? For shame" (*CW*, 11:328). As might be expected, Hawthorne's attempts at humor in such a situation were not universally understood or appreciated.

Such nonfictional sketches helped to augment Hawthorne's income from royalties at a time when he was probably ready to abandon the manuscript of his Septimius romance and had no other book-length work for publication. It was also easier to cull material from his own notations than to work on long fiction when there were interruptions during his working hours. Early in June the English critic Edward Dicey came for a visit. Dicey, who was on an extended tour of the States, had first met Hawthorne in Washington in March, and though their acquaintance was brief, Dicey later showed a remarkable understanding of Hawthorne. He described the novelist as a man who "loving the North, but not hating the South, felt himself altogether out of harmony with the passion of the hour." When Dicey visited at the Wayside, he developed even more appreciation of his host. They strolled together on the hillside behind the house, talking about politics, the war, and some other subjects that Dicey could not recall afterward. When, two years later, he tried to analyze the charm of Hawthorne's talk, he decided that "it lay in the odd combination of clear, hard-headed sense and dreamy fancy."[32]

As the summer heat grew more oppressive, Hawthorne became more restless. Apparently he wrote nothing except a short reminiscence about an old Salem house, "Browne's Folly," and contributed it gratis to the *Weal Reaf,* a sheet published in support of the Essex Institute. He commented in a letter to his sister Elizabeth that the Institute should be pleased, since he usually received $100 for such an article.[33]

In July, Sophia urged her husband and her son, who had recently "poisoned himself in the woods," to take a vacation together at the seashore. This time they went to a farmhouse near West Gouldsborough, Maine, a small settlement on a cove almost opposite Bar Harbor. On this trip Julian kept a journal, to which his father also contributed some brief entries. Julian described how they walked through pastures and along the coast, picking and eating berries as they went. One day they walked seven miles to Prospect Harbor for a more open view of the ocean. Sometimes Hawthorne and his son sat on the rocks while the father smoked a cigar and his son wished that he could also.[34] Finally, much as the two enjoyed their life in Maine, Nathaniel wrote that they could not stay longer; they would be home by September 5. He did not say so, but he was only too well aware of the cost of vacations. Taxes would be due the next month, and as usual he was growing short of funds.[35] This was the last trip on which father and son would find companionship together, for by the following year Julian was absorbed in college entrance examinations and preparations to go away to Harvard.

As soon as they returned to Concord, Hawthorne must have gone to work again on the English sketches, for before the end of September he wrote to Fields that shortly he would have an article on Warwick ready to send, and that he would also have a sketch for the January issue of the *Atlantic*.[36] Writing of his experiences in England must have brought back a flood of memories, since his October letter to Bennoch included a strong renewal of his invitation to visit the family in Concord. "I don't expect ever to see England again," he wrote, and as if to revive Bennoch's memories he enclosed a photograph of himself taken "four or five months ago," probably during the Washington trip.[37]

Once again he was disappointed that Bennoch could not come. Unable to afford a return visit to England, Hawthorne continued to work on his English sketches in spite of steadily failing health. When early in December he wrote to thank Fields for his praise of "Recollections of a Gifted Woman" (a sketch on Delia Bacon submitted in November and published in January), he apologized for the delay in sending another article; it would have been completed before if he had not been "quite ill for some days past."[38] Sophia wrote to Annie Fields that her husband had a feverish cold, similar to those he had had in Rome. The days in that city had been his "first acquaintance with suffering." Now he was "more like an Eolian harp in his spirits . . . and he was once as strong as Atlas while delicate as Ariel." Three days later she was still alarmed by what she called his "Roman cold, with fever and utter restlessness, and it has hardly left him yet."[39] She did not realize that he would not improve except temporarily.

The condition that Sophia had once, in a letter to Elizabeth Peabody, discussed as unlikely was now confronting her husband, even though she did not face its reality. While the family was in England, Sophia had asked Elizabeth not to refer, in letters to Julian or Una, to Nathaniel's or her age or any "coming infirmities as if they were a very agreeable topic for contemplation." At that time she prophesied exactly what his attitude would be:

> To him an infirm, helpless old age is not beautiful for himself, and I can
> see how he would not rejoice in any diminution of power and life. His
> imagination is so potent that he glowers into a condition with his awful
> power of insight. His wonderful and unvarying health and his self poise
> and self helpfulness and independent existence, so peculiarly needless of
> aid or care, I should suppose would make to *him* the picture of tottering
> old age a greater contrast and pain than to most persons.[40]

Nearly ten years had intervened since the letter was written. Now Nathaniel was slowly reaching that very stage of "tottering old age." Undoubtedly he did admit to himself what his wife had feared, for he seemed to realize that he had few years left in life. He worried constantly about family finances and spent as much time on the English sketches as his energy permitted. During the winter of 1862–1863 he stayed at home struggling with attempts at composition for such a long time that he finally wrote to Ticknor, "I don't know whether I shall ever see you again; for I have now staid here so long that I find myself rusted into my hole, and could not get out even if I wished." In return, Ticknor sent him cider and cigars to cheer him up, but did not come to visit.[41]

By spring family matters had changed little: Illnesses, servant problems, and shortage of funds plagued Sophia, and she saw, too, that her husband's health was not much better in warmer weather. During the winter he had refused an invitation from Fields to come to Boston, saying that he would prefer to wait until spring, "though I have now been a hermit so long, that the thought affects me somewhat as it would to invite a lobster or a crab to step out of his shell." When spring came, he pleaded that he was still busy writing. In contrast to previous years, in which he had produced one, two, or at most, three articles per year, in 1863 he turned out four within the first six months, apologizing to Fields each time for some fault he saw in what he was submitting or expressing doubt about the appeal of the whole series: "Heaven sees fit to visit me with an unshakable conviction that all this series of articles is good for nothing; but that is none of my business, provided the public and you are of a different opinion. . . . I mean to write two more of these articles and then hold my hand."[42]

His doubt about the success of his work was characteristic of him as a writer. But now the doubt was much greater, because his efforts to produce the English romance had so far been unsuccessful, and he must have regarded the English sketches as potboilers that only filled the interval until he could make another attempt at fiction. The money was necessary, even though it was insufficient for his family's needs. That fact was the incentive that finally made him agree to Fields's proposal to collect the sketches into a book.[43]

At the end of April he sent in the prefatory article, "Consular Experiences," with the suggestion that it be withheld from the magazine in order to give the book some degree of "freshness." He said he could think of no better title than *Our Old Home; a Series of English Sketches.* He then proposed that if Fields wanted another article for the *Atlantic*, he would compose one final sketch for the August issue, and repeated his former decision: After the book there would be no more articles.[44]

When Fields said that he wanted a dozen chapters for the book, Hawthorne took the manuscript on Uttoxeter that he had submitted to the *Keepsake* back in 1856 (which was reprinted in *Harper's* in April of 1857), added a section on Lichfield, and produced another article that was not printed in the *Atlantic*.[45] Fields may also have suggested the final arrangement of the chapters that gave logical shape to the book: In the first part, all those articles involving Warwickshire; in the middle, those concerned with small towns, such as "A Pilgrimage to Old Boston," "Near Oxford," and "Some of the Haunts of Burns"; lastly, those that had been written most recently and that dealt chiefly with London and its suburbs.

The final chapter, "Civic Banquets," skillfully constructed to pull together the threads of English-American relationships, was delayed by what Hawthorne described as "a cold and derangement of the stomach, making me very uncomfortable and unfit to leave home."[46] When at last he submitted the sketch in June, he sent it to Ticknor—in the absence of Fields, who was on vacation—with the statement that he had been suffering from a kind of dysentery, but that he had recovered. Sophia wrote a note asking Ticknor to send some Marsala wine that she hoped might raise Nathaniel's low spirits: "Till we went to Rome, he never knew what it was to feel ill or dispirited. Now he has lost the zest of life."[47]

Meanwhile, Hawthorne had given some thought to the dedication of the book. He considered dedicating it to Pierce, who had made possible Hawthorne's entire English experience, or perhaps to Bennoch, whose hospitality he had never publicly acknowledged. Eventually he concluded not only to write a brief dedication to Pierce, but also to include a prefatory letter paying tribute to this friend.[48] His decision marked the beginning of trouble. Pierce's unpopularity because of his opposition to the war was so great that Fields was sure the dedication would hurt the sales of the book. But Hawthorne was determined to carry out his decision. Although he modified the dedication slightly, he wrote to Fields that he could not change his stand merely for financial reasons; if Pierce was so unpopular, he needed a friend to stand by him.[49]

If it seems strange today that a furor should arise over the dedication of a book, we should remind ourselves of the high feelings generated by the war. Emerson, Channing, Elizabeth Peabody, and other Concord people objected to the dedication even before the actual publication date; after publication others reacted strenuously, though not so much as Mrs. Stowe, who castigated Hawthorne for praising "that arch-traitor Pierce." To make matters worse, Hawthorne had gone to Concord, New Hampshire, on July 4 and shown support for Pierce by sitting on the platform during the ex-president's Bunker Hill address. Annie Fields, who visited the Hawthornes in July, seems to have been one of the few who defended Hawthorne's dedication. She thought it was a beautiful tribute to his old friend. What Sophia thought about it is not recorded, but of course she would have agreed with her husband, not only because she always supported him, but also because she admired Pierce and appreciated his friendship for Nathaniel.[50]

Before the publication date a visiting Englishman commented on Hawthorne's politics. He was young Henry Yates Thompson, Bright's brother-in-law, who stopped off in Concord during his tour of the United States to observe the war. In his journals he recorded items for his columns in the *London Daily News*. He had come to see conditions in this country; but since he was an Abolitionist at heart, he told his story from the Northern point of view, sometimes rebuking his English relatives, especially his mother, for their Southern sympathies. From New Hampshire he sent Bright a description of his visit to the Wayside. Hawthorne, he said, was a disappointment: He was "frightfully shy" and nervous, though after a time he did become more cordial and calm. Thompson also decided that Hawthorne was a "regular Copperhead" about the war. Above all, Hawthorne shocked his visitor by "anti-negro prejudices." For obvious reasons, Thompson was careful about his phrasing in writing to his brother-in-law.[51]

The paragraph in his diary was shorter than the letter, but more specific and less tactful:

Concord Once More 1869–1864

Saturday, July 18   Concord
Made my call on Mr. Hawthorne. He desired remembrances to Henry
Bright. The son, Julian, was at dinner and took me for a rainy walk
afterwards by the old Manse and across the Concord river. Mr. Hawthorne talked for some time of politics. He is in despair about the war and
the country and he is a copperhead of copperheads. Mr. Hawthorne has
all the prejudices about the negroes—'they smell, their intellects are
inferior', etc., etc. He gave me pleasant California hock, bad claret and
bad beer. He showed me his 'cloister', with the track made by himself in
pacing it, on the top of a rise beyond the house.[52]

Thompson went on to say that copperheads were so called from "the
name of the most disgusting sort of snake in America." They were the
old "pro-South Democrats" who had controlled the Union for the last
forty years "This is the party which established the bad character of the
Union government and pushed forward slavery. Now they are dying to
get into power again."[53]

Many of Hawthorne's readers assumed that because he and Pierce
were friends, he agreed completely with the ex-president on all political matters. Such an assumption certainly promoted discussion about
Hawthorne's dedication, but Fields was probably wrong in thinking
that the dedication would hurt the sale of Our Old Home. It may actually
have helped sales of the book in America. The articles had already
amused and pleased many American readers of the Atlantic, including
those who were antagonized by Britain's failure to remain absolutely
neutral during the war.

In England the reception of Hawthorne's book was quite different.
Some strong reactions to the volume were created, not by the dedication, but by the author's personal comments on the nature of English
people, which were interspersed freely throughout the narrative portions of his book.[54] Magazine and newspaper reviews expressed a wide
range of criticism, from finding fault with petty details to explosions of
wrath or biting satire on the author's attitude toward the British. The
passage cited as most offensive was Hawthorne's picture of the
middle-aged British "dowager," a figure he chose as representative of
some of the crowd on Leamington's Parade:

She has an awful ponderosity of frame, not pulpy, like the looser
development of our few fat women, but massive with solid beef and
streaky tallow; so that (though struggling manfully against the idea) you
inevitably think of her as made up of steaks and sirloins. When she walks,

‡   215   ‡

her advance is elephantine. When she sits down, it is on a great round space of her Maker's footstool where she looks as if nothing could ever move her.[55]

The description was quoted in part or referred to by most of the critics, but there was disagreement among them as to how seriously a reader should take such comments on the "Female Bull."

Personal response came from several of Hawthorne's English friends, who challenged some of his criticisms of their countrymen—or women. In a letter to Hawthorne commenting on his review written for the *Examiner,* Henry Bright took issue with his friend in a light and kindly way for his abuse of English ladies: "It really was too bad some of the things you say. . . . Mrs. Heywood says to my mother, 'I really believe you and I were the only ladies he knew in Liverpool, and we're not like beefsteaks!'—so all the ladies are furious." In addition, Bright pointed out that his second child, a girl, had been born on the sixteenth of that month, and that since she promised eventually to be a typical Englishwoman, he felt called upon to defend his own "ladies." However, he was quick to note Hawthorne's appreciation of himself (though he was not directly named in the book) and of his country in general. The rest of his letter, a chatty recounting of affairs of family and friends, shows that he forgave Hawthorne for this one passage, which Bright said he had written "like a cannibal." Bright's criticism was an illustration of the tilting of lances that the two friends had been accustomed to in Liverpool.[56]

Bennoch did not wait for the publication of the book to mail his response. He wrote to Hawthorne not long after the article "A London Suburb" appeared in the *Atlantic.* First, he gratefully acknowledged Hawthorne's praise of his Blackheath home, for even though his own name had not been given, many readers, he knew, would recognize the place. Then he challenged the author's articles on three points: inaccurate descriptions of English fruits and of the game kiss-in-the-ring, and the ridiculous picture of British women. With his usual good humor he took Hawthorne to task for comparing English women unfavorably with American women by saying, "This won't do! For either grace or loveliness, good bearing or refined gentleness, I'll back England's daughters against the world." Apparently he was thinking of young girls, not the middle-aged "dowager." Almost his last line was the much-repeated question, "When are we to have your new romance?"[57]

There is no indication that Hawthorne responded directly to any of the remarks sent in letters or printed in periodicals, but he was both hurt and surprised by British reactions to his book. To Fields he wrote that in looking over the volume he was surprised to find that whenever he drew comparisons between Englishmen and Americans, he "almost invariably cast the balance against" his own countrymen. He concluded that it was not "a weighty book, nor does it deserve any great amount either of praise or censure."[58]

Hawthorne's English friends and more perceptive readers forgave him for his critical remarks in view of his more important appreciation of English heritage. One of the longest reviews of the book dismissed Hawthorne's abuse of the English by picturing him as sparring with well-padded gloves that dealt blows that fell as lightly as eiderdown; in other words, his "small snarls" were more "amusing than irritating."[59]

But his "small snarls" were not always quickly forgotten. A year or two later one of his greatest admirers, the novelist Anthony Trollope, who had met Hawthorne in September of 1861, still could not resist a gentle slap at the author for his description of British women. In the first of his *Palliser* series, Trollope chose to poke a little good-natured fun at the American writer when he contrasted Lady Monk with Hawthorne's English dowager:

> Lady Monk was a woman now about fifty years of age, who had been a great beauty, and who was still handsome in her advanced age. Her figure was very good. She was tall and of fine proportion, though by no means verging to that state of body which our excellent American friend and critic Mr. Hawthorne has described as beefy and has declared to be the general condition of English ladies of Lady Monk's age. Lady Monk was not beefy.[60]

In spite of the slight sarcasm, Trollope actually paid tribute to Hawthorne by calling him "our excellent American friend and critic." Ever since the two men had met in Boston, Trollope had been frank in publishing his favorable opinion of Hawthorne. In *North America* when he spoke of literary associations in Concord, he described the town as the residence of Emerson and Hawthorne, who was "certainly the first of American novelists." "In point of imagination, which, after all, is the novelist's greatest gift, I hardly know any living author who can be accounted superior to Mr. Hawthorne."[61]

To Hawthorne himself, regardless of praise or blame from his readers, the English sketches remained only a "slight" volume. In spite of his diffidence about the book, he was a better critic than the reviewers and other readers who overemphasized his unfavorable references to the English. A survey of the twelve essays shows that the first three he wrote (on Burns country, Oxford, and Old Boston) are almost straight travelogues. For the most part, the rest of the sketches show an increase in humor as well as in the number of comparisons between British and Americans. *Our Old Home*, though borrowing many incidents from the English notebooks, proves to be far different from the daily jottings begun ten years earlier, but it is still ambivalent in its attitude toward England. Hawthorne had hated much of his consular experience and had been irritated or bored by some people and events; but he loved the scenery, the old castles and cathedrals, he appreciated numerous individual Englishmen, and he longed to return. His feelings were summed up when he wrote about Americans abroad in the introductory chapter: "After all these bloody wars and vindictive animosities, we have still an unspeakable yearning towards England" (*O.O.H.*, CE, p. 18).

The majority of Hawthorne's ninteenth-century readers seem to have overlooked an important point in their judgment of *Our Old Home:* Even in a book intended to be nonfiction, the author became a literary persona. "I" is not Hawthorne, but a figure of his imagination. The prefaces of his romances should have prepared his readers for such a figure. Furthermore, the opening chapter presents Mr. Consul at once as a humorous, almost imaginary character. As soon as he was out of office, Hawthorne wrote, he experienced a sense of illusion: "The retrospect began to look unreal" and he asked himself, "Is it not a dream altogether?" (p. 38). The romancer's stance persisted. The concluding sentence of the Lichfield sketch on places sacred to the literary man says that "sublime and beautiful facts are best understood when etherealized by distance" (p. 138).

Beginning with the sketch "Leamington Spa," Hawthorne's ambivalence toward England shows up especially in his comments about the general nature of English people. Seldom did he exaggerate as much as he did in picturing the middle-aged dowager, and if one searches for remarks that are extremely critical of the British, he finds fewer than he might expect. Most of these are intended to be humorous. In describing the shops at the entrance of the never-to-be-finished Thames tunnel, he wrote, "The Englishman has burrowed under the bed of his great river, and set ships of two or three thousand tons a-rolling over his head, only to provide new sites for a few old women to sell cakes and ginger-beer!" (p. 247). Occasionally there is a sharp edge that makes the comment a more serious generalization, such as his accusation that the common people have no "daily familiarity with" the washbowl or the bathtub. But immediately afterward he notes that "these are broad facts, involving great corollaries and dependencies" (p. 235).

But if Hawthorne found fault with the English, he could also often be generous: "Though the individual Englishman is sometimes preternaturally disagreeable, an observer standing aloof has a sense of natural kindness towards them in the lump" (p. 224). Occasionally he went so far as to give unequivocable praise to the picturesqueness of English scenery or to the warm-hearted hosts who took him into their homes (Spiers of Oxford and the Bennochs, for example). In the concluding paragraph of the Leamington sketch, he summed up his general feeling about England: "An American seldom feels quite as if he were at home among the English people. If he do so, he has ceased to be an American. But it requires no long residence to make him love their island, and appreciate it as thoroughly as they themselves" (p. 64).

The last two sketches, which were written especially for his collection of essays, form a framework that seems to have the most humor, as well as the greatest number of comparisons between British and Americans. These sketches were composed in 1863, when Hawthorne's health was failing rapidly and one might expect the least degree of humor. The introductory chapter, "Consular Experiences," bears out Hawthorne's own statement that in looking over the book he felt he had been harder on his countrymen than on the English. One short passage illustrates his point: "They [groups of Americans] often came to the Consulate in parties of half-a-dozen or more, on no business whatever, but merely to subject their public servant to a rigid examination, and see how he was getting on with his duties" (p. 11).

In the end, Hawthorne succeeded in poking the most fun at himself, or rather at that fictional Mr. Consul, as he rises to make a speech at the Lord Mayor's Dinner in London: "I got upon my legs to save both countries, or perish in the attempt. . . . But as I have never happened to stand in a position of greater dignity and peril, I deem it a stratagem of sage policy here to close these sketches, leaving myself still erect in so heroic an attitude" (p. 345).

Hawthorne was the most successful in stating the purpose of his book. In referring to his sense of futility in writing a sketch so that the scenes would produce pictures in the reader's mind, he wisely concluded, "In truth, I believe that the chief delight and advantage of this kind of literature [travel reminiscences in general] is not for any real information that it supplies to untravelled people, but for reviving the recollections and reawakening the emotions of persons already acquainted with the scenes described" (p. 259). He had thus restated to other readers a point made in the introductory letter to Pierce that the book was "a slight volume" meant for pure pleasure, but not the English masterpiece he had once wished to produce. The reading public could not know the depth of his sense of failure.

In the dedicatory letter to Pierce he had confessed his previous hope that *Our Old Home* would not be all he might write; at first he had planned the sketches only for the "side-scenes and back-grounds" of an ambitious work of fiction. Now this "abortive project" had been thrown aside and would never be completed. The reason was only too clear: "The Present, the Immediate, the Actual, has proved too potent for me. It takes away not only my scanty faculty, but even my desire for imaginative composition, and leaves me sadly content to scatter a thousand peaceful fantasies upon the hurricane that is sweeping us all along with it, possibly, into a Limbo where our nation and its polity may be as literally the fragments of a shattered dream as my unwritten Romance" (*O.O.H.*, CE, p. 4).

It would seem that Hawthorne had thus closed the door on further attempts to write fiction. Publication of the sketches had left him more exhausted than he had ever been. In a spirit of depression he wrote to Fields that he had just read the verses in the *Atlantic* on "Weariness": "I too am weary, and begin to look ahead for the Wayside Inn."[62] Fields, no doubt alarmed by his friend's admission, urged him to begin a new romance. Hawthorne hesitated because he doubted whether he could complete another long piece of work. But financial burdens were pressing, and it seemed that he must write if the Hawthornes were to continue to live in their usual style at the Wayside. Expenses were increasing now that Julian had been accepted at Harvard. Nathaniel had refused a summer trip to the White Mountains because of the high cost of board, although he and Una (who had been ill again that spring) did make a short trip together to Rockport, Massachusetts, in September. He had already written to Ticknor requesting $300 to cover payment of his bills, stating, "I expect to outlive my means and die in the alms-house. Julian's college expenses will count up tremendously." Sophia also emphasized their shortage of funds: "If Mr. Hawthorne did not write, we could by no means make our expenses come within our income, and it is a pain to him to be so hard driven in his present unenergetic condition."[63]

His condition was more than "unenergetic"; it was a steadily increasing weakness. Early in the summer he had had an attack of nosebleeding that lasted more than twenty-four hours. In October, Sophia wrote to Annie Fields that her husband took cold almost every day. Later in the fall he was seriously ill. Sophia referred to the dismal Thanksgiving they had. Part of the weakness near the end of that year probably resulted from an unexpected trip on December 4 to the funeral of Pierce's wife, which took place on a bitter cold day at Andover, Massachusetts. Pierce, though "overcome with his own sorrow," carefully "drew up the collar of Hawthorne's coat to shield him from the wind as they were standing at the grave." Afterward Hawthorne spent the night at Fields's home, reminiscing rather cheerfully about his youth in Maine. Annie Fields, however, was disturbed at how ill and nervous their guest seemed to be. He had brought with him the first chapter of his new untitled book (later to be called *The Dolliver Romance*), but he would not agree to go ahead with the writing until Fields had read that portion and admired it. Even so, Hawthorne said he thought he could never finish the book.[64]

At that time Fields seems to have been the only one who was aware that Hawthorne had returned to the theme of the elixir of life in an American romance. This time the theme was not how to find an elixir, but what to do with it. That first chapter was strongly autobiographical in its picture of an old man struggling to stay alive in order to look after his small granddaughter; only Hawthorne himself had now reached the stage of needing someone to look after him most of the time. Later in December he was seriously ill again, and Sophia became more alarmed. She admitted in a letter to Una, who was away visiting, that Nathaniel was "very thin and pale and weak," even though he was better than he had been. "I give him oysters now. Hitherto he has had only toasted crackers and lamb and beef tea." It seems he had agreed to see a doctor, but he wished to go by himself, and that he was as yet unable to do. "Meanwhile he is very nervous and delicate; he cannot bear anything, and he must be handled like the airiest Venetian glass."[65]

During these days he was unable to do any more writing, though he evidently read the proofsheets for chapter one of the romance. When Fields went to see him in Concord on January 8, he found Hawthorne in his dressing gown, sitting in front of the fire. He said he had done nothing for three weeks. By the seventeenth of the month he was apologizing for not have proceeded with his writing, but he suggested that Fields ought to be thankful that he was not pestered with the kind of "decrepit pages" submitted by an author who still claimed to be "full of the old spirit and vigor." Then once again he prophesied better than he realized: "Seriously, my mind has for the present, lost its temper and its fine edge, and I have an instinct that I had better keep quiet. Perhaps I shall have a new spirit of vigor, if I wait quietly for it; perhaps not."[66]

This first portion of the romance, which had been planned for serial publication in the *Atlantic*, was supposed to appear in February. But as soon as Hawthorne realized he could not go ahead with the story, he wrote to Fields that if the editor wished to print the chapter as a fragment and charge him "with overpayment," he could do so. He could not suggest what kind of explanation Fields might offer to his readers: the author's health? an "addled brain"? Should he announce that the author was not fulfilling his contract? Whatever Fields said, or whether he said anything, would make little difference to the public. That statement alone reveals Hawthorne's mental state. If he forced himself to complete the work, he said, it would be the death of him. Then he went on to explain that he was not "low-spirited, nor fanciful, nor freakish," but he looked "what seem to be realities in the face" and was ready for whatever should come. "If I could but go to England now, I think that the sea voyage and the 'Old Home' might set me all right." It was the old, oft-repeated hope. His last request to Fields was that none of these statements be referred to in the answer that Fields might send to Concord; in other words, he was keeping all such ideas from his family.[67]

That sentence suggests what had slowly been happening in the family relationships. The children were away much of the time. Sophia served as nurse in looking after her husband's physical needs, but more and more he had been withdrawing into himself. In the old days he had always read finished manuscripts aloud to Sophia. (*The Marble Faun* seems to represent one of the few occasions on which Sophia read the story before it was completed.) Since his return from England he had had nothing to read aloud except now and then one of the *Atlantic* sketches. His sense of failure must have haunted him to the end. How much it actually contributed to his slow death we can never tell.

A reading of the first fragment of this last "abortive romance" tells us a good deal about the feelings of its author, a man who had aged prematurely. The chapter presents a clear picture of Dr. Dolliver's physical infirmities in a gentle, whimsical style that recalls Hawthorne's earlier powers. What impresses and saddens the reader is that the author could create some of the finest details in his picture of "Grand-sir" and do it in his usual polished language, but that he had lost the power to control. It looks as if he had intended the Gothic device of the

magic elixir to be the central symbol of his book and then realized that
he did not know what to do with it. If he could finish the book, he wrote
to Longfellow, it might be full of wisdom about matters of life and
death.[68] Perhaps he had been correct in the dedication of *Our Old Home*
when he said that his imaginative faculties were in abeyance, for what
he wrote in this first chapter was realistic description of his own state
before he became as weak as he was late in 1863.[69] "Grandsir" Dolliver,
though feeble, could still potter about the house and had enough vigor
to take care of little Pansie's needs. His creator lacked the ability even to
look after himself.

Whether Hawthorne was sensitive about his declining powers of
imagination or simply lacking in energy to write letters, it is evident that
during that last winter and spring he did not keep in touch with Bright
or Bennoch. A more powerful reason may have been that he could not
admit to himself or to them that he had given up hope of returning to
England. The only incentive now for the voyage would be to improve
his health, yet he was well aware that neither his physical condition nor
his income would allow such a long journey. Furthermore, how could
he, a broken man, with his English romance thrown aside, face those
British friends who had known him in his vigorous days? Any correspondence with them must have become a painful reminder of the
unfortunate events that followed his years in the consulate. Let the old
dream of England remain a dream. Silence on his part was the only
policy left.

He had already warned Bennoch not to expect a steady correspondence, but Bennoch was still concerned when he did not hear from
Hawthorne at all. He waited until March before sending New Year's
greetings, along with the reminder that since Hawthorne owed him at
least a dozen letters, he was writing only a half page "to show you that
we are still in the land of the living, and not forgetful of our dear
American friends so torn and troubled." In spite of his threatened
short note, he devoted two sheets to comments on wars in America and
in Europe. Near the end of his letter he expressed a supposition that
had more truth in it than he realized: that Hawthorne was getting
"venerably gray" and that his grown children were "about ready to
swarm off and form new hives of their own."[70]

When this last letter of Bennoch's reached Concord, Hawthorne was
preparing for a short trip (to Washington again) to improve his health.
The idea was probably Sophia's, though Nathaniel completed the
arrangements by writing a final note to Ticknor, who was to accom-

pany him. In order to meet Ticknor in Boston, Hawthorne stayed overnight at Fields's house. Later Fields wrote a graphic description of his friend as he appeared on the night of March 28:

> I was greatly shocked at his invalid appearance, and he seemed quite deaf. The light in his eye was beautiful as ever, but his limbs seemed shrunken and his usual stalwart vigor utterly gone. He said to me with a pathetic voice, "Why does Nature treat us like little children! I think we could bear it all if we knew our fate; at least it would not make much difference to me now what became of me." Toward night he brightened up a little, and his delicious wit flashed out, at intervals, as of old; but he was evidently broken and dispirited about his health.[71]

On the way south from Boston, stormy weather in New York confined Hawthorne and Ticknor to their rooms at Astor House, but as soon as conditions permitted, the two travelers moved on to Philadelphia. Ticknor wrote to Sophia a number of times to reassure her that her husband was improving somewhat in spite of the bad weather. But in the meantime Sophia had sent to Bridge a long letter describing her anxieties about Nathaniel's health and regretting that he had refused to see a doctor. His attitude had made her feel that nothing was being done "for his relief." The trip with Ticknor should help, and Bridge could see for himself when he met the two men later in Washington.[72]

But they did not get as far as Washington. Ticknor contracted a cold that developed rapidly into pneumonia. Hawthorne wrote to Fields on Saturday, April 9, that although he was concerned about the doctor's treatment of Ticknor, he was optimistic about the recovery. By Sunday morning Ticknor was dead. Hawthorne was left alone and exhausted. In response to a telegram from the hotel management, Ticknor's son Howard came at once to take charge. As soon as Howard arrived, Hawthorne left for Boston. He stayed overnight again with Fields before returning to Concord.[73]

If Fields was shocked by Hawthorne's "invalid appearance" before the trip south, he was even more shocked by his condition when Nathaniel arrived at the Fieldses' house on his way home. His mental state was "healthier," Fields thought, but "the experience had been a terrible one. I can never forget the look of pallid exhaustion he wore the night he returned to us. He said he had scarcely eaten or slept."[74]

Nathaniel walked to the Wayside from the railroad station in Concord because there was no carriage. Sophia was frightened as she looked at his face, "so haggard, so white, so deeply scored with pain and fatigue . . . so much more ill he looked than I ever saw him before . . . his brow was streaming with a perfect rain, so great had been the effort to walk so far. . . . He needed much to get home to me, where he could fling off all care of himself and give way to his feelings, pent up and kept back for so long." Sophia's long letter to the Fieldses thanked them for their hospitality to her husband and told them how much her life was now completely devoted to his welfare. She did not like to have him go up or down stairs alone. She did nothing but sit with him, waiting to see what he needed. "He has not smiled since he came home till today; . . . but a smile looks strange on a face that once shone like a thousand suns with smiles. The light for the time has gone out of his eyes, entirely. An infinite weariness films them quite. I thank Heaven that summer and not winter approaches."[75]

Less than a week afterward, Emerson, who did not realize the seriousness of Hawthorne's condition, offered to take him to the Shakespeare anniversary meeting of the Saturday Club, but of course it was impossible.[76] However, since Ticknor's death, the family felt that if Hawthorne remained in Concord, nothing could save him. What they thought might be a solution was proposed by Pierce: a leisurely trip to Concord, New Hampshire, which the two could use as headquarters for short excursions. Others in the family made the arrangements, though on May 7 Hawthorne himself wrote one last letter to Pierce. The shaky handwriting verifies one of Hawthorne's symptoms, which he himself admitted: "My own health continues rather poor, but I shall hope to revive rapidly when once we are on the road. Excuse the brevity of my note, for I find some difficulty in writing." Sophia enclosed a note saying that she was glad her husband had been able to write, for "he passed a very wretched night last night."[77]

Although Julian was not in Concord when Nathaniel left for Boston on May 9, his account written long afterward shows the son's understanding of his father. Nathaniel must have known, Julian wrote, that this would be his last journey, and although no one else could realize how difficult it was for him to say farewell to his wife, she would be spared the "lingering anguish of seeing him fade out of existence before her eyes."[78]

On the day following Hawthorne's arrival in Boston, Oliver Wendell Holmes, at Sophia's request, met and talked with him, with the idea of making some useful suggestions for the trip. According to his own account, Holmes questioned Hawthorne about his symptoms— stomach "pain, distension, difficult digestion, with great wasting of flesh and strength." He also mentioned the writer's slow, feeble step.

Holmes prescribed a sedative, and Hawthorne, though accepting what little advice the physician could give, spoke as if there was no hope; his work was finished and he would "write no more."[79] He did not say so, but there is no doubt that the only question now was how much longer he would have to endure his present condition.

The next day Fields said good-by. Though he was worried about Hawthorne's ability to reach Brompton House, where he was to meet Pierce, by himself, he feared to offend his friend by offering to take him by the arm. Instead, Fields watched from the door as Hawthorne falteringly went down School Street and turned the corner.[80]

By Wednesday, May 18, Pierce and Hawthorne had traveled as far as the Pemigewasset House in Plymouth, New Hampshire. The next day Pierce sent a telegram to Boston and followed it with a letter to Fields saying that his companion had died peacefully in his sleep during the night. Would he break the news to Sophia? Pierce joined Fields in Boston as soon as possible, and they both went to Concord to be with the family.[81]

From Emerson's journal:

> Yesterday, May 23, we buried Hawthorne in Sleepy Hollow, in a pomp of sunshine and verdure, and gentle winds. James Freeman Clarke [Unitarian minister who had married the Hawthornes on July 9, 1842] read the service in the church and at the grave. Longfellow, Lowell, Holmes, Agassiz, Hoar, Dwight, Whipple, Norton, Alcott, Hillard, Fields, Judge Thomas, and I attended the hearse as pallbearers. Franklin Pierce was with the family. The church was copiously decorated with white flowers delicately arranged. The corpse was unwillingly shown,—only a few moments to this company of his friends. But it was noble and serene in its aspect,—nothing amiss,—and a calm and powerful head. A large company filled the church and the grounds of the cemetery. All was so bright and quiet that pain or mourning was hardly suggested, and Holmes said to me that it looked like a happy meeting.
>
> Clarke in the church said that Hawthorne had done more justice than any other to the shades of life, shown a sympathy with the crime in our nature, and, like Jesus, was the friend of sinners.
>
> I thought there was a tragic element in the event, that might be more fully rendered,—in the painful solitude of the man, which, I suppose, could not longer be endured, and he died of it.[82]

Emerson's account can be supplemented by one or two other statements. Sophia said later that she had objected at first to a large church funeral, but that Annie Fields had persuaded her that her husband's fame demanded it. Fields added that the manuscript of *The Dolliver Romance* was on the coffin during the funeral, but it was removed before Pierce scattered flowers into the grave. Julian later expressed in print a strong appreciation of Pierce for his "rare power of sympathy: thought for others rather than for himself."[83]

Throughout those difficult days Sophia was sustained by a tremendous religious faith. She was certain that her husband was not in Sleepy Hollow; he had entered heaven at once, where she would one day meet him, but because of the children she could not join him soon. She poured out these and other feelings in two long letters to Annie Fields.[84] The children had no such consolation.

A short time later, Longfellow mailed to Sophia a copy of the poem he had sent to the *Atlantic* for publication. She must have been pleased by the description of the day of her husband's funeral, that "one bright day / In the long week of rain," by the picture of the meadow, the Old Manse, and the hilltop of Sleep Hollow "hearsed with pines," and especially by the last stanza paying tribute to the author who "left the tale half-told":

> Ah! who shall lift that wand of magic power,
> And the lost clew regain?
> The unfinished window in Aladdin's tower
> Unfinished must remain![85]

The poem was not published until three months after Hawthorne's death. The news reached England long before then, and Henry Bright wrote for the *Examiner* a moving tribute to his American friend. Bennoch wrote nothing for publication at that time, but neither man ever forgot the pleasure of his friendship with Hawthorne. For the rest of their lives, in words and in deeds, they kept alive his memory.

Nathaniel's children did not express their feelings in print until long afterward. Rose, who wrote perhaps the least about the loss of their father, ended her book with a sentence touching in its brevity. The final line of *Memories* says only, "We have missed him in the sunshine, in the storm, in the twilight, ever since."[86]

‡ 10 ‡

Epilogue

THE DREAM OF ENGLAND as Our Old Home did not die with Nathaniel Hawthorne. The rest of the family eventually returned to live in that country—two of them only temporarily, the other two for the rest of their lives. All four, with the aid of the two Englishmen who had meant so much to Nathaniel, helped to perpetuate his memory by getting his unpublished works into print or by writing about him themselves.

After Hawthorne's death his widow had no intention of leaving the Wayside. For her, life would continue as if he were still there in spirit to guide her in her efforts to look after their children. In less than four years the situation changed completely. Julian was dissatisfied with the technical school in which he had enrolled after leaving Harvard. Una was unhappy over her broken engagement to Storrow Higginson. Rose was amenable to any change. Besides, upkeep of the Wayside became so expensive that Sophia could not manage financially, although she attempted to earn money by copying for publication parts of her husband's notebooks.

In some ways this new work was a welcome task, for it constantly brought back memories of her life with him. But while preparing the American notebooks for publication, she discovered what she thought was careless bookkeeping on the part of Ticknor and Fields. Upon presenting the matter to Fields, she was shocked not only to find herself in debt to him, but also to learn that some years ago the percentage on royalties of her husband's books had been reduced from fifteen to twelve. In spite of the quarrel that gradually developed, she did agree to let Fields's company publish both the English and the French and Italian notebooks. She could scarcely do otherwise, for it was money from the American notebooks that would pay the family's passage to Europe and cover living costs there until the Wayside could be sold.[1]

Sophia explained the family's hopes and plans to Henry Bright about a year before they finally moved. In the end they decided to go *not* to England, as she had implied in her letter, but to Dresden. There Julian could attend an engineering school; the girls could study art and music; and the cost of living, according to Elizabeth Peabody, who recommended the city, would be less than in postwar America.[2] Sophia could do her copying anywhere, and the city, which they had also heard about from other friends, sounded ideal.

They lived in Dresden less than two years. Sophia spent her days, between periods of ill health, copying passages from the French and Italian notebooks and completing her own book, *Notes in England and Italy*, based on the journals she had kept for several years. She gave the manuscript to Putnam's rather than to Fields for publication. In the preface she apologized for sketches she had never intended to publish. Though she did not admit it, she had broken the promise she had made to Fields in 1860 that nothing less than starvation would cause her to publish anything. Perhaps her uncertain income in this strange city seemed to threaten starvation, for the Hawthornes had to be extremely thrifty in their small rented house. Still, Sophia proved that she had not lost her distaste for female writers: Not only did she apologize for her own book, she also refused to sign her name as editor of any of the passages from her husband's notebooks.

While Sophia was busy writing and editing, Una did charity work for the Church of England, of which she had become a member. Rose studied art. Julian studied German and attended technical school for about a year. Then he became engaged to an American girl who was traveling abroad with her family, and he began to plan for a career in engineering in the United States. In the spring of 1870 Sophia and Una made a trip to London to make arrangements for an English copyright on *Passages from the French and Italian Note-books*. They stayed with the Bennochs and visited Annie Bright at Malvern and Fanny Wrigley at Birkenhead. Finally they decided to return to England to live. None of the Hawthornes had liked the Dresden climate, and they thought they would feel more at home in England than anywhere else.[3] The move was made quickly in midsummer because war was breaking out on the Continent and they were afraid of being caught in Dresden. Julian went to New York, where he married May Augusta Amelung and began writing short stories in his leisure time away from his work with the city department of docks. Rose, Una, and their mother found a tiny house to rent in the Kensington area, not far from an art school in which Rose enrolled.

In November of 1870, Henry Bright wrote to Richard Monckton

Una and Rose Hawthorne, ca. 1864

Milnes an account of his visit with the Hawthorne women in Kensington. He said that Sophia had told him a good deal about the last part of her husband's life. The implication in the letter—whether his own or Sophia's, he did not say—was that Hawthorne had died of "no complaint beyond his own melancholy depression and hopeless forebodings." Bright discovered that Sophia was not satisfied with her edition of the English notebooks; she wanted him to help her revise it for a second edition, but he thought it was too late to make changes.[4]

Sophia had not admitted to anyone that her health would not permit more editorial work. She kept up a surprising amount of social life until the London climate once more proved too much to cope with. She was forced at last to go to bed with what seemed to others only a minor illness, but it was the beginning of the end. For Julian's benefit Una wrote a detailed account of her mother's last days. She had not sent him a telegram, because neither of the daughters thought that Sophia's illness was serious. The doctor decided otherwise when he was called in. His diagnosis was typhoid pneumonia that had developed rapidly from her old bronchial condition, aggravated by the English climate. Una, Mrs. Bennoch, and her maid, Louisa Deacon, cared for Sophia in the last week of her life. She died quietly on Sunday morning, February 26, 1871, as the nearby church bells were ringing. The burial was in Kensal Green Cemetery, in a lot a few steps away from the grave of Leigh Hunt, an Englishman whom Hawthorne had admired. On the grave Una and Rose planted ivy and periwinkle from Sleepy Hollow Cemetery. The inscription on the headstone reads simply, "Sophia, wife of Nathaniel Hawthorne." On the stone at the foot is quoted, "I am the Resurrection and the Life."[5]

London friends, both those who had known Nathaniel and the newer Kensington neighbors, came forward with offers to help the girls. Temporarily life went on as before. Rose continued her art lessons. Una, with the assistance of Robert Browning, worked at deciphering the handwriting in the Septimius romance manuscript, which her mother had evidently begun copying. The work was a strain on Una's delicate health. Added to that was the shock of Rose's engagement to G. P. Lathrop, one of two sons in an American family the Hawthornes had met in Dresden. Realizing that she would soon be left completely alone, Una broke down. Dr. Channing, who was then preaching in London and had kept in touch with the family, explained Una's breakdown as "brain fever," a result of the various shocks to her system, weakened ever since the first attack of Roman fever.[6]

When she recovered, Una decided to stay on alone in London, since

Rose and her husband had gone to America, and to continue her charity work for the church. This she did until Julian and his family returned to live in a London suburb. Then Una made her home with them.

For a number of years no more of Hawthorne's works were published. Having given up engineering, Julian was busy starting his own career as a writer of romances. Following a brief try at living in Dresden, he and his family moved to the London suburbs, first to St. John's Wood and then to Twickenham, where they rented a rather large house to accommodate the growing family. After she returned from visiting Rose in America, Una moved into her own room at Julian's and lived there for the rest of her short life. In New York she had met Albert Webster, a tubercular young man making a start at writing for periodicals. They did not become engaged at that time because it seemed that his health would not permit marriage. A trip to the Sandwich Islands was recommended to him. First he spent a year en route to and in California. When his health seemed to be improved, he and Una became engaged by correspondence and began making plans for their marriage in the summer of 1877. Webster sailed for Honolulu, but died three days before the ship landed. The news of his death caused Una to lose all interest in life and gradually to fade away. She died a few months later and was buried in Kensal Green beside her mother. The stone on her grave reads, "Una Hawthorne, Daughter of Nathaniel Hawthorne, Died September 9, 1877."[7]

Meanwhile, as the number of his children increased, Julian had financial troubles in spite of the thriftiness of his wife. Bright and Bennoch did all they could to help by getting loans and a sum from the London Literary Fund to tide him over between publication dates. A diplomatic post in London was suggested as a solution, but Julian decided instead to return to the United States, not because he was better paid there, but because, like his father before him, he wanted his children to be educated in America. In the States Julian published under the title *Dr. Grimshawe's Secret* his version of his father's studies for the unfinished English romance, and also his two-volume biography of his parents. This was only the beginning of a long series of sketches and autobiographical books that included much material on his father's life and literary circle.

The youngest of the Hawthorne children did not keep in touch with her father's English friends after she and George Lathrop settled in America, but she did devote a portion of her long and active life to writing about her parents.[8] Although she published some articles, it was not until 1896 that she finally completed her book of recollections of her father. Since she had been only thirteen when he died, her recollections were rather dim childhood ones; therefore she relied primarily upon her mother's letters, which had been in her keeping since London days. The book was, as the title admits, *Memories*.

So also to some extent was Julian's biography of his parents, for he was not quite eighteen when his father died, but he had the help of his father's friends and was himself by that time an established writer. Henry Bright provided notes for Julian's use in the biography. Though he also supplied some letters, he wrote that he could not furnish for publication much of his and Nathaniel's correspondence. Nor could he write about the most intimate details of their friendship. He was happy, though, that Julian was at last writing a biography that logically should be more accurate than previous attempts by outsiders. Bright did not live long enough to review Julian's volumes as he had the other biographical sketches and Hawthorne's own posthumously published books. Before the time of publication he had been forced to retire from business and to travel to southern France for the sake of his health. Neither France nor a winter on the southern coast of England helped him in his fight against tuberculosis. He returned to the home he had built for his family at Ashfield, near Liverpool, and died a few days later in May of 1884. He was only fifty-four years old.[9]

By contrast, Bennoch, in spite of frequent attacks of gout in his last years, lived to what his contemporaries would have called a ripe old age. After he moved from the suburbs into London and retired as head of his own company, he retained a position as consultant to a number of other organizations. For the Association of Foreign Bondholders, he made a trip to Virginia to investigate the financial situation of that state, which had not paid its foreign debts since the war. In fact, he traveled in many directions and on numerous occasions. One of the delights of his spare time was writing letters about his past life with his American friends, particularly Hawthorne. Not only did he manage the subscription for a London portrait of Hawthorne that was to be shipped to the United States, but he also assisted in the establishment of a memorial to Longfellow in Westminster Abbey.[10]

It was on one of Bennoch's business trips to Paris in August of 1889 that Julian saw him for the last time. They met for dinner, renewed memories of old times, and parted with the feeling that they might never meet again. "Neither spoke of it," Julian wrote later, "but I saw tears in his eyes. Then came once more the genial smile, the hearty handshake, the cheery goodbye."[11] Bennoch lived less than a year after that Paris meeting. In June of 1890, on another of his business trips, he suddenly became ill on the train to Berlin and died before a doctor could be summoned. He was seventy-eight.

When Julian said good-by to Bennoch, all connections between Hawthorne's children and their father's old friends in England came to an end. With the passing years the evidence of Hawthorne's relationship to Our Old Home has become dependent upon the written word. The physical evidence—the consulate building and the houses where the Hawthornes stayed in England—has for the most part disappeared. Only two markers remain. One is the L.C.C. sign on Bennoch's former home in Blackheath: "Nathaniel Hawthorne . . . Stayed Here." With the continuous process of the old making way for the new, it too may vanish. That would leave one other marker, so far undisturbed: the sign on the house at 10 Lansdowne Circus in Leamington, "Hawthorne's Old Home."[12]

Notes

Appendix: Biographical Sketches

Index

Notes

Key to Abbreviations

For quick reference to sources and other information, three categories of materials have been abbreviated for use in the notes:

1. Correspondents. Members of the Hawthorne family are represented by initials unless the name is short:

N.H.	Nathaniel
S.H.	Sophia
U.H.	Una
J.H.	Julian
R.II.	Rose
E.M.H.	Elizabeth, Nathaniel's sister
E.P.P.	Elizabeth Palmer Peabody, Sophia's sister
Mary Mann	Mrs. Horace Mann, Sophia's sister

One outsider, since his name occurs frequently in the notes and is long, is represented as follows:

II.A.B.	Henry Arthur Bright

2. Shortened forms for publications referred to frequently:

AN	*American Notebooks*, ed. Claude Simpson. Ohio State U. Press, 1972.
CE	Centenary Edition, the works of N.H. published to date by Ohio State U. Press.
CW	*Complete Works of N.H.* Boston: Houghton Mifflin, 1883.
EN	*English Notebooks*, ed. Randall Stewart. N.Y.: MLA, 1941; rpt. N.Y.: Russell & Russell, 1962.
F&IN	French and Italian notebooks, N.H. Pearson's transcript for unpublished dissertation, Yale U.; individual volumes numbered according to source also, as MA (Morgan), HM (Huntington), and (Berg). See section 3.
H&HC	*Hawthorne and His Circle*, by Julian Hawthorne. N.Y.: Harper & Brothers, 1903.
H&HP	*Hawthorne and His Publisher*, by Caroline Ticknor. Boston: Houghton Mifflin, 1913.
LL	*Love Letters of Nathaniel Hawthorne, 1839-1863*. Chicago: Society of the Dofobs, 1907; rpt. Washington, D.C.: NCR Microcard Editions, 1972. 2 vols.

LT	*Letters of Hawthorne to William D. Ticknor, 1851–1864.* Newark: Carteret Book Club, 1910; rpt. Washington, D.C.: Microcard Editions, 1972. 2 vols.
Memoirs	*Memoirs of Julian Hawthorne,* ed. Edith Garrigues Hawthorne. N.Y.: Macmillan, 1938.
Memories	*Memories of Hawthorne,* by Rose Hawthorne Lathrop. Boston: Houghton Mifflin, 1897.
NH&HW	*Nathaniel Hawthorne and His Wife: a Biography,* by Julian Hawthorne. Boston: James R. Osgood & Co., 1885. 2nd ed. 2 vols.
P.D. (N.H.)	Pocket diary for 1859 (Berg); the 1856 diary of N.H., seldom referred to, is in Morgan Library.
P.D. (S.H.)	Pocket diary for 1859 (Berg).
Recollections	*Personal Recollections of Nathaniel Hawthorne,* by Horatio Bridge. 1893; rpt. N.Y.: Haskell House, 1968.
Shapes	*Shapes That Pass,* by Julian Hawthorne. Boston: Houghton Mifflin, 1928.
Yesterdays	*Yesterdays with Authors,* by James T. Fields. Boston: Houghton Mifflin, 1900.

Periodicals are represented by standard abbreviations, as *ATQ, ESQ, NEQ,* and *NHJ.*

3. Collections of unpublished materials and/or the libraries where they are found are listed as follows:

Ban.	Bancroft Library, U. of California at Berkeley
Bar.	Clifton Waller Barrett Library of American Literature, U. of Virginia: two collections, N. Hawthorne, no. 6247, and Francis Bennoch, no. 7120. Author's initials in notes indicate which collection is referred to.
Berg	Albert Berg Collection, N.Y. Public Library
Bow.	Library of Bowdoin College, Brunswick, Maine
BPL	Boston Public Library
Clark	Private collection of C. E. Frazer Clark, Jr., Bloomfield Hills, Mich.
Essex	James Duncan Phillips Library, Essex Institute, Salem, Mass.
HM	Huntington Library, San Marino, Calif. Includes Hawthorne collection (chiefly published in *LL* and labeled HM), Fields collection (labeled FI), and vol. V of F&IN (labeled within text as HM 302).
Ho.	Houghton Library, Harvard U., Cambridge, Mass.
MA	Pierpont Morgan Library, N.Y. City
MHS	Massachusetts Historical Society, Boston
Milburn	Ulysses S. Milburn Collection, Owen D. Young Library, St. Lawrence U., Canton, N.Y.
OSU	Ohio State U. Manuscript Collection, Columbus, Ohio
Pearson	Collection originally from notes of Norman Holmes Pearson, now part of Hawthorne Collection at Beinecke Library, Yale U. Some items are transcripts made by Mr. Pearson (including the letters of Ada Shepard); others are originals formerly owned by him.
S.L.	Letters of Ada Shepard, typed copies from the collection of Norman Holmes Pearson at Yale U.; page numbers are of typed sheets.
TCC	Trinity College, Cambridge U., Cambridge, England; includes both the Houghton papers and the Bright papers.

Chapter 1. Departure and Arrival

1. G. P. Lathrop, *A Study of Hawthorne* (Boston: James R. Osgood, 1876), p. 247n. See also Roy Nichols, *Franklin Pierce: Young Hickory of the Granite Hills* (Phila.: U. of Penna. Press, 1958, 2nd ed. rev.), p. 212, where Nichols explains that Pierce never realized what the writing of the biography cost its author.

2. "Mr. Consul Hawthorne," *Home Journal*, N.Y., Sat., Mar. 26, 1853, p. 2, col. 2; quoted in *ATQ*, no. 2 (II Quarter, 1969), p. 34.

3. Ticknor to his wife, Apr. 28, 1853, in *H&HP*, p. 46.

4. Mar. 28, 1853, in *LT*, 1:9.

5. George William Curtis, *Literary and Social Essays* (N.Y.: Kennikat Press, rpt. 1968), pp. 3-4; from the chapter on Emerson in *Homes of American Authors*, 1854.

6. N.H. to Curtis, July 14, 1852, in Lathrop, p. 243. Hawthorne had changed the name of the house from "The Hillside," so labeled by Alcott, to "The Wayside."

7. Ibid., pp. 243-44.

8. Una Hawthorne, born at the Old Manse, Concord, Mar. 3, 1844; Julian, born at the Peabodys' house in Boston, June 22, 1846; Rose, born in the Little Red House, Lenox, May 20, 1851. Sophia's birth year was recorded at the South Church, Salem, as 1809. See Louise Tharp, *The Peabody Sisters of Salem* (Boston: Little, Brown, 1950), p. 342, n. 4. Hawthorne's 1857 statement that Sophia was then 42 is from his request for passports made to Benjamin Moran, U.S. Legation, London, Sept. 15, 1857 (Berg).

9. N.H. to Ticknor, Reed, and Fields, July 5, 1853, in *LT*, 1:11.

10. N.H. to William Manning, July 2, 1853 (Essex). The bird (a cardinal, according to Sophia) survived the journey and lived for several years.

11. J.H. in *Memories*, p. 219.

12. *Shapes*, p. 6. For statistical details of the ship, see Francis E. Hyde, *Cunard and the North Atlantic* (London: Macmillan, 1975).

13. *Boston Daily Courier*, July 7, 1853, p. 2, col. 7, gives a complete list of passengers leaving Boston. Distinguished passengers included both Canadians and British, of whom J. F. Crampton, minister in Washington, D.C., was one; there were some unidentified Europeans and also Señor Pacheco, minister from Mexico to France. Sophia's shipboard journal records the 17 who boarded at Halifax.

14. For the three points of view on Leitch, see *Shapes*, p. 7; Ticknor to his wife, July 22, 1853, in *H&HP*, p. 52; and S.H. to her father, July 7, 1853, in *Memories*, pp. 220-21.

15. *Shapes*, pp. 8-9.

16. Unpublished diary by Sophia (Ban.) is partially quoted in *NH&HW*, 2:16-17.

17. Ticknor to his wife, July 22, 1853, in *H&HP*, p. 52. For details on Train and other people with whom the Hawthornes had contacts, see Appendix.

18. Original sketch in unpublished shipboard journal, dated July 7 (Ban.); another page contains a sketch of a ship's boat, probably made by Sophia.

19. S.H. to her father, in *Memories*, p. 222.

20. Scattered references to Silsbee recur in S.H.'s correspondence: S.H. to her father, Aug. 18, 1854 (Berg); *Memories*, p. 220; incomplete shipboard letter, July 1853 (Berg). Other references appear later. In *H&HC*, p. 81, Julian mistakenly refers to "George" Silsbee as "an American of the Brahman type, a child of Cambridge and Boston, a man of means, and an indefatigable traveler." The ship's passenger list shows Wm. Silsbee, Salem. See Appendix.

21. Scattered comments from the incomplete letter listed in note 20.

22. *H&HC*, p. 79.

23. Howard M. Ticknor, "Hawthorne as Seen by His Publisher," *The Critic,* 45 (July 1904): 52.

24. W. S. Tryon, *Parnassus Corner: a Life of James T. Fields, Publisher to the Victorians* (Boston: Houghton Mifflin, 1963), p. 162.

25. S.H. to Ticknor, Sept. 29, 1854 (Berg).

26. *H&HC,* p. 85.

27. N.H. to H.A.B., July 5, 1855 (Pearson); also in *NH&HW,* 2:65.

Chapter 2. Liverpool, 1853

1. Ticknor to his wife, July 22, 1853, in *H&HP,* p. 52.

2. *Shapes,* pp. 10–11.

3. William Lynn, proprietor of the Waterloo, advertised his hotel as convenient and up to date, with hot and cold showers and American ices and ice creams. *Royal Hotel Guide for 1851,* 4th ed.

4. *Shapes,* p. 11.

5. Ibid.

6. S.H. to her father, July 21, 1853, in *Memories,* p. 224. The soup may have been some of the famous turtle soup advertised for sale by Mr. Lynn. He also shipped live turtles (*Royal Hotel Guide for 1851*).

7. S.H. to her father, July 19, 1853, in *Memories,* p. 224.

8. S.H. to her father, Aug. 1853 (Berg).

9. Ticknor to his wife, July 22, 1853, in *H&HP,* p. 53.

10. *Liver* (pronounced *lyver*) supposedly represented an imaginary bird designed as part of the coat of arms of the city and intended to represent either the eagle of St. John or a sea bird, possibly a cormorant. The name of the city was an early combination of *liver* with *pool* to form a word variously spelled over the centuries: 1194, *Liverpul;* 1211, *Liverpol;* also occasionally *Litherpol.*

11. *EN,* p. 9.

12. Melville's descriptions of Liverpool are mainly in chs. 32–40 of *Redburn* (Evanston: Northwestern U. Press, 1969). For nonfictional accounts, see, for example, Richard D. Altick, *Victorian People and Ideas* (N.Y.: Norton, 1973), pp. 43–44.

13. The most thorough contemporary account of the city is Thomas Baines's 850-page volume, *History of the Commerce and Town of Liverpool, and of the Rise of Manufacturing Industry of the Adjoining Counties* (London: Longman, Brown, Green, and Longmans; Liverpool, pub. by the author, 1852).

14. No date is assigned for Hawthorne's first visit to Young's bookstore, but it was several months after his arrival, for the Hawthornes were then living in Rock Ferry. See ch. 3.

15. *Discourses in America, Works,* vol. 4 (London: Macmillan, 1903): 366.

16. S.H. to Mary Mann, Oct. 9, 1853 (Berg).

17. Terry Coleman, in the chapter "Liverpool and the Last of England," *Passage to America* (London: Hutchinson, 1972), p. 66, describes Goree Piazza (named for the island off Senegal where slavers used to take on cargoes) as having 22 offices in this small area.

18. *Wirral,* the term still in use today, is an Anglo-Saxon word meaning possibly *river meadow* or *a neck* or *spit of land. Hundred,* the term applied to many such divisions of shires, derives from the old system of measuring land by numbers of hides.

19. The Hawthornes moved primarily to save money. The English account book (unpublished original at Essex), p. 2, shows that the bill for 10 days at the Waterloo was

£32 (about $160), plus 12s. for the servants; in comparison, for 9 days at Mrs. Blodget's, Sophia paid £12 12s. (about $62), plus 8s. to the servants.

20. *Shapes*, pp. 31–32.

21. *H&HC*, pp. 175–76. For Julian's reference to Mary Blodget as a "widow," see Appendix.

22. Ibid., pp. 179–80.

23. Donald G. Mitchell, who had worked at the consulate, also emphasized that the office was a "dingy dirty place" in a "very dismal part of the town." He described the staff in 1844 as including Pearce and Wilding (the two men whom Hawthorne retained), plus Davy, and an errand boy. Letter to General Williams, Nov. 14, 1844, in Waldo H. Dunn, *The Life of Donald G. Mitchell* (N.Y.: Scribner's, 1922), p. 92.

24. Walter J. Marx, "The Consular Service of the U.S.," Washington: U.S. Dept. of State Bulletin, Sept. 19, 1955, vol. 33, no. 847, pub. 5995, p. 448. The consular service was organized Mar. 22, 1790, under Thomas Jefferson, first secretary of state, who issued the first formal instructions on Aug. 26, 1790.

25. "Circular to Consuls of the U.S.," Washington: Dept. of State, June 1, 1853, signed by W. L. Marcy, secretary (copy in Milburn).

26. N.H. to Mrs. Auld, Aug. 24, 1853 (Milburn).

27. Compare Aug 18, 1854, and Oct. 12, 1855, in *LT*, 1:60 and 106.

28. July 30, 1857, in *LT*, 2:38.

29. S.H. to H.A.B., Nov. 23, 1870 (TCC). Sophia was quoting a statement made by Nathaniel in F&IN, June 14, 1859 (MA591).

30. See James Heywood, *Academic Reform and University Representation* (London: Edward T. Whitfield, 1860). However, Heywood had been working consistently for reform since his days at Trinity.

31. The *N.Y. Herald* of May 15, 1852, carried a long front-page article, "Arrival of the Great Britain," and a second article on the history of the ship. Her reputation for speed came about because she had left Liverpool on the same day as the Cunarder *Canada*, a ship that had made the fastest run on record to Halifax; yet the *Great Britain* arrived in New York on May 14, only 17½ hours later than the *Canada* reached Halifax.

32. Details are in three previously unpublished notebooks titled "The American Journal" (TCC). I am indebted to Trinity College Library staff and to Mrs. Elizabeth Lloyd, granddaughter of H.A.B., for permission to read and take notes on this ms. It has since been edited by the late Anne Ehrenpreis under the title *Happy Country This America: the Travel Diary of Henry Arthur Bright* (Columbus: Ohio S.U. Press, 1978).

33. H.A.B. to Temple, July 19, 1852 (Glansevern Collection 4883, National Library of Wales, Aberystwyth, Dyfed).

34. Ibid., Sept. 23, 1852 (Glansevern 4884).

35. Ibid.

36. "American Journal," III, pp. 144–45 (TCC); printed in Ehrenpreis, pp. 398 and 400. Bright probably met Tom Appleton at the home of Longfellow, his brother-in-law.

37. "American Journal," III, p. 145; printed in Ehrenpreis, pp. 399–400.

38. Copy, marked by him in pencil, among the Bright papers at TCC.

39. The pamphlet was published in London by Arthur Hall Virtue & Co. and in Liverpool by Deighton, Laughton (1853). For further analysis of H.A.B.'s contacts with blacks and his attitudes, see introduction to Ehrenpreis, pp. 31–35.

40. "Consular Experiences," *Our Old Home*, CE (Columbus: Ohio S.U. Press, 1970), p. 39. (N.H. wrote this chapter in 1863.)

41. *Memories*, p. 225.

42. S.H., Dec. 8, 1853, in *Memories*, pp. 227–28. The visits referred to here were those made after the family had moved to Rock Park.

43. Quoted in *NH&HW*, 2:23–26. The original (Berg) has been wrongly dated as 1855. Julian's version has some errors in deciphering H.A.B.'s handwriting, such as transcribing Charles Morton's father instead of Norton.

44. This page, originally labeled "Inc." (Ho.), proves from the context to be a page that is missing from a letter of Nov. 11, 1853, on the death of Norton's father, Andrew. The date is significant because the Hawthornes had then been in Liverpool four months.

45. Compare Clough to Miss Smith, June 18, 1853, and Clough to Longfellow, Sept. 9, 1853, in *The Correspondence of A. H. Clough,* ed. Frederick Mulhauser (Oxford: Clarendon Press, 1957), 2:450 and 462. See also *The Life of Henry W. Longfellow,* ed. S. L. Longfellow. (Boston: Houghton Mifflin, 1891), 2:250.

46. Entries from G. A. Brown's unpublished diary dated July 25, 1853; Nov. 15, 1855; and Nov. 28, 1855 (Archives Division, William Brown Library, Liverpool).

47. Grace Greenwood had met the Hawthornes when she made a trip to New England in 1851. Neither of the Hawthornes thought much of her writings. See pp. 36–39 of my article " 'Scribbling' Females and Serious Males: Hawthorne's Comments from Abroad on Some American Authors," *NHJ,* 5 (1975). N.H. had met Miss Lynch in N.Y. when he was en route to Washington. N.H. to S.H., Apr. 17, 1853, in *LL,* 2:221.

48. S.H. to her father, Aug. 5, 1853 (Berg).

49. Compare *Shapes,* p. 19, and S.H. to her father, Aug. 9, 1853 (Berg).

Chapter 3. Rock Ferry, 1853–1855

1. Background information on the history of Rock Ferry is from E. Hubbard, "Commuter Country: 1837," *Cheshire Round,* 1, no. 6 (Autumn 1966): 185–87 and 194. Since 1970 a new expressway has changed the coastal area completely. When I first visited Rock Ferry, the esplanade was closed, the Royal Rock Hotel was boarded up, and most of the houses along the riverfront in Rock Park were being demolished. Now that they have been razed, all trace of "Hawthorne House," 26 Rock Park, has vanished.

2. S.H. to her father, Aug. 5, 1853 (Berg).

3. S.H. to her father, Aug. 11, 1853 (Berg).

4. S.H. to her father, Aug. 17, 1853 (Berg).

5. S.H. to her father, Aug. 26, 1853 (Berg).

6. N.H. to Pike, June 7, 1854 (Bow.).

7. S.H. to her father, Aug. 26, 1853 (Berg). Both S.H. and N.H. said that the house was made of stone. Julian later described it as brick covered with gray plaster. He said he could not identify the place precisely, because in the 1850s the houses had not been numbered (J.H. to Thomas H. Sherman, Esq., Dec. 11, 1891 [MA2214]). When nearby residents insisted that the house was no. 26, "Hawthorne House" was painted on the gate pillar. If the house was correctly identified, then it *was* stucco, as the demolition process revealed. Complete discussion of identification is in the series of reports in the "Antiquarian Column," *Rock Ferry and District Herald,* 1891–1892 (Document MD 205/1, *Wirral Notes and Queries,* 1 [1892]: 59, 62, and 66).

8. S.H., to her father, Aug. 26, 1853 (Berg).

9. Ibid.

10. Oct. 12, 1854, in *LT,* 1:66.

11. Expenditures were recorded daily by S.H. in the unpublished English account

book (Essex). It is impossible to refer to specific items by page numbers, since many of the pages are unnumbered and undated.

12. S.H. to her father, Oct. 4, 1853 (Berg).

13. Though Mrs. Isabelle Beeton did not publish her *Complete Book of Household Management* until 1859-1861, she summed up all the household advice and information current during the century. She was regarded as *the* authority.

14. See "A Sophia Hawthorne Journal, 1843-1844," ed. John J. McDonald, *NHJ*, 4 (1974): 1-30.

15. Mar. 3, 1854, in *LT*, 1:31.

16. S.H. to her father, Oct. 4, 1853 (Berg), refers to grapes as costing 1 cent each and peaches 12 cents each. Oranges were always referred to as a special treat.

17. Ibid.

18. Ibid.

19. S.H. to her father, Sept. 2 and 14, 1853 (Berg). For details of Victorian furnishings, see Charles Eastlake, *Hints on Household Taste in Furniture, Upholstery, and Other Details* (Boston: James R. Osgood, 1872, 2nd ed.); though addressed primarily to English readers, it was recommended by its author to the "American public"—one more indication of the influence of British customs upon Americans.

20. Louise Tharp, *The Peabody Sisters of Salem* (Boston: Little, Brown, 1950), p. 252.

21. S.H. to E.P.P., Oct. 25, 1853, Inc. (Berg).

22. S.H. to Mary Mann, Oct. 9, 1853 (Berg).

23. S.H. to her father, Nov. 17, 1854 (Berg).

24. H.A.B. to J.H., Nov. 2, 1883 (Berg).

25. *Memories*, pp. 299-300. Though Rose was not specific about playtime hours, Una wrote that Rose went to bed at 7:30; she and Julian, at 8:00. U.H. to "Grandpapa," Oct. 20, 1854 (Berg).

26. *Shapes*, pp. 25-27.

27. *MS. Diary*, 14 pages of a journal not used for her later *Notes in England and Italy* (Milburn). Calls were "from Mrs. Williams, Mrs. Blodget, Mrs. Brown, Mrs. Warren, and her two children, Mrs. Rawlins, Mrs. and Mr. Watson of Rock Park, Mrs. Banner and Mr. Banner, ditto, Mrs. William Hamilton, and Mrs. and Miss Burton, Mrs. Squarey and her two children, Mrs. Bowman, and Mrs. Loder of notorious memory."

28. Harold Edgar Young, *A Perambulation of the Hundred of Wirral in the County of Chester* (Liverpool: Henry Young & Sons, 1909), pp. 22-23. Mr. Young is quoting his father's comments. Young's bookstore, then located on S. Castle St., is the one referred to in ch. 2. Though it has not been owned by any of the Youngs for 40 years, the store is still in existence on N. John Street.

29. *H&HP*, p. 69, describes the reasons for the delay: Ticknor's busy life in London, including a garden party at Bennoch's house in Blackheath; the stay in Paris with three Bostonians, Mr. F. H. Walley; Mr. Russell, another bookseller; and W. J. Reynolds (pp. 75-76); and the journey to Edinburgh (pp. 85-88). See also Aug. 22, 25, Sept. 7, 10, 1853, in *LT*, 1:14, 16, 18.

30. S.H. to her father, Sept. 29-30, 1853, "copy in unknown hand" (Berg).

31. Oct. 8, 1853, in *LT*, 1:20. See also *H&HP*, p. 64, on N.H.'s pretense, where Ticknor's daughter points out how N.H.'s letters to her father revealed "the freedom of a man who knows that he is so well understood that it does not matter what he says."

32. S.H., to her father, Oct. 5, 1853 (Berg).

33. S.H., Oct. 21 and 23, 1853, in *Memories*, pp. 244-49.

34. N.H. to William Rathbone, Sept. 30, 1853 (Clark).

35. The original of the first note is at Milburn. See also S.H. to her father, Nov., in *Memories,* p. 255, and Nov. 23, 1853 (Berg).

36. S.H. to her father, Nov. 1853, in *Memories,* pp. 252–53.

37. S.H. in *Memories,* p. 262. The letter is dated Dec. 18, but this date must be inaccurate, since the text refers to events of Christmas and after.

38. *H&HC,* pp. 149–50; also *Memoirs,* p. 262.

39. Presentation copy, which had been dedicated by Swain to Bennoch, is in Milburn. For details of the visit, see *Memories,* p. 257. N.H.'s note inviting Bennoch to Rock Park is dated Dec. 3, 1853 (Pearson).

40. S.H. to her father, in *Memories,* pp. 258–60.

41. Ibid., p. 255.

42. S.H., Dec. 18, [?], in *Memories,* p. 260. Boxing Day, though once said to be any day between Christmas and New Year's or to commemorate St. Stephen's Day, is now celebrated as a national holiday on Dec. 26. It seems to have little to do with boxes.

43. S.H. to her father, Nov. 23–24, 1853 (Berg).

44. Compare N.H. to Ticknor, Nov. 25, 1853, in *LT,* 1:23, and N.H. to Pike, Jan. 6, 1854 (HM).

45. See Vernon Loggins, *The Hawthornes* (N.Y.: Columbia U. Press, 1951), ch. 1. For details on the Hawthorne family in England, see Charles Kerry, *History and Antiquities of the Hundred of Bray in the County of Berkshire* (London: Savill and Edwards, 1861); also William Page and P. H. Ditchfield, *Victoria History of the Counties of England,* vol. III: *Berkshire* (London: St. Catherine Press, 1923). The presence of hawthorn trees may be responsible for the name of Hawthorne Hall in Macclesfield, since apparently no Hawthorne family lived there.

46. W. Forster, in his article "An American in Cheshire," *Cheshire Round,* 1, no. 6 (Autumn 1966): 188–94, analyzed N.H.'s interests as revealed in *EN* and discussed some of the walks N.H. took in Cheshire. Mr. Forster also prepared a series of talks for the BBC on Hawthorne in England, especially the Liverpool area.

47. S.H. to her father, Feb. 11, 1854 (Berg), and one marked Dec. 1853[?] (Berg). The date of the second, as is evident from the context, must be Feb. 1854.

48. S.H. to her father, Dec. 1853[?] (Berg), and J.H. in *Shapes,* p. 28.

49. N.H. to Mrs. Heywood, Feb. 16, 1854 (Pearson).

50. Feb. 17, 1854, in *LT,* 1:31.

51. N.H. to Allingham, Feb. 27, 1854, in *Letters to William Allingham,* ed. H. Allingham and E. B. Williams (London: Longmans, Green & Co., 1911).

52. *William Allingham: a Diary,* ed. H. Allingham and C. Radford (London: Macmillan, 1907), pp. 70–71.

53. N.H. to Ticknor, Aug. 17, 1855 (Berg). A letter to Allingham promising to try to help him is dated Jan. 29, 1855 (Milburn).

54. S.H. in *Memories,* pp. 266–67.

55. S.H. to her father, May 12 and 28, 1854 (Berg). On the dinner for Buchanan, see also N.H., Apr. 30, 1854, in *LT,* 1:39.

56. S.H. to her father, May 28, 1854 (Berg). See Eric Midwinter, *Old Liverpool* (Newton Abbot: David & Charles, 1971), p. 85, on the 1854 outbreak of cholera in Liverpool. It seems unlikely that S.H. would have picked up this disease without infecting those around her.

57. S.H. to her father, May 28 to June 22, 1854 (Berg), and Sept. 2, 1854 (Berg).

58. June 27 and July 20, 1854, in *LT,* 1:53 and 56.

59. S.H., excerpts from letters to her father, July 1854 (Manning Hawthorne Scrapbook; Pearson transcript).

60. S.H. to her father, Aug. 18, 1854 (Berg).

61. N.H. to Bennoch, Aug. 31, 1854 (Bar.).

62. S.H., undated, in *Memories,* p. 289. According to the 1851 census for Rhyl, the owners of 2 Mona Terrace were "William Moseley, gentleman, widower," and "Margaret Parr, gentlewoman, his daughter." At that time they were building four new houses, one of which, according to the town map, must have been the one the Hawthornes stayed in during 1854 (information from A. G. Veysey, archivist, County Record Office, Rhyl).

63. S.H. to her father, Sept. 14, 1854 (Berg).

64. S.H. to Ticknor, Sept. 29, 1854 (Berg).

65. S.H. to her father, Oct. 3, 1854 (Berg).

66. *H&HC,* pp. 107-08.

67. N.H.-Milnes correspondence is in Houghton papers, 11-136 and 11-137, at TCC. In the note to Ticknor, Sept. 30, 1854, in *LT* 1:63 64, N.H. requested *Walden, A Week on the Concord and Merrimack Rivers,* Mrs. Howe's *Passion Flowers,* [Mansfield's] *Up-Country Letters,* Mrs. Mowatt's *Autobiography,* and Lowell's *Bigelow Papers.*

68. S.H. to her father, Oct. 3, 1854 (Berg), and S.H. to E.P.P., Oct. 31, 1854 (Berg).

69. N.H. to Longfellow, Oct. 24, 1854 (Craigie House; Pearson transcript).

70. U.H. to Rebecca Manning, Rock Park, Aug. 15-16, 1854 (Essex), stated that Fanny Wrigley, "a pleasant woman," had been with them "only a few months."

71. S.H. to her father, Sept. 2, 1854 (Berg).

72. *Shapes,* pp. 56-58. Fanny was not Lancashire-born; see Appendix.

73. Ibid., pp. 57-58.

74. *Memories,* pp. 476-77.

75. S.H. to her father, Nov. 17, 1854, and Dec. 1854 (Berg).

76. *Memories,* p. 303.

77. The first hint of possible change is in the letter of June 7, 1854, in *LT,* 1:46. References also occur in letters of Aug. 3, Oct. 12, 1854, Jan. 6, Jan. 19, and Mar. 2, 1855, when N.H. reached his first decision.

78. S.H. to her father, late Dec. 1854 (Berg). Her first letter referring to her father's death is dated Jan. 25, 1855 (Berg).

79. N.H. to H.A.B., Jan. 23, 1855 (Rylands Library, Manchester).

80. N.H. seldom mentioned a mayor by name. Since the date of election is not given, though it would seem to be in the fall, the only check is a list of those holding office while Hawthorne was consul: 1853, John B. Lloyd; 1854, J. Aspinwall Tobin; 1855, John Stewart; 1856, Francis Shand; 1857, James Holme.

81. The Hopwood case involved a will disputed between the earls of Derby and Sefton and Hopwood, heir to the estate. S.H. gave a detailed account of this trial and of St. George's Hall in her ms. diary for Apr. 1855 (Milburn).

82. It was finally published in *Nineteenth Century,* 57 (Jan. 1900): 88.

83. Mar. 30, 1855, in *LT,* 1:84.

84. Compare N.H. to Horatio Bridge, in *Recollections,* p. 138, and to Ticknor, June 7, 1854, and Apr. 18, 1855, in *LT,* 1:46 and 85.

85. Mar. 30, 1855 and June 7, 1855, in *LT,* 1:83-84 and 94-95.

86. May 27, 1855, in *LT,* 1:93.

87. *Recollections,* p. 146.

88. N.H. to Pierce, June 7, 1855 (Nat. Archives); also in John Ball Osborne, "Nathaniel Hawthorne as American Consul," *Bookman*, 46 (Jan. 1903): 462–63.

89. U.H. to Richard Manning (son of N.H.'s Uncle Robert), Aug. 29, 1855 (Essex): "The woman who rented the house was very mean. We left the house perfectly nice, and she left it very dirty, and she broke one or two things, and went off bag and baggage without replacing them."

90. S.H. to Mary Mann, May 9–10, 1855 (Berg).

91. *H&HC*, pp. 131–32.

Chapter 4. Leamington, Lisbon, and London, 1855–1856

1. S.H., fragment on the reverse side of the last page of N.H.'s second Italian notebook [MA588].

2. S.H., journal fragment, June 22 and 23, 1855, pp. 284 and 285 (Berg).

3. June 21, 1855, in *LT*, 1:97.

4. The prefix *Royal* was approved by the queen in 1838 after her second visit to the town. The name Leamington seems to be a combination of *leam* (pool or lake), plus *ing* (meadow), and *ton* (town) to form a word that means "a town standing in a meadow on the banks of a pool or lake." See p. 66 of T. B. Dudley, *Complete History of Royal Leamington Spa* (Leamington: A. Tomes, 1896). The Leam is very placid, suggesting *pool* rather than *river*.

5. Ibid., p. 110.

6. The account book for June 19, 1855, shows that the bill for 24 hours at the Clarendon was £2 19s. 6p., plus 3s. 6p. to the servants. A cab fare of £2 6s. from the hotel to Lansdowne Crescent is listed on June 19. Food supplies for the week were recorded on June 20.

7. "Lichfield and Uttoxeter," in *Our Old Home*, CE (1970), pp. 120–39; also *EN*, pp. 147–53.

8. N.H. to H.A.B., July 5, 1855 (Pearson).

9. Details of the entire trip are in *EN*. The only financial record here is a receipted bill from Thomas White to "Mrs. Hawthorne" for meals, July 10 to 14, at a cost of £8 5s. (Berg).

10. Harriet Martineau listed the owner as "C. W. Rotherey, Esq." in *A Complete Guide to the English Lakes* (London: Whittaker & Co., 1855). She did not mention Brown's Hotel in Grasmere, but the *Royal Hotel Guide for 1851*, p. 79, listed Edward Brown, owner, as an auctioneer, appraiser, and general agent. Mr. Brown advertised his furnished lodgings as "overlooking the lake, valley, and church," and he included a long sentence on the beauty of the countryside.

11. N.H. to S.H., July 30, 1855 (HM 11011), and S.H. to N.H., July 31, 1855 (Berg).

12. Detailed plans are in a series of letters: Aug. 1 and 17 and Nov. 23, 1855, in *LT*, 1:100, 102, and 117–18; also to Bridge, Aug. 24, 1855 (Ho.). Notebook entries indicate that a consul could not leave his post for more than ten days in any one quarter without official permission; it was not granted at this time.

13. In addition to the accounts in *EN*, Una's letter to Mr. Pike of Sept. 19, 1855 (Milburn), provides a long list of places where they went and outlines the voyage to Lisbon.

14. *Poems*, by W. C. Bennett (London: Chapman & Hall, 1850), dedicated to Miss Mitford, was inscribed as follows: "N. Hawthorne Esq., with the admiration and respect of the Author" (presentation copy in Milburn).

15. Hunt, pencil notes (HM 2614 and 2617). Barry Cornwall and Hawthorne had corresponded before the family left Concord. See *Bryan Waller Proctor: an Autobiographical Fragment and Biographical Notes* (Boston: Roberts Bros., 1877), p. 296.

16. Compare N.H. to Ticknor, Sept. 27, 1855 (Berg), and N.H. to Fields, Sept. 13, 1855 (Ho. copy).

17. See my article " 'Scribbling' Females and Serious Males: Hawthorne's Comments from Abroad on Some American Authors," *NHJ*, 5 (1975): 35-38.

18. Julian implied this in *NH&HW*, 1:199, when he said that after marriage Sophia "never relapsed into her previous condition of invalidism." But the line between chronic ailments and invalidism is hard to define.

19. Margaret Mare and Alicia C. Percival, *Victorian Best-Seller: the World of Charlotte M. Yonge* (London: George G. Harrap & Co., Ltd., 1948), p. 264.

20. *H&HC*, pp. 185-86, and *Shapes*, p. 37. Huguenin's gymnasium is described in *Shapes*, pp. 30-31, when Julian returned there 20 years later.

21. *Shapes*, p. 34.

22. S.H. to Mary Mann, July 11, 1855 (Berg).

23. *Shapes*, p. 17.

24. Ibid., p. 32, 34-35.

25. Ibid., p. 36.

26. *H&HC*, pp. 187-91.

27. *Shapes*, pp. 27-29.

28. Nov. 9, 1855, in *LT*, 1:114.

29. Nov. 3, 1855, in HM 11012, also *LL*, 2:232, and Nov. 24, 1855, in HM 11018, also *LL*, 2:260; compare Nov. 9, 1855, in *LL*, 2:266-67.

30. HM 11013; *LL*, 2:238-39. The note on the substitution of *see* for *embrace* is from Pearson's copy.

31. HM 11015; *LL*, 2:255-57.

32. N.H. to Mrs. Heywood, Feb. 11, 1856 (Pearson), and notation from the pocket diary of 1856 (MA).

33. *EN*, pp. 273-78; see also "Outside Glimpses of English Poverty," *Our Old Home*, CE (1970), pp. 293-306.

34. HM 11013; *LL*, 2:243 and 244.

35. *Memories*, p. 295.

36. S.H. to E.P.P. [1864] (Ohio State U. Mss. Collection). Sophia explained that Una had been "disgusted with everybody and thing that did not suit her taste and principles and seemed to fail utterly in St. Paul's Charity." At that time Rose seemed to be behaving in the same way.

37. Dec. 13, 1855, incorrectly dated 1858 in *LL*, 2:267-68. For more of Una's personality, see my article "Una Hawthorne: a Biographical Sketch," *NHJ*, 6 (1976): 86-119.

38. Apr. 11, 1856, in *LT*, 2:7.

39. Mar. 15, 1856, in *LT*, 2:5.

40. Apr. 7, 1856, in HM 11015, also *LL*, 2:253.

41. Compare *H&HC*, pp. 92-93 with *Memories*, p. 225.

42. Further details are in my article "Bennoch and Hawthorne," *NHJ*, 4 (1974): 48-74, and in the Appendix.

43. Bennoch to George Holden, Dec. 10, 1884 (enclosing a 25-page description of the trip that he had originally written to Sir Theodore Martin on Nov. 15, 1884) (Bar.).

44. Ibid.

45. *NH&HW,* 2:108–16, quotes verbatim the account of the visit, including the comments given here.

46. Martin Tupper, *My Life as an Author* (London: Sampson, Low, 1886), pp. 246–47. Hawthorne's often-repeated statement to Ticknor and Fields that his notebooks could not be published for many years verifies that he never intended to offend any living person.

47. Details in the letter to Sir Theodore Martin enclosed in the one to Holden. (See note 43.)

48. Sir Theodore Martin, *Helena Faucit (Lady Martin)* (Edinburgh: Blackwood, 1900), p. 259.

49. Charles Mackay, *Forty Years' Recollections of Life, Literature, and Public Affairs* (London: Chapman & Hall, 1877), 2:271–93, tells the story of Jerrold, Hawthorne, and the dinner at the Reform Club.

50. Bennoch to George Holden, Dec. 3, 1885 (Bar.).

51. See also Apr. 7, 1856, in HM 11015, also *LL,* 2:254.

52. S. C. Hall, *Retrospect of a Long Life* (London: Richard Bentley, 1883), 2:202n.

53. Apr. 7, 1856, in HM 11015, also *LL,* 253–54.

54. Apr. 11, 1856, in *LT,* 2:7.

55. N.H. to Bennoch, Apr. 9, 1856 (Bar.).

56. N.H. to Bennoch, June 9, 1856 (Bar.). There is a discrepancy in time here, for the notebooks state that the message was received on June 9. The 1856 pocket diary (MA) cites June 8 for the writing of the sketch and the receipt of the message from Southampton.

57. From Clifton Villa, June 30, 1856 (Bar.).

58. I am indebted to the present owner, Mrs. Edward Street-Porter, for the opportunity of seeing the inside of the house and the garden.

59. An unpublished notebook (Lewisham Public Library) by the late Leslie Baker contains the history of 4 Pond Road. It states that the house was built in 1828, that the rent was £20 per year, and that the Bennochs were the second occupants. Included also is an account of Hawthorne's stay there. The local census quoted in the Baker notebook lists the following residents for April 7, 1851: Francis Bennoch, 38; Margaret Bennoch, 35; Elizabeth Raine, 69, mother-in-law; Clare Rowbottom, 16, manufacturer's daughter, visitor; Francis Carr, 2, nephew; Mary Pousty[?], 43, cook; and Ellen Salby, 22, housemaid. Apparently by 1856 the Bennochs were alone with only two servants.

60. July 17, 1856, in *LT,* 2:20–21.

61. N.H. to J.H., Aug. 16, 1856 (Pearson transcript).

62. See the chapter titled "Decline and Death" in Vivian C. Hopkins, *Prodigal Puritan: a Life of Delia Bacon* (Cambridge: Harvard U. Press, 1959), pp. 245–66.

63. N.H. to Bennoch, Mar. 17, 1857 (Bar.). Compare N.H. to Bennoch, Apr. 9, 1857 (Berg), and N.H. to Ticknor, May 20, 1857 (Berg).

64. "Recollections of a Gifted Woman," *Our Old Home,* CE (1972), p. 116.

65. This photograph by De La Motte is the only known picture from the English period that includes both Sophia and Nathaniel. (Prints in Bancroft and the Bodleian Library.)

66. The description of the volumes is from an unpublished note by Arthur M. Spiers, Esq., Mitre Hotel, Oxford (Pearson transcript).

67. Discussion by Edward Mather Jackson in *Nathaniel Hawthorne: a Modest Man* (N.Y.: Crowell, 1940), pp. 270–78. By contrast, Richard LeGallienne claimed that the Hawthornes when abroad "met everybody worth knowing." See "Hawthorne as His Daughter

Remembers Him," *Literary Digest International Book Review,* 1, no. 9 (Aug. 1923): 8. Both accounts must be inaccurate.

68. Bennoch to George Holden, Oct. 5, 1885 (Bar.).

69. A letter from Milnes, June 30, [1856] (Berg), refers to Hawthorne's failure to get in touch with him on the April visit to London: "You promised to do so, but we sought you in vain. . . . I am quite annoyed at having been so long within the same four seas with you and having seen you so little." The breakfast invitation of July 1856 was Milnes's attempt to improve the relationship, but the two men did not see each other again until 1857. See ch. 5.

Chapter 5. Southport, 1856–1857

1. Probably William S. Crawley, merchant, with offices at 1 N. John St., and residence at Seabank View, Liscard *(Gore's Directory for 1860).*

2. The account book for Sept. 23 shows £3 8s. as the first week's expenses for lodgings, fire, gas, and attendance. From that date on, the rent alone averaged £2 3s. per week. The Hawthornes paid their own coal bill, noted on Dec. 30 as £4 9s. for Sept. to Dec. 30.

3. S.H. to E.P.P., Nov. 19, 1856 (Berg).

4. See F. H. Cheetham, *Nathaniel Hawthorne and Southport,* pamphlet reprinted from the *Southport Visiter,* Jan. 6, 8, and 10, 1903 (Southport Printing Works), and illustration in this chapter.

5. *Souvenir of Southport As It Was in the Beginning: Something Old and Something New,* a photographic record by F. W. Hickson (Birkdale, 1932). Brunswick Terrace was razed in 1880 to make room for the Sandringham Hotel and the new Scarisbrick Avenue. See also *Southport Authors,* vol. 2, *Nathaniel Hawthorne,* clippings available at Atkinson Public Library, Southport.

6. Oct. 10, 1856, in *LT,* 2:28.

7. S.H. to E.P.P., Sept. 23, 1856 (Berg)

8. Ibid.

9. S.H. to E.P.P., marked "[n.d. 1853–60]" (Berg). The fact that Fanny had been with the Hawthornes for 2 years and that Sophia referred to the girl as "nurse for baby" and did not mention the arrival of a governess implies a date of early fall in 1856.

10. Letter by D. Macleod, former general manager, giving the history of the first Adelphi Hotel, which was opened in 1826. After Radley's death in the 1880s the place was rebuilt and resold several times. (See Sir J. A. Picton, *Memorials of Liverpool* [London: Longmans, Green, 1873], 2:232.) When the present building was completed in 1913, *The Midlands Hotels; the History of a Great Enterprise* (Midlands Hotels, 1914) summarized the history and included numerous photographs of the interior. The hotel is now owned and run by British Transport.

11. Charles Dickens, *American Notes* (London: Chapman & Hall, 1890), p. 4.

12. Oct. 10, 1856, in *LT,* 2:28–31. Menu and guest list are included.

13. Recorded on Oct. 5 as "Dinner to 10 gentlemen at Adelphi 22-0-0."

14. Melville had published not only *Moby Dick,* but *Pierre, Israel Potter,* and the *Piazza Tales;* he had also completed *The Confidence Man* and had signed a contract for the American edition before he left the United States. The contract for the English edition was signed by Hawthorne while Melville was on his voyage to the Near East.

15. See Melville's letter of Nov. 25, 1852, in *The Letters of Herman Melville,* ed. M. R. Davis and W. H. Gilman (New Haven: Yale U. Press, 1960), pp. 162–63.

16. Herman Melville, *Journal up the Straits,* ed. Raymond Weaver (N.Y.: Cooper Square, 1971), pp. 4-5.

17. Ibid. Una also described the Wednesday activities in her letter of Nov. 30 to "Aunt Lizzie" [Peabody] (Berg). The game of "fox and geese" (a board with pegs) was a present bought for the children by N.H. when they were at Rock Park. U.H. to "Aunt Lizzie," Mar. 7, [1854] (Berg).

18. Edwin Miller in *Melville: a Biography* (N.Y.: Persea Books, 1975) insists that N.H.'s embarrassment was caused by his previous failure to respond to the demands of a too-close friendship put forth by Melville (p. 286). Other writers have agreed on N.H.'s failure to respond, but Miller goes so far as to suggest that the Hawthornes left Lenox in order to escape from Melville (pp. 247-48). This last point I find impossible to accept. If we take N.H.'s account at face value, we must accept that the embarrassment during this visit was caused by his regret that he had failed to help Melville.

19. *Melville Log,* ed. Jay Leyda (N.Y.: Harcourt Brace, 1951), 2:530.

20. *Journal up the Straits,* p. 5. Here Edwin Miller is in error: He attributes the luncheon and entertainment in Liverpool all to Hawthorne (p. 288). Melville's thank-you note of Nov. 18 (*Letters,* p. 187) testifies that it was H.A.B. who was free to do sightseeing on Friday. N.H. was able to leave the consulate for the trip to Chester because it was a Saturday.

21. N.H. devoted a page or more to the inn where Swift is said to have written three of his typical epigrams on the window. See B. C. S. Windle, *Chester County History* (London: Methuen, 1903), pp. 270-71.

22. *Letters of Herman Melville,* p. 274. See also J.H.'s account of an interview with Melville on Aug. 10, 1883, in N.Y.; it was recorded in *Booklover's Weekly,* Dec. 30, 1901; *Literary Digest International Book Review,* Aug. 1926; and *Dearborn Independent,* Sept. 24, 1922. See also *H&HC,* p. 34.

23. According to N.H.'s pocket diary for 1856 (MA) Miss Browne arrived in Southport on Oct. 18. On Oct. 24 the Hawthornes paid her traveling expenses of £3 3s. (Account Book).

24. S.H. to E.P.P., Oct. 23, 1856 (Berg). Accounts of the life of governesses are vividly given in *The Governess,* a novel by the Countess of Blessington (Phila.: Lea & Blanchard, 1839). Accounts in nonfictional studies, such as E. Royston Pike, *Golden Times: Human Documents of the Victorian Age* (N.Y.: Praeger, 1967), are usually limited to women in domestic service or in industry.

25. S.H. to Mary Mann, Dec. 30, 1856 to Jan. 2, 1857 (Berg). Compare S.H. to E.P.P., Oct. 23, 1856 (Berg).

26. N.H. to Bennoch, Nov. 21, 1856 (Bar.).

27. *H&HC,* pp. 227-28.

28. S.H. to E.P.P., Oct. 23, 1856 (Berg). For J.H.'s attitude, see *H&HC,* p. 228; for S.H.'s criticisms of Miss Browne, see her letter to E.P.P., Dec. 11, [1856] (Berg).

29. S.H. to E.P.P., Dec. 1856 (Pearson transcript): "Mary Herne, efficient as she was, had great faults and was not *true*." Mary had told stories about N.H.; what these were S.H. did not say, but as a result of her experiences she had come to dislike Irish servants.

30. U.H. to Richard Manning, Nov. 30, [1856] (Essex): "I want a home, and do not like the wandering life we lead." See also letters to "Aunt Lizzie," Nov. 6, 1856; Dec. 18, 1856; and Jan. 14, 1857 (Berg).

31. N.H. to Ticknor, Dec. 18, 1856 (HM 2859). The banquets later appeared in "Civic Banquets," final chapter of *Our Old Home.*

32. U.H. to "Aunt Lizzie," Dec. 3[?] (Berg). For use of the microscope, see incomplete letter from J.H. to U.H., Aug. 24, 1857 (Milburn).

33. S.H. to Mary Mann, Dec. 30, 1856 to Jan. 2, 1857 (Berg).

34. On Feb. 13, 1857, N.H. sent the following statement to the president: "I beg permission to resign my office as Consul of the United States at this Port, from and after the date of August thirty-first, 1857" (Nat. Archives). The resignation was sent to Bridge with the request that he deliver it to Buchanan after the inauguration.

35. S.H. to E.P.P., May 7, 1857 (Berg).

36. Ibid. N.H. to Fields on March 27 reported that *both* thieves were sentenced to be transported: "So England will have two rogues the less on my account" (Ho.).

37. Details of the burglary from the *Southport Visiter* of Feb. 19, 20, and Apr. 2 were reprinted in *NHJ*, 4 (1974): 142–48.

38. U.H. to "Aunt Lizzie," Mar. 9, 1857 (Berg). The date of Fanny's return is not given, but it must have been in April.

39. U.H. to S.H., July 10, [1857] (Berg).

40. Compare U.H. to Richard Manning, Mar. 9, 1857 (Essex), and U.H. to Rebecca Manning, Mar. 25, 1857 (Essex). See also S.H. to U.H., May 23 and 24, 1857 (MA). S.H. tried to compensate for her daughter's staying at home by writing long, detailed letters about their trips. These pages probably became part of *Notes in England and Italy*, minus, of course, the personal comments.

41. "Outside Glimpses of English Poverty," *Our Old Home*, CE (1972), pp. 306–09. The comparison from the original edition of *Passages from the English Notebooks* was quoted extensively in "Hawthorne in Manchester," *Manchester Guardian*, July 4, 1904, p. 10, col. 1.

42. Brown's offer to finance the library was reported in the *London Times*, Jan. 2, 1857, p. 10, col. e. Shaw's Brow had been named for Alderman Thomas Shaw and other members of the family whose potteries were moved to Dale Street. The new street was named William Brown Street.

43. Photographs of the ceremonies are reproduced on pp. 213 and 214 of *NHJ*, 2 (1972). N.H. is shown in the photo on p. 213. He is directly behind Brown, the central figure in the front row.

44. *Documents and Proceedings Connected with the Donation of a Free Public Library and Museum by William Brown, Esq., M.P. to the Town of Liverpool*, ed. A. Hume (Liverpool: T. Brakell, printer, 1858).

45. Ibid., p. 56.

46. Ibid., p. 57.

47. Ibid., p. 58. Speech reprinted in *NHJ*, 2 (1972): 208–10, as part of the report of the 1971 Hawthorne Exhibition in Liverpool. The reprint begins with a section of Milnes's introduction, not identified as such.

48. Ibid., p. 58. When the library was completed in 1860, Hawthorne's successor, Beverly Tucker, was present, but did not make a speech. Report of the acceptance proceedings is in the same binding as the booklet on the cornerstone laying.

49. Apparently because N.H. made his dislike of Southport well known, there was scarcely any mention of him in local histories until F. H. Cheetham wrote extensively about him at the beginning of this century. See "Nathaniel Hawthorne Did Not Like Southport," *Southport Journal*, June 24, 1964, and Cheetham's *Nathaniel Hawthorne and Southport*, referred to in note 4.

50. Apr. 9 and 24, 1857, in *LT*, 2:49 and 2:50–51.

51. Ms. journal later published as part of *Notes in England and Italy* (Milburn).

52. June 5, 1857, in *LT,* 2:56.

53. In this incomplete section from S.H.'s journal (Milburn) the items not used later in the book were put in parentheses or crossed out with red pencil. Fortunately the reader can easily decipher the omitted passages.

54. The modern Benn's *Blue Guide to England,* p. 382, quotes N.H.'s description of the scenery around Matlock. The *Manchester Guardian* (see note 41) quoted his favorable comments on Matlock in order to compare them with his unfavorable comments about Southport.

55. Compare N.H. to Bennoch, Mar. 27, 1857, and June 13, 1857 (Bar.).

56. Moray McLaren, *If Freedom Fail: Bannochburn, Flodden, and the Union* (London: Secker and Warburg, 1964), pp. 105–06.

57. N.H. to Ticknor, July 17, 1857, in *H&HP*, pp. 204–05.

58. Ibid., p. 205.

59. N.H. to Bennoch, June 13, 1857 (Bar.).

Chapter 6. Manchester, Leamington, and London, 1857–1858

1. Hawthorne mistakenly dated this first notebook entry from Manchester as Thursday, July 22, instead of 23.

2. Rent payments for their first lodgings were made to "Mrs. Richmond," according to the account book. The only Richmond listed in the *Manchester Register for 1856* was Thomas Richmond, surgeon, at Chorlton Lodge, Stretford New Road.

3. First-day expenditures for food in Manchester were similar to those in Rock Park: potatoes, steak, eggs, butter, cheese, bread, sponge cake, oranges, wine, beer, and milk. Later expenditures were much more extensive. As in Southport, they bought a padlock to lock up their wine bottle in a cupboard.

4. Aug. 29, 1857, in *LT,* 2:61: "I have been well enough contented to wait hitherto, because I live at Uncle Sam's expense, and do him very little service—the old scoundrel! But it is getting late in the season, and I ought to be in Italy in little more than a month."

5. *Irish Quarterly Review,* 7, no. 15 (March 1857): 905.

6. Ibid., pp. 945–46. The author's figures seem to be exaggerated, for the highest attendance record, according to London and Manchester papers, averaged 11 or 12 thousand on any one day.

7. Plan of the Exhibition is from the *Catalogue of the Art Treasures* (London: Bradbury and Evans, 1857[?]) and from the *London Quarterly Review,* 9 (Oct. 1857): 78–103. Also included were the total dimensions of the building—724 feet deep and 200 feet wide—and those of the Great Hall, the central portion—600 feet by 104 feet.

8. Opening-day ceremonies were described in detail in the *London Times,* Wed., May 6, 1857, p. 9, col. a, b, and c, beginning with the statement that Manchester was the scene of "an event almost unique in the history of art in England, or perhaps in the world." "Her Majesty's Visit to Manchester" appeared in the *Times* of Tues., June 30, 1857. See also the *Manchester Guardian,* July 1 and 2, and the *Illustrated Times,* July 11 and 18.

9. For comparisons see *The Crystal Palace and Its Contents: an Illustrated Cyclopaedia of the Great Exhibition of 1851,* nos. 1–27 (London, 1851–1852). For changes in Manchester, see the *London Times,* Wed., June 10, 1857, p. 5, col. b.

10. S.H. to E.P.P., in *Memories,* p. 331.

11. Ibid., p. 333. The date is uncertain. This may refer to a second occasion on which the Hawthornes saw the Tennysons.

12. Ireland to Fields, Apr. 15, 1871 (FI 2803, Pearson transcript).

13. Ireland to Moncure D. Conway, Southport, Apr. 6, 1890 (Bar.). It seems strange that the *Examiner*'s list of distinguished visitors included Tennyson and Woolner for the week of July 29, but Hawthorne was not mentioned until Fri., Sept. 4, when he was listed as "among those present."

14. See "Charles Allen Duval," *Art-Treasurer's Examiner* (Manchester, 1857), pp. 189–91, for illustration and discussion of his two paintings.

15. S.H. to Mary Mann, Aug. 28, 1857 (Berg).

16. J.H. to U.H., Aug. 24, 1857 (Milburn). There are 4 incomplete letters from Julian in Manchester; the other 3 are among the J.H. papers in Bancroft. The account book records fares for Una and Rose to York and 1 pound for Una "to cover expenses while gone." This was undoubtedly a visit to Fanny's family.

17. S.H. to E.P.P., Sept. 9, 1857 (Berg).

18. The houses in the Circus were designed in 1835–1836 by William Thomas (1800–1860), architect of houses in nearby Holly Walk and Lansdowne Crescent. Though the exteriors were similar, there were individual interior variations. Number 10 was purchased in Dec. 1973 by Don and Ann Locke, who are now restoring the house so that it will be closer to the way it looked in the 1850s when the Hawthornes rented it from Mrs. Edith Maloney (see *Warwickshire Directory for 1850*). As it appears from the present floor plan, the house consisted of kitchen (the original stone floor is still there), pantry, laundry, wine cellar, and coal hole in a semibasement; drawing room, dining room, and central hall on the first floor; 3 bedrooms on the second floor; and 2 small rooms, plus 2 tiny storage rooms, under the eaves in the attic. There was a small back garden surrounded by a brick wall. Since all the rooms are rather small, the Hawthornes, with 7 in the household by October, must have felt crowded.

19. S.H. to E.P.P., Sept. 9, 1857 (Berg).

20. N.H. to Fields, Sept. 9, 1857 (copy at Ho.).

21. Thomas Brigden in *Stray Notes on Some Warwickshire Worthies* (Warwick, n.d.) refers to N.H. at Leamington from 1853 to 1857; the *Complete History of Leamington Spa*, by T. B. Dudley, mistakenly lists him as a resident at 10 Lansdowne Circus in 1853; George Morley includes a chapter titled "In the Footsteps of Hawthorne: a Rural Sketch" in *Sketches of Leafy Warwickshire Rural and Urban* (Derby: Moray Press, 1895), pp. 97–102. A local man also reprinted passages from N.H. for the benefit of "visiting Americans": *Leamington Spa, Warwick, Stratford-on-Avon by Nathaniel Hawthorne, Author of Our Old Home, Seven Gables, Scarlet Letter*, etc. (Warwick: Henry H. Lacy, n.d.).

22. S.H. to Mary Mann, July 16, 1857 (Berg).

23. S.L., pp. 86, 91, and 96.

24. *H&HC*, pp. 229–30. A photograph of Ada in the Pearson collection verifies Julian's description.

25. S.L., Oct. 4, 1857, p. 91.

26. S.L., Oct. 14, 1857, p. 119.

27. S.L., Oct. 18, 1857, p. 125.

28. S.L., Oct. 7, 1857, p. 103. Una's letter to "Aunt Lizzie," Oct. 30 (Berg), may reflect changes made after Ada reviewed the competencies of her pupils. Una listed arithmetic at 7:30 A.M.; breakfast at 8:30; chronology from 9:30 to 11:00; dinner; study from 2:00 to 5:00; gym for 15 minutes; French until 6:00; then tea and reading in the evening.

29. S.L., Nov. 3, 1857, pp. 164–65.

30. Oct. 9, 1857, in *LT*, 2:64. Parenthetical passage, omitted in the printed version, is in the original (Berg).

31. N.H. to Bennoch, Oct. 16, 26, and 28, 1857 (Bar.), covers plans for their moving.

32. S.L., Nov. 10, 1857, p. 176. *London Directory* for 1857 lists Mrs. Sievers as landlady at 24 Great Russell Street.

33. Full report of the bankruptcy case appeared in the *London Times* of Nov. 28, 1857, p. 7, col. b. In the previous December, Bennoch's firm had shown a profit. In November of 1857 there was a deficit of £101,446 5s. 3p. The deficit, which occurred over a relatively short time, probably represented the "speculations" of his partners to which Bennoch referred.

34. S.L., p. 277. Evidently N.H. missed seeing Patmore when he called a second time with a new edition of his poems. N.H. to Patmore, Jan. 5, 1858 (Pearson), is a thank-you note for the book.

35. N.H. to Benjamin Moran, American legation in London, Sept. 15, 1857 (Berg). See also ch. 1, note 9, on ages of family members.

36. S.L., Dec. 23, 1857, p. 259. Ada's letter to her sister Kate, from Paris, Jan. 10, 1858, p. 1189, explains why Fanny went to York to live with her stepmother and also says that the Hawthornes planned to wait until they reached Rome to find a suitable servant to replace Fanny. This was never done.

37. N.H. to Fields, Sept. 9, 1857 (copy in Ho.), states the number of ms. volumes as seven. Number 7 in the Stewart edition spans Oct. 1857 to Jan. 3, 1858. Since it ends with ms. page 112 and the French and Italian notebooks begin with page 114, it is most likely that N.H. carried this portion with him to the Continent.

38. N.H. to H.A.B., in *NH&HW*, 2:168–69.

39. July 30, 1857, in *LT*, 2:60.

40. While he was in Liverpool waiting for his successor to arrive, N.H. received praise for his work as a "servant" of the government from Lewis Cass, secretary of state in Washington. See *NH&HW*, 2:163.

41. N.H. to H.A.B., Jan. 4, 1858 (Pearson). Subsequent letters from Wilding to N.H. show that he did stay on at the consulate.

42. F&IN, Jan. 6, 1858 (I, 113, MA587), and Jan. 7, 1858, in *LT*, 2:70.

43. In *NH&HW*, 2:169, Julian mistakenly set the date of departure as Jan. 3. N.H.'s last entry of Sun., Jan. 3, said that they expected to leave on Tues., which would be the fifth. Farewell note to H.A.B. from London was written on Jan. 4.

Chapter 7. Italian Interlude, 1858–1859

1. See his discussion of anticipation vs. reality in an early sketch, "My Visit to Niagara," *CW*, 12:42–50.

2. For Hawthorne's complete F&IN I have used a film of Norman Holmes Pearson's transcription made from the manuscripts, most of which are in the Morgan Library. The 1980 published edition from OSU became available only in time for a final check of end notes and biographical sketches. In comparing Sophia's edition of *Passages from the French and Italian Note-books,* I have used the Houghton Mifflin edition of 1883 (*CW*, 10). Sophia's own *Notes in England and Italy* (N.Y.: Putnam's, 1869) are of use only occasionally, because they include very little of family life or personal comments.

3. N.H., F&IN (I, 115, MA587). Hereafter page and volume numbers will occur within the text in the form used by Pearson. Those from the Morgan Library are indicated by MA; the Huntington volume, V, is HM; III is from the Berg.

4. Sophia chose to omit this passage from her edition. Instead of attempting to draw

detailed comparisons between the two editions, I shall depend upon N.H.'s version for the most part. Ada Shepard's letters are used to supplement N.H.'s accounts whenever they provide more detailed information or a different point of view.

5. Ada insisted that Hawthorne pretended that he could not speak French, although he knew the language "very well" (S.L., ca. Jan. 5, 1858, p. 284). She was only partly correct: He had a reading knowledge of French.

6. S.L., ca. Jan. 5, 1858, p. 282.

7. Visitors included M. Husson, Una's French teacher from Liverpool days; the Pickmans from Concord; and Fanny MacDaniel, former Brook Farmer.

8. S.L., Jan. 15, 1858, p. 302.

9. *Passages from the French and Italian Note-books*, p. 47. This is typical of one kind of change made by S.H. in later years. In all fairness to her it should be pointed out that she made changes in wording that she thought her husband would have considered in better taste than the original. Unfortunately her edition gives a rather false picture. On this subject see also Stewart's introduction to his edition of the *English Notebooks*.

10. *Memoirs*, p. 203. The only additional point made by Ada in her account of the journey was that before they left Civitavecchia, she helped with the language problem by buying food for the trip—dried beef, cheese, bread, apples, oranges, and walnuts—so that the family could eat as they rode along in the carriage (S.L., ca. Jan. 22, 1858, p. 322).

11. *Memories*, pp. 354 and 356. N.H. had nothing to say about food in Rome, and Rose's only recollection was the monotonous repetition of rice pudding on the dinner menu. The Hawthornes must have studied the advice in Murray's *Hand book of Rome and Its Environs* (Part II of *The Hand-book for Travellers in Central Italy*, 5th ed. 1858), which recommended this system of contracting for dinners from a trattoria as the most economical method of providing for meals.

12. Later in the spring Ada wrote almost exactly the same description of Roman streets as "very ugly" and "narrow and dirty." The buildings were high and not beautiful. Laundresses hung clothes in front of the upper windows of houses so that wet clothes seemed to be everywhere (S.L., Apr. 9, 1858, p. 508).

13. Extract from a letter of Feb. 16, 1858, from *Maria Mitchell: Life, Letters, and Journals*, ed. Phebe Mitchell Kendall (Boston: Lee & Shepard, 1896), p. 90. She added that Hawthorne had "a horror of sightseeing and of emotions in general," but "I like him very much." Miss Mitchell accompanied the Hawthornes in their sightseeing much of the time until she left Rome for Berlin on May 8.

14. Ibid., p. 90.

15. The first person the Hawthornes called upon in Feb. was W. W. Story. It was not until ms. vol. III of the notebooks, begun in Mar. 1858, that N.H. started to show any real interest in life in Rome.

16. S.H. to E.P.P. (n.d.), in *Memories*, pp. 354-55.

17. It is not the purpose of this biography to make detailed comparisons between the Italian notebooks and *The Marble Faun*. Occasionally a statement of opinion or an incident from the notebooks is quoted because of its significance in revealing how the ideas for the romance originated.

18. The Barberini Palace is described in Henry James's *William Wetmore Story and His Friends* (N.Y.: Grove Press, rpt. 1903). Story's letter to C. E. Norton about the apartment, dated May 21, 1857, is quoted on pp. 351-52.

19. Mary E. Phillips, who gave the description of the studio in her *Reminiscences of William Wetmore Story* (Chicago: Rand McNally, 1897), p. 103, said that Story's first studio

had been on Via Sistina, but that it was at the second studio, on Via San Nicolo di Tolentino, that N.H. visited with him while he worked. She equated this studio, rather than Miss Lander's, with Kenyon's in the romance.

20. James C. Hooker was a partner in Packenham and Hooker, bankers with offices at 20 Piazza di Spagna. The company did more than operate as an exchange; it forwarded packages, received mail, and performed other such services. Ada wrote that Packenham was "a myth," that Hooker was the only one in the company (S.L., ca. Jan. 28, 1858, p. 343).

21. Julian in *NH&HW,* 1:259–62, quoted N.H.'s unflattering remarks about Margaret Fuller's marriage, thereby stirring up some controversy.

22. Ada recorded that at first impression Hatty seemed too "mannish in her bearing" (S.L., Feb. 26, 1858, p. 400). Later she admitted on one occasion that Hatty was "quite a charming person" (p. 567). No friendship developed between the two. To Ada, Miss Mitchell was a much more agreeable person; in fact, no one woman is more highly praised in Ada's letters than Maria Mitchell. When the astronomer left Rome, Ada wrote that there would be a great gap in her life.

23. For Miss Bremer's account of her first meeting with N.H., see *Homes of the New World, Impressions of America,* trans. Mary Howitt (N.Y., 1853), 2:597. She did not realize that Hawthorne failed to understand her; she admitted that he was a kind person who tried to make her comfortable, but "we could not get on together in conversation." The description of his appearance that follows these comments is approximately the same as N.H. gives in his notebook.

24. N.H. to Bennoch, Mar. 16, 1858 (Bar.). There are comparatively few letters by the Hawthornes during their stay in Italy. S.H. compensated for her failure to write many letters by sending home her journal with Miss Lander (S.H. to Mary Mann, May 16, 1858 [Berg]). Ada wrote many letters in the hope that Clay would keep them as a form of journal of her experiences (S.L. to Lucy [Shephard], Mar. 27, 1858, p. 1235).

25. April 14, 1858, in *LT,* 2:71. Hawthorne's only attempt at fiction during this spring was noted by Ada in her letter (S.L., April 13, 1858, p. 519), in which she said that he had begun a new book. This was apparently the sketch later called *The Ancestral Footstep.*

26. April 14, 1858, in *LT*, 2:71–72.

27. S.L., May 16, 1858, p. 587. A month earlier, in explaining the Hawthornes' need for economizing, Ada wrote that the family would travel more if they could afford it. "As it is, we have not been out of Rome since we entered it, except for walks and drives of a few miles" (p. 532).

28. To her sister Kate, S.L., Feb. 1, 1858, p. 1221.

29. To her sister Kate, S.L., Oct. 19, 1857, p. 1135.

30. To Ratie and Nellie [nieces or little sisters?], S.L., Mar. 1, 1858, p. 1222.

31. The first mention of Ada's being asked to stay a second year occurred in her letter of Mar. 15, 1858. At that time Ada was not sure that she wished to stay on. She received no salary, the hours were so long that she could not do much studying on her own, and she had not even begun to do any work on German; in short, she was not convinced that the advantages outweighed the disadvantages. Gradually she changed her mind, possibly after being advised by Maria Mitchell. Clay may also have implied some uncertainty about job possibilities at Antioch. One other incentive for remaining was Sophia's suggestion that in the fall Ada could make some money by taking on several more pupils—the Story and the Thompson children.

32. Powers had not met the Hawthornes before. Arrangements had been worked out

through their friends in Rome, when Akers, or Story, or both, wrote to Powers that the Hawthornes were coming to Florence and would want a house.

33. As one faced the Porta Romana, Casa del Bello was about three-quarters of a mile from the gate, on the right side of Via de Serraglio, according to Laurence Hutton in *Literary Landmarks of Florence* (N.Y.: Harper's, 1897), p. 65. See also John Arthos, "Hawthorne in Florence," *Michigan Alumni Quarterly Review,* 59 (Feb. 21, 1953): 118-29. In addition to the rent the Hawthornes paid only $6 per month for a servant to clean the house and prepare breakfasts and teas. The dinners were brought in, as they had been in Rome, at a fixed charge of twelve pauls (about $1.20) a day, plus one paul for a bottle of red wine.

34. *Notes in England and Italy,* pp. 336-37.

35. S.L., ca. June 9, 1858, p. 646.

36. Julian aroused ill feeling in Robert Browning by implying that the Brownings were present at the séance on Bellosguardo when "Mary Rondel's" spirit spoke to the group (*NH&HW,* 1:30-33). The Brownings, however, had left Florence a month before this occasion, as proved by Browning's letter to Story, Dec. 28, 1884. See G. R. Hudson, *Robert Browning to His American Friends* (N.Y.: Barnes & Noble, 1965), p. 185.

37. S.L., June 3, 1858, p. 637.

38. Ibid., p. 639.

39. S.L., ca. June 14, 1858, p. 697.

40. Lucy P. Stebbins and Richard P. Stebbins, *The Trollopes: the Chronicles of a Writing Family* (N.Y.: Columbia U. Press, 1945), p. 185. Isabella Blagden has been the subject of much speculation, but there are few known facts about her life. See Appendix.

41. S.L., ca. July 6 and 27, 1858, pp. 688 and 720.

42. According to Pearson's notes this preliminary sketch has never been found. Possibly Hawthorne destroyed it when he completed the romance in England.

43. The contract (original owned by Pearson) with Andrea Radice, signed by C. G. Thompson, called for rental fee of 65 scudi per month, with maid service at 8 scudi, excluding board. See Pearson's dissertation, end note 373.

44. Ada to her sister Kate, S.L., Oct. 20, 1858, pp. 1305 and 1315. Although Sophia had suggested in the spring that all the Thompson and Story children be tutored, the Story boys—Thomas Waldo and Julian—seem to have been too young. (Joseph, the oldest after Edith, had died of fever in Nov. 1853). The 3 Thompsons, the Motley girl, and Edith Story verify Ada's total of 5 pupils in addition to the Hawthorne children. Ada listed the studies as "Reading, Spelling, Writing, Composition, Latin, Greek, German, French, Italian, Arithmetic, Algebra, Geometry, Geography, and Chronology," all individually taught according to age and ability.

45. In S.L., Jan. 17, 1859, p. 936, Ada states that Hawthorne wrote diligently "all his mornings." His pocket diary for 1859 (Berg) records January 23 as the day on which he could not "scribble" on his romance. January 30 was the day on which he recorded having finished the rough draft.

46. S.L., ca. Nov. 12, 1858, p. 861, refers to Miss Cushman and 1 or 2 of the many other callers.

47. S.L., ca. Mar. 12, 1858, p. 996. Since the Thompsons had decided to return to the U.S., Ada could go with them on the *Vanderbilt* in June while the Hawthornes went on to England. N.H. wrote for passage for her.

48. S.H. to E.P.P., July 3, 1859 (Essex): "[Pierce] was divinely tender, sweet, sympathizing and helpful. He took Mr. Hawthorne to walk and wrapped him round with the most

soothing care. He would not let him fall into solitary reverie. It was a benign Providence that he was there. No one else could have supplied his place." This long letter was the first that gave the full story of Una's illness. From it we learn all the details that Sophia had been unable to write at the time. The news that she had sat up with Una for 30 nights explains why Sophia was exhausted for so many months afterward.

49. P.D. (S.H.), Apr. 5, 1859 (Berg); (N.H.), Apr. 8, 1859 (Berg).

50. Pierce's sorrow had been caused by the greatest shock a father could experience: He witnessed the death of his only remaining son, aged 11, in a railroad accident when the family was en route to Concord, N.H. Two other sons had died in very early childhood. See "Tragedy," ch. 29, in Nichols, *Franklin Pierce.*

51. N.H.'s pocket diary entries from January to May list dozens of callers whom the Hawthornes had met in 1858—artists and other friends, both American and English. Ada also mentioned particularly Mrs. Story, Mrs. Motley, Mrs. Browning, and Mrs. Farrar (friend of S.H.; widow of John Farrar, former Harvard professor) as people "who did things" (S.L., ca. Apr. 7, 1859, p. 1028). Browning himself was so concerned that he wrote to Isa Blagden, "The Hawthornes are horribly off, Una suffering from Roman fever, changed so that you would not recognize her, she that never was ill before, her mother says." See *Letters to Isa Blagden* (Waco, Texas: Baylor U. Press, 1923), p. 11. In May he wrote to his sister, "Una Hawthorne is better (miraculously all considered)" (*New Letters of Robert Browning*, eds. W. C. DeVane and K. L. Knickerbocker [New Haven: Yale U. Press, 1950], p. 118).

52. In the spring of 1859 the Hawthornes visited a number of artists' studios. In addition to the Americans mentioned in this chapter, other people listed either in the pocket diary or in the notebooks are: William Page, portrait painter; Randolph Rogers, sculptor; Joseph Ropes, painter and drawing instructor; Peter Frederick Rothermel, historical painter; Luther Terry, portrait painter; John R. Tilton, landscape painter; and Hamilton G. Wilde, landscape painter. There were also innumerable callers, including especially Charles Sumner, former senator from Mass. See ch. 1 for Sumner's first comment on N.H.'s appointment to Liverpool.

53. S.L., ca. May 29, 1859, p. 1071.

54. S.L., Apr. 7, 1858, p. 500; S.L., June 23, p. 664; and S.L., June 27, 1858, p. 693, are only a few examples from Ada's letters. Both N.H.'s Italian notebooks and S.H.'s *Notes in England and Italy* are so concerned with art works and sightseeing that personal matters, especially health, are minimized.

55. N.H. to Bennoch, June 17, 1859 (Pearson). Compare with N.H. to Fields, Sept. 3, 1858 (FI 2294 at HM; Pearson transcript): "One grows old in Italy twice or three times as fast as in other countries. I have three gray hairs now, for one that I brought from England, and I shall look venerable indeed by next summer when I return."

56. The family had disliked Mrs. Sievers, the landlady at 24 Great Russell St., too much to wish to stay there again. In this 1859 letter to Bennoch, Hawthorne also said that he longed for England "just as if I were a native John Bull."

57. When N.H. sent the note to Wilding, he expressed in his notebook some uneasiness at the thought of returning home—that it might not turn out to be his home any longer (VII, 60, MA591). Nevertheless, at that time he had no intention of staying in England longer than necessary to await the ship that would return them to Boston.

58. *H&HC*, p. 366. Ada gave no account of the parting, because any letter to Clay written after Switzerland would be apt to go on the same ship with her, and he was to meet her in New York. The last letter in the collection of Ada's correspondence was to her brother, Horace, dated from Paris, June 18, 1859.

Chapter 8. England Again: Yorkshire, Leamington, and Bath, 1859–1860

1. In 1860, N.H. added four passages from Leamington, one from Bath, and one from London. See VII, MA 591. In her edition of *Passages from the French and Italian Note-Books*, Sophia also included an excerpt from a letter and a paragraph from a journal kept in the summer of 1862 in West Gouldsborough, Maine.

2. P.D. (N.H.), 1859 (Berg). Hereafter notation will appear within the text as P.D., plus the date; the same system will be followed for Sophia's P.D. (also Berg).

3. Fields's first wife, Eliza Willard, died about a year after their wedding in 1850; he married Annie Adams in Nov. 1854. This trip was a kind of delayed honeymoon. Records of their travels are in Annie Fields's 1859–1860 Diary (MHS), and *James T. Fields: Biographical Notes and Personal Sketches,* ed. Annie Fields, (1881; Port Washington: Kennikat Press, rpt. 1971).

4. Even before the bankruptcy in 1857, the Bennochs had moved to a smaller (and less expensive?) house at The Knoll, Eliot Hill, which was somewhat nearer to London and reached from Greenwich, not Blackheath, station.

5. This trip was part of an excursion with the Society of Archimagi, to which Bennoch seems to have belonged. Fields must have left the group because of business with Smith and Elder, for by the time N.H. met him again on Tuesday morning he had completed the contract with the publishers.

6. S.H. to E.P.P., July 15, 1859 (Berg). The reference to Una as "fading" in London does not correspond to the letter from Perceval Spencer to H.A.B., Oct. 2, 1860 (TCC), in which he describes a girl he met at Lady Harrington's ball. He decided that she was a Hawthorne from her appearance, references to Italy, and statement that she would not see another season in London. I have found no mention of this ball in any Hawthorne records.

7. The sole official record of their week's stay in Whitby is an erroneous entry of "A. Hawthorne and family. America." at the Angel Hotel; *Whitby Gazette* "Visitors' List" for Aug. 6, 1859. The Hawthornes were not listed at any time in July when they should have been.

8. St. Hilda was the first abbess in this religious house built on one of 12 sites to commemorate the victory of Oswy, Christian king of Northumbria, over Penda, pagan king of Mercia. During her lifetime (to A.D. 680) the abbey became the most celebrated religious house and center of learning in the northeast area. One of her most important contributions was her encouragement of Caedmon, a farm laborer, in his efforts to "sing." The cross marking the supposed burial place of this poet still stands on the hill below the abbey. Historical information is from 2 pamphlets published by the British Ministry of Public Works: *St. Hilda of Whitby, Historical Notes by Norman Moorsom,* 1970, and *Whitby Abbey, Official Handbook by the Late Sir Alfred Clapham,* 1969 ed.; see also *The Streets of Whitby and Their Associations,* by the late Hugh P. Kendall (Whitby Literary and Philosophical Society, 1971). Numerous nineteenth-century guides to Whitby, all published locally, would have been available to the Hawthornes.

9. Legends from *St. Hilda of Whitby,* p. 13.

10. The bank and its surroundings in Grape Lane are described in *The Streets of Whitby.*

11. H.A.B. to N.H., July 29, 1859 (Berg), refers to H.A.B.'s having sent a letter to Whitby, where he thought the Hawthornes were, asking N.H. to write a letter to Milnes in support of the latter's coming speech on the ship cruelty question. H.A.B.'s letter of Sept. 8 to N.H. in Redcar (Berg) explains Mrs. Gaskell's plans for her novel.

12. Redcar (supposedly named for Ivo de Redcar, A.D. 1231, who gave 43 acres to a

Guisborough religious house) was for centuries a small fishing village. After the railroad was extended to the town in 1846, it became a "fashionable watering place of a quiet kind." W. Page, *History of the County of York, North Riding* (London: St. Catherine Press, 1923), 2:401. Redcar's main attraction, the beach with "broad, firm, and smooth sand" extended then from the mouth of the Tees River to Saltburn, "a distance of ten miles." John W. Ord, *History and Antiquities of Cleveland Comparing the Wapentakes of East and West Langbargh, West Riding, County York* (London: Simpkin and Marshall, 1846), p. 364.

13. S.H. to E.P.P., July 31, 1859 (Berg). On a watercolor map of the town in the nineteenth century, the corner of High Street and King Street is lettered "Home of the American Author." A photograph of the house formerly at this location, given to me by the former librarian at Redcar, Mr. H. Moore, tallies exactly with the Hawthornes' descriptions. Before her death Mr. Moore's mother assured him that the photograph was that of the house at 120 High Street.

14. N.H. to Bennoch, July 23, 1859 (Berg).

15. F&IN, Florence, June 13, 1858 (V, 78, HM).

16. *H&HC*, p. 368. Hawthorne's P.D. has notations on 63 different days of such walks with Julian.

17. J.H., Boyhood Diary, Southport, May 1857 to the fall of 1859, in Leamington (MA1377). With characteristic inaccuracy Julian stated that the family had arrived in Redcar on "Friday, *June* the twenty-second 1859 after a sojourn in France and Italy" (italics mine).

18. *Memories*, p. 351.

19. U.H. to "Aunt Lizzie," Aug. 13, 1859 (Berg).

20. S.H. to H.A.B., Sept. 12, 1859 (Berg).

21. Ibid.

22. *Memories*, p. 350.

23. S.H. to E.P.P., Oct. 2 and 20, 1859 (Berg).

24. S.H. to E.P.P., Oct. 20, 1859 (Berg).

25. S.H. to Mary Mann, [before Apr. 8, 1860] (Berg).

26. N.H. to Fields, Oct. 10, 1859 (FI 2314 at HM). Evidently Fields misinterpreted this letter. Years later in *Yesterdays* he reversed the Redcar and Leamington residences, putting Leamington first for the writing, then Redcar for recuperation, and finally Leamington again for the winter.

27. N.H. to Fields, Nov. 17, 1859 (Berg).

28. U.H. to Richard Manning, Dec. 2, 1859 (Essex).

29. S.H. to E.P.P., Oct. 20, 1859 (Berg).

30. N.H. to Fields, Nov. 28, 1859 (Ho. copy); also N.H. to Bennoch, Nov. 29 (Bar.).

31. Dec. 1, 1859, in *LT,* 2:85. On Oct. 6 he had apologized for having neglected Ticknor. Since his last letter from Rome on May 23, he had not even told Ticknor about Redcar until after they had left the place.

32. S.H. to Fields, Nov. 28, 1859 (BPL). This part is in S.H.'s handwriting; page 2 is a transcript by Annie Fields.

33. Ibid. All of this passage except the last sentence is in Annie Fields's writing.

34. N.H. to Fields, Nov. 28, 1859 (BPL).

35. N.H. to Bennoch, Nov. 29, 1859 (Bar.).

36. N.H. to Bennoch, Dec. 22, 1859 (Bar.).

37. Compare Jan. 26, 1860, in *LT,* 2:90, and S.H. to E.P.P., Feb. 27, 1860 (Berg).

38. S.H. to E.P.P., Feb. 27, 1860 (Berg).

39. S.H. to Mary Mann, Feb. 29, 1860 (Berg).

40. Jan. 26, 1860, and Feb. 10, 1860, in *LT*, 2:90 and 96.

41. See Claude Simpson's introduction to *The Marble Faun*, CE, pp. xxviii–xxix.

42. Francis Bennoch, *Poems, Lyrics, Songs, and Sonnets* (London: Hardwicke and Bogue, 1877), p. 267.

43. The verse escaped destruction and is at present in the Milburn Collection (#136). It is marked *n.d.,* but the last line, "Bath St. Number 21," identifies the place and occasion.

44. N.H. to Bennoch, Mar. 4, 1860 (Bar.).

45. N.H. to Smith and Elder, Mar. 7, 1860 (Pearson transcript). The same plan was indicated in his letter of Mar. 9, in *LT*, 2:97.

46. *Examiner,* Mar. 31, 1860, p. 197, cols. b and c.

47. N.H.'s note from Bath was dated Apr. 23, 1860 (Pearson). In 1936 the ms., bound in 2 volumes, was given to the British Museum in memory of her father by Bright's daughter, Mrs. Elizabeth Merivale. Two letters — 1 from Hawthorne, Mar. 10, 1860, and 1 from John Elliott Hodgkin, artist — have been inserted in the front of volume 1.

48. Apr. 6, 1860, in *LT*, 2:100. For summaries of reviews, see the introduction to *The Marble Faun*, CE, pp. xxx and xxxii, n. 47.

49. N.H. to Motley, Apr. 1, 1860 (Berg)

50. S.H. to E.P.P., n.d., in *Memories*, pp. 343–46. Names were suggested by the Manning family property at Raymond, Maine, and an old claim to further property that was reflected in the plot of *The House of the Seven Gables.*

51. *Memories,* p. 346. The house on Charles Street was demolished when all the older buildings on that side of the street were razed. The houses that are left on the opposite side suggest that the one rented by the Hawthornes must have been small and unpretentious.

52. S.H. to Mary Mann, Feb. 29, [1860] (Berg).

53. Compare S.H. to Mary Mann, Mar. 14, 1860 and from Bath [before Apr. 8, 1860] (Berg).

54. S.H., to Mary Mann, May 27, 1860 (Berg).

55. N.H. to Fields, May 3, 1860 (Ho. copy).

56. S.H. to Mary Mann, Mar. 14, 1860 (Berg).

57. Apr. 6, 1860, in *LT*, 2:99-100. For American reviews, see reference in note 48.

58. Maria Mitchell, May 12, 1860, in *Maria Mitchell: Life, Letters, and Journals*, p. 171. The correspondent is not named.

59. Longfellow to Wadsworth, in Edward Wagenecht, *Longfellow: a Full-Length Portrait* (N.Y.: Longmans, Green, 1955), p. 26.

60. In Samue Longfellow, *Life of H.W. Longfellow* (Boston: Houghton Mifflin, 1887), 2:351.

61. Hosmer to Wayman Crow, May 20, 1860, in *Harriet Hosmer: Letters and Memories*, p. 156.

62. Temple to H.A.B., Apr. 7, 1860. On Aug. 12, 1855, he wrote to H.A.B. that he had been reading *Mosses from an Old Manse* and that he had been "greatly taken with *Goodman Brown* and *Earth's Holocaust.*" On Jan. 9, 1883, he referred to a review in the *Athenaeum* of *Dr. Grimshawe's Secret*, which he assumed was Bright's. It was. (All correspondence at TCC.)

63. J.A.V. Chapple and Arthur Pollard, eds., *The Letters of Mrs. Gaskell* (Manchester U. Press, 1966; Harvard U. Press, 1967), pp. 592–93 and 575. For further comparisons, see Section IV, "Rome, the Storys, and *The Marble Faun*," in Anne Ehrenpreis, "Elizabeth Gaskell and Nathaniel Hawthorne," *NHJ*, 3 (1973) : 89–119.

64. Apr. 19, 1860, in *LT,* 2:103 and 104.

65. Fields to N.H., May 2, 1860 (Pearson transcript).

66. N.H. to H.A.B., May 5, 1860 (Pearson).

67. N.H. to Bennoch, Apr. 26, 1860 (Bar.).

68. S.H. to Mary Mann, May 27, 1860 (Berg).

69. N.H. to S.H., May 17, [1860] (HM 11016); also N.H. to U.H., May [16], attached to the first letter.

70. Bright had made his arrangements for May 19 (if the day should be "sunshiny enough") with John Edwin Mayall, photographer of 224 and 226 Regent St. The extensive correspondence (Bar.) between Bennoch and George H. Holden, a native of Salem living in Providence, R.I., in the 1880s, led Holden into an argument over the three Mayall photographs with Robert C. Hall, another "admirer" of N.H. In answer Hall published his "Portraits of Hawthorne" (*Athenaeum,* June 1887). See Holden's letters to the *Salem Gazette* and Hall's scrapbook (Berg). I am indebted to Buford Jones of Duke University for calling my attention to the latter items. Much of the discussion in Bennoch's letters to Holden concerns the photo from which the artist Johnston painted the portrait now at Bowdoin College.

71. N.H. to U.H., May 25, 1860, in *NH&HW,* 2:259-60.

72. Hammond to H.A.B., May 20, 1860 (TCC).

73. Hammond to H.A.B., Apr. 27, 1860 (TCC).

74. H.A.B. to J.H., in *NH&HW,* 2:259. Listing of events appeared in the *Cambridge Chronicle and University Journal* and in the *Cambridge Independent Press,* both for May 26, 1860.

75. N.H. to Mrs. S. C. Hall, May 20, 1860 (Berg). Annie Fields's diary notes that N.H. was present at this dinner.

76. N.H. to H.A.B., in *NH&HW,* 2:242.

77. N.H. to W.C. Bennett, June 15, 1860 [mistakenly dated Mar. 15] (Bar.). Sonnets are quoted in *NH&HW,* 2:253-54. Letters to Sturgis (Fruitlands Museum) and to Brown (Pearson transcript) both were written on June 10.

78. S.H. to Ticknor, May 16, 1860 (Berg).

79. Annie Fields's diary (MHS) gives the date as June 12, but the next entry is June 14, "a quiet day" in Liverpool.

80. Annie Fields's diary for June 18, 1860. Compare *Yesterdays,* pp. 92–93.

81. *Yesterdays,* p. 92.

82. N.H. to Fields, Apr. 26, 1860 (FI 2300 at HM).

83. For example, the passage in his letter to H.A.B. quoted in *NH&HW,* 2:242.

84. *H&HC,* p. 372.

Chapter 9. Concord Once More: Memories of "Our Old Home," 1859–1864

1. Longfellow, diary for June 30, 1860 (Craigie-Longfellow House), in W. S. Tryon, *Parnassus Corner: a Life of James T. Fields, Publisher to the Victorians,* p. 248.

2. *Recollections,* p. 164.

3. Alcott kept an exact record of dates. For references to his journal, to Hawthorne writings on the subject, and for floor plans, photographs, uses of the rooms, etc., see *The Wayside: Homes of Authors,* by Robert D. Ronsheim (1968 report) and *The Wayside: Historic Grounds Report,* by Anna Coxe Toogood (1970 report), both publications from Minute Man National Historical Park (U.S. Dept. of Interior: National Park Service). Though the first report has more historical background on the early years of the house, there is

some duplication in the 2 reports, especially on the years of Hawthorne ownership.

4. Dec. 28, 1860, in *LT,* 2:111.

5. Alcott, journal notations (vol. 35, p. 369?), quoted in Ronsheim, note 132, p. 72.

6. U.H. to Richard Manning, July 20, 1860 (Essex). Compare Sept. 27 and Oct. 3, 1860, in *LT,* 2:106–07. As Una's history shows, she never did recover completely. See *NHJ*, 6 (1976): 86–119.

7. For an account written by Julian, see "Frank Sanborn" and "Life at Sanborn's School," in *Memoirs,* pp. 77–90. His mother's reactions were recorded by Sanborn in *Hawthorne and His Friends: Reminiscence and Tribute* (Cedar Rapids, Iowa: Torch Press, 1908), pp. 13–17.

8. Daily entries in the diary (microfilm from Ban.) are full of comings and goings by the rest of the family, but N.H. is seldom mentioned.

9. On his greater ease, see M. D. Conway's "My Hawthorne Experience," *Critic,* July 1904, pp. 22–25; on his shyness, see Sanborn, p. 10.

10. N.H. to Motley, Apr. 1, 1860 (Berg).

11. May 16, 1861, in *LT,* 2:114.

12. Also reprinted in *The American Claimant Manuscripts: The Ancestral Footstep, Etherege, Grimshawe,* CE 12 (Columbus: Ohio State U. Press, 1977), pp. 472–73. Subsequent page references to this volume occur within the text, together with identification of the particular manuscript.

13. H.A.B. to N.H., Sept. 8, 1860, in *Memories,* pp. 464–66.

14. Bennoch to N.H., Jan. 8, 1861 (Berg). Compare Bennoch to N.H., Dec. 14, 1860 (Berg); N.H. to Bennoch, Dec. 17, 1860 (Bar.).

15. May 26, 1861, in *LT,* 2:115.

16. S.H. to N.H., July 27, 1861 (Berg). Julian dated this letter "Saturday Evening, July 25, 1861" (*NH&HW*, 2:282). The original has been marked "July 25 [1862]." In neither year was July 25 on a Saturday. S.H.'s diary for 1861 (Ban.) states that the 2 men had left for Pride's Crossing on Saturday, July 27, a correct date for 1861.

17. Aug. 8, 1861, HM 11022; *LL,* 2:275–76.

18. Fields was mistaken in his recollections. In *Yesterdays* (p. 96) he wrote as if the story N.H. outlined was that of *The Dolliver Romance* instead of *Septimius.* See also the discussion on p. 562 of "Historical Commentary" in *The Elixir of Life Manuscripts,* CE 13 (Columbus: Ohio State U. Press, 1977). As with the English romance, references to this volume occur within the text along with identification of the particular manuscript.

19. Discussed in note 7, pp. 558–59 of "Historical Commentary," CE 13; also in my article "Hawthorne and the Magic Elixir of Life: the Failure of a Gothic Theme," *ESQ,* 18, no. 2 (2nd qtr., 1972): 97–107.

20. *NH&HW*, 2:301. Note, however, that Julian mistakenly dated the Septimius romance as being written before the Grimshawe story.

21. Oct. 10, 1856, and March 13, 1857, in *LT,* 2:29 and 46.

22. May 16, 1861, in *LT,* 2:114. Compare N.H. to Bennoch [1861], in *NH&HW*, 2:290–92.

23. N.H. to Bridge, May 26, 1861, in *NH&HW,* 2:276–77. Compare H.A.B. to N.H., Sept. 10, 1861, in *NH&HW*, 2:296. Bridge's summary of N.H.'s letters, 1861–1862, was printed in "Hawthorne's Loyalty," *Century Magazine,* 13 (Nov. 1887–Apr. 1888): 489–90.

24. H.A.B. married Mary Elizabeth Thompson, oldest daughter of Samuel H. Thompson of Thingwall Hall, near Liverpool. Their first child, Allan Heywood, was born on Sat., May 24, 1862, the queen's birthday. See H.A.B. to N.H., May 30 [1862] (Berg).

25. N.H. to Bennoch, [Sept. 1861] referred to by J.H. but not quoted; later printed as "My Dear B," in "Nathaniel Hawthorne," *Once a Week* (June 27, 1868), p. 563.

26. On Feb. 14, 1862, N.H. had declined Bridge's invitation; in March he accepted, according to *Recollections,* pp. 171–74.

27. Leutze, a German painter most famous for historical scenes, had settled in the U.S. in 1859.

28. N.H. to Fields, [Apr. 2, 1862], in *Yesterdays,* p. 96.

29. S.H. to Annie Fields, May 7, 1862 (BPL). Details of Thoreau's last days and funeral are in Walter Harding's *The Days of Henry Thoreau* (N.Y.: Knopf, 1965), ch. 20.

30. Correspondence on the article began with N.H. to Fields, May 7, 1862 (Milburn) and continued on May 23, 1862 (Pearson transcript). Nine years later Fields decided that it was safe to print the deleted passage. (*Yesterdays,* p. 101)

31. "Chiefly About War Matters," from *Complete Works* (1883 edition), 11:318. Other references occur in parentheses within the text.

32. Edward Dicey, *Macmillan's Magazine,* 19 (July 1864): 241–46. This article was his tribute to N.H. following the author's death. S.H. to Annie Fields, June 13, 1862 (BPL), describes Dicey's visit.

33. N.H. to E.M.H., in *NH&HW,* 2:314.

34. This journal is partly reproduced in *NH&HW,* 2:315–20. N.H.'s entries are comments on various Maine natives and on the departure of soldiers to the war. Two paragraphs on the latter subject are quoted by S.H. at the end of her edition of *Passages from the French and Italian Note-books,* pp. 561–62, as an indication of her husband's "state of mind at an interesting period of his country's history."

35. Oct. 27, 1862, in *LT,* 2:119.

36. N.H. to Fields, Sept. 27, 1862 (Berg).

37. N.H. to Bennoch, Oct. 12, 1862 (Bar.).

38. N.H. to Fields, Dec. 6, 1862 (FI 2316 at HM); another portion of the same letter is quoted in part in *Yesterdays,* p. 103.

39. S.H. to Annie Fields, Dec. 14 and 17, 1862 (BPL).

40. S.H. to E.P.P., marked "Private," [between 1853 and 1859] (Berg).

41. Jan. 6, 1863, in *LT,* 2:120. The thank-you notes were sent by N.H. on Feb. 22 and Apr. 30, 1863, in *LT,* 2:122–23. The note of Feb. 8, in *LT,* 2:121–22, refers to Ticknor's and Pierce's failure to visit him.

42. N.H. to Fields, Feb. 14 and 22, *Yesterdays,* pp. 103–04.

43. At first N.H. received $100 for each article in the magazine; later this payment was increased. His income from all of the articles on England was estimated at about $1,300. See Claude Simpson's introduction to *Our Old Home,* CE 5, p. xxxvii, n. 56, in which he estimates N.H.'s lifetime income from the articles and the book, both English and American editions, as slightly over $3,000.

44. N.H. to Fields, Apr. 30, 1863 (FI 2309 at HM), reprinted in part in *Yesterdays,* pp. 104–05.

45. See Fredson Bowers, "Textual Introduction," CE, pp. cxiii–cxiv.

46. N.H. to Lowell, dated before June 4, 1863 (Pearson transcript).

47. June 7, 1863 (Pearson transcript with S.H.'s note), and June 18, 1863, in *LT,* 2:123–24.

48. N.H. to Fields, July 1, 1863 (FI 2303 at HM); also in *Yesterdays,* p. 106. Neither Bright nor Bennoch was named in the book, though each is referred to obliquely — Bright in connection with his visits to the consular office in Liverpool; Bennoch as his dear friend, sitting near him at the Lord Mayor's Dinner. Later Sophia decided to

remedy the omission of Bennoch's name by dedicating *Passages from the English Note-books* to him.

49. N.H. to Fields, July 18, 1863 (Ho); also in *Yesterdays,* pp. 107–08.

50. For the various reactions to the dedication, see Annie Fields, *Authors and Friends* (Boston: Houghton Mifflin, 1897), pp. 15, 72, and 184.

51. Thompson to H.A.B., July 20, 1863 (TCC).

52. *An Englishman in the American Civil War; the Diaries of Henry Yates Thompson, 1863* (N.Y.: N.Y.U. Press, 1971), p. 46.

53. Ibid., p. 52.

54. For a summary of reviews, see Claude Simpson's introduction, CE, p. xxxi.

55. *Our Old Home,* CE 5, p. 60. Subsequent notations on this volume occur within the text.

56. H.A.B. to N.H., Oct. 24, 1863 (Berg). The *Examiner* article was in no. 2907, Oct. 17, 1863, pp. 662–63.

57. Bennoch to N.H., Mar. 28, 1863 (Berg), reprinted in *NH&HW,* 2:306–08.

58. N.H. to Fields, Oct. 18, 1863 (FI 2313 at HM); also in part in *Yesterdays,* p. 109.

59. Review in the *London Times,* Nov. 9, 1863, p. 10, cols. 1–3.

60. Anthony Trollope, *Can You Forgive Her?* (London: 1864–1865; rpt. Oxford U. Press, 1948), 1:342.

61. Anthony Trollope, *North America* (N.Y.: Harper's, 1862), p. 69. An account of the dinner in Boston where Trollope and N.H. met was given by Lowell on Sept. 20, 1861. See *J. R. Lowell: a Biography* by Horace Scudder (Boston: Houghton Mifflin, 1901), 2:83–84.

62. N.H. to Fields, Oct. 24, 1863 (FI 2296 at HM); also in *Yesterdays,* pp. 109–10.

63. S.H. to Elizabeth (Peabody) (O.S.U. Ms. Collection, dated 1864, but more likely late in 1863, since she refers to "this autumn"). Compare July 27, 1863, *LT,* 2:124.

64. For details on N.H.'s deteriorating health, compare S.H. to Annie Fields, Oct. 11, 1863 (BPL), with Fields's account in *Yesterdays,* p. 113 ff., and Annie Fields's descriptions in *Memories of a Hostess* (Boston: Atlantic Monthly Press, 1922), pp. 57–61.

65. S.H. to U.H., Dec. 19, 1863, in *NH&HW,* 2:333.

66. *Yesterdays,* p. 115.

67. N.H. to Fields, Feb. 25, 1864, in *Yesterdays,* pp. 115–16.

68. N.H. to Longfellow, Jan. 2, 1864 (Pearson transcript from Ho).

69. In her final chapter of *The Shape of Hawthorne's Career* (Ithaca: Cornell U. Press, 1976), Nina Baym discusses the shift of Hawthorne's writing away from romance toward realism. She points out that Hawthorne was trying a new approach to his role as artist.

70. Bennoch to N.H., Mar. 8, 1864 (Berg).

71. *Yesterdays,* p. 117.

72. Details of the trip are in a series of letters: Mar. 18, 1864, in *LT,* 2:126; Ticknor's letters quoted in *NH&HW,* 2:339–43; and S.H. to Bridge, Apr. 5, 1864 (*Recollections,* pp. 189–92).

73. *Yesterdays,* p. 118.

74. Fields's diary account, dated Mar. 28 and Apr. 1864, is from *Memories of a Hostess,* pp. 62 and 63–64.

75. S.H., Apr. 18, 1864 (BPL), quoted in part in *Yesterdays,* pp. 118–20.

76. Emerson to J. R. Lowell, Apr. 21, 1864, *Letters of R. W. Emerson* (N.Y.: Columbia U. Press, 1939), 5:373. See also R. Rusk, *Life of Ralph W. Emerson* (N.Y.: Columbia U. Press, 1939), p. 424.

77. N.H. and S.H. to Pierce, May 7, 1864 (Bar.).

78. *NH&HW*, 2:345.

79. Holmes, introduction written to accompany ch. 1 of *The Dolliver Romance* in *Atlantic Monthly*, 14 (July 1864): 98–101. It has been suggested that N.H.'s illness was possibly a gastrointestinal cancer. This would account for the symptoms described here, but not for the earlier ones of colds and nosebleeds.

80. *Yesterdays*, p. 122.

81. Pierce's letter of May 19 is quoted in *Yesterdays*, p. 123. He wrote much the same to Bridge; see *Recollections*, pp. 176–79. Bridge, who would have been expected to attend the funeral, was notified in Washington, where he was confined to his room by an accident. (See p. 175.)

82. *The Heart of Emerson's Journals*, ed. Bliss Perry (Boston: Houghton Mifflin, 1926) pp. 305–06. The funeral was reported in detail and the address by James Freeman Clarke reprinted in the *Boston Evening Transcript* of May 24, 1864; reprinted in *NHJ*, 2 (1972): 257–61.

83. For the additions, see S.H. to Anne O'Gara, Sept. 4, 1864, in Maurice Bassan, "A New Account of Hawthorne's Last Days, Death, and Funeral," *AL*, 27 (Jan. 1956): 562–65. Also in this letter to their former servant is a description of the flowers. They included lilies of the valley, N.H.'s favorite, inside the church; and two wreaths—one of apple blossoms from the Old Manse orchard, and one of white hothouse flowers (tea roses, orange flowers, gillyflowers, and others). See also *Yesterdays*, p. 124.

84. One letter was published in *Biographical Notes and Personal Sketches of James T. Fields*, pp. 92–95; the other was included in Annie Fields, *Memories of a Hostess*, pp. 70–72.

85. "Hawthorne. May 23, 1864" in *The Poetical Works of Henry Wadsworth Longfellow*, Household Edition (Boston: Houghton Mifflin, 1882–1883), p. 319.

86. *Memories*, p. 480.

Chapter 10. Epilogue

1. From analysis of S.H.'s letters (BPL) Randall Stewart published a series of articles on the affairs of the family during that period, including S.H.'s quarrel with Fields. See, for example, *More Books*, 20 (1945) and 21 (1946); also *NEQ*, 17 (1944): 418–23. The Hawthornes had no funds from the Wayside until after July 1870, when it was finally sold.

2. S.H. to Bright, May 10, 1868 (TCC), where she explains another reason for leaving the Wayside: Her husband had never been happy there.

3. Ibid. Sophia's and Una's journals from Dresden (Berg) give full details of their life in that city, but do not cover the year 1870. Passages from Julian's diary for 1868–1869 are quoted in Maurice Bassan, *Hawthorne's Son* (Columbus: Ohio S. U. Press, 1970).

4. H.A.B. to Lord Houghton, Nov. 18, [1870], in T. Wemyss Reid, *Life, Letters, and Friendships of Richard Monckton Milnes, First Lord Houghton* (N.Y.: Cassell, 1891), 2:242. The letter is quoted as if it were related to events of 1865, but the contents establish the date as 1870.

5. Una's account is in *NH&HW*, 2:353–71. Moncure Conway published two accounts of the funeral: "A Fresh Grave in Kensal Green," an article in *Harper's Weekly*, Apr. 22, 1871, pp. 369–70, and his chapter on N.H. and S.H. in *Emerson at Home and Abroad* (London: Trübner, 1883). Information on the graves is from my own visits to the cemetery.

6. Letters to Bright in the fall of 1871 from Channing and from a Kensington neighbor, Jane Tennant, are in TCC. Both E.P.P. and R.H. applied the term "insanity" to

Una's violent condition. Channing disagreed. Subsequent accounts by outsiders were no doubt exaggerated, for Una apparently had no recurrence of violence after the attack in 1871. Details are also in my article, "Una Hawthorne: a Biographical Sketch," *NHJ*, 6 (1976): 86–119.

7. Information on Webster and his writings is also in the article on Una in *NHJ*. The date of Una's death was given by newspapers and by J.H. and T. W. Higginson as Sept. 10. I cannot account for the date on the tombstone.

8. Rose's life has been covered in several biographies, including Theodore Maynard's *A Fire Was Lighted* (Milwaukee: Bruce Pub. Co., 1948).

9. Biographical material on Bright may be found in a number of sketches and in his correspondence at TCC.

10. Some details on Bennoch appear in my article, "Bennoch and Hawthorne," *NHJ*, 4 (1974): 48–74. Subsequent research has been in Scottish and English newspapers. See especially the obituary in *Dumfries and Galloway Standard,* July 5, 1890. The memorial to Longfellow is referred to in a catalogue note on a letter sold in 1977 by Sotheby's of London.

11. J.H., letter to the editor, the *Critic,* July 19, 1890, p. 36.

12. Present owners, Mr. and Mrs. Don Locke, are much involved in restoring the house. See note 18, ch. 6.

Addendum

English readers of this book will already be familiar with a news item not known to most American readers: Not long ago the screw steamer *Great Britain*, described in Chapter 2, was discovered beached in South America; the ship was towed to Bristol, the port where it had been built, and is now (1980) being restored. It joins a very small group of ships that have been restored as a significant part of British naval heritage.

Appendix:
Biographical Sketches

The following are thumbnail sketches of individuals who had some contact with the Hawthornes or who were sources of information about the family during and after their experience abroad. For the most famous authors and for details of other biographies, the reader is referred to the *Dictionary of National Biography* (1921 ed.), the *Dictionary of American Biography* (1957–1958 ed.), and the *National Cyclopedia of American Biography* (use 1978 index volume for specific individuals). Annotations in the 1980 Ohio State University Press edition of *F&IN* identify people, places, and works of art on the Continent. The forthcoming edition of *EN* will do the same for England.

Adolphus, John Leycester (1795–1862), barrister, author, judge of county court circuit, 1844 to death in London; guest at Haywood's dinner in Liverpool attended by N.H., 1857. Author of *Letters to Richard Heber, Esq., Containing Critical Remarks on the Series of Novels Beginning with "Waverley," and an Attempt to Ascertain Their Author,* 1821. Obit. in *Gentleman's Magazine,* 14 (1863): 246

Aikin, John, Liverpool merchant and insurance broker; host at dinner for N.H. and the sons of Robert Burns, Oct. 1, 1853. Partner in J. Aikin Son & Co. and in Rawson, Aikin & Co., 21 Exchange Bldgs., Liverpool. Residence: 4 Windermere Terrace, Prince's Park. (Or possibly James Aikin, also merchant and shipowner, of 1 Alfred St., Liverpool, partner in Aikin Son & Co., merchants and shipbrokers of 2 Drury Lane. Because of the address, John is more likely to have entertained the group.)

Ainsworth, Peter (1790–1870), owner of Smithill's Hall, Bolton le Moors, guest at Heywoods' dinner with N.H., Apr. 1855, and host to N.H. at Smithill's Hall, Aug. 1855. M.P. for Bolton, 1835–1847. The hall had a cavity somewhat resembling a footmark in the stone step, giving rise to the tradition of the "bloody footstep." See Baines, ed., *History of County Palatine and Duchy of Lancaster* (London, 1868): I, 543–47.

Akers, Paul (1825–1861), Am. sculptor, met N.H. in Rome. Supposed by readers to have been the model for Kenyon in *The Marble Faun*. Son of a sawmill owner in Sacarappa, Maine, he first trained to be a printer, then studied plaster-casting in Boston. Studio for 2 yrs. in Portland. A year of study in Florence, 1852; then a winter in Washington, D.C. Returned to Italy, 1854. In ill health for several yrs. Returned home, 1858.

Allingham, William (1824–1889), Irish author, first visited N.H. at Liverpool consulate, 1854; his poems promoted by N.H. in 1855. Son of branch bank mgr. in Ballyshannon, Ireland, he was a self-educated man. Began work in bank at age 13. Gov. appointments to customhouses. Tried literary life in London twice, 1854 and 1870, when he became sub-editor of *Fraser's*. Friend of many literary men, including Leigh Hunt, Thomas Carlyle, Coventry Patmore, Tennyson, and the pre-Raphaelites. First book, *Poems,* pub. 1850. Biog. in *Letters to William Allingham* (London, 1911) and in *William Allingham: a Diary* (London, 1907).

Apthorp, Robert (1811–1882), real-estate broker of Boston, whose family met Hawthornes in Rome, introduced by Wm. Story. He was father of *William Foster Apthorp* (1848–1913), who was taken at age 8 to Europe to study languages, art, and music. Family did not return to the U.S. until 1860. Wm. became a famous music critic, writing for *Atlantic Monthly* under W. D. Howells, editor. *Mrs. Eliza (Hunt) Apthorp* (1817–1903), wife of Robert, and her sister, *Sarah Henshaw Hunt* (1815–1895), were both much admired by Ada Shepard. Their friendship with Theodore Parker is explained in note 199.16, p. 970, *F&IN* (OSU ed., 1980).

Babcock, Benjamin Franklin, Liverpool merchant, host to N.H. at an "American style" dinner, Jan. 1856; guest at N.H.'s dinner for Bennoch, Oct. 4, 1856. Office in the Commercial Bldgs., 17 Water St., Liverpool; residence: Hayman's Green, West Derby.

Bacon, Delia (1811–1859), Am. lecturer and author, aided by N.H. in publication of her book on Shakespeare for which he wrote the preface. b. Tallmadge, Ohio. Father died, 1817, leaving wife and 6 children. Delia attended school of Catherine Beecher in Conn. until age 15. Tried to establish a school in 3 different locations. Successful lecturer in N.Y. Sailed for England, 1853, to do research on Shakespeare. Spent 3 yrs. in relative poverty. Taken home by nephew to Hartford, where she died reportedly insane. Details in Theodore Bacon, *Delia Bacon: a Biographical Sketch* (Boston, 1888), and Vivian D. Hopkins, *Prodigal Puritan: a Life of Delia Bacon* (Cambridge, 1959).

Badger, Henry Clay (1833–1894), fiancé of Ada Shepard. Did not meet Hawthornes, but corresponded and knew much about them through Ada. b. Honeoye Falls, N.Y. Grad. Antioch College, 1857, and became engaged to Ada. Attended Harvard Divinity School. m. Ada Shepard, 1859. Taught at Antioch, 1858–1861. Worked with Sanitary Commission, 1862. Ordained

Unitarian minister, 1865. Assumed pastorate, Christ Church, Dorchester, Mass. Suffered breakdown in health that led to pact with his wife re insanity. (See *Shepard*.) After her suicide he spent later yrs. in charge of map dept. at Harvard Library. Details in fictionalized biography, pub. posthumously: *Bethlehem, or Border Lands of Faith, a Historical Novel,* 1895. See also Robert L. Straker, "Romance Pathetique," *Antioch Alumni Bulletin,* 8, no. 2 (Feb. 1937).

Bailey, Dr. Gamaliel (1807–1859), Am. journalist and antislavery agitator, visited Hawthornes, 1853, in Rock Ferry on way home from first trip abroad. Known nationally for editorship of the *National Era,* to which prominent contributors were Whittier, Grace Greenwood, Theodore Parker, and Mrs. Stowe (first publication of *Uncle Tom's Cabin*). His home in Washington, D.C., was a social center for abolitionists. Made second trip abroad, 1859, for his health. Died at sea on the way home, but was buried in the U.S. See *DAB,* 1:496.

Bailey, Philip James (1816–1902), Eng. poet, guest at numerous parties of literary people in London, where he met N.H. several times. Barrister and son of proprietor of *Nottingham Mercury.* Fame as a poet rested almost entirely upon a single work, *Festus,* begun at age 20, pub. 1839, with 11 eds. in England and 30 in U.S. See A. H. Miles, editor, *Poets and Poetry of the Century* (London, 1859), 4:467.

Bartholomew, Edward Sheffield (1822–1858), Am. sculptor whose studio Hawthornes visited in Rome. After trying several careers, attended Academy of Design, N.Y. Became curator of Wadsworth Gallery, Hartford, at age 23. Went to Italy, 1850, to study sculpture. Moved to Naples for change of air to improve health. Died there, 1858, one month after Hawthornes met him. Death recorded by Ada Shepard in letter of May 8, 1858. See Henry T. Tuckerman, *Book of the Artist,* 2nd ed. (N.Y.: J. F. Carr, 1969), pp. 609–12.

Bennett, William Cox (1820–1895), Eng. jeweler and poet. N.H. first bought a watch from him by correspondence. Bennett, who had long admired N.H.'s writing, presented a copy of his *Poems* (London, 1850) to him sometime before they met in London, 1855. In 1860 he wrote sonnets about *The Marble Faun.* b. Greenwich, Eng. Son of John Bennett, clock and instrument maker for Royal Observatory. Bus. address: 65 Cheapside, London. Pub. about 14 vols. of poems.

Bennoch, Francis (1812–1890), London poet and bus. man; first met N.H., Dec. 1853, at Rock Park, introduced through correspondence with Fields. Host to Hawthornes at Blackheath for summer, 1856, and on other occasions. After N.H.'s death Bennoch helped S.H. and the children. b. Drumcrool, Durrisdeer, Scotland, sixth of 9 children of Robert Bennoch, farmer, and Jean Kennedy Bennoch. Moved to London, 1828, to work as a clerk. m. Margaret Raine, d. of Wm. Raine of Staindrop, Durham and York counties, June 28,

1838. No children. Established own bus., Bennoch, Twentyman, & Rigg, wholesalers in silks and ribbons, 77 Wood St., City. Took active part in meetings of Burns Society, wrote poetry, and pub. first vol. privately, 1830s. Sailed to U.S. on *Niagara*, 1848, and visited numerous Am. writers. Civic work in London as member of common council, deputy of a ward, and commissioner of lieutenancy for City; pub. pamphlets on metropolitan improvements. Memberships: RSA, 1852; Noviomagians (dining club connected with Society of Antiquarians); Royal Blackheath Golf Club, of which he was captain, 1860–1861. After recovery from bankruptcy, traveled to U.S. on bus. for Council of Foreign Bondholders, 1880; served as advisor for 5 or 6 other companies. Continued to write poetry and to visit in Scotland as long as his parents lived at Thornhill, near Dumfries. Successive residences: Diamond Terrace, Greenwich; Pond Rd., Blackheath; the Knoll, Eliot Hill, Lewisham; Tavistock Square, London. On one of many bus. trips, fell ill on train to Berlin and died suddenly.

Bill, John, Esq., ribbon mfr. of Coventry, host at dinner for Bennoch and N.H., Feb. 1860. Charles Bray (q.v.) and wife were the other guests. Residence: Barrs Hill, Radford Road, Coventry.

Blagden, Jane Isabella (Isa) (1816–1873), Eng. writer, met Hawthornes at Brownings' in Florence. Lived then at Villa Bricchieri, near Villa Montauto. As friend of the Brownings she had settled in Florence, 1849. Helped nurse both Elizabeth Browning and Theodosia Trollope in their final illnesses. After death of the former, Isa went to Paris with Robert and his son. Returned to Florence and lived there until death. Wrote essays and sketches for *Cornhill* and *Athenaeum*. Pub. several novels, 1861–1869. *Poems, with a Memoir by Alfred Austin* (London, 1873) gives little biog. information. Some details in correspondence with Browning, but nothing of her background.

Blodget, Mary (1794–1862), wife of Samuel Chase Blodget (q.v.), famous for managing lodging houses for Americans. Hawthornes stayed at her Duke St. house in Liverpool on numerous occasions. First listed in 1834 Gibraltar census as b. London, married, aged 40, resident 19 yrs. Possibly second wife of Samuel, since son, Samuel Blodget, Jr., aged 22, was listed as b. in America, resident of Gibraltar only 1 yr. (1834 census). Date of move to Liverpool not given. After Samuel's death, 1855, she was listed as lodging house keeper at 153–155 Duke St. Outlived her husband by 7 yrs. Buried in St. James's Cemetery, Liverpool.

Blodget, Samuel Chase (1781–1855), possibly an Am. merchant. Though still living at Duke St. in 1853, he is not mentioned by Hawthornes; evidently he retired because of poor health. Yrs. later J.H. wrote in error of Mary Blodget as "widow" when his family was in Liverpool. S. C. Blodget was first listed, 1839, as commission agent, partner in Blodgett (*sic*) and Henrickson, residence at 10

Appendix: Biographical Sketches

Colquitt St., off Duke St.; in 1841 and 1843, listed as ship chandler; in 1851–1855, labeled "gentleman" and "lodging house keeper" at 133 (renumbered 153) Duke St. Not included in Gibraltar census, 1834. Death certificate described him as aged 74, retired; date: May 30, 1855; cause: asthma, paralysis, and pneumonia.

Boott, Elizabeth Otis Lyman (1846–1888), Am. artist, d. of Francis (q.v.), met N.H. at Brownings' soirée in Florence, 1858. R.H. described her as a very young artist who made a watercolor sketch of N.H. that was not a good likeness (*Memories*, pp. 398–99). In 1870s, after some yrs. of study in Europe, she sent pictures to exhibitions in U.S., but later returned to studio in Boston. m. Frank Duveneck, artist, 1886. See *NCAB* under *Duveneck*, 20:87–88.

Boott, Francis (1813–1904), Am. composer, met Hawthornes in Florence through the Brownings with whom he was friendly. See *Letters of Robert Browning to His American Friends*, ed. A. J. Armstrong (Waco, Tex.: Baylor U. Press, 1923). Resident of Villa Castellani, Florence, and Cambridge, Mass. Composed string quartets and songs. Left fund of $10,000 for annual prize at Harvard for 4-part vocal work.

Bowman, young accountant (in 1856), resident at 32 St. James's Place, London, with office on Old Broad Street, City. Assisted N.H. on his first visit to London by arranging for accommodations at his own lodging house and by showing N.H. around the city until Bennoch took over that function. In May 1858, Bowman met N.H. in Liverpool for trip to Scotland. Since the two men had not met before London trip, arrangements had obviously been made by correspondence, probably through Bowman's relatives living either in Liverpool, where he had visited, or possibly in Manchester. No further mention of Bowman in N.H.'s writings.

Bowman, William (1803–1863?), merchant in Am. trade; resident at 6 Rock Park, Rock Ferry, 1853; and partner in Bowman Tetley & Co. (later Bowman, Grinnell & Co.), 8 Fenwick Chambers, Fenwick St., Liverpool, owners of Swallowtail Line of ships to Boston. Elizabeth (or Eliza) Ann Bowman, Wm.'s second wife, called upon S.H. when they were neighbors in Rock Park. Census records include Bowman's older daughter, Elizabeth (aged 22 in 1853), b. London, child of a first wife, and 2 children by the second wife, both b. near Liverpool: Lucy Ann (aged 13 in 1853), and Wm. R., aged 8. Though N.H.'s writings provide no clues, family's connection with London is clearly indicated by several bits of evidence, including the move of Wm.'s family after his death to South Kensington, where all except the son, Wm. R., spent the rest of their lives. (Wm. R. died in America.)

Bracken, Annette, Eng. friend of Isa Blagden and of Brownings, met Hawthornes in Florence and later in Rome. d. of Mary Egerton Smith Bracken, referred to in Browning letters. Her father was dead at the time she was in Italy, but the uncle, William, was in Rome for winter of 1858–1859. For notes on Bracken family, especially the mother and the son, Willy, who was a particular friend of Pen Browning, see Armstrong, *Letters of Robert Browning to Isa Blagden;* also *Browning to His American Friends,* ed. G. R. Hudson (N.Y.: Barnes & Noble, 1965).

Bradford, George Partridge (1807–1890), Am. educator, visited Hawthornes in Rock Park, 1854, and was then introduced to Bennoch through N.H.'s correspondence. Grad. Harvard Divinity School, 1828. Opened own school at Plymouth. Taught at Brook Farm, where he first met N.H., 1841. Made 7 trips abroad, besides teaching, gardening, and editing. See Zoltan Haraszti, *The Idyll of Brook Farm* (repr. from BPL's *More Books*), also Lindsay Swift, *Brook Farm* (N.Y., 1961).

Bramley-Moore, John (1800–1886), Liverpool merchant, host to N.H. in Liverpool and guest at N.H.'s dinner for Bennoch, Oct. 1856. Chairman of Liverpool docks and head of Bramley-Moore & Co., merchants of Orange Ct., 37 Castle St. Mayor of city, 1849; M.P. for Maldon, 1854, and for Lincoln, 1862. Residence: Carioca Lodge, Aigburth. One of the large docks was named for him.

Bray, Charles (1811–1884), Eng. journalist, guest at Mr. Bill's dinner for N.H. and Bennoch, Feb. 1860, where George Eliot was important topic of discussion. Ribbon mfr. from 1835–1856, when he retired. Known as free-thinking social reformer. Purchased *Coventry Herald and Observer* and edited it for nearly 30 yrs. Author of *The Philosophy of Necessity,* 1841, and *Phases of Opinion During a Long Life,* 1885. Residence: 3 Barrs Hill Terrace, Coventry. For his connections with George Eliot, see "The Holy War" in Gordon Haight, *George Eliot: a Biography* (Oxford, 1968).

Bremer, Fredericka (1801–1865), Swedish novelist, first met N.H. in Concord during her travels in U.S., 1849–1851. Later entertained Hawthornes in Rome. b. near Abo, Finland. Brought up near Stockholm. Traveled in Italy, England, U.S., Greece, Palestine. Two vols. on travels: *Homes in the New World* (which includes her descr. of N.H.) (N.Y.: Hacher, 1853) and *Life in the Old World,* 1862. Also wrote *Sketches of Everyday Life, America of the Fifties,* and novels dealing with emancipation of women. First writer to paint realistic picture of Swedish family life. Biog. in *Life and Letters,* edited by her sister (translated, 1868).

Bridge, Horatio (1806–1893), classmate of N.H. at Bowdoin, lifetime friend, N.H.'s chief link with Washington, D.C., while abroad. Bridge's *Personal Recollections of Nathaniel Hawthorne,* 1893, gave information on family after N.H.'s death. After Northampton Law School he practiced in Maine for 10 yrs.

Appointed purser, U.S. Navy. Pub. *Journal of an African Cruiser,* 1845, edited by N.H. Appointed chief of bureau of provisions and clothing, 1853–1868; paymaster general, 1868; chief inspector of provisions and clothing, 1869. After 35 yrs. of service, retired, 1873, to country home, Bradford Co., Pa. See *NCAB,* 4:358.

Bright, George Charles, cousin of H.A.B. and student at Rugby, 1859, had dinner with N.H. and H.A.B. in Rugby hotel on night when latter was visiting N.H. in Leamington, 1859. Fifth son of Richard Bright, M.D., of Savile Row, London. Like his father became a physician; practiced in Cannes for most of his life. See Sir Bernard Burke, ed., *History of the Landed Gentry of Great Britain and Ireland,* 1898, 9th ed., for family relationships.

Bright, Henry Arthur (1830–1884), Eng. bus. man, literary critic, author, first met N.H. in Concord when touring U.S., 1852; friendship continued in Liverpool and thereafter by correspondence. N.H. gave him original ms. of *The Marble Faun* (later given to Br. Museum by his granddaughter). b. Liverpool, oldest son of Samuel Bright, of Gibbs, Bright, & Co., and of Elizabeth Anne, d. of Hugh Jones, Liverpool banker. Ed. Rugby and TCC. Because of ruling against Nonconformists could not take degree until 1857. Became partner with father in shipping bus. Resided until 1861 with family at Sandheys, West Derby. m. Mary Elizabeth Thompson, d. of Samuel H. Thompson of Thingwall and sister of Henry Yates Thompson (q.v.,), 1861. Children: Allan Heywood, Henry Yates, Hugh, Elizabeth Phebe, Marianne Harriette (d. in infancy), and Mary Honora. Built home for family at Knotty Ash, Ashfield, near Liverpool. Friend and acquaintance of many literary people. Active Unitarian, especially in writing for the *Inquirer, Christian Reformer,* and *Christian Life.* Noted for charitable work, particularly against abuses in mercantile marine. Memberships: Philobiblon Society, Roxburghe Club, local historical and literary organizations. Ardent collector of autographs and manuscripts. For many yrs. wrote for *Examiner* and *Athenaeum.* Because of pulmonary disease spent some months in southern France and a winter in Bournemouth. Returned to his home at Ashfield, where he died on May 5. Details in "In Memoriam," by his cousin, Lord Houghton, in *Philobiblon Society Miscellanies,* 1884, vol. 15; also in introduction by Anne Ehrenpreis, editor of his Am. journal, pub. as *Happy Country This America* (Columbus, Ohio, 1978).

Bright, Samuel (1799–1870), Liverpool shipowner, host to Hawthornes and to N.H. alone on numerous occasions at Sandheys estate, West Derby; also to J.H. when family was away, 1856. Ed. Edinburgh. Partner in Gibbs, Bright & Co., shipowners of Eagle Packet Line, Royal Ins. Bldgs., 1 N. John St., Liverpool. m. Elizabeth Jones, d. of Hugh Jones, banker, of Lark Hill, near Liverpool, 1828. Eight children: Henry Arthur, Heywood, Hugh, Samuel, Sarah, Elizabeth, Harriette, and Anna Maria (the Annie who became Una Hawthorne's best friend).

Brown, George Alexander, Liverpool merchant, banker, cousin of William Brown, M.P. His unpub. diary gives accounts of meeting N.H. several times in Liverpool. b. Baltimore. Began bus. career in U.S. Moved to Liverpool branch of Brown Shipping & Merchandising Co., but did not become a partner.

Brown, George Loring (1814–1889), Am. artist whose studio was visited by Hawthornes in Rome. Began career in Boston by illustrating children's books. Studied with Allston before going to Paris, 1833. Under influence of Claude, turned to landscape painting for the rest of his life. Moved to Italy, 1840, and stayed 20 yrs. Studio in Boston from 1860 on. See Tuckerman, *Book of the Artist,* pp. 346–54; *NCAB,* 7:466.

Brown, William, Esq., M.P., Liverpool merchant, banker, philanthropist, guest of honor at dedication ceremony of library, 1857, where he met N.H. In 1810 he established Brown, Shipley & Co. and W. & J. Brown & Co., importers. For company history, see Aytoun Ellis, *Heir of Adventure, the Story of Brown, Shipley & Co., Merchant Bankers, 1810–1860* (London, privately printed). In 1857 Brown donated funds for building a Liverpool City Library, which was then named for him. Residence: Richmond Hill, near Liverpool, and Fenton's Hotel, St. James's, when he was in London.

Buchanan, James (1791–1868), fifteenth president of U.S., corresponded with N.H. and met him in Liverpool and in London. Allowed N.H. to stay in the consulship for 4 full yrs. in spite of change in administrations. Served as congressman, minister to Russia, senator, sec. of state, and minister to Gr. Britain under Pierce. Planned to retire, but was elected president and served 1857–1861. His niece, Harriet Lane, was his hostess in London, Washington, and at his home, "Wheatland," near Lancaster, Pa. See George Curtis, *Life of James Buchanan* (N.Y., 1883); also *DAB*, 2:207–14.

Burder, Thomas Henry Carr (1831–1855), Eng. traveling companion of H.A.B., met N.H. in Concord briefly, 1852. Grad. Eton and TCC. Admitted to Inner Temple, 1849. Moved from London to Cambridge for his health. Suffered from asthma attacks during his visit to U.S. with H.A.B. Died in England of rheumatic fever at age 24. Biog. sketch in J.A. Venn, *Alumni Cantabrigienses,* (Cambridge, 1947).

Channing, Barbara, Am. tourist abroad, visited Hawthornes in Rock Park, 1854. S.H. had been a patient of Barbara's father, Dr. Walter Channing, first professor of obstetrics at Harvard. Barbara's brother was Ellery Channing, poet friend of Thoreau and other Concord authors. Barbara lived with her grandfather in Boston until ca. 1850. From 1856 on kept house for her father and two of Ellery's children after death of their mother.

Channing, William Henry (1810–1884), Unitarian minister from Boston, knew Hawthornes before and during their Eng. residence. Associated previously with Brook Farm, where N.H. met him. Spent 3 yrs. at Renshaw St. Chapel, Liverpool, where S.H. attended services from 1854–1855. He baptised Hawthorne children while they were living in Southport, 1857. See *DAB*, 2, pt. 2:9–10.

Chorley, Henry Fothergill (1808–1872), Eng. author and critic, first Englishman to recognize N.H.'s genius as s.s. writer in 1830s before periodical printings were signed. Host to Hawthornes in London, 1859. Some correspondence on *The Marble Faun*. A Lancashire native, ed. in Liverpool, he moved to London, 1833, and became critic for lit. dept. of *Athenaeum* until 1866; for music dept. until 1868. See *Autobiography, Memoirs, and Letters*, ed. H. G. Hewlett, 1873; *DNB*, 3:273–74.

Clarke, James Freeman (1810–1888), Am. Unitarian clergyman, married Hawthornes and gave N.II.'s funeral sermon. See *DAB*, 2, pt. 2:153–54.

Cranch, Christopher P. (1813–1892), Am. writer and artist, met Hawthornes and Brownings in Rome, winter of 1858–1859. Spent early life as preacher. During illness took up painting. First trip abroad after marriage to Elizabeth Windt. Joined Am. colony in Rome. Second trip with family, chiefly in Paris, 1853–1862. Spent winter of 1858–1859 alone in Rome in studio on Via Sistina, while family remained in Paris. Details in *Life and Letters of Christopher Pearse Cranch*, ed. by his daughter, Leonora Cranch Scott, 1917.

Crittenden, Thomas Leonidas (1819–1893), Am. lawyer and soldier, Liverpool consul preceding N.H., called on N.H. at Waterloo Hotel, July 1853, after latter arrived to take office. Helped initiate N.H. in duties at consulate. Served in Mexican War as lt. col. on staff of Gen. Taylor. Appointed to Liverpool by Taylor, 1849, after presidential election. In Liverpool, Crittenden and his wife lived at Mrs. Blodget's. After war he retired from army to live in his home on Staten Island. See *DAB*, 2, pt. 2:549.

Crosland, Camilla Toulmin (1812–1895), Eng. writer, described her impressions of N.H. on occasions when she met him in Blackheath at various parties. See her *Landmarks of a Literary Life*. b. Aldemanbury, London. Chiefly self-educated. At early age contributed to periodicals. Well known as writer when she married Newton Crosland (q.v.) in 1848. Lived for 38 yrs. in Blackheath. Pub. 12 vols. of sketches, poems, etc. See *DNB* under *Toulmin*, 19:1008–09.

Crosland, Newton (1819–1899), Eng. wine merchant and author, first called on N.H. in Liverpool; met him again in Blackheath at parties, 1856. b. Philadelphia of Eng. parents who had emigrated to U.S.; moved to Montreal for 3 yrs.

After death of father family returned to England, where Newton was educated. Moved to London and worked as clerk for wine importer. Started own business, 1852. m. Camilla Toulmin, already well-known author, 1848; thereafter also led a literary life. Reminiscences of Eng. writers are in *Rambles Round My Life, an Autobiography (1819–1896)*.

Cushman, Charlotte (1816–1876), Am. actress, met N.H. in U.S. before his consulship; while she was staying with her sister near Liverpool she visited N.H. at consulate and was invited to stay overnight at Rock Park. Met Hawthornes later in Rome. b. Boston. Studied music; first on stage as singer in New Orleans. N.Y. debut as actress, 1836. In Liverpool she acted with sister, Susan, who later married an Englishman, Sheridan Muspratt, and retired from the stage. After success in both U.S. and Eng., Charlotte established residence in Rome, where she entertained many Americans. Continued acting in U.S. until forced to retire by illness, 1875. Died of cancer, 1876. See Joseph Leach, *Bright Particular Star: the Life and Times of Charlotte Cushman* (New Haven, 1970); also *DAB*, 3:1–2.

Dallas, Eneas Sweetland (1828–1879), Eng. journalist, host to N.H. twice in spring, 1856. b. Jamaica, son of John Dallas, physician. Ed. U. of Edinburgh. Resident of London most of life. Contributor to numerous periodicals; correspondent for many yrs. for the *Times*. Edited *Once a Week*. m. actress Isabella Glyn, widow of Edward Wills, first in Scotland, 1853, again in London, 1855. Divorced her on petition, May 10, 1874.

Dallas, George Mifflin (1792–1864), vice-president of U.S., 1845–1849, diplomat in London during N.H.'s stay there before Hawthornes left for Italy. (See comments in *EN.*) b. Philadelphia. Ed. Princeton. Trained in father's law office. Served as district attorney, senator, minister to Russia, and vice-president under Polk. Appointed minister to Gr. Britain on resignation of Buchanan, 1856. Returned to U.S., 1861. See *DAB,* 3:38–39.

De La Motte, Philip Henry (1821–1889), Eng. artist and pioneer photographer, photographed group of guests at Spiers' home in Oxford, 1856, that included N.H., S.H., and others. Son of William Alfred De La Motte, also an artist. b. Royal Military College, Sandhurst. First trained in art, then took up photography. Elected FSA, 1852; professor of landscape drawing and perspective, 1855–1879, and of fine art, 1879–1887, King's College, London. Exhibited at Royal Academy. Instructor in drawing to princes and princesses. Pub. 14 books, incl. *Practice in Photography,* 1853, and *Views of Crystal Palace,* 1855; illustrated 56 other books.

Dicey, Edward James Stephen (1832–1911), Eng. author and journalist, met N.H. in Washington, D.C., in spring, 1862, and later visited at Wayside; wrote tribute to N.H. in 1864. b. Claybrook, Leicestershire. Ed. at home and for 2 yrs. at King's College, London. Grad. from TCC, 1854. Traveled abroad and became interested in foreign politics, especially in Eastern Europe, Egypt, U.S., and South Africa. Visited U.S., 1862, and wrote on war for *Macmillan's* and *Spectator.* Worked for *Daily Telegraph*, 1861–1869; edited *Observer*, 1870–1889. Pub. 5 vols. of own works, some reprints of periodical articles.

Durham, Joseph (1814–1877), Eng. sculptor, guest at S. C. Hall's soirée, May 1856, where he met N.H., and at Spiers' home in Oxford, Sept. 1856, along with Hawthornes, Bennoch, Halls, etc. Well-known pupil of E. H. Bailey in London. Created busts of Jenny Lind and Queen Victoria; also designed statue of prince consort for gardens of Horticultural Society, 1863. FSA, 1853; ARA, 1866. See *DNB*, 6:256.

Duval, Charles (1808–1872), Eng. painter, met N.H. at Manchester Exhibition; invited him to dinner at his home, 1857. He had moved from Liverpool to Manchester, 1833. From 1836 to yr. of death exhibited 20 pictures at Royal Academy, plus pictures at local exhibits. Wrote 5 pamphlets on Am. Civil War, 1863. Also contributed to *North of Eng. Magazine.* For artwork, see notes on Manchester Exhibition in ch. 6; also *DNB*, 6:270–71.

Eckley, David and *Sophia (Tuckerman)*, of Boston, friends of Brownings, met N.H. at Brownings' party, Florence, 1858. Sophia Eckley was a special friend of E.B.B., 1858–1859, supposedly because of interest in spiritualism. After death of E.B.B., who had already ended friendship, R.B.B. broke off relations entirely, because of scandal about Eckleys' marital relationship. See Hudson, *Browning to His American Friends*, pp. 88, 120–21, 123, 132–33, 139–40.

Ely, Richard, Liverpool merchant, guest at N.H.'s dinner for Bennoch, Oct. 1856. Agent to New Orleans Canal & Banking Co., 9 Bedford St., South, Liverpool. Mrs. R. L. Ely (his wife?) and her mother visited Hawthornes, 1853. Rose interpreted the initials as *R.S.,* not *R.L.,* and said that the younger Mrs. Ely was Am.

Fields, Annie Adams (1834–1915), second wife of James T. Fields, friend of Hawthornes, especially S.H. Her journal of the European tour, 1859 (MHS), has references to Hawthornes abroad. See also her later correspondence with S.H., now at BPL. She wrote verse, essays, biog. of authors she had known. Famous as hostess to literary people in Boston home. See *DAB*, 3, pt. 2:377–78.

Fields, James T. (1817–1881), Am. editor, author, publisher; published N.H.'s books and was close friend of the family until the quarrel with S.H. in late 1860s, after N.H.'s death. At age 16 went to work as office boy for Carter & Hendee, booksellers, Boston. After Allen & Ticknor bought out retail dept.,

1832, Fields served as office boy, then jr. and sr. clerk, finally partner. Headed the co. after death of Ticknor. Editor of *Atlantic Monthly,* to which N.H. was prominent contributor from 1861 to 1864. First m. Eliza Willard, 1850, who lived only a short time; then m. Annie Adams, 1854, who outlived him by 34 yrs. On N.H. see Fields, *Yesterdays with Authors;* also see biog. by J.C. Austin, W. S. Tryon; *DAB*, 3, pt. 2:378–79.

Franco, Dr., homeopathic physician, attended Hawthornes in Rome. Ada Shepard's letters refer to his undesirable lovemaking to her. She may have imagined this, since the Hawthornes seemed unaware of his attentions to her. See Pearson's summary of her statements in notes to his ms. of *F&IN*. Franco was listed in Murray's *Guide to Rome* as an English-speaking Maltese, residing at 81 Via della Croce, and "much employed by foreign visitors in Rome."

Gaskell, Elizabeth Cleghorn (Stevenson) (1810–1865), Eng. novelist, wife of Wm. Gaskell, Unitarian minister in Manchester; never met Hawthornes, but wrote about N.H. Hawthornes admired her works, especially *Mary Barton, Ruth,* and *Cranford.* H.A.B. tried to bring about a meeting between her and N.H., but plans did not work out. See biog. by Winifred Gerin (Oxford, 1976); also Anne Henry Ehrenpreis, "Elizabeth Gaskell and Nathaniel Hawthorne," *NHJ,* 3 (1973): 89–119; *DNB,* 7:928–33.

Gayangos, Emilia, Spanish guest at Haywood's Liverpool dinner, 1857, where N.H. met her. She was daughter of Pascal de Gayangos y Arce, who was professor of languages at U. of Madrid, interpreter for Foreign Office, and editor of catalogues of Spanish mss. for Br. Museum. Emilia assisted her father in most of this work; also said to have assisted George Ticknor (q.v.).

Gibson, John (1790–1866), Eng. sculptor, met N.H. at Read's dinner, Rome, 1858. b. Wales, son of market gardener. Ed. in Liverpool. Left England for Rome, 1817, and worked for a time with Canova and Thorvaldsen. Spent rest of his life in Rome, with occasional visits to England. In F&IN, N.H. discussed Gibson's use of color on statues and of classical drapery in the Greek tradition. See *DNB,* 7:1157–60.

Gilman, Arthur (1821–1882), Am. architect, passenger on *Niagara,* July 1853. Made drawing in S.H.'s shipboard journal. Left Trinity College, Hartford, in jr. yr. and gave 2 successful series of lectures on architecture before going abroad for further study. First important building designed by him was Arlington St. Unitarian Church, Boston, 1861.

Glyn, Isabella (Gearns) (1823–1889), Eng. actress, met N.H. at her husband's supper party after she returned from evening performance at the St. James. She was on stage in Manchester before moving to London. m. Eneas Sweetland Dallas, 1853 and 1855; divorced by him, 1874.

Godwin, George (1815–1888), Eng. architect, guest at dinner party given by Stevens, the book collector, Apr. 1856, London, where he met N.H. Chief founder of Art Union of London. Editor of the *Builders.* Vice-president of Royal Institute of Br. Architects. Author of many books on architecture.

Greenwood, Grace (Sara Jane Clarke Lippincott) (1823–1904), Am. author, first met Hawthornes when she was on tour of New Eng., 1851. Met them in Liverpool, 1853, as she was returning from 15-month tour of Europe. Upon return to U.S. m. Leander K. Lippincott of Phila., 1853. Pub. *Haps and Mishaps of a Tour in Europe,* 1854. Contributed to numerous magazines and newspapers. N.H. classed her among the "scribbling females." See under *Lippincott* in *DAB,* 6:288–89.

Hall, Anna Maria (1800–1881), Eng. novelist and prolific contributor to periodicals, was hostess to N.H. at Firfield and in London. Much admired by N.H. and an exception to his general attitude toward "scribbling females." b. Dublin, but moved to England, 1815. m. S. C. Hall, 1824. Edited *Art Journal,* 1849; *Sharpe's London Magazine,* 1852–1853; *St. James Magazine,* 1862–1863. Fifty publications in addition to many short writings. Together she and her husband pub. over 300 vols. See *DNB,* 8:938–39.

Hall, Samuel Carter (1800–1889), Eng. editor and author, host to N.H. on several occasions, described N.H. in both autobiogs. b. Geneva barracks near Waterford, Ireland, while father was in army. Moved to London and at age 21 became a reporter in House of Lords. Contributor to and editor of numerous magazines, incl. *Art Union Journal;* not many original works. Extensive circle of lit. friends and acquaintances described in *Book of Memories,* 1871, and in *Retrospect of a Long Life,* 1883. See *DNB,* 7:971–73.

Hammond, Lemprière (1829–1880), Eng. educator, host to N.H. at TCC commencement, May 1860; also wrote about N.H. to H.A.B. B.A. from TCC, 1852; M.A., 1855; Fellow from 1853 on. Called to the bar; became governor of Christ's Hospital, 1866, governor of Westminster School, and sec. to Duke of Devonshire. Close friend of H.A.B. Biog. in Venn, *Alumni Cantabrigienses.*

Haworth, Fanny Euphrasia (1801–1883), Eng. author, one of first to visit N.H. at consulate, calling without her promised letter of introduction from Charlotte Lynch; great admirer of N.H. They met in Florence, 1858, and in Rome, 1859. She was introduced to Robert Browning, possibly 1839. Corresponded with Brownings before visiting them in Florence, 1858. Pub. *St. Sylvester's Day & Other Poems,* 1847, and *Stories for Idle Afternoons,* 1875.

Haywood, Francis (1796–1858), Liverpool bus. man and writer, host to N.H. and others at dinner at his Edgelane Hall, 1857. Translated Kant's *Critique of Pure Reason,* 1838, and Wilhem Ibne's *Researches into the History of the Roman*

Constitution. Wrote *Analysis of Kant's Critick of Pure Reason,* pub. 1844. Known as great friend of Antonio Panizzi of Br. Museum. Biog. in Fagan, *Life of Antonio Panizzi.* Obit. in *Gentleman's Magazine,* Aug. 1858, p. 201.

Helps, Sir Arthur (1813–1875), Eng. secretary and ghost writer, guest at Stevens' dinner party, Apr. 1856, where he met N.H. b. Streatham, Surrey. Private secretary to chancellor of exchequer; also served as chief secretary for Ireland. Clerk, privy council, 1860 to death.

Heywood, John Pemberton (1803–1872), Liverpool banker, host to Hawthornes on numerous occasions. Mrs. Heywood was great favorite with N.H. Family visited Heywoods at Norris Green, West Derby, and at London home in Connaught Place. Mrs. Heywood was Anna Maria Jones, d. of Hugh Jones, of Lark Hill, near Liverpool, and sister of Elizabeth Jones Bright, wife of Samuel, Sr. Heywoods were, therefore, uncle and aunt to H.A.B. See Burke, *Landed Gentry.*

Hillard, George Stillman (1808–1879), Am. lawyer and literary man, first helped N.H. by arranging loan after latter lost Salem Custom House job. Corresponded with and visited Hawthornes in Leamington, 1859. Lifelong friend of N.H., though never so close as Ticknor or Pierce. First law office with Charles Sumner, Boston, where N.H. visited. Served in Mass. House of Rep., state senate, and as U.S. attorney, district of Mass. Well known for both writing and editing. Traveled in Italy, 1847–1848, and pub. *Six Months in Italy,* 1853. See *DAB,* 5:49–50.

Hoar, Elizabeth (1814–1878), close friend of S.H. in Concord, visited Hawthornes in Rome while she was touring Europe, 1859. Formerly engaged to Charles, brother of R. W. Emerson. She had gone to Europe with Elizabeth Hallett Prichard, of N.Y., and with her own brother, Edward Hoar. Latter two were married by Am. consul in Florence. From there Elizabeth H. went on to Rome, where she helped S.H. during Una's illness. From Rome she traveled to Florence and north again. See R.H., *Memories,* pp. 366–68.

Holland, Charles, Liverpool merchant, host to Hawthornes at dinner, Oct. 1853, and guest of N.H. at dinner for Bennoch, Oct. 1856. Bus. address: 17 Tower Bldgs., North, Liverpool; residence: Liscard Vale, suburb in Wirral near Birkenhead.

Hosmer, Harriet (1830–1908), Am. sculptor, met Hawthornes in Rome when she was working at Gibson's studio. b. Watertown, Mass. At age 16 sent to Lenox, Mass. for 3 yrs. to be taught by Mrs. Sedgwick. Studied anatomy in med. division of St. Louis U. and lived at home of former Lenox schoolmate. Girl's father, Wayland Crow, became "Hatty's" patron. Met C. Cushman (q.v.) 1852, and was persuaded to go abroad. Obtained place in Gibson's studio. Later worked in both U.S. and Britain. Biog. in Cornelia Carr, *Harriet Hosmer: Letters and Memories*, 1912; see also *DAB*, 5:242–43.

Howitt, Mary (Botham) (1799–1888), Eng. writer and editor, met Hawthornes in Blackheath and in London at parties. Autobiog., edited by her daughter Margaret, 1889, discusses literary life, but has no mention of N.H. m. William Howitt, 1821. Together they wrote and edited many books. Joined R.C. Church and received by Pope, Jan. 1888. Died at her home in Rome. See *DNB*, 10:122–23.

Howitt, William (1792–1879), Eng. editor, guest at Bennoch's dinner, Apr. 1856, and on other occasions when Hawthornes were present. Started as druggist and chemist in Nottingham. Became editor and translator of long list of books. With his wife he edited the *People's Journal* (later *Howitt's Journal*). Residences in Heidelberg and Australia as well as England; in Rome from 1870 on. See *DNB*, 10:124–25.

Hunter, Joseph (1784–1861), Eng. clergyman and antiquarian, guest at Milnes's London breakfast, July 1856, where he met N.H. b. Sheffield. Ed. in York. Presbyterian minister at Bath, 1801–1833. Moved to London, 1833, where he served as assistant keeper of public records. Obit. in *Gentleman's Magazine*, 10 (May–June, 1861): 701–03.

Ingram, Herbert (1811–1860), Eng. journalist, guest at Bennoch's dinner, Milton Club, Apr. 1856; host at dinner for N.H. and Bennoch, 1856. b. Boston, Lincolnshire. Journeyman printer, 1832–1834; printer and bookseller, Nottingham, 1834. Started *Illustrated London News*, 1842. Bought various other papers, incl. *London Journal*. Gave mgt. of *Illustrated London News* to Charles Mackay, 1852. Elected M.P. from Boston, 1856. Drowned on lake trip in U.S., 1860.

Ireland, Alexander (1810–1894), Eng. writer and editor, guest at Bennoch's Manchester dinner, May 1856; also met N.H. at Manchester Art Exhibition, 1857. Famous for promoting education for workingmen. Managed Emerson's 1847–1848 lecture tour. Organized Manchester Free Library, 1852. Newspaper writer for yrs. See Townsend Scudder, *The Lonely Wayfaring Man: Emerson and Some Englishmen*, 1936; also *DNB*, 22 (Supplement): 905–06.

Jameson, Mrs. Anna Brownell (1794–1860), Eng. art historian, hostess to N.H. in Rome. m. Robert Sympson Jameson, barrister, 1825. Resided in Germany, 1833–1836 and 1845. Studied art in Italy, 1847. Wrote various books of commentary on art. Met Brownings in Paris and went to Italy with them. Last stay in Italy began in 1857. Died in London. Gibson's bust of her is in National Portrait Gallery, London. See *DNB*, 10:667–69.

Jerdan, William (1782–1869), Eng. journalist, visited Hawthornes in Dec. 1853 in Rock Park, along with Bennoch, and met them later in London. N.H. read parts of Jerdan's autobiog., but did not care for it. Edited *Literary Gazette;* wrote for a number of papers. Retired, 1853, on civil pension to Bushey Heath, Hertfordshire, but continued free-lance writing. At age 70 began 4-vol. autobiog. See R. H. Stoddard, ed., *Personal Reminiscences by Moore and Jerdan,* 1875; also *DNB,* 10:773–75.

Jerrold, Douglas (1803–1857), Eng. author and editor, guest at dinner with N.H. at Reform Club, Apr. 1856, but event not mentioned in biog. by his son, Blanchard. See Charles Mackay for account of dinner. Started as writer and producer of dramas. Edited *Douglas Jerrold's Shilling Magazine,* 1845–1848; *Jerrold's Weekly Newspaper,* 1846; *Lloyd's Weekly Newspaper,* 1852 to death. Leading contributor to *Punch.* See *DNB,* 10:786–89.

Jewsbury, Geraldine (1812–1880), Eng. novelist, guest at S. C. Hall's London soirée, May 1856, where she met N.H. No mention of meeting in her letters. Native of Manchester and friend of the Carlyles from 1841 on, she moved to Chelsea in 1854 to be near Jane Carlyle, who satirized her as "Miss Gooseberry." Details in Mrs. Ireland's introduction to *Letters of G. E. Jewsbury to Jane Welsh Carlyle,* 1892. See *DNB,* 10:821–22.

Jones, John Edward (1806–1862), Eng. sculptor, guest at Stevens' dinner party, Apr. 1856, where he met N.H. b. Dublin. Civil engineer in London for 7 yrs. From 1846 on worked as sculptor; 108 pieces exhibited at Royal Academy. Best-known sitters were the queen, Prince Albert, Louis Philippe, and Napoleon III.

Kirkup, Seymour (1788-1880), Eng. friend of artists and writers; resident of Florence, Italy, from 1820 on. Famous for collections, "spiritualistic activities," and unusual personality, he was visited by many Am. and Eng. tourists. Regina Ronti (1837–1856), Italian peasant, on her deathbed claimed Kirkup was the father of four-year old Imogen, who was living with Kirkup at the time Hawthornes visited him. Browning and many others were certain that the woman's claim was fraudulent. N.H. seems to have agreed. However, he was much interested in the situation; no doubt Kirkup and Imogen influenced his portrayal of Grandsir and Pansie years later in *The Dolliver Romance.* These two were also supposedly referred to by Kenyon (in ch. 28 of *The Marble Faun*) when he responded to Donatello's question about the "necromancer" and "a bright-eyed little girl." See notes 390.29, p. 1039, and 393.12, p. 1040, in *F&IN,* CE (OSU, 1980).

Lander, Maria Louisa (1826–1923), Am. sculptor from Salem, Mass., with studio in Rome. Made bust of N.H. that he later decided was not a good likeness.

(Statue now in Concord Free Public Library). First went to Rome in 1855, where she worked with Thomas Crawford until his death. Left Rome for U.S. in 1865. For relationship with Hawthornes that was broken off see John Idol, Jr., and Sterling Eisiminger, "Hawthorne Sits for a Bust by Maria Louisa Lander," *HCEI*, 114, no. 4 (Oct. 1978): 207–12; also note on Lander, 77.26 of *F&IN* (OSU, 1980).

Layard, Sir Austen Henry (1817–1894), Eng. archaeologist and diplomat, speaker at 1855 luncheon on the *Donald Mackay*, described by N.H. in *EN*, but not mentioned in autobiog., nor in Arnold Brackman's *The Luck of Nineveh* (1978 biog.). Famous for excavations in Mesopotamia, Babylon, and Nineveh, and for Assyrian art shipped back to Br. Museum. Minister to Spain, 1869–1877; ambassador to Constantinople, 1877–1880. Pub. numerous books about his archaeological work and reports on the Crimean War. See *DNB*, 22 (Supplement): 954–57.

Lind, Johanna Maria, or *Jenny* (1821–1887), Swedish singer, guest of honor at S. C. Hall's London soirée, July 1856, where N.H. met her. Appointed court singer and member of Swedish Academy of Music, 1840. Sang in Sweden and Germany before going to London in 1847. Tour of U.S., 1850–1852; of Germany, Austria, and Holland, 1854–1855; of Great Britain, 1855–1856. m. Otto Goldschmidt, musical conductor, 1852. Became professor of singing, Royal College of Music, London. See *DNB*, 11:1152–54.

Littledale, Harold, Liverpool broker, guest with Hawthornes at Hollands' dinner party, Oct. 1853. Partner in Thomas & Harold Littledale & Co., 12 and 13 Exchange Bldgs., Liverpool. Residence: Liscard Hall, Cheshire.

Lynch, Anne Charlotte (1815–1891), Am. poet and hostess of literary circle, met N.H. at her home in N.Y. when he was en route to Washington, D.C., 1853; then later that year in Liverpool. Grad. Albany Female Academy, 1834. Taught there and at Shelter Island, N.Y. Settled in Providence and educated young women in her home. Moved to N.Y.C., 1845. Made trip abroad, 1853, to study art. m. Professor Vincent Botta, 1855. He had come to U.S. to study schools, but stayed and became Am. citizen. Their home at 25 W. 37 St., N.Y., became famous as a literary salon.

Mackay, Charles (1814–1889), Eng. poet and journalist, met N.H. in London and served as host at dinner, Reform Club, spring 1856. Wrote about N.H. in first autobiog. From 1834 on, wrote for numerous papers. Editor, *Illustrated London News*, 1852. Toured U.S., Oct. 1857–June 1858, with letters of introduction to Am. authors received from N.H. (Letter of Sept. 23, 1857, to N.H., now at U. of London Library.) Special correspondent for *London Times*, 1862–1865, in N.Y. during the war. Pub. 14 vols. of poems, then *Collected Songs*,

1859. Prose works included two autobiogs.: *Forty Years' Recollections of Life, Literature, and Public Affairs (1830–1870)* 2 vols., 1877, and *Through the Long Day, or Memorials of a Literary Life During Half a Century,* 2 vols., 1887. See *DNB,* 12:564–65.

Mansfield, John Smith, stipendiary magistrate, of 50 Mount Pleasant, Liverpool, met N.H. at dinner, 1855, at Norris Green, Heywoods' home; conducted N.H. and Mrs. Heywood on tour of West Derby Work House shortly afterward.

Marston, John Westland (1819–1890), Eng. playwright, guest at Stevens' dinner, Apr. 1856, where he met N.H. b. Boston, Lincolnshire. Articled to uncle who was solicitor in London, 1834. Edited *National Magazine,* together with H. Saunders, 1856–1857. Author numerous plays.

Martin, Lady Helena, wife of Sir Theodore Martin (q.v.), known as Helena Faucit on stage, served as hostess to Bennoch and N.H. in Hastings, 1856. See *DNB,* 22 (Supplement): 627–30.

Martin, Sir Theodore (1816–1909), Eng. writer, host to N.H. and Bennoch at luncheon, Hastings, Mar. 1856. Ed. at Edinburgh High School and University. Solicitor in Edinburgh and London. Contributed comic sketches and poems to *Tait's* and *Fraser's* under pseudonym of Bon Gaultier. W. E. Aytoun became partner until 1844. Blackwood's pub. *The Book of Ballads, Edited by Bon Gaultier,* 1845, later criticized by N.H. Martin became translator and biographer. Pub. biog. of his wife, *Helena Faucit,* 1900.

Martineau, Harriet (1802–1876), Eng. writer, met N.H. in Liverpool, 1854, introduced by H.A.B. Afterward S.H. wrote disparagingly of *Athenaeum* account of cure of Martineau's illness by mesmerism, 1845. Two other works may have been known to Hawthornes: *Restrospect of Western Travel* (U.S.) and *Complete Guide to the Lake District,* 1855. Built the Knoll, at Clappersgate, near Ambleside, 1845–1846, where she spent the latter part of her life. See *DNB,* 12:1194–99.

Martineau, James (1805–1900), Eng. Unitarian minister, brother of Harriet, met Hawthornes in Liverpool and was much admired by S.H. as a speaker. First pastorate in Dublin; then minister at Paradise St. Chapel, Liverpool, 1848; Hope St. Chapel, Liverpool, until 1857; chapel in Little Portland St., London, 1857–1872. Gained international distinction during long career. See *DNB,* 22 (Supplement): 1018–22.

Mason, John Young (1799–1859), Am. minister to France when N.H. called on him at Paris office, 1858. Native of Greensville Co., Va. Attended law school, Litchfield, Conn. Practiced in Greensville, Southampton Co., and Richmond;

served in General Assembly and Congress, and as federal judge and sec. of navy. Minister to France, 1853–1859.

Mayall, John Jabez Edwin (1810–1901), daguerreotypist, generally considered Am. (though cited by Newhall as possibly b. Birmingham), made 3 photographs of N.H. at his Regent St. studio on May 19, 1860. One of these used by Alexander Johnston (commissioned by Bennoch) when he painted oil portrait of N.H. now at Bowdoin College. Mayall learned daguerreotype process from Paul Beck Goddard and Hans Boye, 1840. First appeared in Phila. as lecturer in chemistry, 1842; opened photographic studio. Moved to London, 1846; opened Am. Daguerreotype Institution at 322 West Strand. Introduced from France the albumen glass negative process, 1851; obtained Br. patent on vignetting device, 1853. Opened second studio, 1852, at 224 Regent St. In 1860s made large sums of money photographing members of royal family and producing "cartes de visite." Popularity is said to have developed because of skill in "art photography," patience in making portraits, and superiority of his glass plates over Eng. ones. Moved to Brighton, 1864; mayor, 1877–1878. See *Royal Heritage* (BBC, 1978); Beaumont Newhall, *The Daguerreotype in America* (Dover, 1976); and Helmut Gernsheim, *History of Photography* (Oxford, 1955).

Melly, George, Liverpool merchant, partner in Melly, Romilly & Co., of 5 Bedford Place, guest at N.H.'s dinner for Bennoch, Oct. 4, 1856, at the Adelphi. Melly became H.A.B.'s brother-in-law.

Milnes, Richard Monckton (First Lord Houghton) (1809–1885), correspondent and host of N.H. Toastmaster at 1857 dedication ceremony, Liverpool library, where he introduced N.H. as speaker. Ed. by private tutors. M.A. from TCC. Traveled and lived on Continent until 1835. M.P. for Pontrefact, Yorkshire, 1837–1863. Country residence: Fryston, Wakefield. m. Annabella Hungerford, d. of John, Second Lord Crewe, 1851. City home on Upper Brook St., London, became famous for entertainment of literary people. Milnes helped establish Philobiblon Society in 1853. Wrote poems, monographs, and *Life and Letters of John Keats*, and contributed to *Quarterly* and *Edinburgh Reviews*. Widely known as patron of writers. Standard biog. is T. Wemyss Reid, *Life, Letters, and Friendships of Richard Monckton Milnes, First Lord Houghton,* 1891; see also *DNB*, 13:465–68, and Houghton papers at TCC and Crewe papers at U. Library, Cambridge.

Mitchell, Maria (1818–1889), Am. astronomer, took letter of introduction to N.H. at Liverpool consulate, 1857. In Paris, 1858, she asked to accompany Hawthornes to Italy because she did not want to travel alone (her companion had been called home unexpectedly). Impressions of N.H. recorded in biog. listed below. d. of Wm. and Lydia (Coleman) Mitchell, Quakers of Nantucket. Ed. in astronomy by working with father. Became librarian at Nantucket

Athenaeum and worked at computations for Harvard. Received Daniel Medal for discovery of comet by telescope, 1847. First European trip, 1857; second trip, 1873. Professor of astronomy and director of observatory at Vassar from 1865 on. First woman admitted to Am. Academy of Arts and Sciences. Also elected to Hall of Fame. See *Maria Mitchell: Life, Letters and Journals*, ed. Phebe Mitchell Kendall, 1896; also *DAB*, 7:57–58.

Moon, Sir Francis (1796–1871), retired Eng. printmaker, host to N.H., Bennoch, and Fields in Brighton, July 1859. Youngest son of a goldsmith, he was first employed by a book and print seller. Became best-known printmaker of his time. Served as common councilman, alderman, and Lord Mayor of London, 1854–1855. Created first baronet, May 1855. Residences in London and Brighton.

Motley, John Lothrop (1814–1877), Am. historian and diplomat, had known Hawthornes in Boston in 1840s. His stay in Rome, winter of 1858–1859, was for a rest from work on 2-vol. *History of United Netherlands* (pub. 1860–1861). Ada Shepard taught daughter Lily (Elizabeth), along with Hawthorne children. Motley moved back to Eng., 1859, and entertained N.H. in London, 1860. Admired N.H.'s writings, especially *The Marble Faun*. Served briefly as Am. minister to Gr. Britain. Died and was buried in England. See *DAB*, 7:282–87.

Mott, Albert, Liverpool wine merchant, guest at N.H.'s dinner for Bennoch, Oct. 4, 1856, at the Adelphi. Member of firm of J. Mott & Sons, Castle St., Liverpool. Residence: Orchard Hey, Rice Lane, Walton.

Mozier, Joseph (1812–1870), Am. sculptor, called on Hawthornes in Rome; much of discussion was on Margaret Fuller's marriage. (See note 155.4, pp. 945–52, in *F&IN* [OSU, 1980].) b. Burlington, Vt., but spent earliest part of life in Mt. Vernon, Ohio. Merchant in N.Y.C., 1840s. Moved to Rome, 1845, for rest of life except for 1 visit to U.S. As sculptor he preferred draped ideal figures. For artwork see Tuckerman, *Book of the Artist*, pp. 590–91.

Norton, the Honorable Mrs. Caroline (1808–1877), Eng. author and editor, invited N.H. to be her guest, Nov. 1853, but did not meet him until Mrs. Hall's dinner in London, May 1860. d. of Thomas Sheridan, granddaughter of dramatist R. B. Sheridan. Aunt of Lord Dufferin of Clandeboye, Ireland. Edited the *Keepsake* and the *Drawing-Room Scrapbook*. Among best-known works are *A Voice from the Factories* (poem on child labor), 1836, and *English Laws for Women in the Nineteenth Century*, 1854. See *DNB*, 14:651–53.

Ogden, William Butler (1805–1877), Am. real-estate dealer and railroad president, traveled abroad in 1853 and visited N.H. at Liverpool consulate in Nov. Invited to stay overnight in Rock Park home, where he told of his Oct. trip to

Bacon's grave with Delia Bacon. In U.S. he had bought up properties in Midwest and become president of various railroads. First mayor of Chicago, 1837. Contributor to educational and charitable institutions. Sponsored Delia Bacon's N.Y. lecture course. Arrived in London with wife, brother-in-law Charles Butler, and Charlotte Lynch, Aug. 1853. See *DAB*, 7:644–45.

O'Sullivan, John Louis (1813–1895), Am. diplomat, knew N.H. in U.S.; visited Hawthornes in Liverpool, 1854; host to S.H. and daughters in Lisbon, winter of 1855–1856. Son of U.S. consul to Barbary States, he was born on Br. man-of-war in Bay of Gibraltar during plague. Ed. in Fr. and Eng. schools; grad. Columbia College. As editor of *Democratic Review* published many of N.H.'s s.s. before collected editions. Member of N.Y.S. Assembly; regent of U. of N.Y.S.; minister to Portugal, 1854–1858. Lived abroad until 1871 or later. Spent last 20 yrs. in N.Y. See *DAB*, 7, pt. 2:89.

Palfrey, John Gorham (1796–1881), Am. Unitarian clergyman, educator, historian, guest at Milnes's London breakfast, July 1856, where he met N.H. Dexter Professor of Sacred Lit. at Harvard until 1839. Served in Mass. legislature, as sec. of commonwealth, and in U.S. Congress. Traveled to England to do research for *History of New England*, 4 vols., pub. 1858–1875. See *DAB*, 7, pt. 2:169–70.

Patmore, Coventry (1823–1896), Eng. poet, visited Hawthornes in London, fall of 1857, and gave them copy of his poems, since they were great admirers of *Angel in the House*. Assistant in Dept. of Printed Books, Br. Museum, 1846–1866. Emily Augusta Andrews, the "Honoria" of *Angel in the House*, was his first wife. After her death he married twice (1864 and 1881) and outlived both wives. Converted to Roman Catholicism, 1864. Biog. in *Memoir and Correspondence*, ed. Derek Patmore, great-grandson. See *DNB*, 22 (Supplement). 1121–24.

Pierce, Franklin (1804–1869), fourteenth president of U.S., began friendship in Bowdoin College with N.H. that led to N.H.'s writing of Pierce's campaign biography and the reward of Liverpool consulship. Visited Hawthornes in Rome daily during Una's illness. Afterwards aided and advised family, especially Julian in college. At his death Pierce left $500 to each of the Hawthorne children. He had served in N.H. Gen. Court, U.S. House of Representatives, and U.S. Senate. Practiced law in Concord, N.H. Served in Mexican War. Became "dark horse" candidate of Democratic party, 1852. During presidency, 1853–1857, lost popularity because of position on slavery issue. Succeeded by Buchanan in 1858. See *DAB*, 7, pt. 2:576–80.

Pollock, Joseph (1818–1858), Eng. barrister and judge, guest at N.H.'s dinner for Bennoch, Oct. 4, 1856; also at Duval's dinner in Manchester, 1857. b. Co. Down, Ireland. Ed. Armagh College and Trinity College, Dublin. Law training in London. Barrister from 1842. Went on Northern Circuit, then practiced in Manchester. Judge of Salford Court of Record to Nov. 1851; County Court of Liverpool, Nov. 1851–1857. Retired on pension, Oct. 1857. Died following spring in London.

Power, Marguerite (1815–1867), Eng. writer, friend of Bennoch's and editor to whom N.H. contributed "Uttoxeter" at Bennoch's request; so far as is known, she and N.H. did not meet. She was niece of Marguerite, Countess of Blessington. Began writing at early age. Resided with aunt at Gore House, Kensington, to Apr. 1849, then went with her to Paris. Served as assistant in editing the *Keepsake;* upon death of countess, Marguerite Power became editor and retained position to 1857. For work on the *Keepsake,* see Michael Sadleir's *The Strange Life of Lady Blessington* (Boston, 1933); also *DNB,* 16:258.

Powers, Hiram (1805–1873), Am. sculptor, whose family were friends and neighbors of Hawthornes in Florence. b. Woodstock, Vt., fifth of 9 children of farmer. At age 14 moved to Cincinnati, where father died of fever. Hiram found various jobs and learned modeling in leisure time. Two yrs. training in Washington, D.C. Aided financially for his trip to Italy, 1837. Spent most of remaining 36 yrs. in Florence. Most popular work was "The Greek Slave." See *DAB,* 8:158–60.

Proctor, Bryan Waller (1787–1874), Eng. poet, corresponded with N.H., 1852; visited Rock Park, 1854; met N.H. again in London. Began career in law in London, 1807. Contributed poems under pen name of Barry Cornwall. After retirement as gov. employee, continued to edit and pub. poetry. See *Autobiographical Fragment and Biographical Notes,* 1877, and *DNB,* 16:416–18.

Rathbone, Richard, brother of William (q.v.), Liverpool acquaintance of N.H. His wife also visited S.H. Probably a retired merchant, he was listed as "gentleman" of Woodcote, Aigburth, Liverpool. His wife illustrated and contributed drawings for *Poetry of Birds* (Liverpool, 1832). Rathbone family discussed in Baines's *History of Liverpool.*

Rathbone, William, Liverpool merchant, host to Hawthornes, guest at N.H.'s dinner for Bennoch, Oct. 1856. Partner in Rathbone Brothers & Co. and insurance broker in R. Martin & Co., agents to East India Co. Office: Water St., Liverpool. Residence: Greenbank, Wavertree, 1853; Toxteth Park, 1857. See Baines for family history.

Read, Thomas Buchanan (1822–1872), Am. writer and artist, host at dinner in Rome to artists and to N.H. Though b. on farm in Chester Co., Pa., he spent much of his life in Phila. Lived in Italy in 1850s. Came back to U.S. when Civil War broke out, but returned to stay in Rome until health failed. Died in N.Y. few days after return there. His narrative poem, "Wagoner of the Alleghanies, a Poem of the Days of Seventy-six," 1862, paid tribute to N.H. in an introductory stanza. He sent a copy to N.H. in Concord after Hawthornes returned from England.

Reade, Charles (1814–1884), Eng. novelist and dramatist, guest at Dallas's supper party, Apr. 1856, where he met N.H. Oxford fellow and barrister; author of numerous plays and novels, incl. the famous *Cloister and the Hearth*. Among those works read by Hawthornes were *Christie Johnstone*, *It Is Never Too Late to Mend*, and *Love Me Little, Love Me Long*. *The Memoir of Charles Reade*, compiled by Charles R. Reade and Rev. Compton Reade, 1887, does not mention N.H., but includes *The Scarlet Letter* among famous books that Reade knew and liked. See *DNB*, 16: 797–801.

Reynolds, William J. (1814–1865), Am. bookseller, passenger on the *Niagara*, July 1853; also one of the group who toured Paris with W. D. Ticknor later that summer. b. Salem, Mass. Moved to Roxbury after death of father, Davidson H. Reynolds, builder. Short, active life as bookseller, publisher, and member of common council and state legislature (1863–1865). Traveled abroad on book-buying trips. Whether he knew Hawthornes before 1853 is uncertain.

Salomons, Sir David (1797–1873), Lord Mayor of London when Bennoch and N.H. attended his official dinner and sat across from Cecilia Salomons (N.H.'s "Jewess"), 1856. Second son of Levy Salomons, merchant and underwriter, he began commercial life at an early age. One of founders of London & Westminster Bank, 1832. Underwriter, 1834. Sheriff for London and Middlesex; alderman for Aldgate; high sheriff of Kent; magistrate and deputy lieutenant for Kent, Sussex, and Middlesex. Commissioned as first Jewish magistrate. Political career as Liberal. Defeated twice, but elected for Greenwich, 1851. Lord Mayor of London, 1855–1856. Created baronet, 1869. Six publications, chiefly on oath required of office holders and on money markets. m. twice: Jeanette, d. of Solomon Cohen; Cecilia, widow of P. J. Salomons, David's brother, 1872.

Sanborn, Franklin Benjamin (1831–1917), teacher, writer, abolitionist, did not meet N.H. until 1860, when Ellery Channing recommended his school to Hawthornes for J.H.'s college preparatory work. A Harvard grad., Sanborn conducted private school in Concord according to "progressive" methods such as those used by Thoreau and Bronson Alcott. Assisted in operation of underground railroad and in plans for John Brown's raid. Edited *Boston Commonwealth* and *Springfield Republican*. Pub. books on Alcott, Brown, Emerson, Hawthorne, Dr. S. G. Howe, and Thoreau. Worked for improvement of prisons, insane asylums, orphanages, etc.

Shepard, Ada Adaline (1835–1874), tutor to Hawthorne children from fall 1857 to summer 1859. Went to Europe immediately after graduation from Antioch

College. On return to U.S. she married Henry Clay Badger (recipient of most of her letters concerning Hawthornes). From 1859–1861, professor of modern languages at Antioch. Together with husband she had post in the Sanitary Commission, 1862, arranged by Dr. Bellows, Unitarian minister. After move to Cambridge, Ada opened school for girls on Spring St. Following husband's breakdown in health, each partner feared insanity and agreed that if either one lost reason, the other would not have the afflicted one committed. Because of misinterpretation, Ada became convinced that Clay thought her to be insane. Leaving a note asking sons' forgiveness, she took the Fall River boat for N.Y. and jumped overboard off Pt. Judith. Clay, sensing her intentions, tried to prevent suicide by reaching the boat. He was too late; her body was never found. For biog. see sources listed under *Badger*.

Silsbee, William (1813–1890), Am. Unitarian minister, passenger on the *Niagara*, July 1853; visited Hawthornes, 1854 and 1857. b. Salem, Mass. Grad. Harvard, 1832. Began preaching, 1840. Taught private school in Cincinnati, 1851–1853. Traveled in Europe from July 1853 to Sept. 1854 and again probably in 1857. Pastor, Second Congregational Church, Northampton, 1856–1863; Cambridge, 1863–1867; Trenton, N.Y., 1868. m. twice: Charlotte Lyman (died 1848); Maria P. Woodward. Biog. in *Biog. Clippings*, 46:51 (Essex), and *HCEI*, 17:288; also in correspondence of Henry W. Bellows, Unitarian minister (MHS).

Sinclair, Catherine (1800–1864), Scottish writer and charity worker, guest at S. C. Hall's soirée in London, July 1856, where she met N.H. d. of Scottish baronet, she served as his secretary, 1814–1835. Well known for charitable work in Edinburgh as well as for writing popular fiction and nonfiction. Visited sister, Lady Glasgow, in London. Moved to house of her brother, Archdeacon Sinclair, in Kensington. Obit. in *Gentleman's Magazine,* Nov. 1864, p. 659–60.

Smith, Albert Richard (1816–1860), Eng. author and lecturer, host to N.H. and Bennoch at Evans's Supper Rooms, Apr. 1856, after one of his lectures. Son of a surgeon, he began career by practicing with father. Turned to writing plays, became famous contributor to *Punch.* Ascent of Mont Blanc, Aug. 1851, followed by lecture series from 1852–1858, led to his being labeled "Albert the Great"; also butt of jokes by *Punch* staff because of his self-advertising. Biog. in N. H. Spielman, *History of Punch,* 1895; see also *DNB,* 18:418–20.

Stevens, Henry (1819–1886), Am. book collector and seller, host to N.H. at dinner, Apr. 1856, at "Vermont House," his home in Camden Town, London. b. Barnet, Vt. Grad. of Yale. First trip to London, 1845, as hunter of books for famous Am. libraries. Also hired to add Am. books to collection in Br. Museum. Settled in England and passed bookselling bus. on to son and grandson. See *DAB,* 9:611–12.

Story, William Wetmore (1819–1895), Am. sculptor and writer, one of N.H.'s closest friends in Rome. b. Salem, Mass. Grad. Harvard, 1838, and law school, 1840. In Boston joined firm of Hillard and Sumner, both of whom N.H. already knew. Early writings: poetry and biog. of father, Chief Justice Story. After start at sculpture, he was commissioned to make statue of his father. First went to Rome, 1851. Spent most of his life abroad, with frequent visits to U.S. and England. Became center of social group of artists in Rome. Children included Edith, girl of Una's age, who was also taught by Ada Shepard; two boys, Thomas Waldo and Julian Russell; third son, Joseph, died of fever, 1853. Biog. in Henry James, *William Wetmore Story and His Friends* (Boston, 1903); see also *DAB*, 9, pt. 2, 109–11.

Sturgis, Russell (1805–1887), Am. bus. man, banker, father of Russell Sturgis, architect and writer; served as financial advisor of Hawthornes in England. Later the son was consulted about helping J.H. financially during the latter's days in London in the 1870s–1880s. Sturgis, Sr., had been shipping merchant and commissioner of pilots in N.Y.C. Member of firm of Russell & Co., Canton, China. Moved to England and spent 30 yrs. as partner in Baring Brothers, bankers, of London.

Sumner, Charles (1811–1874), senator from Mass., met Hawthornes in Rome, 1859, again in London, 1860. N.H. had known him since 1840s, when he was Hillard's law partner. He went to Europe twice to consult physicians about an injury. In the U.S. senate chamber he had been attacked for opposition to slavery and struck on the head by Preston Brooks of S.C. By the time he met Hawthornes in 1859, his health had improved somewhat.

Swain, Charles (1801–1874), Eng. poet and engraver, guest at Bennoch's dinner in Manchester, May 1856; also host to Hawthornes at his home, summer of 1857. Native of Manchester, he began career as engraver, printer, and lithographer. Wrote poetry as avocation. First pub. vol., 1827; total of 11 vols., collected in 1867. Honorary professor of poetry at Manchester Royal Institute; lectured there on modern poets. Biog. sketches in John R. Swann, *Lancashire Authors*, 1924, pp. 202–03, and John Evans, *Lancashire Authors and Orators*, 1850, pp. 260–68.

Taylor, Tom (1817–1880), Eng. dramatist and editor of *Punch*, guest at dinners in London, where he met N.H. several times. Ed. Glasgow U. and TCC. Professor of Eng. lit. and language, London U., 1845–1847. Barrister at Inner Temple, 1846. Art critic for *Times* and *Graphic* for many yrs. One of his best-known plays, *Our Am. Cousin*, was at Ford Theater on night of Lincoln's assassination. See *DNB*, 19: 472–74.

Temple, Robert (1828–1902), classmate and friend of H.A.B. at Rugby and TCC; did not meet N.H., but admired his works and wrote about him to H.A.B. Vicar of Lache, Wales, at time of H.A.B.'s Am. tour, 1852. Inspector of schools for 36 yrs. Retired to rectory of Ewhurst, near Guilford, Surrey. See correspondence with H.A.B. at TCC. Information from Montgomeryshire Collections, 33 (1902): 293–94, courtesy of R. McDonald, Dept. of Mss. and Records, Nat. Library of Wales.

Thompson, Cephas Giovanni (1809–1888), Am. painter, close friend of Hawthornes in Rome. Had painted N.H.'s portrait in Boston, 1850. Brother-in-law of Anna Cora Ogden Mowatt, Am. actress, whose autobiog. N.H. praised highly. b. Middleboro, Mass. Taught by father. Worked in Providence and N.Y. In 1852 he and his wife, Mary Ogden, went to Rome for 7 yrs., where he maintained a studio. Their children were taught by Ada Shepard along with Hawthornes': Cora, Una's age; Eddy, Julian's age and "his bosom friend"; and Herbert, aged 10. Family returned to N.Y.C., 1859; spent rest of their lives there. Thompson's studio was at 68 Via Sistina. For his artwork see Tuckerman, *Book of the Artist,* pp. 490–91; see also *DAB,* 9, pt. 2: 452–53.

Thompson, Henry Yates (1838–1928), Eng. newspaper correspondent touring U.S. during war, visited N.H. in Concord, July 18, 1863, with letter of introduction from H.A.B. Oldest son of S. H. Thompson, Liverpool banker, he became brother-in-law of H.A.B. Ed. Harrow and TCC. Friend of Wm. Everett, son of Edward Everett, at whose Boston home he stayed off and on during 6 months' tour of U.S. Notations from diary of 1863 trip sent as articles to *London Daily News.* Lectured about his tour, 1864, in England in defense of Northerners' views. Private sec. to Spenser, Viceroy of Ireland, 1868–1874. m. Elizabeth Smith, d. of George Smith, publisher, 1878. Proprietor of *Pall Mall Gazette,* 1880–1892. Traveled on Continent and built up collection of illuminated mss., donated eventually to Roxburghe Club and to Br. Museum. Biogs. in Venn, *Alumni Cantabrigienses* and *An Englishman in the American Civil War; the Diaries of Henry Yates Thompson, 1863,* ed. Sir Christopher Chancellor (N.Y., 1971). See also correspondence with H.A.B. in TCC.

Ticknor, George (1791–1871), Am. editor and author; knew N.H. in Boston in early 1850s; guest at Milnes's London breakfast, July 1856, when he met N.H. again. Professor of French and Spanish at Harvard. In Europe with family, 1835–1838. Spent 10 yrs. working on *History of Spanish Lit.,* pub. 1849. One of founders of BPL, 1852. Again in Europe, 1856, buying books. Bequeathed entire Spanish collection to BPL. See *DAB,* 9, pt. 2:525–28.

Ticknor, William Davis (1810–1864), cousin of George Ticknor; Am. publisher whose friendship with N.H. began about 1850, when Fields (q.v.) was negotiating for printing of *The Scarlet Letter.* Close relationship with N.H. lasted until Ticknor's death, 1864. b. Lebanon, N.H. At age 17 went to Boston and worked in brokerage office of his uncle, Benjamin Ticknor. Founded small co., Allen &

Ticknor, booksellers, 1832. After partners separated, 1834, he published by himself until 1843. Joined by Fields and others, he headed the co. that became famous for insisting on copyright laws; eventually the co. was bought out and became Houghton Mifflin. See Caroline Ticknor, *Hawthorne and His Publisher,* 1913; *The Cost Books of Ticknor & Fields & Their Predecessors, 1832–1858,* ed. Warren S. Tryon and Wm. Charvat, 1949; and *DAB*, 9, pt. 2:528–29.

Train, Enoch (1801–1868), Am. merchant and shipowner, passenger on the *Niagara,* July 1853, together with his second wife, Almira Cheever (m. 1836), and his son, Enoch, Jr. Made his fortune from shipping bus. established in competition with Cunard Lines. Probably best known for commissioning the famous *Flying Cloud,* which he later sold to Grinnell, Minturn & Co., of N.Y., for $90,000, double its contract price. See *DAB*, 9, pt. 2:625.

Tucker, Nathaniel Beverly (1820–1890), Am. bus. man and politician, met N.H. in Liverpool, 1857, when he arrived to assume consulship as N.H.'s successor. In bus. in Richmond, he had lost capital and acquired debts. Began political career as result of work representing claims before Congress and fed. depts. during Mexican War. Edited *Washington Sentinel,* 1853–1857. After Liverpool office, joined Confederate army and became Confederate agent. Accused of being in plot to murder Lincoln. Case dismissed for lack of evidence. Described in warrant for arrest as "a large man, upwards of fifty [1861], florid complexion" with "plausible and boisterous manners." Ended life writing for newspapers and fighting illness and poverty. See *DAB*, 10:36–37.

Tupper, Martin Farquhar (1810–1889), Eng. author, host to N.H. and Bennoch, Apr. 1856. His *My Life as an Author,* 1886, included severe criticism of N.H. for comments about himself printed by J.H. after N.H.'s death. b. Marylebone, London. Ed. Charterhouse and Christ Church, Oxford. Called to bar, 1835, but did not practice. Writer of both prose and poetry. Most popular work, *Proverbial Philosophy,* also much criticized. Visited U.S., 1851 and 1876. Collected works in 39 vols. See *DNB*, 19:1245–47.

Warren, Samuel (1807–1877), Eng. author, guest at dinner at Bramley-Moore's, 1854, where he met N.H. Studied medicine, Edinburgh, 1826–1827. Admitted to Inner Temple, 1828. Author of *Popular and Practical Introduction to Law Studies,* 1835; *Passages from the Diary of a Late Physician* (written 1829), pub. at intervals in *Blackwood's,* 1830–1837; *Select Extracts from Blackstone's Commentaries,* 1837; *$10,000 a Year,* 3 vols., completed 1841; *Now and Then,* 1847; 3 other legal manuals. M.P. for Midhurst, 1856–1859. Many republications of his works. See *DNB*, 20:880–83.

Watson, Charles (1815–1874), Eng. merchant and J.P., guest at Bennoch's dinner in Manchester, May 1856, where N.H. met him and admired him for his frank conversation about Americans. Member of the firm of Carlton, Walker, Watson & Co. of 14 George St. and 11 and 13 Mosley St., Manchester. Self-made man who started as clerk in countinghouse and became its head. Died suddenly (supposedly of Bright's disease) one evening after leaving his office. Obit. in Manchester Library newspaper cuttings F920.04273.01, p. 42.

Weston, The Misses, 5 daughters of wealthy family in Weymouth, Mass., of whom at least 2 were in Rome in 1858. N.H. had lunch and spent afternoon with them. N.H.'s daughters also visited them. The Westons who were abroad probably included Anne Warren, Caroline, and Emma Forbes. An elder sister, Maria Weston Chapman, was a prominent abolitionist. For the 7 children of Capt. Warren and Nancy Bates Weston, see *Weymouth Vital Records to 1850,* vol. I, *Births;* Weston family correspondence in BPL; and references in note 141.16, p. 940 of *F&IN* (OSU, 1980).

Wight, Orlando W. (1824–1888), Am. physician, passenger on the *Niagara,* July 1853; toured Liverpool in company of Wm. Silsbee (q.v.). b. Centerville, N.Y. Ed. Westfield Academy and Rochester Collegiate Institute. Ordained Unitarian minister; apparently did not preach. Taught Latin and Greek in 2 academies. Listed as physician and author, but did not study medicine at Long Island College Hospital until after return from 1853 European trip. Surgeongeneral and health officer in Milwaukee. Last position as health officer in Detroit. Long list of writings.

Wilkinson, James John Garth (1812–1899), Eng. homeopathic doctor, physician to Hawthornes in London, 1857, introduced them to Coventry Patmore. Office at 13 Stone St., 1837–1847; then at 24 Finchley New Road, London, 1853–1867. Member of Swedenborg Society and author of biog. of Swedenborg, 1849. Long list of publications, incl. some on spiritualism, a belief he rejected in later yrs., according to his wife, who objected to J.H.'s account in *NH&HW*.

Williams, Anne, younger sister of Mary Blodget (q.v.), helped run the lodging house on Duke St., Liverpool, where Hawthornes stayed several times. b. London. Listed in Gibraltar 1834 census as aged 30, unmarried, and living with Mary Blodget. Moved to Liverpool with her and continued to run the lodging house for some yrs. after her sister's death.

Woolner, Thomas (1825–1892), Eng. sculptor, accompanied Tennyson at Manchester Art Exhibition, 1857, where he was observed by N.H. but did not meet him. b. Hadleigh, Suffolk. Ed. Ipswich. Studio in London. Well-known sculptor with works at Royal Academy. Met Tennyson through Coventry Patmore. His bust of Tennyson, 1857, is still in the library of TCC. See *DNB*, 21:905–07.

Wrigley, Frances Augusta (Fanny) (1829–1878), nurse and maid in Hawthorne household in England. b. Halifax, d. of Watts Wrigley, associated with John Wrigley & Co., cotton brokers of Liverpool (later listed as farmer in Malton, Yorks.). No information on mother or on childhood. Hired at age 25 by Hawthornes, though she had no working experience except caring for invalid stepmother, Catherine Elizabeth Wrigley. Her family moved to Malton sometime between 1854 and 1857. Service with Hawthornes ended temporarily in Dec. 1857 when her father drowned. She returned to Malton to live with stepmother until 1859, when Hawthornes came back to England. Moved to Redcar, Leamington, and Bath with them, 1859–1860. Planned to go to U.S. with them, but not to stay unless health improved. Only circumstantial evidence (in letters of S.H.) exists, since Cunard passenger lists have been destroyed. S.H. sent Fanny her "things" from Concord, March 1861. Census for 1871 shows Fanny and stepmother (then aged 63) living at Union Villas, 12 New Ferry Park, Birkenhead. S.H. and U.H. visited there in spring, 1870. Last reference: letter of R.H. from London, Aug. 1870, in which she said she had not yet seen her "old nurse." In or after 1871 the Wrigley women returned to Malton. Fanny died of cancer of the throat, aged 49, at Greengate, Malton, Oct. 7, 1878. Informant: M. A. Copperthwaite, cousin, of Beech Grove, Old Malton.

Index

Index

Index